PUL ELIYA

PUL ELIYA

A VILLAGE IN CEYLON

A STUDY OF LAND TENURE
AND KINSHIP

BY

E. R. LEACH

Reader in Social Anthropology in the
University of Cambridge

CAMBRIDGE
AT THE UNIVERSITY PRESS
1961

PUBLISHED BY
THE SYNDICS OF THE CAMBRIDGE UNIVERSITY PRESS
Bentley House, 200 Euston Road, London, N.W. 1
American Branch: 32 East 57th Street, New York 22, N.Y.

©

CAMBRIDGE UNIVERSITY PRESS

1961

Printed in Great Britain at the University Press, Cambridge
(Brooke Crutchley, University Printer)

CONTENTS

LIST OF ILLUSTRATIONS

vii

DIAGRAMS

TABLES

ACKNOWLEDGEMENTS

The research on which this monograph is based was carried out during the period June to December 1954, and was supplemented by a further brief visit to Ceylon during August 1956. This work was made possible by the grant of leave of absence by the General Board of the University of Cambridge and by financial grants from Leverhulme Research Awards and from the Wenner Gren Foundation. Preparation of the work for publication has been assisted by a personal grant-in-aid from the Behavioral Sciences Division of the Ford Foundation.

Work in the field was only made possible by the generous help and co-operation afforded by a large number of friends and officials both in Ceylon and the United Kingdom. I feel particularly indebted to Mr B. H. Farmer, Fellow of St John's College, Cambridge, Mr P. E. P. Deraniyagala, Director of Museums, Ceylon, Dr Ralph Pieris, lately Head of the Department of Sociology, Ceylon University, Mrs E. C. Fernando of Colombo, Mr R. B. Weerakoon, C.C.S., and Mr G. P. Elangasinhe, Divisional Revenue Officer, Nuwaragam Palata (East), all of whom gave me very direct assistance with problems arising in the course of my investigations.

A different and special acknowledgement must be made to Dr N. O. Yalman, a fellow Cambridge anthropologist, whose field-work in Ceylon overlapped with my own. Dr Yalman was working in another part of the Ceylon Dry Zone where demographic and ecological conditions are very different from those described in this book, but even so there was a great deal of common ground between our two fields of study. Dr Yalman's investigation covered a period of 15 months and the very general degree of agreement that exists between us provides me with some defence against the obvious criticism that my study of Pul Eliya covered too short a period to be of real scientific value.

Finally to the people of Pul Eliya itself I offer my thanks and my apologies.

NOTE TO THE READER

The written form of the Sinhalese language distinguishes 35 consonants and 14 vowels. Transcription into the roman alphabet is necessarily conventional and the conventions have varied considerably over the past 80 years. The conventions adopted in this book are as follows:

(1) Ordinary Sinhalese words, if they occur in the glossarial index to Ralph Pieris, *Sinhalese Social Organisation* (1956), are normally so spelt.

(2) Exceptionally, certain commonly occurring technical terms are differently spelt, either for simplicity or in order to accord with the usage of previous authors. These terms are: *elapata* (instead of *älapata*), *pangu* (*paṃgu*), *andē* (*anda*), *Vidāne* (*Vidāna*), *bethma* (*betma*).

(3) Other ordinary words, if they occur in Charles Carter, *A Sinhalese English Dictionary* (1924) are romanised according to the spelling of that dictionary.

(4) Colloquial terms which do not appear in that dictionary are romanised more or less phonetically.

(5) Personal names are written phonetically and without diacritical marks; for example, I write Sinni Etani where a 'correct' romanisation should be Siṃni Ethani.

(6) Titles are written in roman and not italic script but are distinguished from personal names (which they resemble in sound) by the inclusion of diacriticals; for example, in the names Appurala Vidāne and Punchirala Gamarāla, Appurala and Punchirala are personal names, but Vidāne and Gamarāla are titles.

(7) Place-names are spelt as in the survey maps of the area even when such spelling is bizarre. The name Pul Eliya does not

appear on the survey map, but is an orthodox romanisation of the Sinhalese original.

(8) The names of castes, whether written in romanised Sinhalese or in English translation, are written in roman script with capitals, while occupational groups are written with lower-case initials; example: 'Goyigama' and 'Washermen' both denote caste groups, 'washermen' denotes persons pursuing the calling of laundryman.

NAME CODE

The names of the places and people recorded in this book are the actual names recorded by me in the field. In the case of residents of Pul Eliya, both past and present, the mention of a name is usually accompanied by a code number, thus: V. Menikrala (B1:7), A.V. Punchi Etani (B1:A1), U.V. Pinhamy (C1:W).

The use of this code is explained in full at pp. 191–2.

In brief: Every code number is divided in the middle by a colon. The letter and figure to the left of the colon indicate the Pul Eliya compound in which the individual ordinarily resides. Letters and figures to the right of the colon indicate where the individual was born.

If the individual resides as an adult in the same compound as that in which he or she was born the right-hand portion of the code-number contains figures only, no letters. If the right-hand portion of the code number contains letters then the individual in question was born in a compound other than that in which he or she normally resides as an adult.

In the above examples, V. Menikrala (B1:7) was born in Pul Eliya Compound B1 and still resides there; A.V. Punchi Etani (B1:A1) resides in Compound B1, but was born in Compound A1; U.V. Pinhamy (C1:W) resides in Compound C1, but was born in Wiralmurippu village.

An index to personal names, arranged according to Compounds, is given in Appendix 3 (pp. 321–31). With certain exceptions, the genealogical position of all those who have been given code numbers is shown either in Chart *i* (at end of book) or on Chart *h* (p. 312).

REFERENCES

Books and articles quoted are given in the form of the author's name and the date of publication. Full details will be found in the list of references at p. 334.

CHAPTER I

INTRODUCTION

This monograph has two aspects. First, it is an addition to the already substantial literature relating to Ceylonese land tenure (*Bibliography*, 1951; Codrington, 1938, Bibliography; Wickremasinghe, 1924); as such its value is narrowly regional and ethnographic, but not exclusively anthropological; there is matter here which has relevance both for the historian and for the general sociologist. Secondly, the book is an academic exercise designed to provide a critical test of certain features of the theory and method of contemporary British social anthropology; in this latter respect I presuppose an audience of professional anthropologists with interests in the general field of kinship theory.

In this opening chapter I try to strike the balance between these two presentations. I first describe the nature of the book considered as a contribution to Ceylon studies; I then go on to outline my objectives as a professional exponent of academic social anthropology.

'PUL ELIYA' AND CEYLON LAND TENURE STUDIES

My formal subject-matter covers an extremely narrow field. The book contains a detailed account of the land tenure system prevailing in a single village in the North Central Province in the year 1954. The total population of the village at that time was 146 individuals and the total area under irrigated cultivation was approximately 135 acres.

The village in question is similar to other villages in the vicinity, but I do not suggest that it is in any special way 'typical' of all such villages or that it is in any sense a statistically 'average' village. The numerical quantities which appear in various parts of this book are not generalised statistics, but particular figures which relate to a single particular place at a single particular time. It is this fact which distinguishes this study from all its predecessors in the same field.

There are already a number of publications which purport to include sociological descriptions of village life in the North Central Province; all of these are, in different degrees, synthetic. Ievers's (1899) account is based partly on personal observation, but mainly on a study of the Administration files relating to land disputes occurring during the decade 1870–80. Although he appears to have misunderstood his sources in certain particulars, his account may be regarded as generally valid for most villages in the area at that time, but in detail it applied to none.

Codrington (1938) was more concerned with ancient history than with contemporary fact. He uses Ievers's synthesis and supplements this with his own observations made in the Vavuniya District around 1909; he then adjusts the synthesis to fit ancient documentary sources dating back to the ninth century or earlier. Codrington's analysis certainly has some relevance for most contemporary villages in the North Central Province area, just as Magna Carta may be said to have some relevance for all contemporary parliamentary systems, but the detailed illumination that it provides is not very great.

Pieris (1956) relies heavily on Ievers and Codrington, and although he introduces a large body of additional documentary source material, the outcome of his analysis is of the same kind as before. His 'Nuvarakalāviya village' is an ideal type, a phenomenon of history. Its relationship to any particular village of the present day is not examined.

The case of Ryan is rather different. This author devotes a ten-page section of his important study of Sinhalese caste (Ryan 1953 a) to the description of a single actual village to which he gives the pseudonym 'Vanniaveva'.[1] He describes it as: 'a village near the border of the North Western and North Central Provinces which is, in its ecology, social structure and attitudes, similar to hundreds of other settlements in the great north central dry zone', (p. 251), but he does not explain how he has managed to locate

[1] Professor Ryan kindly divulged to me the true name of this village.

a single village which can be regarded as typical of all other villages in the region.

Since Pul Eliya is not very far from 'Vanniaveva' it might have been interesting to draw some direct comparisons, but Ryan's statements, when placed against the Pul Eliya context, become difficult to understand. For example, he asserts that: 'as is practically universal in Ceylon, there are different Gē having somewhat different statuses...the Goyigama of Vanniaveva are divided into three Gē groups or Houses' (p. 253). Now Ryan's definition of a 'Gē group' is such that an anthropologist would infer that the Goyigama population of 'Vanniaveva' comprises three patrilineal lineages, each with its ancient family name (*vasagama*), and each contracting a separate set of marriage alliances with other similar lineages in other villages.[1] This is quite unlike anything which I have recorded for the case of Pul Eliya.

However, my own separate inquiries indicated that in fact there are no patrilineal lineages in 'Vanniaveva', and that all the Goyigama inhabitants share the same *vasagama* name. If then, as Ryan asserts, the population is split into 'three status groups' the nature of these groups is obscure.

My purpose here is not to denigrate Professor Ryan's very notable contributions to Ceylon sociology, but simply to urge that too much should not be inferred from the apparent differences between 'Vanniaveva' and Pul Eliya. 'Vanniaveva', though based on an actual case, is not in any genuine sense a case history. Because Ryan makes use of unanalysed general concepts such as 'Gē group' the picture he presents is as much an ideal type as are the descriptions of Northern Dry Zone villages which appear in Ievers, Codrington and Pieris.

The present study of Pul Eliya is not comparable to any of these, for my first concern is not with general characteristics, but

[1] Ryan, 1953*a*, p. 26; 1953*b passim*; but cf. 1958, pp. 46–51 which includes the statement that 'neither the *Ge* nor the family can be conceived as a lineage in the proper sense of that word'. The discussion of the terms *gedera* and *pavula* in chapter IV of this book will throw light on Professor Ryan's confused terminology.

with the workings of a particular social system in all the details of its singular particularity.

It is often forgotten that the social facts which are of relevance to sociologists fall into two quite distinct classes which call for fundamentally different techniques of investigation. First, there are facts which are essentially statistical; these include nearly everything which is relevant in the study of economics and of demography. If one is investigating birth-rates, death-rates, production-rates, consumption-rates, prices, living standards, etc., then the techniques of survey and statistical generalisation are fundamental. It would clearly be entirely unscientific to make a study of a single village, however detailed, and then generalise from these particular facts so as to claim knowledge of an entire region. And I frankly admit that for a great many practical administrative purposes it is the 'generalised', 'average', 'typical' truth which matters.

But there is another class of social facts where this is not the case. In the field of law, general principles are certainly important, but particular instances, actual precedents, are crucial. A mere statement of the rules, an assertion that 'this is the custom', tells us extremely little until we have observed in detail a particular application of the rules. It is only when we have observed the practice that the rule, as an ideal type, acquires meaning.

This is particularly noticeable in the present instance. Ievers, Codrington and Pieris have given quite competent descriptions of the general legal principles which apply to the holding of land in the North Central Province. Hayley (1923) likewise has accurately stated the general principles governing kinship, marriage, and inheritance among the Kandyan Sinhalese. Yet from none of these descriptions could one formulate an even approximately accurate guess at the kind of society that is to be found in the village of Pul Eliya. The Pul Eliya villagers do in fact apply, with considerable rigour, the legal principles which are recorded in Ievers and Hayley, but it is not until one has worked right through the detailed facts of the case that this becomes apparent.

In sum, all previous studies of North Central Province village

4

organisation have been descriptions of an ideal type. The present study consists of the detailed study of a particular instance. Both in the economic and in the legal spheres the two types of analysis supplement one another. From the viewpoint of a specialist in Ceylon studies, the particular value of this book is the light it may throw on the academic treatises to which I have already referred. *Pul Eliya* is a case history; it does not refute what has been said before, but it exemplifies past statements in a way that for most readers must be unexpected.

'PUL ELIYA' AS A CONTRIBUTION TO ACADEMIC SOCIAL ANTHROPOLOGY

Regarded as a contribution to technical social anthropology, my topic might be summarised as follows: This is a study of a small peasant community subsisting by the cultivation of rice in irrigated fields of fixed size and position. The emphasis is on the relevance of kinship and marriage for the practices relating to land holding and land use. Unilineal descent is not a factor in the situation. Although the ethnography has an extremely narrow range the community has an ecology which has parallels in many parts of the world; for that reason some aspects of the analysis are of general significance.

The factual evidence is in certain respects very detailed and some parts of it have a time depth of 65 years. This 'excessive' detail brings into prominence the question of how far the anthropologist's concept of social structure refers to a set of ideas or to a set of empirical facts. This is a general theoretical issue which concerns all social anthropologists.

All British social anthropologists would agree that during the period 1935–54 the most important developments in anthropological theory were concerned with the enlargement of our understanding of the nature and significance of unilineal descent groups. This work stemmed directly from a series of theoretical papers by Radcliffe-Brown[1] and from the influence of Evans-Pritchard's

[1] Reprinted in Radcliffe-Brown (1952).

brilliantly simplified study of the Nuer (1940). Fortes (1953) has provided an admirably argued summary of this whole development. Like all successful theses the theory of unilineal descent groups serves to generate its own antithesis.

Throughout his writings Radcliffe-Brown consistently exaggerated the importance of unilineal as opposed to bilateral (cognatic) systems of succession and inheritance. Likewise, he constantly stressed the legal aspects of kinship relations as manifested in rights of inheritance in contrast to the economic aspects manifested in work co-operation. The lineage and not the family was the focus of attention.

The bias in favour of unilineal exogamous descent structures was remarkable. In an 85-page general survey of kinship theory published in 1950 the whole Arab world was dismissed in three lines (Radcliffe-Brown, 1950, p. 69). In the same essay, cognatic systems proper which, though uncommon in Africa, are widely distributed throughout the rest of the world, were treated simply as an eccentric historical peculiarity of the Teutonic tribes (Radcliffe-Brown, 1950, pp. 15–18; cf. 1952, p. 48).

Such bias should make us cautious. A number of far-reaching generalisations have been derived from Radcliffe-Brown's theoretical argument and the field-work which resulted from it. The generalisations stand up well in most lineage type societies. But how far do they apply in societies which do not conform to the unilineal pattern to which Radcliffe-Brown attached so much importance?

For example, it has been argued, very cogently, that in societies with a lineage structure the continuity of the society as a whole rests in the continuity of the system of lineages, each of which is a 'corporation', the life span of which is independent of the individual lives of its individual members. But in societies which do not have unilineal descent groups, what kind of 'corporation' takes the place of the lineage in providing the nexus of continuity between one generation and the next?

By implication Fortes himself, in the paper I have cited, posed precisely this problem and a quotation may usefully serve as a text for my whole investigation.

We see that descent is fundamentally a jural concept as Radcliffe-Brown argued in one of his most important papers (1935); we see its significance, as the connecting link between the external, that is political and legal aspect of what we have called unilineal descent groups, and the internal or domestic aspect. It is in the latter context that kinship carries maximum weight, first, as the source of title to membership of the groups or to specific jural status, with all that this means in rights over and toward persons and property, and second as the basis of the social relations among the persons who are identified with one another in the corporate group. In theory membership of a corporate legal or political group need not stem from kinship, as Weber has made clear. In primitive society, however, if it is not based on kinship it seems generally to presume some formal procedure of incorporation with ritual initiation.... Why descent rather than locality or some other principle forms the basis of these corporate groups is a question which needs more study. It will be remembered that Radcliffe-Brown (1935) related succession rules to the need for unequivocal discrimination of rights *in rem* and *in personam*. Perhaps it is most closely connected with the fact that rights over the reproductive powers of women are easily regulated by a descent group system. But I believe that something deeper than this is involved, for in a homogeneous society there is nothing which could so precisely and incontrovertibly fix one's place in society as one's parentage (Fortes, 1953, p. 30).

It will be found that in the Sinhalese village of Pul Eliya it is locality rather than descent which forms the basis of corporate grouping, even though the final sentences of the quotation remain valid. The circumstances in which this comes about suggest some interesting reflections on Fortes's thesis.

First, it should be observed that Fortes is here writing in general terms and not exclusively of unilineal systems. Negative evidence will thus throw doubt upon the whole theory.

The issues at stake are far reaching. If anthropologists come to look upon kinship as a parameter which can be studied in isolation they will always be led, by a series of strictly logical steps, to think of human society as composed of equilibrium systems structured according to ideal legal rules. Economic activities come to appear of minor significance and the study of social adaptation to changing circumstance is made impossible.

But an alternative possibility is to regard economic relations as 'prior' to kinship relations. In this case the continuity of the kinship system need not be regarded as intrinsic; it is, at every point in time, adaptive to the changing economic situation.

In Evans-Pritchard's studies of the Nuer (1940, 1951) and also in Fortes's studies of the Tallensi (1945, 1949a) unilineal descent turns out to be largely an ideal concept to which the empirical facts are only adapted by means of fictions. Both societies are treated as extreme examples of patrilineal organisation. The evident importance attached to matrilateral and affinal kinship connections is not so much explained as explained away.

The basic thesis which underlies these writings has been thus summarised by Fortes: 'The tendency towards equilibrium is marked in every sector of Tale society and in the society as a whole; and it is clearly *the result of the dominance of the lineage principle* in the social structure.... The almost complete absence of economic differentiation... mean(s) that *economic interests do not play the part of dynamic factors in the social structure*' (Fortes, 1945, p. x. (My italics.)). But the factual evidence presented in support of this thesis is highly selected and the time depth very shallow. To the more sceptical it might appear that, if the evidence were more specific and more historical, the discrepancies between the ideal of patrilineal descent and the facts of empirical behaviour might well become still more prominent. In that case both the 'equilibrium' and the 'dominance of the lineage principle' would be little more than academic fancies.

In later writing Fortes has treated the concept of social structure in a different way (Fortes, 1949b). Whereas in the Tallensi books structure is a matter of jural rules, the ideal form of which can be represented as a paradigm, Ashanti social structure is shown to emerge as a statistical norm. Fortes himself does not contrast these two arguments and he perhaps intended to imply that the statistical pattern must always converge towards the normative paradigm. But this could only be a presumption. If in reality the ideal order of jural relations and the statistical order of economic relations do not converge, then the significance which we attach to the 'structure of unilineal descent groups' will need careful reconsideration.

It is my thesis that jural rules and statistical norms should be treated as separate frames of reference, but that the former should always be considered secondary to the latter.

In this book I examine the quantitative ('statistical') facts of a particular case and show that these possess a structural pattern which is independent of any ideal paradigm. This does not imply that ideal relations are irrelevant, but it does emphasise that the ideal order and the statistical order are not just one and the same thing.

In an earlier publication (Leach, 1954) I have stressed this dichotomy in a different way. I there argued that the ideal order tends to be a constant which is reinterpreted to fit the changing circumstances of economic and political fact, but I also suggested that the latter—the facts of empirical reality—are, in every variation, constrained by the ideas which people hold about what is supposed to be the case.

In my Sinhalese story I want to make a different point. Here again the ideal model of society and the empirical facts are distinct. Indeed, despite tremendous empirical changes, the ideal order is still close to that described by Ievers nearly 60 years ago. The remarkable manner in which this ideal system has constrained actual behaviour is clearly demonstrated, especially in chapter VI.

But the Pul Eliya community does not only operate within an established framework of legal rules, it also exists within a parti-cular man-made ecological environment. It is the inflexibility of topography—of water and land and climate—which most of all determines what people shall do. The interpretation of ideal legal rules is at all times limited by such crude nursery facts as that water evaporates and flows downhill. It is in this sense that I want to insist that the student of social structure must never forget that the constraints of economics are prior to the constraints of morality and law.

9

Although I am pleading that my specialist study of Pul Eliya has general implications, I am not proposing a classification. Since I have used a quotation from Fortes as my text, this must be stressed.

The theory of unilineal descent groups is, on the face of it, well established; it would, therefore, be tempting to offer Pul Eliya as a contrary type—a 'bilateral' as opposed to a 'unilineal' structure. I am not proposing any such typology, for I am sceptical of all typologies.

Radcliffe-Brown's generalisation (1950, p. 14) that 'there are few if any societies in which there is not some recognition of uni-lineal descent' is itself invalid, but the corollary, that no clear distinction is possible between societies which recognise unilineal descent and those which do not, is correct. There are a large number of societies which possess some of the superficial attri-butes of unilineal systems yet lack clearly defined unilineal descent groups. The English with their patrilineally inherited surnames provide one example; Sinhalese society is another. The precise nature of the 'unilinearity' present in these marginal cases calls for close investigation, but it would be prejudging the whole issue to assume that the presence or absence of lineages was a diacritically significant factor.

Other writers have suggested that patrilineal lineages occur in Sinhalese society (Ryan, 1953a, p. 26; Pieris, 1956, pp. 219–22). In my view that is fallacious, yet it is perfectly true that the Sinhalese do possess, in certain respects, a patrilineal ideology. Is this patrilinearity of the Sinhalese an enduring characteristic of Sinhalese culture or is it a reflection of the way in which Sinhalese order their economic lives? Has it the lasting quality of a prin-ciple of law or is it simply descriptive of a temporary state of affairs?

I might put it this way. We can learn a great deal about the nature of unilineal descent groups by pursuing to its limit the terminological issue as to whether it is or is not correct to say that Sinhalese society is patrilineal. Conversely we can learn a great deal about the nature of cognatic (bilateral) systems if we pursue the question: Why is it functionally useful in a society such as that of Pul Eliya, which lacks unilineal descent groups, to have a concept of descent at all? But the outcome of this inquiry will be to blur rather than to intensify the distinction between unilineal and non-unilineal systems; Pul Eliya itself does not belong to either 'type'.

Kinship as we meet it in this book is not 'a thing in itself'. The concepts of descent and of affinity are expressions of property relations which endure through time. Marriage unifies; inheritance separates; property endures. A particular descent system simply reflects the total process of property succession as effected by the total pattern of inheritance and marriage. The classification of whole societies in terms of such a parameter can only be meaningful in an extremely crude sense.

What we need to understand about a society is not whether it is patrilineal or matrilineal or both or neither, but what the notion of patrilinearity stands for and why it is there.

Again and again I found my Pul Eliya villagers asserting of a particular piece of ground that the owner's rights were *purāna* ('from the beginning') or *paravēni* ('ancestral'), even when I knew as an unquestionable fact that the land in question had recently been acquired by purchase. Why this scheme of values? What does continuity with the ancestral past 'mean' in such a society?

Such answer as I can give is a special answer which applies in its particularity only to the special case of Pul Eliya. But it is a special answer with general implications; it has relevance for the much wider issue of the distinction between unilineal and bilateral kinship systems on the one hand, and between jural and economic relationships on the other.

Finally I would add a more technical point. The case-history method of presenting anthropological arguments has now been in vogue for many years. It was practised by Malinowski and it has been practised in much the same way by some of his most vociferous critics. But case-history material in anthropological writings seldom reflects objective description. What commonly happens is that the anthropologist propounds some rather preposterous hypothesis of a very general kind and then puts forward his cases to illustrate the argument. The technique of argument is still that of Frazer. Insight comes from the anthropologist's private intuition; the evidence is only put in by way of illustration.

Now the special conditions under which the anthropologist makes his observations and his analyses make it very difficult to avoid this kind of subjectivism, and I do not pretend that I have escaped from it in this book. But I have tried to do so. The case-history material in this book is very extensive, but the cases are not simply there to illustrate a particular theoretical principle. On a larger scale the isolated examples all fit together into a single case-history, and the material is there in sufficient quantity for the reader to exercise his scepticism where and how he will. The interpretation of the evidence is of course still *my* interpretation, but I have tried to avoid offering a 'take it or leave it' solution. I claim that the evidence 'speaks for itself'. Even if this is not entirely the case I feel that I have been more honest with my readers than some of my colleagues have managed to be with theirs. The extra detail goes in at the cost of readability, but I cannot avoid that. The result is not bedside reading, but there is plenty to exercise the acrostic-making talent of the industrious undergraduate.

CHAPTER II

PUL ELIYA: THE GENERAL BAC[

The purpose of this chapter is to provide a broad outline of the
general context within which the Pul Eliya social system exists.

TOPOGRAPHY AND HISTORICAL CONTINUITY

Pul Eliya is a village in the Kende Kōralē of the Nuvarakalāviya
District of the North Central Province of Ceylon. It lies about
12 miles to the north of Anurādhapura. It is a Sinhalese-speaking
village inhabited by members of the Goyigama caste. Most other
villages in the immediate vicinity are similarly Sinhalese-speaking,
but to the south-west there are some Tamil-speaking villages of
which the inhabitants are Moslem (*marakkal*); Hindu Tamil
villages are to be found a few miles to the north-west.

Because the ancient Sinhalese kingdom was for many centuries
centred on Anurādhapura and Mihintalē, the region is one
which is of very special interest to Ceylon historians. Contemporary documents of the early Sinhalese kingdom scarcely
exist. Far more than in Europe the medieval historian must rely
on archaeological evidence and the decipherment of cryptic,
fragmentary stone inscriptions. In such circumstances it is not
surprising that scholars, in endeavouring to find meaning in these
defective records, have looked for clues among the modern
practices of the Sinhalese villagers living nearby. Unfortunately
Tylor's doctrine of cultural survival has here often been employed
in an entirely uncritical fashion.

In using twentieth-century materials as evidence for ninth-
century custom it has come to be assumed that rural Ceylon
continues from century to century almost unaffected by the
passage of history. Documents from the tenth, twelfth, sixteenth,
eighteenth, nineteenth and twentieth centuries are repeatedly cite
side by side as if they all referred to the same thing. This is pa

cularly true with regard to the region covered by the modern North Central Province. Codrington in 1938 and Pieris in 1956[1] alike take it for granted that customs prevalent in the North Central Province at the beginning of the twentieth century were necessarily a perpetuation of something which formerly prevailed uniformly throughout the Sinhalese kingdom.

I must emphasise very strongly that no such assumptions are implicit in the present volume. This book is concerned with the state of affairs in Pul Eliya in 1954. There is archaeological evidence that a village also existed on the same site in ancient times, and there are grounds for thinking that in certain respects this ancient village must have been rather similar to the present one. But that is all. I do not claim that Pul Eliya is a typical Nuvarakalāviya village, still less do I suppose that the social system which I describe was once universal throughout the Kandyan kingdom or any of its predecessors.

For historical reconstruction of the type favoured by Codrington and Pieris the key document has been Ievers's *Manual of the North Central Province* (1899), a book which contains a general description of the manners and customs of the Sinhalese of the area as observed between 1870 and 1890.

The detailed reliability of this important work is less than has been commonly supposed. Ievers's account of land tenure is synthetic, being based mainly on the diary records of a series of land cases tried by Mr J. F. Dickson, Government Agent, Anurādhapura, in the period 1870 onwards. Ievers, who succeeded Dickson in this post, was mainly interested in irrigation and his official diaries show little concern with the finer intricacies of native law and custom. Reference to Dickson's original manuscript notes[2] suggests that Ievers at times misunderstood his source.

Nevertheless, Ievers's idealised account does have great relevance for our understanding of Pul Eliya, and in chapter v

[1] Pieris (1956, p. 235) fully appreciates the nature of the assumptions involved.
[2] Held at the Ceylon Government Archives, Nuwara Eliya; cf. also Dickson (3).

I shall recapitulate certain sections of Ievers's versic
to me crucial.

When Ievers wrote his account nearly all villa
North Central Province were still held under ru¹
and custom. By 1954 the position was very differ....
a proportion of the land of most villages was still held according
to supposedly traditional rules, other lands (*sinakkara*) were now
held freehold on a registered title, while still other holdings, known
as *badu idam*, were held on a kind of perpetual Crown lease. The
diversity of these modern tenures has important implications for
the present-day villagers, which I shall endeavour to explain in
due course.

The historians' assumption of long-term structural stability in
the society of the Nuvarakalāviya District can be justified by
certain ecological arguments. Geographically considered, the
region is a very special one. It forms part of the Dry Zone of
Ceylon. Rainfall is around 50–75 inches a year which, under
tropical conditions, is meagre. Most of this rain is concentrated
into two periods, October–December and April–May. The
terrain is nearly flat. The soil cover is thin and markedly lacking
in humus. Rain, when it comes, is usually heavy; there is then
a rapid run-off, the rivers become torrents for a few hours and
then relapse. In a few days everything is just as dry as before.
The natural cover is forest, but it is very dry forest which, once
it has been felled, grows up again only very slowly. To anyone
accustomed to the lush pastures of Europe such conditions offer an
uninviting prospect. Robert Knox, writing in the seventeenth
century, treated the whole area as an uninhabitable wilderness.
Yet, paradoxically, this was the centre of the first Sinhalese
civilisation. The whole region is thick with the archaeological
remnants of its romantic past.

The ancient civilisation endured from about the second century
B.C. to the middle of the thirteenth century A.D. Political decay
and depopulation then followed and continued for several
centuries. Only in quite recent times has the land once again been
required to support a large and growing population. Even in

ıevers's day the villages were still very small and widely scattered. Chronologically, there is thus a wide discontinuity between the prosperous present and the glories of the historical past. Nevertheless the newly emergent society is, in a curious way, conditioned and restricted by the civilisation that flourished a thousand years ago. If it be true that the present-day society is in any sense similar to the ancient one—and that is very difficult to demonstrate—it is because the new society has had to adjust itself to a rather special and difficult set of ecological conditions which have remained constant through the centuries. There has been no substantial historical continuity in the society itself.

The classical Sinhalese kingdom, with its capital at Anurādhapura, was a striking and characteristic example of what Wittfogel has called 'hydraulic civilisation' (Wittfogel, 1957; but cf. Leach, 1959). A region of poor natural fertility was made to support a large and flourishing population by resort to irrigation engineering. Statements about demographic conditions in the ancient kingdom tend to be fabulous rather than exact, but, around the tenth century A.D., the population of the Nuvarakalāviya District can scarcely have been less than it is today.

The Chinese traveller Fa Hsien described the Anurādhapura of the late fourth century A.D. as a large and prosperous city. He had been told that there were then over sixty thousand monks in the Sinhalese kingdom and he accepts the possibility that in Anurādhapura alone there might have been five or six thousand monks directly dependent on the king's bounty. Even allowing for some exaggeration it is evident that the Sinhalese economy of this period was such that the State could afford to maintain a large number of unproductive individuals.

The high productivity, per unit of labour, which Fa Hsien's account implies, had gradually become possible through the accumulated capital investment represented by ever-extending irrigation works. Although in later centuries most of these works were abandoned it is essentially the same system of irrigation which has now been restored and refurbished. It is thus probable that the distribution of population on the ground is today rather similar to what it was in Fa Hsien's time. (See Brohier, 1934/5.)

The present-day villagers go much further than that; they claim that their whole system of organisation has been handed down intact from the most ancient times. That they should hold this opinion and thus put a value upon traditional ways and social stability is a fact of sociological significance, but it is not a fact of history. We know nothing at all about the organisation of village life in the ancient Sinhalese kingdom.

The modern irrigation works of Nuvarakalāviya, like their ancient predecessors, fall into two distinct categories. There are the small reservoirs (tanks) associated with individual villages and the very much larger central reservoirs and feeder canals which now, as formerly, are under the control of the central government. The latter class of works do not immediately concern us. Pul Eliya is not today connected with any central irrigation system and, so far as can be judged, it never has been so connected in the past.

Of the smaller reservoirs—the village tanks—there are today several thousand in actual use. Almost all are of ancient origin, but only a few have been in continuous use over the centuries. The great majority have been abandoned at various times and then restored again.

In this economy the basic valuable is scarce water rather than scarce land; it is the total water-supply available to a community which sets a limit to the area of land that may be cultivated and hence to the size of the population which may survive through subsistence agriculture. The same is true of the district as a whole. In 1954 additional sources of irrigation water were becoming very scarce and expensive to control and this suggests that, by 1954, the population of this district was rapidly approaching the maximum that could be supported from local resources alone. A similar situation seems to have arisen around the eleventh century A.D.

A village tank is created by damming up a natural stream and building a long earthwork wall to hold the water up behind it.

The resulting reservoir (when full) is usually about seven feet deep immediately behind the earthwork ('bund'). Very roughly, the full tank covers much the same area of ground as the land below it which it is capable of irrigating. Clearly, the location of tanks must conform to the natural lay of the ground. Although, in a generally flat terrain, the villager has some choice about how he constructs minor works, the site of the larger tanks is predetermined from the start.

The village of Pul Eliya today has a main tank of about 140 acres. Archaeological evidence in the shape of an ancient spillway and two *bisōkotuva* type sluice works demonstrates conclusively that the present bund occupies exactly the same position as the bund of an ancient tank of the eleventh century or earlier.

This particular village has been occupied continuously since the British records begin around 1838. For earlier periods we have no evidence. It is a tank that is exceptionally well situated, the length of the bund in relation to the area of water being relatively short. This means that the tank can be fairly easily kept in good order. Moreover it is a tank which very seldom dries up completely even in years of drought. A reliable tank such as this would seldom have been abandoned for very long even in periods when the population was at a minimum, and it could be the case that Pul Eliya has been continuously occupied from the beginning. This we cannot know. On the other hand the remnants of various subsidiary irrigation works show that the overall system of water control has not always been quite what it is today.

The present villagers have a romantic tradition that their village was founded in the time of Dutthagāmani, which would imply a date round the second century B.C. They also maintain that they formerly possessed a palm leaf 'book' which was kept in the temple and which recorded that the original grant of their land dated from remote antiquity. This book is said to have been 'stolen' by a certain government official some years ago.

Claims of this general type are common to all the villages around and have no particular historical significance. In the days of the Kandyan kings most village lands were held by virtue of a title deed recorded on palm leaf (*ōla*). A Ceylon Government Commission appointed in 1869 to investigate these ancient titles[1] declared that most of the *ōla* documents produced before it were valueless forgeries. The name Pul Eliya does not appear in the surviving files of the Commission's proceedings. The evidence is thus negative. It is possible, though improbable, that the villagers possessed an ancient title deed until quite recent times.

The villagers themselves clearly believed in the authenticity of their story. They declared that the principal details of the ancient *ōla* were reproduced on the letter of appointment of Mudalihamy Vel Vidāne (B1:3) who was given the title Badderāla[2] around 1930. But here again verification eluded me—Mudalihamy's son (P:B1) admitted to having had the document, but said he had lost it.

Pul Eliya theory is that in Kandyan times the village was classed as *nindagam* land over which the ancestors of the present Bulankulame Disava exercised ultimate title as hereditary feudal lords (*gamladdā*).[3] This is very probable.

The Disava's family have both a ritual and an historical claim to aristocracy. They are hereditary guardians of the Sacred Bo Tree at Anurādhapura and also descendants of the eighteenth-century Vanniyar—the Lord of the Vanni—whose baronial status was almost that of an independent prince.

To Pul Eliya villagers of the Kandyan period the Vanniyar, who lived only twelve miles away, must have appeared an absolute potentate from whose decisions there was no appeal. If the Vanniyar ever deferred to anyone it was probably to the Dutch, who had a garrisoned frontier post a few miles to the north-west of Pul Eliya. The Sinhalese king in Kandy was far away (Pieris, 1956, pp. 249–51; cf. Tennent, 1859, II, p. 625; Nevill, 1887).

When the British colonial regime was established in 1815 village administration was for a while completely disrupted, but

---

[1] 'Report', 1869–76; cf. 'Papers', 1869; Dickson, 1870–2.
[2] See p. 71.
[3] Pieris, 1956, Part II, chapter VII. The Disava died in 1959.

by 1838 a type of indirect rule had been established in which all effective authority was in the hands of a native official generally known as the Ratēmahatmayā. The office was in practice virtually hereditary. The Ratēmahatmayā responsible for Pul Eliya affairs was invariably a member of the ancient Vanniyar family.

The villagers' belief in continuity with the past is thus something more than a romantic dream. The Vanniyar in the days of the Dutch and the Ratēmahatmayā in the days of the British were persons of very similar status; they were individual members of the same family. The present generation of villagers are probably quite correct in thinking that between 1800 and 1938 the relations between themselves and their feudal overlord scarcely changed at all.

The villagers' interest in descent is linked with this fact. As we shall see, the village lands are today divided into a very large number of separate holdings, individually owned. For the majority of these holdings no documentary title exists or has ever existed; the sanction which preserves the rights of one owner against another is appeal to government authority, first to the Vel Vidāne, then to the Village Cultivation Officer (V.C.O.) and finally to the Divisional Revenue Officer (D.R.O.)[1] which is the modern name for the office formerly filled by the hereditary Ratēmahatmayā. The manner in which such validation is achieved is by reference to the past and to principles of descent. I shall discuss this point again in chapters IV and V.

Apart from its good situation the Pul Eliya tank is not in any way exceptional, though it is somewhat larger than a number of those round about. Administration records show that the tank was in reasonably good condition in 1870; they also record government-assisted tank repairs in 1900 and 1940. A cadastral survey of the village lands was made in 1900 and from that date onwards we have a fairly complete set of data concerning the changes in land tenure.

I must stress again that we know little for certain about the remote past. The location, the size, and even the general layout

[1] See p. 69 n.

of the modern village may well be ancient, but we have no right to assume that the modern society closely resembles that of antiquity. This is a society which has ancient traditions but a shallow history. Documentary records for any period before 1886 are negligible, both in quantity and quality. At the same time it is sociologically significant that the villagers should themselves firmly believe that their customs have continued unbroken from the remote past; they constantly cite the great names of Duttha-gāmani and Parākrama Bāhu as justification for all they do. Even I myself, as anthropological observer, surrounded on all sides by visible evidence of a past civilisation, found it difficult to avoid thinking that the present was in some way a survival from antiquity. Yet factually such assumptions are unjustified and mis-leading. We can take it as certain that some modern customs are derived directly from practices that prevailed in the middle of the nineteenth century—but how much further back their genealogy can be traced is a matter of pure guesswork.

The air photograph Plate I (between pp. 24 and 25) includes Pul Eliya (58 on Map A) and three neighbouring villages—Diwulwewa (56), Kalawel Potana (61) and Tulawelliya (59). The villages are spaced roughly 1½ miles apart and this distribution is normal throughout the area. Map A records the position of all the villages in the immediate vicinity of Pul Eliya. Throughout this book the numerals shown in brackets after village names refer to this map. As may be seen in Plate I each village is an entirely separate unit with its own tank or tanks and its own set of fields dependent on those tanks. On Map A the position of the tanks and 'Old Field' is sketched in only for villages 55–8.

The village houses are ordinarily located immediately below the tank bund; they therefore lie between the tank and the field which it serves. The pressure of water in the tank maintains a high water table in this house-site area (*gamgoda*) and this makes it possible to grow coconuts, plantains and certain other 'wet zone' fruits. Most of the dry 'highland'[1] which surrounds the village can be

[1] This term does not denote hillside, but simply ground inaccessible to irrigation.

cultivated occasionally by shifting cultivation (*hēna*) techniques, but this is a precarious business. For their main livelihood the villagers are dependent on the rice which they can grow on the irrigated land below their tank.

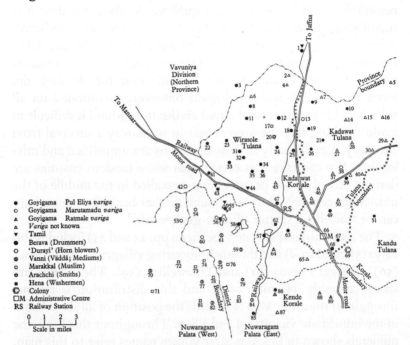

Map *A*. Map of western end of boundary zone between Kende and Kadawat Korale, North Central Province, showing distribution of villages distinguished by *variga*. In the case of Bellankadawala (55) and Diwulwewa (56), Wiral-murippu (57) and Pul Eliya (58) only, the position of the tank and Old Field is shown in outline. Villages in the Vavuniya Division other than those mentioned in the text are not included.

These circumstances imply that the people living immediately below a particular tank are closely bound together by common economic interest to the exclusion of others. Many features of the associated society stem from this fact.

The population of the area, taken as a whole, is very diverse. As between one village and the next there may be very great differences of language, religion and caste. Yet in any one village the population is ordinarily homogeneous. This is a special feature peculiar to this part of Ceylon.

THE CASTE ORDER

The local Sinhalese have a word, *variga* (variety, kind) which they use to denote categories of human beings of all kinds.[1] Thus the Tamils—a linguistic category—form a *variga*, but so do the Moslems (*marakkal*)—a religious category. The castes of Washermen and Drummers, which are social categories, are *variga*, but so are the Väddā, and that is a cultural-racial category. No matter what the type of *variga* may be, the ordinary expectation is that in any one village the regular inhabitants will be members of one *variga* only. Exceptions occur, but the general principle is that only members of one particular *variga* shall have rights to the water in any one village tank. I shall have much more to say later on about this equation between one village and one 'caste'. But some preliminary elaboration of this *variga* concept is necessary even at this stage.

In the Sinhalese conception the essential characteristic of a *variga* is its endogamy. Members of one *variga* should intermarry with one another, but are strictly forbidden from marrying with the members of any other *variga*. In the ideal, therefore, the members of one village community are not merely of one religion and one language, they are also kin, being members of one endogamous *variga*. All kinds of exceptions to this ideal pattern occur and, for a variety of reasons, are tending to increase. But in 1954 the norm was still quite clear. Ordinarily all the inhabitants of any one village recognised one another as quite close kin. Of the villages round about some were recognised as belonging to kinsmen, others not. A man might properly seek a wife only in one of the related villages.

Pul Eliya is inhabited by members of one particular *variga* of

[1] The Pul Eliya villagers pronounced this word *varigē* and it is so written in some published work. I write *variga* throughout.

23

the Goyigama (cultivator) caste of the Sinhalese. This *variga* has no particular name; it is simply known as 'our *variga*'. The inhabitants of about twenty-five other villages are recognised as being of the same endogamous group.

The Pul Eliya villagers like to think of themselves as culturally and socially superior to most of their neighbours. They claim to be more modest and traditional in their clothing and in their housing; they claim to be better Buddhists and to be more strict in adhering to the rules of *variga* endogamy, and they pride themselves on the very limited extent of their social and economic relations with neighbouring groups of Tamils.

It is very difficult to know whether these claims to cultural distinctiveness correspond to any genuine reality. Certainly, in appearance, Pul Eliya looked more of a 'traditional' village than most, but mere conservatism was not what the villagers had in mind. Another village which they claimed was notable for its respectability was Mahā Diwulwewa (39). This large community which is adjacent to a main road has none of the old world appearance of Pul Eliya, but it was the home of a retired Kōrāla[1] who was related by marriage to various members of the Ceylon Government. Social snobbery is certainly closely linked with the idea of adhering closely to orthodox caste behaviour, but kinship with the influential is equally important.

If the members of the Pul Eliya *variga* are really culturally distinct from their near neighbours it is certainly only in very minor matters. Judging by appearances the land tenure system recorded in this monograph is very similar to that of nearly all other villages in the vicinity, whether they are of the same *variga* or not. Some of the features of Sinhalese society which I describe may be peculiar to members of the Goyigama caste or even to members of one particular *variga* of the Goyigama caste, but I have no particular grounds for supposing that the peoples of Pul Eliya are in any way exceptional.

There are, however, differing degrees to which members of separate *variga* can be considered socially distinct. The most

[1] See p. 69 n.

24

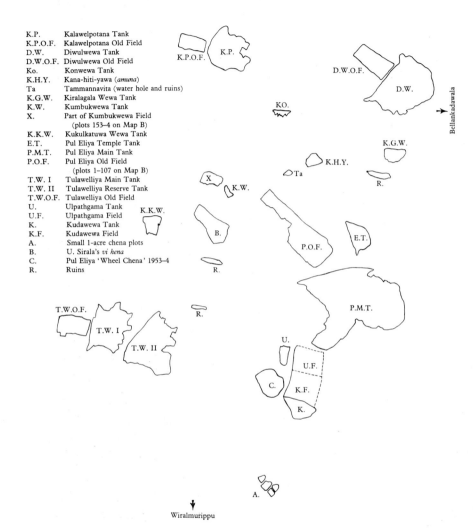

K.P.	Kalawelpotana Tank
K.P.O.F.	Kalawelpotana Old Field
D.W.	Diwulwewa Tank
D.W.O.F.	Diwulwewa Old Field
Ko.	Konwewa Tank
K.H.Y.	Kana-hiti-yawa (*amuna*)
Ta	Tammannavita (water hole and ruins)
K.G.W.	Kiralagala Wewa Tank
K.W.	Kumbukwewa Tank
X.	Part of Kumbukwewa Field
	(plots 153–4 on Map B)
K.K.W.	Kukulkatuwa Wewa Tank
E.T.	Pul Eliya Temple Tank
P.M.T.	Pul Eliya Main Tank
P.O.F.	Pul Eliya Old Field
	(plots 1–107 on Map B)
T.W. I	Tulawelliya Main Tank
T.W. II	Tulawelliya Reserve Tank
T.W.O.F.	Tulawelliya Old Field
U.	Ulpathgama Tank
U.F.	Ulpathgama Field
K.	Kudawewa Tank
K.F.	Kudawewa Field
A.	Small 1-acre chena plots
B.	U. Sirala's *vi hena*
C.	Pul Eliya 'Wheel Chena' 1953–4
R.	Ruins

Bellankadawala

Wiralmurippu

PLATE I

The surroundings of Pul Eliya. (See key opposite and pp. 21, 64, 240)

radical types of *variga* contrast are those which correspond to differences of language and religion. The Sinhalese as a whole, the Tamils as a whole and the *Moslem marakkal* as a whole, are members of different societies. Their interrelations with one another are kept to an absolute minimum. At this level, we may speak of Dry Zone Ceylon as possessing a 'plural society' in Furnivall's sense (Furnivall, 1939, ch. XIII). Tamils and Moslems often own shops at which Sinhalese peasants trade, Sinhalese peasants sometimes hire individual Tamil labourers, but relations seldom get closer than that. Such cross-cultural relationships as exist are almost exclusively economic.

In contrast, within the Sinhalese section of this totality, all the different *variga* are Buddhist by religion and Sinhalese by speech. In this case the context in which the *variga* concept is used is relatively narrow and relates mainly to the closely linked themes of sex relations and commensality. *Variga* in this sense is fairly translated as 'sub-caste'.

In Pul Eliya theory it would be considered intensely shocking for any woman of 'our *variga*' to have sex relations with any male of another *variga*, even if the other *variga* was of Goyigama caste. On the other hand less intimate forms of inter-*variga* association are not only permitted but prescribed. Although the actual inhabitants of Pul Eliya are exclusively of Goyigama caste, members of several other Sinhalese castes regularly partake in the Pul Eliya village rituals and various non-Goyigama Sinhalese are regularly employed as labourers in the Pul Eliya fields. But inter-*variga* contact of this sort is specifically a cross-caste phenomenon; there are no traditionally established relationships between the inhabitants of Pul Eliya and persons of Goyigama caste of *variga* other than their own, and contacts of this latter sort are consciously kept to a minimum.

Named Sinhalese castes are distinguished from one another mainly in terms of traditional service duties. These are not in any total sense occupational categories. The Washermen are only ritual washermen; the Drummers are only religious drummers; in their ordinary life Goyigama, Washermen, Drummers and the rest are all alike cultivators of the soil. This was so in the past just as it is now. In the past, however, the non-Goyigama were quite definitely of lower status in the feudal hierarchy. The service duty—that of providing a certain number of washers, drummers, dancers, palanquin bearers, etc. as the case might be on specified occasions—was something which was attached by title deed to a particular piece of land. This meant that only members of the appropriate caste group could work such land, and if the land in question was transferred by grant from one member of the feudal aristocracy to another, the peasant occupiers were transferred too, virtually as tied serfs.

The Goyigama villagers likewise formerly held their lands in fee either from the king or from one of his feudal lords, but they were not required to perform menial services as part of their rent, and they were not bond servants to their overlords in the manner of the service tenure villagers.

The Pul Eliya villagers of 1954 were keenly aware of these past social distinctions and were constantly complaining of the presumptuous behaviour of their non-Goyigama neighbours.

But caste difference is not simply an anachronistic relic of the feudal past, it still plays a very positive function in the total society. A village occupied by a group of Washermen or a village occupied by a group of Drummers looks no different from a village occupied by a group of Goyigama. But because the members of the traditionally menial castes are still prepared to perform ritual duties for their Goyigama neighbours in the traditionally prescribed form on traditionally prescribed occasions, caste difference serves to draw together the members of different *variga* who would otherwise tend to maintain a social life of total segregation.

This point needs to be emphasised. The traditional caste system in its full operation did not consist simply of an enumeration of different castes of different ritual status. The essence of the traditional caste system lay in the mesh of inter-caste relationships—the service duties which were performed not merely as an obligation but as a right. With the decay of caste, the social separation of the *variga* groups tends to become greater, not less.

26

The caste system as a whole may be thought of as having two major aspects. On the one hand the principle of endogamy serves to produce small exclusive localised groups of people who consider themselves to be of the same 'sub-caste' (*variga*) and of the same social status; on the other hand the system of caste rituals and caste duties provides an institutional framework through which members of different sub-castes are brought into relationship. These relationships extend to economic, religious and political spheres; only kinship is excluded. As the caste system atrophies, it is the institutional framework of caste which decays first; *variga* endogamy is as clearly marked as ever.

The Pul Eliya villagers were themselves aware of this trend and even of some of its causes. One man remarked that while the maternity service recently established by the Government had clearly brought enormous benefits, it had certain drawbacks. Now that all the women had their babies in hospital the rewards of the ritual office of washerwoman were no longer worthwhile. The traditional link between the Pul Eliya Goyigama and the Hēnayā (Washermen) people of Lindahitidamana (62) was thus breaking down, since it was becoming difficult to persuade any member of the Hēnayā caste to turn up at the annual village festivals. Formerly attendance at a birth was the most regular and the most lucrative of the washerwoman's various caste obligations.

To summarise: the inhabitants of Pul Eliya are associated with the inhabitants of a group of neighbouring villages on the grounds that they are kinsmen of the same Goyigama *variga*. They are also associated with the inhabitants of certain other Sinhalese villages because of their special technical-ritual functions. These functions are those of mediumship, drumming, washing, pot-making, blacksmithing, horn-blowing and temple-painting. Each of these functional activities is carried on as an hereditary craft by the members of a distinct *variga*. Pul Eliya villagers have contractual economic and religious relations with members of several of these functional *variga*, but do not intermarry with them. Finally there are, in the vicinity of Pul Eliya, various other villages inhabited either by Tamils, or by Moslems, or by Goyigama Sinhalese of different *variga*. With all such the Pul Eliya villagers endeavour to avoid contact altogether.

ADMINISTRATION

In most villages governmental authority is exercised through the Vel Vidāne (Irrigation Headman) who is, in theory, elected by the villagers themselves as their spokesman and leader. Once a man has been appointed to this office he is likely to hold it for many years until he either resigns or is dismissed for malpractice. It is an office which entails a large amount of tedious clerical work for which the direct rewards are small, but in a prosperous village the indirect advantages which accrue to the Vel Vidāne through his position of influence can be very great. No Vel Vidāne of Pul Eliya has ever vacated his office except on grounds of ill-health or old age.

Although Coomaraswamy writes of this office as if it were ancient I cannot trace any reference to it prior to 1867 and I am inclined to think that it is a British administrative invention instituted for the express purpose of creating a single responsible village head.[1] The Vel Vidāne's authority is mainly economic. His first responsibility is to see that government regulations regarding the fair distribution of tank water are fully adhered to. In such matters the Vel Vidāne's immediate superior is a government official, the V.C.O. (Village Cultivation Officer). Since one V.C.O. may be responsible for fifty or more villages the Vel Vidāne is in general left to his own devices. He can, if he so chooses, exercise wide and autocratic powers. The office of V.C.O. is a quite recent creation and in the days of the Ratēmahatmayā before 1938 the Vel Vidāne's local authority must have been complete.

In legal, as opposed to agricultural matters, the Vel Vidāne is only an informer. He is expected to report to the *tulāna* Headman.

[1] Coomaraswamy, 1956, p. 30; cf. Ceylon Government Ordinance no. 21 of 1867.

28

The *tulāna* Headman (misleadingly entitled 'Village Headman') is responsible for a dozen or more villages. His duties are mainly clerical.[1] Almost every matter which calls for administrative decision, even of the most trivial kind, has to be referred to still higher authority. This higher authority is the D.R.O. (Divisional Revenue Officer) of whom there were in 1954 five for the whole of the North Central Province. The ordinary villager seldom has any direct contact with any higher officer of the administrative hierarchy. Above the D.R.O. stands the Government Agent, but to the ordinary villager this high official seems remote. For most practical purposes the D.R.O. personifies the government. In this respect he has taken over the role of the former Ratē-mahatmayā.

Today the D.R.O. is a civil servant in permanent government employ who is liable to be transferred from one district to another, but in the Pul Eliya area, it was only in 1938 that the Ratēma-hatmayā relinquished his D.R.O. functions. In 1954 this same Ratēmahatmayā was serving as Minister of Lands in the Central Government. At this date the local D.R.O. was an extremely efficient regular civil servant but he also, as it happened, was a member of the local aristocracy affinally related to the former rulers. His sympathetic understanding of traditional custom was greatly appreciated by the villagers.

In 1954 the local *tulāna* Headman was K.V. Appuhamy (A 2:7), himself a resident of Pul Eliya, while the office of Pul Eliya Vel Vidāne was held by V. Menikrala (B 1:7). The two men were cross-cousins, the Vel Vidāne being the older man. So far as village affairs were concerned it was the *latter* office which mattered most.

Over the years the Ceylon Government has endeavoured to soften the rigidities of direct colonial administration by creating a supplementary system of local self-government. In the North Central Province these legislative measures have led to a great deal of administrative duplication, but have seldom brought any

[1] Unlike the Vel Vidāne who was (until 1958) rewarded with a commission on the crop, the Village Headman is a salaried government official.

29

obvious benefits to the individual villager. In 1954 the term Village Committee represented an institution roughly comparable to an English Rural District Council with greatly reduced powers. Members of the Village Committee were elected on a constituency basis, each member representing a group of villages. This Village Committee had control of certain funds intended to be used for village improvements such as roadmaking, well-digging and so on. In this monograph I shall avoid detailed reference to this institution. The Village Committee which was supposed to look after the welfare of Pul Eliya village had its headquarters some seventeen miles away and its incursions into Pul Eliya affairs were very slight. It was said to be an institution of great profit to its Chairman. In 1954 there was no member of the Village Committee actually resident in Pul Eliya itself. The local constituency member was a member of the Vanni-Väddā *variga* from Tulawelliya (59) village, two miles to the south.

COMMUNICATIONS DEVELOPMENT

To those familiar with the present-day North Central Province my account of Pul Eliya may suggest an unusual degree of isolation, but Pul Eliya is not really atypical in this respect. Communications in the Nuvarakalāviya District are deceptive. A network of fine motor roads joins the main centres and in good weather many minor village roads are easily motorable. It is usually possible to reach Pul Eliya from Anurādhapura in less than an hour.

Now it is true that villagers do not own motor-cars, but many of them do own bicycles. In 1954, Pul Eliya villagers frequently visited Anurādhapura and some went even further afield. Yet it was a curiously lopsided type of mobility. The villager could go outside into the Great World, but the inhabitants of the Great World never came to see the villager. Had it not been for my presence no 'outsider' would have visited Pul Eliya during the whole period of my stay there. If we ignore those villages which are actually sited on a main arterial road, this situation may be regarded as normal. The only visitors to a village are those who have relatives there or else some regular duty to perform.

Obviously the improvement in communications over the past half century has had important social consequences, but it is only in certain special ways that the isolation of the village has been eliminated.

For one thing the villager can no longer escape the eye of government officials; this is a most important change. Administrative records make it obvious that prior to 1890 senior officials very seldom managed to pay serious attention to any village which was 'off the beaten track'. Consequently tax evasion was rampant; regulations were applied simply according to the whim of the local Ratēmahatmayā, an arrangement which probably suited the villagers very well. The building of the motor roads brought an end to this particular aspect of indirect rule. Even so, there is a sense in which Pul Eliya, lying three miles from a main road, is rather more 'off the map' than it was a century and a half ago.

At the very beginning of the period of British administration Pul Eliya was easily accessible. Schneider's map of 1822 gives an alignment of the main road north from Anurādhapura which, in the vicinity of Pul Eliya, closely follows the trace of the present railway line. This road passes through Wiralmurippu (57), Kadawatgama (47) and Weditibbagala (45). It lay therefore about two miles to the east of Pul Eliya.

By 1840 there had been a change; the normal road now lay three miles to the west through Tammane-Elawake (54). Then, in the 1850's, the Mannar Road was constructed on its present alignment. This became the main transit route for Indian labourers making their way from India to the Kandyan Highlands. After mid-century, English government officials, moving north on tour from Anurādhapura, invariably made straight for Medawachchiya (66). The evidence suggests that during the next forty years European officials only visited Pul Eliya on four or five occasions altogether, and then only very briefly.[1]

---

[1] Evidence from official tour diaries preserved in Government Archives, Nuwara Eliya.

31

From 1885 onwards communications improved rapidly and administration became generally more intensive. The routine statistical records collected since that date imply regular visits by a wide variety of administrative officials.

From the villagers' point of view the most important consequence of improved communications has been an economic one. All surplus production can now be marketed quickly and, in times of famine, government aid can be anticipated with confidence. Harvest is thus no longer the occasion for acute anxiety that it was in the past. For the nineteenth-century Sinhalese villager the threshing and storing of grain were matters of crucial significance and were the focus of many elaborate rituals and taboos. Most of these picturesque customs have now disappeared. Magical hocus-pocus has been replaced by guaranteed prices and a government mill at Medawachchiya railway station. Folklorists may lament, but the modern villager finds himself living in a golden age.

Better communications have also had very important effects for the health of the villagers; since 1947 government insecticide teams have appeared in the village at regular intervals, and the formerly endemic malaria has become a nightmare of the past. Today most pregnant women regularly make the seven-mile journey to Medawachchiya (66) to attend the government antenatal clinic. To add to this a government medical officer visits the village by car roughly once a week. This does not imply that the traditional *ayurvedic* doctors (*vedarāla*) or the magical practitioners (*anumätirāla*) have been driven out of business, but they are now faced with competition. These medical and sanitary improvements have recently resulted in an extremely rapid increase in population, but in this monograph I shall scarcely consider this particular problem. (See Table 14, p. 333.)

All these are important matters, but sociologically they are not the most fundamental. The really crucial fact about recent changes is a negative one. Development in the North Central Province has *not* so far provided the ordinary villager with any alternative avenues of employment. There is still no local industry. Although some members of Pul Eliya village had moved away from the community altogether, there was, in 1954, no one who could be considered an 'absentee resident'. There was no one with a permanent job in Anurādhapura or in Medawachchiya or in any other urban or semi-urban centre, whose 'real home' was at Pul Eliya. All the inhabitants of Pul Eliya spent their whole working lives there. It is this circumstance, the coincidence of the residential group with the local working community, which makes Pul Eliya village a suitable object for an anthropological style of analysis.

The Pul Eliya people are not 'primitive' in the sense that that word is commonly used by anthropologists. But they have this in common with primitive peoples: they live and work in the same place so that the various institutional aspects of community life overlap. That which is a co-residential group from one point of view may also be a kinship group, a labour team, or a religious congregation according to the circumstances of the case.

EDUCATION

Pul Eliya has its own government elementary school which in 1954 was attended not only by the Pul Eliya children, but also by children from two or three other villages in the vicinity. The standard attained was not high and very few pupils had ever passed on to any form of higher education. Even so, nearly all the male adult members of the present community are literate after a fashion. In this respect the junior generation will be no worse than their elders.

This is a society in which the individual achieves adult status very young. Girls are considered adult as soon as they have had their first menstruation and they commonly bear children very shortly afterwards. There is probably some tendency for the age at which women have their first pregnancy to rise, but this is not yet obvious. Mothers of fifteen or sixteen years of age are common. Boys usually start getting 'married' at about the age of eighteen. This, as we shall see later, is not such a final commitment as the word 'marriage' might ordinarily imply.

33

MAN, NATURE AND DEITY

During the past century the increase in the human population of the North Central Province has been matched by a corresponding decrease in the population of other animals. In the thirties of the last century, elephants were so numerous as to be considered a major pest. Some idea of their numbers may be gauged from the statement that between 1831 and 1847 3561 elephants were slaughtered in the Mannar and North Central Province areas alone.[1] Today, of course, the herds of elephant have been enormously reduced but, even so, the Kende Kōralē of the North Central Province is still a region where the existence of wild life has positive implications for the villagers' existence. Between July and December 1954 two men were killed by wild elephants within three miles of Pul Eliya and throughout that period the Pul Eliya rice fields were repeatedly damaged by elephant herds. Crocodiles too are still to be found in the village tanks and constitute a real, though minor, hazard to life.

Such natural dangers were much more potent in the past and their social influence must then have been very great indeed. Many institutions in contemporary village life still reflect this active hostility between Man and Nature.

The attitude expressed towards elephants epitomises this. The elephant has a very special symbolic connotation for all Sinhalese. The sacred tooth relic which has for many centuries served both as the supreme symbol of Buddha's power and as the crucial essence of Sinhalese nationhood is, in its material form, the tip of an elephant's tusk. Tusked elephants have a leading role to play in nearly all great religious ceremonials throughout the island—the great *perahära* rituals of Kataragama, Kandy, Ratnapura and elsewhere are cases in point—but in the jungle villages of the north-west the elephant is much more than an impressive and ornamental religious symbol. To the Pul Eliya villager the elephant appears as a creature of benign yet terrible power and almost superhuman intelligence. Stories of 'were-elephants'

[1] Archives: A.G.A.'s Diary, May 1847.

34

(*holman*) are recounted endlessly and without number, and always with a strange blend of wonder, admiration and terrified respect.

The villagers are Buddhists, but they also recognise various 'village gods'. If we go twenty miles or so further south we find that the chief of these minor deities is the goddess Pattini, but here in Pul Eliya we are within the domain of Pulleyar (Pillaiyar), the elephant god, who is, in origin, a Tamil version of the Hindu Ganesha. His emblems in village ritual are blatantly phallic. (See Plate III B, facing p. 241.)

Pulleyar is worshipped at an open shrine called a *kōvil* (see Map *C*, p. 45) in rites which emphasise very strongly the male role in procreation and fertility. Complex interpretations of symbolism would be out of place, but it seems legitimate to comment that there is a certain similarity between the attitude of the Pul Eliya villagers to elephants and the attitude of Pul Eliya sons towards their fathers.[1] Fathers and elephants are both necessary evils whom one tolerates with respect but avoids as much as possible!

Pulleyar has no female counterpart. Further south the goddess Pattini presides over fertility much as Pulleyar does here, but in Pul Eliya she has no standing. The ideology of masculine superiority was quite emphatic. 'Brahma (Mahā Bamba)' I was told, 'is a sculptor (*hitāra*) who fashions the form of human beings. For this end male semen is the clay and the mother's womb only a carrying basket.'

But theology apart, the villagers were less confident of the supremacy of the male. The experts were agreed that women as well as men possess *dhātu*, a term meaning 'elemental substance', which is applied not only to the potency of seeds, but also both to sacred relics and sexual excretions. For conception to occur the

---

[1] In normal Tamil theogony Pillaiyar ('the son') is the son of Shiva and Parvati. He is an example of 'the slain god risen again'. Sinhalese Pulleyar is more explicitly a phallic deity concerned with the fertility of crops and women and the health of young children. He is the younger brother of Ayiyanari (*ayiyā* = 'elder brother') who is a son of Shiva and Mohini and whose role is that of village guardian. Cartman (1957) gives some relevant details of mythology. Cf. Parker (1909), p. 206.

dhātu of the man and the *dhātu* of the woman must fuse in the moment of sexual orgasm.

I have made this digression into the ideology of procreation and the association between elephants and sexual potency for two reasons. In the first place it illustrates a very general tendency among these jungle villagers to personify the forces of Nature. It is not unusual to come across abandoned house-sites, gardens and fields, but where the observer might suppose that a man has given up a particular garden for the perfectly rational reason that it has proved too dry or because he preferred to live somewhere else, the Pul Eliya villagers were likely to say that it was because the place was haunted by a demon (*yaksha*) or by a spirit guardian of ancient sacred treasure (*bahīravaya*).[1]

They would then go on to expound a complicated theory as to just why this particular demon should have a grudge against this particular victim.

Generalising, one may say that the villagers tend to attribute all misfortune and illness to sin—that is to misdemeanours of a moral kind. Punishment for sin is inflicted by the activities of demons, and is manifested in a hostile Nature. The 'severe father' attributes of elephants which have been discussed above are simply a special case of this general feeling that the forces of nature serve to exert moral sanctions on human beings.

The second aspect of Pulleyar worship that deserves attention is that it reminds us that this is a male-dominated society. From puberty onwards the sexes are segregated from one another to an extreme degree. The women together and the men together lead separate social lives; and in the totality it is the men who govern and who take the managerial decisions. But there is a sharp distinction here between political rights, as asserted in religious ceremonial, and property rights, as manifested in the inheritance system. Men are the rulers and managers, yet women as well as

[1] Digging for buried treasure among the ruins of ancient temple sites is regarded as the characteristic behaviour of bad characters. Such men are supposed to be possessed of special magical techniques for 'binding' the *bahīravaya*.

men are owners of land. Rights over property are commonly exercised by men, yet they are transmitted through women as easily and as frequently as through men. It is around this 'inconsistency' that the main theoretical problems of this monograph tend to cluster.

In passing it may be remarked that a rather similar type of property law prevails also in Burma and Thailand, the other main centres of Hinayana Buddhism.

ORTHODOX RELIGION

In matters of orthodox Buddhist religion the Pul Eliya villagers are adherents of the Siam sect, a feature of which is that members of the priesthood are recruited exclusively from the Goyigama caste. Although the village possesses a temple (*vihāra*—see Map C, p. 45) there is at the present time no resident priest. The Pul Eliya temple is considered to belong to the high priest of Kadawatgama (47) Temple and he has the right to appoint a resident priest to Pul Eliya. While the benefice is vacant the revenues of the Pul Eliya go direct to the high priest personally. On the occasions when the presence of a priest is considered essential, of which the most important is a funeral, the temple priest from Periyakkulam (33), 4½ miles to the north, is usually called in. This man was born in Wiralmurippu (57) and is a relative of the Pul Eliya villagers. He is likely to succeed to the office of high priest at Kadawatgama within a few years. In 1954 a young boy from Pul Eliya was undergoing training for the priesthood,[1] and it was the obvious hope of the villagers that ultimately they would have this young man as their resident priest. The Kadawatgama high priest comes under the jurisdiction of the Mahā Vihāra at Kandy, but the exact nature of the control that is exercised is not known to me.

By virtue of his office the Kadawatgama high priest is the largest landowner in the district, but his economic functions are less significant than might be expected. This is because the

[1] A son of U. Wannihamy (A 2:6).

37

status of the high priest as landlord rests on a feudal tradition which has now lost its sanction.

It is a general feature of this part of Ceylon that temple property is extensive but very badly maintained. The temple estates are, for the most part, a residue from the days of the Kandyan kingdom. In earlier times the tenants, who were always members of the inferior castes, cultivated the temple lands as part of their service duties, and such service was enforceable. Today such land is still usually cultivated by members of these same inferior castes, but the cultivators are sharecropping tenants of the temple priest, and the rights of the priest-landlord are un-supported by government sanction.

Two examples may be cited. Kalawel Potana tank (Plate I, pp. 24–5) is the property of the Kadawatgama temple. In ancient times it was cultivated by members of the Vanni-Väddä caste from Tulawelliya (59). The caste profession of these people is that of priest-medium (*kapurāla*). The *kapurāla*'s main priestly functions are carried out in a temple building (*dēvāle*) which is usually an annexe of the Buddhist temple proper (*vihāra*). Although the 'village gods', whom the *kapurāla* serves, are deities of Hindu origin, their existence is tacitly recognised by the Buddhist Church, but, just as the 'village gods' are considered to be servants of the Lord Buddha, so also their *kapurāla* priests are considered to be servants of the orthodox Buddhist priesthood. The Vanni-Väddä tenancy of Kalawel Potana was an expression of this relationship.

There are still Vanni-Väddä people living at Kalawel Potana, but it is notorious that for many years they have paid scarcely any rent to the Kadawatgama high priest. In reprisal the latter refused to finance repairs to the tank, which gradually became nearly derelict.

In 1954 the Kadawatgama high priest had embarked on a new policy. He had persuaded several families of Hēnayā (Washer-men) caste to move to Kalawel Potana (61) from the overcrowded village of Lindahitidamana (62). The terms were that the new tenants should pay a cash rental instead of a share of the crop. The

38

priest had also surrendered certain of his ownership rights to the government in return for a promised tank-repair subsidy. In other words, the feudal authority of the priest was gradually changing over into that of a normal landlord. Much the same was happening in Pul Eliya itself where the property of the village temple includes a small tank and some four acres of land lying beneath it. In 1954 the tank was nearly derelict. The land was formerly worked by temple servants of low caste status who lived in the Vihāra compound, and by a family of Washermen who lived in the village itself. But now the Kadawatgama high priest, as landlord, has great difficulty in finding any tenant, for this service-tenure land has a low-caste taint about it which is potentially contaminating for a man of Goyigama caste.

In 1954 the land was being worked by the village schoolmaster in return for a cash rental. This suited everyone. The schoolmaster, as an outsider, did not feel sensitive on caste issues and, as recipient of a government salary, it was easy for him to pay a cash rental. Nevertheless it was significant that no locally born Pul Eliya villager, other than the 'outcaste'[1] R. Punchirala (X:4), would admit to having ever worked this land in the past.

Because of such facts as these, it is very difficult to make any detailed assessment of the influence of the Buddhist priesthood in Pul Eliya affairs. On paper the Church appears to be very wealthy and the villagers are very free in recounting tales of the avarice and immorality of the priesthood. Yet in practice the Church seemed to impinge on ordinary village affairs only to a very limited degree. The two priests with whom the villagers had direct dealings—those of Kadawatgama (47) and Periyakkulam (33)—were treated not only with the utmost deference but also, it seemed, with genuine affection.

LIVESTOCK

While the main economic activities of Pul Eliya are agricultural, the villagers are also owners of livestock, mainly buffaloes and

[1] See Appendix 2.

cattle. Since the animals are mostly allowed to run wild, the villagers can hardly be regarded as herdsmen or cattle breeders. Even so, livestock forms an important item of property.

The buffaloes can be trained for ploughing and for threshing and can then be let on hire to yield a cash rent. In a small minority of cases the cows yield a certain amount of milk. A small proportion of the cattle are trained to pull a cart, but the rest have value to their owners only as objects for cash sale.

As Buddhists, the Sinhalese are, in theory, vegetarians. Theory and practice do not coincide but no villager would willingly eat beef. The cattle are mostly disposed of to travelling Moslem traders who are said to transport the animals down to Colombo for sale on the meat market there.

FOREST REGULATIONS AND LITIGATION

In the terminology of Ceylon, Pul Eliya village is situated in the Vanni—that is, in the forest. Today, as a result of the increase in population and the depredations of shifting cultivators, the forest cover is mostly very thin. But it is still the case that large sections of the total map area are officially treated as reserved forest and controlled by the Government Forest Department. It is impossible for any villager to fell any useful type of timber tree without either infringing a government regulation or spending futile weeks in endeavours to obtain a felling licence.

If any villager is seen to be putting up a new building of any kind, it is almost certain that he has committed some technical offence in order to obtain the timber.[1] I need not go into details. It will suffice to say that the forest regulations are a constant source of grievance to the villager and a standing source of illicit income to the Forest Rangers. The passing of anonymous reports to the Forest Office is a widely practised form of spiteful behaviour between near neighbours.

[1] Holders of *badu* (leasehold) land titles have freer access to building timber than the owners of freehold property. The unfairness of this discrimination against the supposedly wealthy will become apparent in later chapters.

40

Litigation might be described as a favourite village sport. Cases usually originate in written petitions addressed in the first instance to the Government Agent at Anurādhapura. In most instances these are then dealt with by the D.R.O. at his monthly informal assize ('Division Day').

Alternatively a formal legal action may be brought before the Stipendiary Magistrate at his Rural Court, an institution which has lately superseded the less formal Village Tribunal[1] which fell under the jurisdiction of the Kōrāla. The latter office is now extinct.

Petitions usually concern land titles, water rights and the alleged malpractices of minor government officials; Rural Court cases are brought by one villager against another and appear to be largely concerned with theft and assault and verbal abuse. Perjury by witnesses is widespread and obvious, and the magistrate, being aware of this, frequently tests the reliability of witnesses by the technique of ordeal. When accused and accuser both swear in court to a diametrically opposed set of facts they may be required to proceed to Anurādhapura and there solemnly swear to the truth of their statements before one of the great relic shrines or even before the Sacred Bo Tree itself. In some cases at least this unusual legal procedure elicits the truth.

I should stress, however, that while the Pul Eliya villagers are likely to go to law on the slightest provocation, none of them really expects to settle his internal disputes by this kind of reference to external authority. Litigation is simply one among many possible ways of making things awkward for one's opponents.

CONCLUSION

This rambling chapter has not provided a complete picture of the background of Pul Eliya village, but it has touched briefly on certain crucial elements in that background. I have said something of the history and of the ecology; I have given in crude outline the main features of the administration as they affect village life; I have explained the general nature of the local

[1] See pp. 70 ff.

population in relation to caste and I have drawn attention to one or two particular features of the total range of religious institutions. Bearing in mind that my central problem is concerned with the relation between land holding and kinship, this limited range of materials seems to me sufficient.

We are now in a position to examine the facts of the Pul Eliya situation in greater detail.

CHAPTER III

THE PUL ELIYA LAND MAP

My purpose in this chapter is to give a detailed picture of the ecological situation in Pul Eliya village as it affects the pattern of land use and residence. My account is primarily an elaboration of the two village maps. Map *B* shows the whole of the village land, while Map *C*, on a larger scale, shows the detailed position of the various buildings in the village as they were in 1954. These buildings are mostly clustered together on the damp land immediately below the main tank. This is the usual pattern of all villages in this part of Ceylon.

TANKS

There are two tanks. The larger one is deemed to be on Crown land; the smaller one belongs to the temple. Here again we are dealing with a typical situation. It was the general policy of the British administration to presume that, in the absence of very specific evidence to the contrary, all village tanks belong to the Crown. It is by virtue of this Crown ownership that the customary *corvée* work known as *rājakāriya*, which is used to maintain the tank in good condition, is given a legal enforcement.

A minority of tanks are *not* the property of the Crown. These fall into three classes. First there are a few which have been from ancient times the property of feudal landlords. Mostly the villages associated with these tanks are those of lower castes such as Palanquin Bearers, Drummers, and the like. In former days a considerable proportion of all village tanks fell into this category, but in the course of the nineteenth century the British Colonial administration managed to whittle down their number to a small minority. None of the village tanks in the immediate vicinity of Pul Eliya falls into this category.

Secondly there are tanks which belong to temple authorities. Acting on the general principle that interference with religious

43

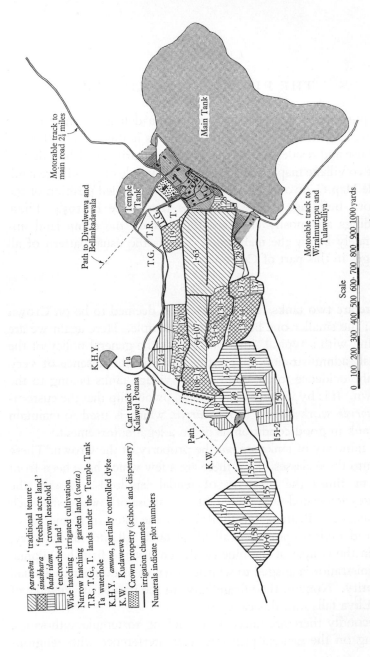

paravēni 'traditional tenure'
sinakkara 'freehold acre land'
badu idam 'crown leasehold'
'encroached land'
Wide hatching irrigated cultivation
Narrow hatching garden land (vatta)
T.R., T.G., T. lands under the Temple Tank
Ta waterhole
K.H.Y. Kudawewa
K.W. amuna, partially controlled dyke
Crown property (school and dispensary)
— irrigation channels
Numerals indicate plot numbers

Main Tank

Temple Tank

Motorable track to
main road 2½ miles

Path to Diwulwewa and
Bellankadawala

Motorable track to
Wiralmurippu and
Tulaweliya

Cart track to
Kalawel Potana

Path

K.H.Y.

K.W.

Ta

Scale

0 100 200 300 400 500 600 700 800 900 1000 yards

T.G. T.R. T.G. T.

1-63

129

128

137

132

130

138-44

131-6

120

64-107

123-8

121-3

124

125-7

108-13

145-7

149

148

150

151-2

153-4

155

156

157

158

159

60-6

Map *B*. Pul Eliya irrigated fields distinguished according to tenure.

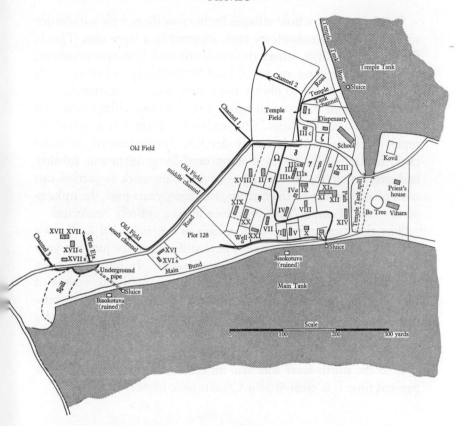

Map *C*. Layout of Pul Eliya house-site area showing compound boundaries. All permanent buildings are shown and distinguished by roman numerals (see Table 1 (p. 55)). The Greek letters indicate plots of garden land (*vatu*) lying within the *gamgoda* area but not containing any residential building in 1954. The ownership of these plots is recorded at pp. 211–16.

affairs should be avoided whenever possible, the British authorities were always extremely cautious about questioning the title of any lands or tanks claimed by temple authorities. Consequently the number of such tanks is considerable. Temple Tanks receive no financial assistance from the Government Irrigation Department and most of them are now in a very bad state of repair. The associated villages are commonly both poor and small.

Besides owning whole villages in this way the temple authorities sometimes own a subsidiary tank adjacent to a large one. This is the case in Pul Eliya, where the small side tank is temple property, as are the four acres or so of land immediately below it. It is probable that down to about 1900 there was no substantial difference between the state of upkeep of the main village tank and that of the Temple Tank. But today the former is in excellent repair while the latter is nearly derelict. In the case of the main tank, major repairs are now supported by government subsidy and every year the annual *rājakāriya* repair work is carried out with official backing. In contrast, for many years past, the upkeep of the small Temple Tank has been almost entirely neglected.

The third category of tank which is not regarded as Crown land is that known as *olagama*. There still exist in the jungle a very large number of ancient abandoned tanks. It has long been official policy that anyone who goes to the trouble and expense of repairing such a tank shall be entitled not only to the land of the tank itself but also to any area of land below it which can thereby be irrigated. Kudawewa and Ulpathgama just to the east of Pul Eliya are privately owned *olagama* of this type, Bellankadawala (55) to the north-west was also an *olagama* in origin, but at the present time it is treated as a Crown tank of normal type.

LAND CATEGORIES

The present-day categories of land within the Pul Eliya village boundaries derive from a cadastral survey made about 1900. At this date, all villages in this area were officially surveyed by the government and the principle was adopted that only land in active use should be recognised as private property, everything else being treated as Crown land. By this rule, house-sites and gardens, which were in good condition, were recognised as being *paravēni* property, that is 'private property from ancestral times'. Likewise, land that was already 'asweddumised', that is, laid out in rectangular flat terraces for rice cultivation, was also mostly recognised as private property. Where such private tenure was admitted, the government made no inquiry as to how these lands were divided up among different individual holdings; nor has there been any later inquiry as to how they have been inherited or otherwise disposed of. Production statistics, collected on behalf of the Agricultural Department, record indirectly the ownership of such holdings, but such returns have no legal standing. In theory, the transmission of *paravēni* land is still governed by traditional Kandyan customary law.

Disputes as to title are, in practice, settled by the Vel Vidāne acting under the aegis of the Village Cultivation Officer (V.C.O.). The Vel Vidāne submits annually to the V.C.O. at a public village meeting two elaborate returns. The first, the 'Pangu List', specifies the total irrigated area held by each shareholder in the village lands and provides the basis of assessment for *rājakāriya* repair work on the tank bund. The second is the 'Paddy Census', mentioned above, which purports to record the acreage, seed sown, yield, ownership and leasehold history of every individual plot in the entire village. Both returns are produced by copying down the record from the previous year and then taking note of changes. The Vel Vidāne is required to justify any changes to the V.C.O. in the presence of his fellow villagers. The village meeting which I attended was a distinctly lively affair and I should judge that the sanctions against 'fraudulent conversion' on the part of the Vel Vidāne are reasonably effective. Since errors are self-perpetuating the Paddy Census figures for acreages, yields, etc. are wildly inaccurate, but the facts regarding title over individual plots appear to be correctly recorded.

Old Field

The original 'Old Field' of Pul Eliya which was held, or thought to be held, on *paravēni* tenure in 1900 is shown on Map *B* with diagonal hatching and plot nos. 1–63, 64–107.

The British administrators of the latter part of the nineteenth century, influenced by current theories concerning the origins of Aryan society (Phear (1880), pp. 179–205), believed that Ceylon

47

villagers held their land on some kind of a communal basis. They supposed that the basic principles of Sinhalese law were essentially those of the patrilineal Hindu joint-family as it appears in various parts of India. The following extract from Codrington (1938, p. 3) is in line with this general trend of thought:

The cultivated land in the village was divided into *pangu* or shares, each *panguva* usually consisting of paddy land, of gardens, and, subject to the reservation made below, of chena. For purposes of service the *panguva*, whatever the number of the co-heirs may be, is indivisible and the co-heirs jointly and severally are liable for the service. It seems to be a survival of the Hindu joint-family estate. Of the joint-family all the male members own and have a right to the family property; no coparcener is entitled to any special interest in the property nor to exclusive possession of any part of it. Private property belonging to a single person is unusual except in the case of self-earned property or gifts. The joint-family property is generally managed by the eldest member. Dissolution takes place by mutual consent or by application to a court of law, but this division of the property generally is made only when the relations amongst the coparceners grow remote.

This is represented as a description of the state of affairs in Ceylon in the tenth century A.D. Although Codrington recognises that present-day Sinhalese tenure is of a more private kind, he seems to imply that a thinly disguised primitive communism is still latent in the system.

The facts are quite otherwise. In Pul Eliya every adult individual, male or female, is treated as a separate economic unit, separately entitled to own property and separately entitled to derive benefit therefrom. Indeed, where livestock are concerned, even small children are independent owners. Even when close relatives team up together they consider themselves to be working a 'sharecropping partnership' (*andē havula*) rather than to be coparceners.

Again, as we shall see, there are several plots of inherited land in Pul Eliya which are 'undivided'. But the owners of such land, 'the heirs of *X* the previous owner', are not coparceners; they do not pool the proceeds of the land and share it out in common—

they are rather shareholders or partners, each of whom has a separate title to a particular mathematical proportion of the total. The system has its analogue in English law. When a man leaves his estate in trust to his children with an annuity to his widow with the proviso that the trust terminates on the death of his widow, he does not thereby establish a joint family estate. On the contrary, each of the individual heirs is jealously conscious of his private individual rights. So too with 'undivided' property in Pul Eliya.

Although there is no evidence for the existence of anything remotely resembling 'communal' tenure anywhere in Ceylon during any part of the British Colonial period, the *belief* that such communal elements were present, plus the general nineteenth-century prejudice against egalitarian ideas, provided the basis for official policy. The supposed village communism was condemned on principle, and it became the publicly declared objective of government to replace this 'primitive' form of organisation by a system of peasant proprietorship. Official policy was explicitly designed to favour the relatively wealthy peasant at the expense of his poorer neighbour, the theory being that the richer man must be, *ipso facto*, the more enterprising.

Freehold 'acre land' ('sinakkara')

Accordingly, rules were introduced whereby individuals could purchase Crown land outright and thereby acquire freehold areas over and above whatever they might hold in the supposedly communal village fields. It was quite consistent with this policy that these Crown lands were sold only in relatively large plots so that the poor peasant was excluded from the market. In theory, no plot of Crown land sold for use as rice land could be less than a five-acre block. The obvious intention was that each village would ultimately consist of a large number of separate small-holding farms.

Such a notion conflicts, not only with the traditional theory of land holding, but also with technological common sense. It is, therefore, hardly surprising that, from the start, the villagers resorted to a variety of devices to get around the law, both as regards the purchase of this freehold Crown land and its inheritance.

Land purchased freehold from the Crown in this way was always officially surveyed; formal title deeds were then registered at the Government Land Office in Anurādhapura. These title deeds show land areas in English acres which explains why this category of land has come to be known, in the villagers' terminology, as *sinakkara*, which may be translated 'freehold acre land'. House-sites and gardens were also sometimes purchased from the Crown on freehold *sinakkara* title. In this case the plots were much smaller.

The government policy of selling 'acre' land outright continued until 1935. By that date, most of the ground in the immediate vicinity of the original Pul Eliya *paravēni* field had passed into private hands. This acre land is shown on Map *B* by diamond hatching. The principle of marginal utility applies here. Naturally the Old Field—that is the land already under cultivation in 1900 (Map *B*—diagonal hatching)—represents the land which can be most easily irrigated. When Crown lands began to be sold, the plots which were first taken up were those which could most easily be provided with irrigation water simply by extending the original irrigation channels of the Old Field itself. Thus in general the later the date of sale the more disadvantageous the position of the land, though occasionally the buyers made mistakes; one plot of acre land sold in 1919 proved to be incapable of irrigation and has never been 'asweddumised' at all.

Crown leasehold ('*badu idam*')

As the ideology of self-government began to supersede that of imperialist colonialism a new socialistic mood came to prevail in government circles, and the concept of the 'peasant proprietor' underwent a sea change. The outright sale of freehold Crown lands had been intended to encourage the smallholder capitalist; the new emphasis was on preserving the peasantry from exploitation.

Land regulations introduced under the *Land Development Ordinance* of 1935 were designed to assist a supposed category of 'landless peasants'. It was definitely intended that these new regulations should operate to the disadvantage of the owner of freehold land who now began to be thought of as a wealthy parasitic absentee landlord. In terms of the over-simplified categories of popular politics, all owners of freehold land became tyrannous rent collectors, while all landless peasants were *ipso facto* virtuous and exploited serfs. (For details see Farmer, 1957, pp. 123–8.)

Under the 1935 regulations no Crown land at all could be sold outright. Instead, land was granted in two-acre plots on permanent lease. The individual villager acquired a documentary title to his land and, provided he behaved himself and continued to pay quite a nominal rental to the government, the land was inalienable.

Certain defects in this legislation may well be mentioned from the start. The leasehold land, which in Sinhalese is known as *badu idam*, was to be allocated only to poor peasants. But the regulations failed to provide any adequate definition of a poor peasant. In Anurādhapura District Village Headmen were required to produce lists of all adult male individuals owning less than one acre of freehold rice land, and these were deemed to be automatically worthy of *badu* allocations. In practice this meant that the newly married son-in-law of the richest man in the village might be granted a *badu* lease, but his neighbour, who happened to own just over one acre in the Old Field, could be excluded.

Secondly, the rules included the proviso that, while *badu* plots could be inherited, they could only be transmitted to a single heir specified in the lease. On the death of the holder of a *badu* plot, the title would be transferred to this individual without fragmentation. The consequences of this well-intended regulation, which conflicts radically with the ordinary principles of Sinhalese land inheritance, will be discussed later.

Finally, the leasehold character of *badu* tenure, whereby the government retained the right to eject the holder in certain special circumstances, was one which the Sinhalese villagers themselves bitterly resented. In 1954 very few *badu* tenants had in fact ever been evicted but the villagers expressed an exaggerated anxiety lest this might happen. The real source of their hostility to the leasehold element in the system was that the ultimate insecurity of tenure precluded a tenant from using such land as security for a mortgage. *Badu* land is a source of income but it cannot be converted into capital, even temporarily.

The *badu* land in Pul Eliya in 1954 is shown on Map *B* (p. 44) by vertical shading. Although the regulations concerned date from 1935, they did not become fully effective until after the war. Thus, most of the *badu* holdings in Pul Eliya in 1954 had only been cultivated for a few years. It is obvious from the map that, because the Old Field and the freehold acre land between them had previously taken up all the best ground, all *badu* land is very disadvantageously sited. It seems likely that a good deal of it can never be properly irrigated, except at extravagantly uneconomic cost.

IRRIGATED CULTIVATION

The whole Pul Eliya cultivation area taken together, the Old Field plus the freehold acre land plus the *badu* land, amounted in 1954 to about 135 acres. This is approximately the same area as that covered by the main tank when full. This coincidence is not an accident. The Irrigation Department, which issues regulations on these matters, seems to have a rule of thumb that a village tank is capable of irrigating an area of land equivalent to itself.[1]

The increase in total cultivation area since 1900 does not imply a corresponding increase in the productive capacity of the village, since there is insufficient water to supply the whole area during both cropping seasons. In recent years the Old Field has normally only been cultivated for the *Yala* harvest (September) and the acre land only for the *Mahā* harvest (March); in former times, when the total asweddumised area was less, much of the land was made to yield two crops a year.

[1] See Park, 1908.

52

The decision as to what fields are to be cultivated in any particular season is made at a public village meeting and formally declared to the V.C.O. The issue is a subtle problem of economic choice since, if the water resources of the irrigation system are over-extended, the outcome may be total crop failure. The village meeting makes its collective decision on the basis of the level of water in the tank and a gambling estimate of the prospect of rain in the weeks to come. In a normal year the *Mahā* rains will be much heavier than the *Yala* rains and it is therefore logical that attempts to irrigate the outer fringes of the irrigation system should be confined to the *Mahā* season.

TANK BED CULTIVATION

To recapitulate, I have so far mentioned three main categories of ground. First, there is tank ground. When the tanks are full, this is covered with water, but at other times of the year it is soft pasture. In the dry weather the moist grassland in the rear of the tanks provides the main grazing grounds for the cattle and the buffaloes. At one time it was common practice to cultivate this ground for rice, but for many years now this has been prohibited. The reason for this is that the villagers often found it easier to cultivate in the empty tank bed than in the orthodox fields and ill-disposed persons were liable to break the bund of the tank on purpose. The prohibition on tank bed cultivation applies only to government-owned tanks and this form of cultivation is still practised from time to time in the small *olagama*.

HOUSE-SITES AND GARDENS

The second main category of ground is that on which the village buildings stand. Each dwelling-house is in a small compound (*vatta*, plural *vatu*) in which there are a few coconut trees, plaintains, areca palms and the like. In some cases there are several distinct dwelling-houses within the one compound. There are also, in Pul Eliya at the present time, two garden compounds

53

which contain no dwelling-house at all. These will be discussed later. A few further points of detail deserve to be noticed.

First, the house-sites fall into two distinct classes; there are those which have been in existence since antiquity and which are on ground which was accepted as *paravēni* land when the survey of the village was made in 1900. These ancestral house-sites are all clumped together near the northern end of the main tank bund. In contrast, the three house-sites numbered I, XVI and XVII in Map *C* are of more recent origin. They are located on ground which has been purchased or leased from the Crown. All the occupants of these 'outside' houses have for one reason or another an 'outsider' status *vis-à-vis* the rest of the community.

Each of these outsider compounds had a distinctive name[1] but the *paravēni* compounds were lumped together under the expression *mahā gam mada* ('main village mudland') which corresponds to the *gamgoda* of other authorities.[2]

A house is simply known by the name of the owner. Nevertheless the boundaries of the various compounds seem to have considerable permanence; the right to erect a house within a particular compound area is an inherited right and one to which considerable value attaches. In later chapters there will be extended discussion of the nature of these rights and of the relationship between house ownership and compound group membership. The facts are summarised briefly in Table I.

The names are those of the thirty-nine individuals resident in Pul Eliya in 1954 who were recognised as having the status of domestic family head; all are adults and all were either married or had been married in the past. The roman numerals relate to Map *C* and show where these thirty-nine individuals and their families were living in 1954. The thirty-nine individuals are also grouped into thirteen 'compound groups'. In general, a compound group is simply a group of individuals who occupy houses within a

[1] House-site I: *egoda-läga-gedara*—'the house perched on the other side'. House-site XVI: *akkara langa gedara*—'the house next to the acre field'. House-site XVII: *pahala vatta*—'the lower garden'.
[2] Codrington, 1938, Appendix 1; Farmer, 1957.

Table I. *The 'family heads' of Pul Eliya and their compound groups*

Compound group	House no. (Map C)	Domestic family head
A2	XII	U. Kadirathe (A2:4)
	XII	K.V. Appuhamy (A2:7)
	XIA	K. Murugathe (A2:3)
	XI	K. Dingiri Banda (A2:B2)
	XIA	B. Siriwardena (A2:Z5)
	XIV	U. Sirala (A2:5)
	XIV	P. Herathamy (A2:C1)
	XV	U. Wannihamy (A2:6)
	XIII	B. Ausadahamy (A2:Y)

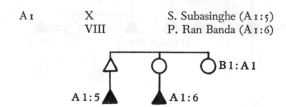

A1	X	S. Subasinghe (A1:5)
	VIII	P. Ran Banda (A1:6)

55

Table I (*cont.*)

Compound group	House no. (Map C)	Domestic family head
F	IX	K.V. Kapuruhamy (F:Dw)
D2	V	Punchirala Gamarāla (D2:C)
	V	P. Kirala (D2:1)
C2	VII	P. Kapuruhamy (C2:D2)

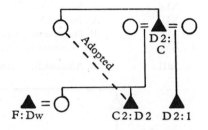

{D1	VI	K. Punchi Etani (D1:6)
	VI	S. Jaymanhamy (D1:9)
{Dx	XVIIc	J. Punchirala (Dx:2)
	XVIIA	N. Punchi Banda (Dx:4)
	XVIIB	N. Ran Manika (Dx:5)
	XVII	M. Naidurala (Dx:Y)

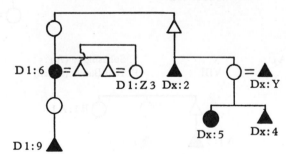

H	IV	U.G. Pinhamy (H:A2) (brother of A2:4)
	IVA	K. Ukkurala (H:(S)) (servant status)

Table I (*cont.*)

Compound group	House no. (Map C)	Domestic family head
C1 (Cx)	XIX	M. Kirala (C1:2)
Cx	XVI	K. Tikiri Banda (Cx:2)
	XVIA	K. Nanghamy (Cx:3)
		A. Ranhamy (Cx:Y)
		A. Sitti Etani (D1:Z3)
		(sister-in-law of D1:6; servant status)
C1	XXI	U.V. Pinhamy (C1:W)

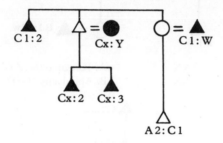

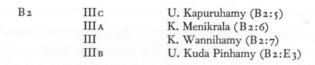

B2	IIIc	U. Kapuruhamy (B2:5)
	IIIA	K. Menikrala (B2:6)
	III	K. Wannihamy (B2:7)
	IIIB	U. Kuda Pinhamy (B2:E3)

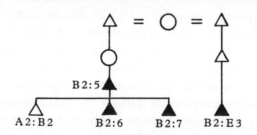

Table I (*cont.*)

Compound group	House no. (Map *C*)	Domestic family head
B1	XVIII	V. Menikrala (B1:7)
	II	A.V. Punchi Etani (B1:A1)
	II	M. Herathamy (B1:Dw)

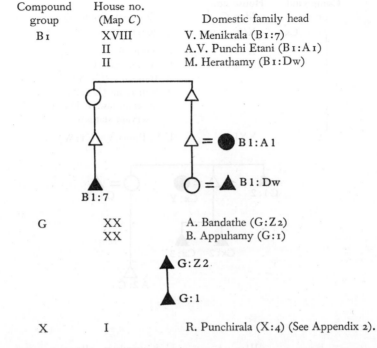

G	XX	A. Bandathe (G:Z2)
	XX	B. Appuhamy (G:1)

| X | I | R. Punchirala (X:4) (See Appendix 2). |

single compound (*vatta*) surrounded by a continuous fence. But two exceptions may be noted. The various occupants of house-site XVII, which is outside the main house-site area, belong to the same compound group (D1–Dx) as the occupants of house-site VI. The other seeming exception is the case of compound C1–Cx (see Map *D*, p. 100, for the location of compounds). Reference to Map *C* will show that house-sites XIX and XVI are separated by a considerable space of open ground. This ground, however, is the property of various members of compound Cx and the two house-sites form one collectivity even though there is no common fence around them.

The skeleton genealogies on Table 1 show the relationships between the domestic family heads of each compound group, the individuals named being shown in black. It should be noted that an individual born into a compound group ordinarily derives his or her status in that group from one parent only, sometimes the father and sometimes the mother.

Besides ordinary houses, Map C also includes several public buildings. The temple compound contains a very ancient temple with its associated Bo tree and also a newly built temple which has not yet been consecrated. The ancient temple serves the dual function of *vihāra*—(Buddha shrine)—and *dēvāle*—(shrine to the village gods). It was not clear whether the new temple would also incorporate a *dēvāle*. The same compound also contains a well-built dwelling-house suitable for the village priest. In 1954 there was no such priest resident in the village. Across the road, immediately below the bund of the Temple Tank, is the village school, which is government property. This includes accommodation for the schoolmaster and his family. The schoolmaster was a Sinhalese from another part of Ceylon. The small building nearby, marked 'Dispensary', is a derelict structure put up originally by the Village Committee, of which mention has already been made. It was supposed to be for the use of the travelling medical officer who stops at the village for an hour or so roughly once a week. When I arrived at Pul Eliya in 1954, the dispensary had no roof. Later, after some temporary repairs, it became my accommodation. The area marked *kōvil* (immediately across the road from the temple compound) contains no building. It is the location of a small shrine dedicated to the God Pulleyar (Ganesha) (see chapter II, p. 35).

Most of the buildings in the village have mud walls, rough wooden roof-poles and thatched roofs. The only exceptions are the school, which has a corrugated iron roof, the several buildings in the temple compound, all of which have tiled roofs, and finally the village shop. This last is the dwelling-house numbered IX in Map C (p. 45). It is a well-built, tiled-roofed structure which had been completed about one year before my arrival.

It is worth remarking here that the strictly traditional type of architecture favoured by the Pul Eliya villagers (Diagram 1), was

59

out of favour in official circles. In 1954 the government was prepared to pay a subsidy to any villager who constructed a new house according to a standard house-plan issued from Colombo. M. Naidurala (Dx:Y), the principal owner of house-site XVII, was engaged in erecting such a house while I was in the village. It did not appear to me that the finished product was going to be very impressive.

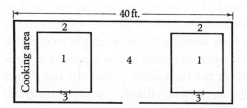 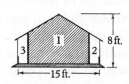

Diagram 1. Common type of traditional-style house-plan. 1. Walled room—sleeping accommodation for married couples and children (*kāmaraya*). 2. Back verandah—*passā istōppuva*. 3. Front verandah—*issaraha istōppuva*. 4. Unwalled room—sitting and sleeping accommodation for bachelors (*sālaya*).

Where several domestic families live under one roof cooking and sleeping accommodation is wholly distinct, but the verandahs (*pila*) are continuous. The walls of the house rooms and of the verandahs are of sun-dried earth obtained from termite heaps. Roofs are of thatch. (Cf. Plate IIIA.)

By European standards the ordinary village dwelling-house is damp, cramped and rather insanitary, and the villagers had been under some pressure from official circles to move their entire village to high dry ground some hundreds of yards further to the north. It was even rumoured that ultimately they might be compelled to make this move. The villagers' attitude to the matter was mercenary and cynical, but also illuminating. On the one hand they reckoned that a new house and a new well could be built for very much less cash outlay than the government subsidy for such constructions, so they had all applied for plots of Crown land on which to build their new houses. But they disdained the notion of a planned village site; each man wanted a house-site situated close to his existing holding of *sinakkara* or *badu idam* rice land. Privately the Village Headman admitted to me that there was no possibility that the wells would ever contain any water, so that even if the new houses were built it was most unlikely that anyone would live in them! The third main category of ground, the irrigated rice land, has already been discussed. A detailed analysis of the use and ownership of this land provides the main subject-matter of chapters v and vi.

'HIGHLAND' AND SHIFTING CULTIVATION

Finally, those parts of the map which do not fall into any of these three main categories are, for the most part, rough scrub jungle. The ground surface is rocky and uneven and it is covered with a coarse type of forest including much thorn and cactus. If we exclude the very rocky areas and certain temple ruins, nearly every part of this rough jungle has at one time or another been cleared for shifting cultivation. This is clearly apparent from the air photograph between pp. 24 and 25. After more than a century of administrative indecision, official policy on the use of such land remains very obscure.

Formal government opposition to shifting cultivation (*hēna*: anglicised as 'chena') of all sorts goes back almost to the beginning of British administration. Colombo government officials have usually taken the view that forest trees are a valuable commercial asset which ought not to be destroyed. Forest lands should therefore belong to the Crown and be looked after by the Forest Department. Villagers should be confined to their irrigated farm-lands. These general principles are sensible enough when applied to the ecological conditions which prevail in the wet south-west zone of Ceylon, but they ignore altogether the realities of the North Central Province.

In the first place, there is very little commercial value in the timber of the low-grade secondary forest which surrounds villages such as Pul Eliya. Secondly it is a demonstrable fact that droughts and floods and other natural disasters are so frequent in the North Central Province that if the villagers did not from time to time resort to shifting cultivation they would all have to starve.

61

There have been brief periods during the past century when shifting cultivation has been officially prohibited altogether. There have also been brief periods when it has been allowed without restriction. But for the most part the legal rules have been similar to those which apply today. Roughly, the present legal position is that if a Village Headman will certify that one of his villagers has a number of dependants and cannot be expected to support himself from the irrigated land which he works, then this man can apply for a licence to clear a one-acre plot for shifting cultivation, for one year only, at a nominal rent. Such rules are unworkable and practice is very far removed from the legal theory. The principal actual effect of the present regulations is to ensure that all shifting cultivation is carried out in the most inefficient manner possible!

From an agronomist's point of view the ideal way to work shifting cultivation would be to clear any particular piece of land only at very long intervals. The Ceylon Dry Zone jungle has a very slow natural recovery rate, but if land were cleared only once every twenty or twenty-five years the leaf fall from the trees would provide a fairly considerable humus; crop yields would then be good and the erosion following cultivation would be small. The regulations, however, instead of ensuring that shifting cultivation shall only take place on land which has *not* been cleared recently, contain the specific instruction that where land is cleared for shifting cultivation it must be jungle which is 'not more than ten years old'! This implies that the fertility of this cleared ground shall be as low as possible and it also, incidentally, makes it certain that the resulting erosion shall be the maximum possible!

It is certainly manifest that shifting cultivation, as at present practised in the North Central Province, is very destructive to the forest cover; it can readily be seen that areas where this kind of cultivation has been regularly practised have become heavily eroded, and it is this fact which is repeatedly used as justification for the official attitude that shifting cultivation ought to be suppressed. Yet the erosion is not due to shifting cultivation as such; the real cause of the trouble is the stupidity of the government regulations.

In 1954 amended chena regulations had recently been introduced. These were so manifestly unworkable that all the villagers in the district had gone on strike. They declared that they would starve rather than apply for licences under such a scheme.[1] This extreme behaviour was presumably exceptional, but shifting cultivation is a field of activity in which lack of co-operation between the villagers and the government may be considered normal.

While the irrigated lands are devoted exclusively to rice, the shifting cultivation areas can be used for a variety of alternative crops. Traditionally the most important of these is a species of millet, known as *kurakkan*. In years when there has been a rice crop failure this may be a very important standby item of diet. But shifting cultivation can also be used for a number of important cash crops, such as gingelly and mustard. It is this which makes the problem so peculiarly difficult from the administration's point of view.

If all restrictions were withdrawn, many of the villagers would probably devote their entire energies to the cultivation of cash crops by shifting cultivation. They would then count on being able to purchase foodstuffs in the open market with only a proportion of the cash they obtained from their cash crop. At current (1954) prices they would be better off than if they had stuck to their ordinary occupation of rice cultivation. Such behaviour is sensible for the individual farmer but, if carried out on a large scale, might have quite disastrous consequences for the general economy of Ceylon.

In this monograph the wider problem does not concern us. It is sufficient to point out that, so far as the individual villager is concerned, the position seems quite simple. He considers that, by ancient tradition, he has the right to clear land for shifting cultivation where and when he will. He looks upon this shifting cultivation as his main means of earning a cash income in contrast to

---

[1] The chena activities described in this book represented recultivation of existing clearings and did not require a licence.

his ordinary activities as a rice farmer which provide him with a subsistence living. For over a hundred years successive governments have expressed their disapproval of shifting cultivation; there is a constant threat that it may be prohibited altogether. The villager looks upon this attitude of government as merely vindictive. He sees it as a persecution designed to prevent honest men from earning a decent cash income.

One further point may be made here regarding the jungle areas. The air photograph (between pp. 24 and 25) reveals a few portions of jungle which have never been cleared at all in recent times. Some of these localities are rocky and could not be cultivated in any case, but there are others where the only deterrent against cultivation is that the site contains, or is thought to contain, the ruins of a *dāgoba* (relic shrine) or of an ancient *vihāra* (temple). Sinhalese villagers have an elaborate set of beliefs concerning the dangers pertaining to land which has formerly been devoted to sacred purposes. Generally speaking they will not knowingly trespass on such land. As we shall see, disagreement as to whether particular plots of land in and around Pul Eliya are, or are not, sacred ground is of some importance for our analysis.

IRRIGATION DITCHES

The final map feature which I wish to consider in this chapter is that of the irrigation ditches. As I have already stressed, the basic scarce commodity is water. Economic and political influence throughout the community is determined by control of water and it is this factor which has made the office of Vel Vidāne (Irrigation Headman) so important. The tank water is conveyed to the house gardens and the irrigated fields by way of a sluice (*horovva*) and then by ditches (*vel*). Operation of the sluice is an exclusive prerogative of the Vel Vidāne personally. Every house-site garden in the village proper has access to a particular length of irrigation ditch, and the same basic principle governs the division of land in the Old Field. Under the traditional system, holders of land in the Old Field owned rights in a certain length of irrigation ditch rather than rights in a particular area of ground. A plot-holder owned rights in water; he could cultivate as much or as little land as he chose.

Now so far as the Old Field is concerned, ditch maintenance is simple. The general obligation is that each plot-holder must maintain that part of the main irrigation ditch which passes by or flows through his plot. Since nearly every villager has a plot in the Old Field, the obligation to maintain the original main irrigation ditch is, in practice, a widely distributed general duty.

But the development of 'freehold acre lands' and *badu* areas has created a new situation. To feed these new lands several new main irrigation ditches have had to be constructed, but these ditches are private property. They belong to those particular individuals whose land the channel serves. These private rights in irrigation ditches are jealously guarded and are becoming of very special significance in the developing polity of the village. The position of the main irrigation ditches is shown on Map *B* (p. 44).

Individuals who work land served by the same irrigation channel have an inescapable obligation to co-operate. This fact is a most potent source of friendship alliances, but it is also a major source of hostility. Several examples of this fact will be studied in detail at a later stage of the monograph.

CONCLUSION

These then are the categories of land over which the Pul Eliya villagers exercise rights of usufruct and ownership. My task is to examine in detail what these rights are, how they are exercised and how they are transmitted from individual to individual and from generation to generation.

The frame of reference in terms of which this transmission takes place is that of kinship, and before I present the detailed facts of individual landholdings I propose to analyse the role played by kinship in the overall organisation of the Pul Eliya community.

Social anthropologists are prone to make a specialism of kinship and to treat it as a separate dimension. Such presentation can be very misleading. Kin groups do not exist as things in themselves without regard to the rights and interests which centre in them. Membership of such a group is not established by genealogy alone. Properly speaking, two individuals can only be said to be of the same kinship group when they share some common interest—economic, legal, political, religious as the case may be—and justify that sharing by reference to a kinship nexus. The anthropological problems that then arise are: What are these common interests? What individuals share them? What is the nature of the nexus? Why is kinship rather than some other principle of incorporation used to provide the sanction of legitimacy?

In the case of Pul Eliya we shall find that property rights adhere, not only to individuals, but also to the groups which I have listed in Table 1 (pp. 55–8) as 'compound groups' and even to still vaguer entities which the Pul Eliya villagers describe as *pavula* ('families'). Moreover, rights of all kinds can be transferred by loan and mortgage and outright sale as well as inheritance. It is, therefore, to the nature of kinship grouping and inheritance rules that we must now turn our attention.

CHAPTER IV

THE KINSHIP SYSTEM

We are concerned in this chapter with the inter-connections between landholding and kinship. Land in Pul Eliya is owned by individuals of either sex. Every child at birth becomes a potential heir to each of its parents considered as an individual. The distribution of property within the community at any one time is thus greatly affected by the pattern of marriage and residence adopted by its individual members over a series of past generations. These are matters to which the Pul Eliya villagers devote very great attention.

To understand the significance of such behaviour we need to know the rules and practices of inheritance, but discussion of these latter must wait until the end. Inheritance takes place within an existing kinship system and my first task is to describe the nature of this social framework. But I must stress from the start that the application of kinship 'rules' is highly flexible and is constantly being re-adapted to fit the relatively immutable physical facts of the agricultural terrain and the irrigation system.

When Pul Eliya villagers discuss their own society certain category words are constantly employed. One of these is *pavula* ('family'), another is *variga* ('sub-caste'). The heart of my problem is to explain to the reader the precise relationship between these two terms. It is a complicated matter and I must proceed slowly.

THE 'VARIGA' COURT

As mentioned already in chapter II, the inhabitants of Pul Eliya all consider themselves to be members of a single endogamous *variga* of the Goyigama caste. All the villagers are, therefore, kinsmen of one another. Let us examine this statement in detail.

There are three common Sinhalese words which the dictionary translates as 'caste'; *jati* and *variga* both have the sense of 'variety' or 'kind', *kula* means 'colour' and was no doubt originally the equivalent of the Vedic term *varna*. The Pul Eliya villagers seldom used the term *jati* but were at pains to distinguish between *variga* and *kula*. They said, for example, 'we people of Pul Eliya (58) and the people of Marutamadu (52) are of the same *kula* but of different *variga*; but the people of Tulawelliya (59) are of different *kula* as well as being of different *variga*'. In such a context as this, *variga* refers to a quite specific institution which is today peculiar to the Nuvarakalāviya District.

Although the literature on Ceylon caste is extensive this particular institution has attracted little attention. Bryce Ryan in his *Caste in Modern Ceylon* (1953) discusses *variga* (*varige*) only very briefly in a rather misleading footnote at p. 246. Pieris (1956), after summarising certain published and unpublished sources, sums up by saying: 'the whole subject of *variga* is little understood' (Pieris, 1956, p. 252 n.; cf. Kapuruhamy, 1948). A rather lengthy discussion is therefore justified.

The majority of modern Sinhalese castes are historically derived from groups which filled particular economic roles in the feudally organised Kandyan kingdom. These economic roles ceased to exist when the feudal hierarchy was abolished in the 1830's and since that time most of the castes have ceased to serve any political or economic function. The Nuvarakalāviya *variga* system provides an exception to this generalisation. It is peculiar in that the *variga* served a very definite political function throughout the latter part of the nineteenth century and continued to do so until 1938. This function was not an historical survival from the days of Kandyan feudalism, but an element in the British colonial system of indirect rule. If we are to understand why the *variga* played a major role in Pul Eliya village affairs during the period 1886–1940, it is necessary to consider the wider aspects of *variga* organisation during this colonial phase of Ceylon history.

When I myself observed the Pul Eliya *variga* organisation it was a system in decay, but this decay was recent and was not due to any basic change in the kinship sentiments of the villagers. The cause was political. When, in 1938, the functions of D.R.O.

(Divisional Revenue Officer) were transferred from the hereditary Ratēmahatmayā to a civil service bureaucrat, the sanctions which had maintained the *variga* system in being came to an end. Thereafter the *variga* structure, as a formally organised institution, began slowly to collapse.

During most of the British period the rule of government was essentially indirect. The British Colonial administrator (Government Agent) issued his orders to the local Sinhalese 'chieftain', the Ratēmahatmayā, a member of the local aristocracy. Although the Ratēmahatmayā was held responsible for law and order within his district,[1] he was provided with very little administrative apparatus through which he might legitimately assert authority. A Ratēmahatmayā was supposed to be able to control his district simply because he was a man of influence. Just what sort of influence this might be was never made explicit.

The administrative theory was that the Ratēmahatmayā exercised his jurisdiction in his capacity as president of the Village Tribunal, a kind of informal rural assize court of British origin. This Village Tribunal was formally empowered to deal with almost every variety of legal problem, but in practice disputes relating to matters of caste, marriage and inheritance were usually treated separately under the category 'matters of native law and custom'. Issues of this kind were only handled by the Village Tribunals in exceptional circumstances; ordinarily the villagers were expected to settle such matters for themselves. For this purpose the villagers made use of a specific institution, the *variga* court (*variga sammutiya*). This court had no official standing and is never

---

[1] In this respect Pul Eliya lies within the district (*palata*) of Nuwaragam Palata (East) which has an area about five times that covered by the whole of Map *A* (p. 22). A *palata* was formerly divided into several *kōralē* each under a Kōrāla. Each *kōralē* was divided into several *tulāna*, each under a Headman, formerly called a Lēkama. Today the office of Kōrāla has been abolished and the Ratēmahatmayā has been replaced by the Divisional Revenue Officer (D.R.O.). The executive head of each individual village is called a Vel Vidāne. In matters relating to general administration the Vel Vidāne takes his instructions from the *tulāna* Headman; in matters relating to agriculture he takes his instructions from the Village Cultivation Officer (V.C.O.). The *tulāna* Headman takes instructions from the D.R.O. The V.C.O. is an official of the Irrigation Department (see also chapter II, pp. 28–9).

mentioned in British official documents, but we must suppose that the more alert of British Government Agents at least knew of its existence.

In name, the *variga* court was a survival from Kandyan times, but we know nothing of its operations during the pre-British period. All the evidence that we have seems to relate to dates later than 1870.[1] From this it appears that each *variga* had its own court but that the Ratēmahatmayā was hereditary head of each such court.

A significant implication of this arrangement was that the territorial area covered by a *variga* court never coincided with the territorial area covered by a Village Tribunal, but the Ratēmahatmayā was *ex officio* chairman of both. He was head of the *variga* court by hereditary right; he was head of the Village Tribunal by virtue of his office. A single *variga* court exercised jurisdiction over all members of one particular *variga* wherever they might be located; a single Village Tribunal operated within the limits of a single *kōralē*, that is the administrative district of a Kōrāla. Now the Kōrāla was subordinate to the Ratēmahatmayā in the administrative hierarchy; but whereas the office of Ratēmahatmayā was (in practice) that of an hereditary feudal chief, the Kōrāla was (in theory) appointed by the British Government Agent. One aspect of the *variga* court was that it was an instrument through which the Ratēmahatmayā influenced such appointments.

The *variga* court dealt with nearly all disputes that might arise between members of the same village community, while the Village Tribunal concerned itself with major crimes, disputes between villagers and the Crown, and property disputes between members of different *variga*. In this division of functions, it was the *variga* court that assumed greatest prominence in village affairs. The Ratēmahatmayā's importance for the average villager

---

[1] See Kapuruhamy (1948). Courts known as *gamsabha*, *ratasabha* and *varigasabha* existed in Kandyan times, but their precise functions are not clear. In the British period the term *gamsabha* was applied to the institution here described as the Village Tribunal, which was a British invention. Pul Eliya villagers referred to their local caste court as *variga sammutiya* rather than *variga sabha*. For the history of the 19th-century Village Tribunal see Goonesekere (1958).

stemmed from the fact that he was supreme lord (*loku nāyaka*) of the *variga* court; his role as president of the Village Tribunal appeared relatively remote and secondary. Every *variga* court decision had to be referred to the Ratēmahatmayā for his personal confirmation; all *variga* court officials were personal appointees of the Ratēmahatmayā.

These officers of the *variga* court were men of influence and affluence in the villages of the *variga* concerned. In return for suitable gifts, the Ratēmahatmayā bestowed titles and robes of office which enabled the recipient to sit in judgement upon his fellow villagers. Any individual mentioned in this book whose name includes one of the titles Mohottāla, Badderāla, Lēkama, is likely to have been a member of the local *variga* court.

Most present-day disputes, which are internal to the village community, have their focus in some kind of quarrel over rights to irrigation water. In apparent contrast to this, most of the cases which came before the *variga* court were formally concerned with issues of caste and sex. This difference is, however, more apparent than real.

It will be evident from the analysis of inheritance rules given later in this chapter that disputes over irrigation water will ordinarily arise between the owners of adjacent plots of paddy land and that the householders concerned are likely to be, from a kinship point of view, either 'brothers' or 'brothers-in-law'. In such a dispute the objective of the stronger party is to force his opponent out of the village and the traditional way of doing this was to get him convicted by the *variga* court.

The obvious way to drive an opponent from the village is to convince the other villagers that he is a 'stranger', a member of another *variga*. Most *variga* court cases in fact took this form— a '*binna*-married husband' (that is, a man living uxorilocally with his wife) was accused of being a member of an outside *variga* and hence of breaking the rules of *variga* endogamy. A smaller group of cases had the form that a man born and bred in the local community—and therefore clearly not a 'stranger'—was accused of committing incest, that is, co-habiting with a close classificatory

71

'sister', accuser and accused being 'brothers'. This offence was the less serious of the two.

In both types of case the transfer of the argument from the field of economics to that of sexual sin turned the issue into one of witchcraft.

It is the common assumption of these villagers that all kinds of personal and general calamity are attributable to the sins of sacrilege and caste pollution. No *variga* court could possibly afford to admit that it allowed its women to be tainted by sexual sin.

Yet it would be a serious mistake to suppose that the function of the *variga* court closely resembled that of the Inquisition. The court's interest in sexual morality was distinctly hypocritical.

This will be apparent from a bare statement of the normal sequence of legal procedure.

No matter whether the accusation was one of incest, that is of a woman having sex relations with too close a kinsman, or one of exogamy, that is of a woman having sex relations with a man who was not a kinsman at all, the judgements of the *variga* court were of the same type and were always designed to maintain, as a fiction, the caste dogma that only kinsmen standing in the relationship of *massinā-nāna* ('classificatory cross-cousins') may legitimately co-habit.

The court achieved its purpose by discriminating between two possible judgements. It might declare that the breach of customary behaviour was heinous, in which case the guilty woman was expelled from the *variga* altogether. This verdict implied expulsion from the village and from the village lands, and the penalties might extend to many of the erring woman's close kinsmen. Alternatively the court could punish the paramour with a fine. Payment of the fine then constituted a purging of the offence, and in the case of exogamy offences was tantamount to a *variga* admission fee.

An actual case will serve to illustrate the principle. At the beginning of this century there was resident in Pul Eliya one Ranhamy (C:N) who came from Nawana in Kurunegala District, more than forty miles away. He lived in Pul Eliya because he was a cousin (*massinā*) of the priest. In due course he set up house with Walli Etani (C:7), daughter of Kadirathe Gamarāla (C:3), one of the leading men of the village. Ranhamy was summoned before the *variga* court. With the priest as his kinsman and Kadirathe Gamarāla as father-in-law the case was not in doubt. After payment of a fine Ranhamy was recognised as a member of the local *variga* and formally married to Walli Etani.

The priest in question had a gardener who was also called Ranhamy (X:1). He and his wife both came from Randänigama, a village close to Nawana. When the gardener's sons grew up they sought wives from the Pul Eliya area. Eventually one of them induced a girl from Yakawewa (43) to set up house with him. This time the judgement of the *variga* court was that the girl and her whole family be expelled from the *variga*.

In the first example Ranhamy (C:N), the priest's cousin, was of Goyigama caste with respectable connections; in the second Ranhamy (X:1), the gardener, was of dubious caste origins and a man of no substance. The second case occurred around 1938 at a time when the power of the *variga* court was waning and the judgement was ineffective (see Appendix 2), but the discrimination in the rulings is revealing. The principle involved is clear. Where the 'sinner' is a desirable relative, his offence is purged with a fine; where he is undesirable he and his accomplices are cut out of the *variga* altogether.

It follows as a consequence of such proceedings that however often the strict rule of *variga* endogamy may be broken, all persons resident in one village at any one time will recognise one another as members of the same *variga*. The court did not in fact ensure that the *variga* was strictly endogamous, it merely made it appear that this was the case. Negatively the court did ensure that members of the local *variga* were without effective kinship links with members of any other *variga*. Or to put it another way, endogamy is not here a rule saying that every man shall marry a woman of his own *variga*, instead it is a rule saying that if a woman of the *variga* has a paramour, that paramour cannot have the status of husband to the woman and of father to her children

73

unless he also is recognised as a member of the local *variga*. In a small number of cases where a man has brought in a woman from a wrong (Goyigama) *variga* to live with him, no one seems to have made any fuss, though her offspring were liable to suffer some discrimination. I did not meet with any case where a man had set up house with a woman of wrong caste (*kula*) in this way. I was told that sex relations with Vanni-Vädda women would be tolerated, but that a man who kept a mistress of 'low caste' (*adukulaya*, that is, Washermen, Drummers, etc.) would be expelled from the community. This might well be the case, particularly if the woman had children, though I must stress that here, as in other caste systems, the emphasis is upon preserving the caste purity of the women rather than upon controlling the sexual behaviour of the men (Stevenson, 1954; Yalman, 1960).

This discrimination deserves comment. The emphasis on the purity of the women corresponds to the rabbinical doctrine that only the children of Jewish *women* are Jews. Though frequently found in association with strongly patrilineal ideologies, such a principle implies a theory of conception by which the child derives its bodily substances equally from both parents. Strict matriliny denies the parenthood of the father;[1] strict patriliny allows a man to have 'legitimate' children by concubines of alien and inferior birth,[2] only a 'bilateral' ideology should logically require the mother to cohabit only with men of her own status. But the ultimate concern is with the children of the woman rather than with the woman herself. In principle, in the Sinhalese system, children derive property rights from both parents, but it is the father and not the mother who manages the whole of the household property. In these circumstances it is perfectly logical that an uxorilocally married (*binna*) stranger husband should be intolerable; he must either be fully incorporated into the group or driven out. But a virilocally married (*dīga*) stranger wife is of less moment, provided always that the husband repudiates his affinal links with his wife's kinsmen.

[1] For example, Trobriands.
[2] For example, Ottoman Turks.

The ideological distinction between women of Vädda caste and women of 'low' caste also deserves attention. The caste status of the Vädda is a special one. Vädda communities in the vicinity of Pul Eliya are *gam-Vädda*—settled Vädda. The local Goyigama regard them as a primitive people, yet though they claim that the Vädda were formerly their tied servants, they do not say that they are 'low caste'. By tradition the Vädda are descendants of a union between Vijaya, the first king of Sinhala, and a spirit princess (*yakkini*),[1] a myth which establishes both their high caste and their special capacity for mediumistic powers.

The 'aristocratic' status of the Vädda is widely recognised. For example, the descendants of the former Vanniyar rulers of Nuvarakaláviya are locally regarded as constituting a distinct *variga* (Pieris, 1956, p. 251) but in Pul Eliya it was implied that this *variga* was of Vädda rather than Goyigama origin, and the Vädda villagers of Tulawelliya (59) were quite positive that the Vanniyar had been *their* relatives. It was on this account that they claimed that their caste name was Vanni (*not* Vädda) and that their *vasagama* name was Vannisingha (Wannisinghe).[2] Elaborating on this they asserted that 'in the old days' it was they, the Vanni, who had issued orders to the neighbouring Goyigama and not vice versa. They claimed that even today there are members of the aristocratic Bulankulame family who are prepared to recognise the humble Vanni as kin.

Local belief in such kinship is evidently long established. In 1850 the then Government Agent visited Magurihitiyawa (75), a Vanni-Vädda village a few miles south of Pul Eliya, and noted in his diary: 'The village is inhabited by domestic Veddo; one of the peons said that all the headmen here except the Kalagam Kohrala Noomerawewe formerly belonged to this caste, but this must be a mistake...'.[3]

In support of these rival theories as to the mutual status of

---

[1] Mahāvaṃsa, VII, 59–68 (see Geiger, 1950). Cf. Seligman (1911), pp. 48–57.
[2] The relevance of this is that the Bulankulame Disava's full name is Soori-yakumara *Wannisinghe* Punchi Banda Bulankulame.
[3] Archives, file 42, fo. 167, entry 1850; 29 April.

Vanni-Vāddā and Goyigama there was a picturesque clash of mythologies.

The Goyigama of Pul Eliya claimed that their high status was evidenced by the fact that the duty attached in ancient times to the Pul Eliya lands had been to supply water lilies to decorate one of the great shrines at Anurādhapura on occasions of festival ('Pul Eliya' means 'flowery open space'). The Vanni of Tulawelliya said that this was true enough but the flowers had to be delivered for measurement to the Vanniyar's officer at Tulawelliya ('Tulawelliya' means 'place of the weighing machine')!

After this digression we may return to our consideration of the *variga* court. The value of the court to the villagers is clear, but why should the Ratēmahatmayā have bothered to support such an institution? I think that the essence of the matter is that through his influence over the *variga* courts the Ratēmahatmayā was able to control appointments within the official administrative hierarchy associated with the village tribunal.

The administrative categories of the British Colonial period were a systematisation of those used under the Kandyan feudal system. In the North Central Province a British officer (Government Agent) administered the province as a whole, which was divided into several *palata*, each with its hereditary Sinhalese Ratēmahatmayā; each *palata* consisted of several *kōralē* administered by a Kōrāla; each *kōralē* contained several *tulāna* administered by one or more Lēkama, the equivalent of the modern *tulāna* Headman (see pp. 29, 69 n.). Since the principal instrument of judicial decision, the Village Tribunal, covered one whole *kōralē*, the Kōrāla was the key official in the day-to-day running of the administration. In the last analysis, the power of the Ratēmahatmayā depended on his ability to keep control of the various Kōrāla.

Now the territorial boundaries of any one *variga* court ordinarily lie within the boundaries of a single *palata* but are not confined within any one *kōralē* or any one *tulāna*.

For example, in the case of the Pul Eliya *variga*, about half the villages are in the Wirasole and Kadawat *tulāna* of Kadawat *kōralē*, another third in Wew *tulāna* of Kende *kōralē*, and the rest are in other administrative districts (see Map *A*, p. 22). But almost all the villages of the *variga* are within the former boundaries of the Nuwaragam *palata*, the jurisdiction of one particular Ratēmahatmayā.

The operations of the *variga* court which tended to confine the members of each *variga* to particular named villages and which served to prevent the recognition of kinship between members of different *variga* were thus directly in the Ratēmahatmayā's interest. They ensured that, within any one administrative sub-district of his total *palata*, the villages would be split up into tiny *variga* factions each competing for his personal favour. By bolstering the influence of *variga* officials in village matters, the Ratēmahatmayā could circumscribe the potentially independent influence of the Kōrāla.

In short, the Ratēmahatmayā's monopoly right to bestow the coveted *variga* court titles was a valuable form of patronage.

One important way in which the title-holders could recompense their benefactor was in the matter of elections. The British liked to think that they ran their administration according to 'democratic' principles. When appointing junior native officers such as Kōrāla, Lēkama, etc., the Government Agent was prone to consult the villagers most concerned. An actual case will serve to illustrate the kind of thing that happened:

In 1850 there were five approved candidates for the vacant post of Kōrāla, Kende *kōralē*. The candidates were:

(1) The acting Kōrāla, formerly a *tulāna* Lēkama.
(2) A nephew of (1) 'one of the Lēkama of Kende *tulāna*'.
(3) A cousin of (1) 'also a Lēkama in Kende *tulāna*'.
(4) An uncle of (1) without any official post
(5) A non-relative.

Thirty-six village representatives voted. Candidate no. 1 was elected and candidate no. 5 received no votes at all. The Establishment was taking no chances!

Now the electoral body in such a case would consist of one

leading citizen from each principal village in the *kōralē*. Nearly all the voters would be individuals with the *variga* titles of Mohottāla, Badderāla, Lēkama, etc. We may be quite certain that every successful candidate was the Ratēmahatmayā's nominee. The Ratēmahatmayā's nomination was bound to succeed because in his alternative capacity of *variga* lord he had already hand-picked the titled village elders whom the British Government Agent called upon to act as an electoral body! In the above example several closely related candidates were allowed to stand so as to allow for the possibility that the British administrator might be specially prejudiced against one or more of them.

This element of political patronage explains why such an apparently archaic institution as the *variga* court should have retained a lively vitality as late as 1938. At this date not only was the hereditary office of Ratēmahatmayā converted into the bureaucratic office of D.R.O., but the intermediate office of Kōrāla was abolished. At much the same time the Village Tribunal was replaced by the Rural Court, an orthodox legal institution presided over by a professional stipendiary magistrate. Precisely from this time the Ratēmahatmayā lost interest in the maintenance of the Nuvarakalāviya *variga* institutions.

Since 1938 very few new *variga* titles have been bestowed. Although it is still possible, in theory, for the Pul Eliya *variga* court to meet and pass judgement, it has in fact never done so since 1939. Members of the present younger generation treat stories of the *variga* court's former activities as matters of ridicule.

Let me sum up this section. For a proper appreciation of the Pul Eliya kinship system it is important to understand that the Nuvarakalāviya *variga* is a relatively corporate type of social group. It is a much more precisely institutionalised entity than the ordinary caste or sub-caste encountered in other parts of Sinhalese Ceylon. The *variga* is corporate in that its representative leaders (the members of the *variga* court) ultimately decide who is and who is not a member of the group but also because the *variga*, as an aggregate, has title in all the lands of all the villages comprising the *variga*; furthermore *variga* membership is directly

78

linked with this title in land. Since it is land rights and place of residence rather than descent which provide the ultimate basis for *variga* status, the translation of the term *variga* as 'sub-caste' must be used with caution.

By 1954 the corporate nature of the Pul Eliya *variga* had become blurred because of the disintegration of its representative body, the *variga* court. Nevertheless, during most of the period to which this book refers the existence of the *variga* as an organised corporation had been a crucial factor in the total situation.

This lengthy discussion of the interconnection between the *variga* court as a persisting legal institution and the persistence of the *variga* itself as a kinship and territorial corporation bears directly on the general theoretical argument of this book. In the villagers' conception, the *variga* court is the representative body of the *variga* which exists in its own right, but, as I have described it, the *variga* concept is something of an abstraction. The structure of relationships to which the term refers at any one time is not intrinsically self-perpetuating. The *variga* was formerly a kind of idealist projection of a more concrete cultural phenomenon, the *variga* court. With the disappearance of this latter objective feature of the politico-legal context, the *variga* has ceased to be functional; there is nothing in the kinship structure *per se* which will keep the *variga* in being.

'VARIGA' ENDOGAMY AND THE DISTRIBUTION OF MARRIAGE

But now let us look more closely at the actual working of the *variga* rules. We have seen why the maintenance of *variga* organisation was advantageous to the Ratēmahatmayā, but why was it attractive to the villagers?

When I asked a Pul Eliya villager how he knew who was, and who was not, a member of his own *variga*, the answer was always given in the form of a list of village names. 'Members of our *variga* live in such and such villages.' The genealogical evidence which I obtained tended to confirm that the only recognised kinship links, either of descent or of affinity, were with members of these named *variga* villages.

Map *A* (p. 22) shows the position of most of these villages in relation to Pul Eliya. They form a roughly contiguous grouping of all Goyigama villages in the extreme north-west corner of the Nuwaragam *palata*. In most of these villages all the Sinhalese inhabitants were said to be of the one Goyigama *variga*. But in some villages on the edge of the area members of more than one Goyigama *variga* are present—this is the case for Mahā Diwulwewa (39), Diwulwewa (56) and Ambagahawewa (86), a circumstance which suggests that *variga* boundaries are less rigid than the villagers like to pretend. Some of the villages on the map (e.g. Ulukkulama (3), Iratperiyakulam (1) and Bellankadawala (55)) are joint Sinhalese-Tamil communities, but it was alleged that in all such cases the Sinhalese and the Tamil sectors are socially quite separate. Observation seemed to confirm this claim. At Bellankadawala (55), for example, there are actually two distinct village tanks, one Sinhalese, the other Tamil.

A large proportion of the village names in this region are plainly of Tamil origin, but this does not reflect any recent migratory movement. The population of Wiralmurippu (57) (a Tamil-sounding name) is just as 'purely Sinhalese' as that of Pul Eliya (58) (a Sinhalese name) and both villages appear to have existed from antiquity. Members of Pul Eliya were prone to accuse their Sinhalese neighbours (from other *variga*) of intermarrying with Tamils. I have no direct evidence of such marriages, but it is quite possible that, with the decay of formal *variga* organisation, villagers in some parts of the area have become more tolerant of wrong *variga* marriages, even to the extent of permitting relations between Buddhists and non-Buddhists. No such toleration was observable in the group of villages with which I myself had close contact, namely Pul Eliya (58), Wiralmurippu (57), Bellankadawala (55), and Diwulwewa (56). Here wrong *variga* marriages had certainly occurred, but they were neither forgotten nor forgiven.

In theory, any girl from any village of the right *variga* who is not a classificatory sister (*akkā, naṃgi*) is an appropriate mate for a man, but marriages are by no means randomly distributed over the whole *variga* area. In Tables 2 and 3 I have analysed two sets of marriages so as to show the territorial distribution. Table 2 concerns the thirty-nine latest marriages of domestic family heads resident in Pul Eliya in 1954. Table 3 concerns one hundred such marriages which have existed at one time or another since 1890. In all cases one or both spouses were born in Pul Eliya, but in thirty-one of the marriages in Table 3 the conjugal home was set up in some village other than Pul Eliya.

Both tables agree that in just on 50 per cent of all marriages a Pul Eliya spouse has found his or her mate in one of the four 'daily contact' villages—Pul Eliya (58), Wiralmurippu (57), Diwulwewa (56) and Bellankadawala (55). Rather over 20 per cent found their mates in one of the three 'regular contact' villages, Yakawewa (43), Kadawatgama (47) and Walpola (63), all of which lie within three miles of Pul Eliya itself. The remaining 30 per cent of all marriages were distributed widely over some eighteen different villages. Four of these lie outside the area of the map. Some of the villages on the map, though listed as belonging to the Pul Eliya *variga*, do not appear in this sample at all. This is a significant point since it shows that recognition of *variga* kinship is not entirely dependent upon the existence of a recent affinal link. For example, Pul Eliya people recognised the inhabitants of Kidawarankulama (12) as being 'people with whom we marry' although no one could remember any such marriages having ever taken place.

In these tables the terms *dīga* and *binna* denote virilocal and uxorilocal residence respectively. This is a distinction to which Sinhalese profess to attach great importance. These terms do not have a great deal of practical significance when applied to marriages in which both spouses come from the same community, but where the spouses are from different villages the relative statuses of husband and wife are greatly affected.

Although property is transmitted through women as well as through men, it is men who are the farmers and the managers of

Table 2. *Extant marriages of living residents of Pul Eliya* (1954)
(*including latest marriages of widows, widowers and divorced males*)

Village of origin of incoming spouse
(village no. from Map *A*)

Pul Eliya resident	58	57	56	55	43	47	36	33	22	85	25	21	3	Ralapa-nawa	Not recorded
B1:7	×	.	.	.	.	.	.	.	.	.	.	.	.	.	.
A2:7	.	.	.	.	.	.	.	.	.	×	.	.	.	.	.
A2:4	.	.	.	.	.	.	.	.	.	×	.	.	.	.	.
Dx:Y	.	.	.	.	o	.	.	.	.	.	.	.	.	.	.
A1:5	.	×	.	.	.	.	.	.	.	.	.	.	.	.	.
H:A2	o	.	.	.	.	.	.	.	.	.	.	.	.	.	.
A2:5	.	×	.	.	.	.	.	.	.	.	.	.	.	.	.
A2:6	.	.	.	.	.	.	.	×	.	.	.	.	.	.	.
A1:6	.	.	.	.	.	.	.	.	.	.	.	×	.	.	.
C2:D2	.	×	.	.	.	.	.	.	.	.	.	.	.	.	.
B2:E3	.	.	.	.	.	×	.	.	.	.	.	.	.	.	.
A2:3	.	.	.	.	.	.	×	.	.	.	.	.	.	.	.
Cx:2	×	.	.	.	.	.	.	.	.	.	.	.	.	.	.
C1:W	o	.	.	.	.	.	.	.	.	.	.	.	.	.	.
G:Z2	.	.	.	.	.	.	.	.	.	.	.	.	.	.	o
C1:2	.	×	.	.	.	.	.	.	.	.	.	.	.	.	.
A2:B2	.	.	.	.	.	×	.	.	.	.	.	.	.	.	.
X:4	.	.	.	.	×	.	.	.	.	.	.	.	.	.	.
Dx:4	.	×	.	.	.	.	.	.	.	.	.	.	.	.	.
B2:6	×	.	.	.	.	.	.	.	.	.	.	.	.	.	.
B2:7	×	.	.	.	.	.	.	.	.	.	.	.	.	.	.
F:Dw	.	.	o	.	.	.	.	.	.	.	.	.	.	.	.
Dx:2	.	.	.	.	.	.	.	.	.	.	×	.	.	.	.
D2:C	.	×	.	.	.	.	.	.	.	.	.	.	.	.	.
D1:9	.	.	.	.	×	.	.	.	.	.	.	.	.	.	.
G:1	.	.	.	.	.	.	×	.	.	.	.	.	.	.	.
A2:Z5	.	.	.	.	.	.	.	.	.	.	o	.	.	.	.
A2:Y	.	.	.	.	o	.	.	.	.	.	.	.	.	.	.
Dx:Z	.	.	.	.	.	.	.	.	.	.	.	.	.	o	.
B1:Dw	.	.	o	.	.	.	.	.	.	.	.	.	.	.	.
B2:5	o	.	.	.	.	.	.	.	.	.	.	.	.	.	.
Cx:3	o	.	.	.	.	.	.	.	.	.	.	.	.	.	.
D2:1	.	.	.	×	.	.	.	.	.	.	.	.	.	.	.
H(S)	.	.	.	×	.	.	.	.	.	.	.	.	.	.	.
A2:C1	o	.	.	.	.	.	.	.	.	.	.	.	.	.	.
B1:A1	×	.	.	.	.	.	.	.	.	.	.	.	.	.	.
D1:6	.	.	.	.	.	o	.	.	.	.	.	.	.	.	.
D1:Z3	.	.	.	.	.	×	.	.	.	.	.	.	.	.	.
Cx:Y	.	.	.	.	×	.	.	.	.	.	.	.	.	.	.

Totals

Diga marriages (×), wife from another village	21
Diga marriages (×), wife from Pul Eliya (58)	5
Binna marriages (o), husband from another village	8
Binna marriages (o), husband from Pul Eliya (58)	5
	39

Table 3. *Analysis of* 100 *marriages extant at various dates between* 1890 *and* 1954 *of which at least one partner was born in Pul Eliya*

Distance (miles)	Birthplace of spouse of Pul Eliya citizen (village nos. from Map *A*)	Dīga	Binna	Total	Whether Pul Eliya residents own land in the village (1954)	Degree of contact (1954)
0	Pul Eliya (58)	15	5	20	×	
1½	57	16	5	21	×	Daily
	56	1	3	4	×	
	55	3	1	4	×	
3	43	6	4	10	×	Regular
	47	6	1	7	×	
	63	3	2	5	.	
4–6	34	0	1	1	.	Occasional (between close kin only)
	49	1	0	1	.	
	36	2	0	2	.	
	33	1	0	1	.	
6–10	86	0	2	2	.	Occasional (between close kin only)
	85	2	2	4	.	
	25	0	1	1	.	
	18	0	2	2	.	
	21	0	2	2	.	
	8	1	0	1	.	
	3	1	2	3	.	
10–15	Ralapanawa	0	1	1	.	Occasional (between close kin only)
	Wewelketiya	1	0	1	.	
40+	Vilava	0	1	1	.	None
	Nawana	0	1	1	.	
3	54 (wrong *variga*)	2	0	2	.	None
Unknown	—	0	2	2	.	None

the family land. Every man aims to live off the produce of his own land rather than to exist simply as a manager for his wife. Now a man can ordinarily only inherit land in the villages where his own two parents were born. Suppose we call these *A* and *B* and assume that the young man has been brought up in village *A*.

If he establishes a *binna* marriage he will ordinarily find himself living in a village where he has no prospect of inheriting land in his own name. However, an important exception to this will occur if he married *binna* a girl in village *B*, for then he will reside in *B* and be able to enjoy not only his wife's land, but also property of his own derived from the parent who was born there.

These general facts explain the two most commonly expressed assertions regarding marriage. First, every Pul Eliya male, without exception, expressed a strong verbal preference for *dīga* marriage. Secondly, it was very commonly asserted that a man had a 'right' to marry his *āvässa nānā* (true cross-cousin), though at the same time it seemed to be regarded as a rather feeble sort of thing to do.

Let us look at the facts. In Table 3, if we omit those cases in which both spouses were born in Pul Eliya, we find that *binna* marriages (33) and *dīga* marriages (37) are almost equally frequent. Table 2 on the other hand shows a bias of 21 to 8 in favour of *dīga* residence.

Although my sample cannot be regarded as strictly random it contains no intended bias. I believe that the contrast in proportions shown in these tables does represent a rather recent shift in the direction of *dīga* residence. This is a consequence of the expansion of the irrigated land area under the Pul Eliya tank. Several landless young men, who might ordinarily have been expected to contract *binna* marriages, have in fact established *dīga* households on the strength of holding land on lease (*badu*) from the Crown. Except where there are special factors of this type at work, my evidence suggests that the general incidence of *binna* marriage is between one third and one half of all matings in which the spouses come from different villages. In a proportion of cases, however, the *binna/dīga* distinction is indeterminate. A married couple may settle first as *binna* and then revert to *dīga* status, or vice versa.

But if *binna* marriage is regarded with disfavour why is it that the proportion of actual *binna* marriages is so high? A check of the details shows that *binna* marriages are not randomly distributed through the population. The preference for *dīga* residence is not simply a verbal formula. *Binna* residence is only resorted to in certain special types of case. *Binna* marriages are, by and large, those of overprivileged females or of underprivileged males.

First, where a girl has no brothers but stands to inherit substantial property from her parents, the latter are likely to insist that she marries a husband in *binna* so as to carry on the parental home. Secondly, a young man without property or inheritance prospects of any kind is likely to be willing enough to marry a wife in *binna* and work for his father-in-law, even if this father-in-law himself is a man of small means. Since it is deemed humiliating for a young man to enter into this kind of dependent relationship, a man who is contemplating such a marriage likes to move as far as possible from his own natal village to escape the jeers of his near relatives. Thirdly, young men whose families have somehow become tainted by an infringement of caste rules may have difficulty in finding a mate in villages near their home even though the *variga* court has formally purged the offence. Such men may find it simpler to travel far afield and marry in *binna*.[1] Fourthly there are cases of cross-cousin marriage, especially those in which a man marries his true mother's brother's daughter.

Marriages of this last kind are not common, but many of those that do occur are *binna* marriages. These again are often cases where a man's prospects of inheritance from his own father are poor; by returning to his mother's natal village and asserting his right to marry a daughter of his mother's brother (*māmā*) a man may lay claim to his mother's hereditary property. In effect he is repudiating his patrilineal connections and attaching himself to the family group of his mother's brother who thereby takes on the responsibilities of the father. There is less tendency to marry a father's sister's daughter although this girl also is an *āvässa nānā* and her father is also a *māmā*. The reason is clear. A man

---

[1] The importance of this type of factor may be seen from the large number of *binna* marriages included in the 'caste scandal' genealogy in Appendix 2 (see Chart *h*, p. 312).

who is entitled to 'claim' in another village an *ävässa nānā* who is his father's sister's daughter will be the son of a *binna*-married father and the odds are that this *ävässa nānā* is herself a girl of no property.

Marriage with a true cross-cousin is linked up with the notion of the 'solidarity of the *pavula*' to which further reference will be made later. A *pavula* (kindred) which is short of resources, either of men or of property, conserves its assets. The men marry endogamously and neither men nor dowries are lost. Correspondingly when a formal marriage is staged with ceremony it is an alliance between different *pavula*. A prominent feature of the ritual in such cases is that the male cross-cousin of the bride symbolically surrenders his claims to the outsider, the bridegroom from the other *pavula*. As we shall see in a moment, these ceremonial marriages only occur when a *pavula* is prosperous and pursuing a policy of expansion.

Still another cause of *binna* residence is exchange marriage. It is not uncommon to find that two brothers marry two sisters at much the same time. Then one of these households is likely to be *binna* and the other *dīga*. One case in my records provides a variation of this theme. A brother and a sister married a sister and a brother. Both households started as *dīga*; one household later reverted to *binna* status and the other promptly did the same.

Analysis of the details given in Table 3 will show the incidence of these variations; in this table the five *binna* husbands who came from more than ten miles distant were all landless men. One was also his wife's cross-cousin. Of the eleven *binna* husbands who travelled six to ten miles to find a wife, three were landless, three had been exiled from their home village for caste offences, and four married relatively wealthy heiresses; the eleventh man married his cross-cousin.

In the four- to six-mile range nothing much is known about the economic status of the *binna* husband from Kuda Kumbukgollewa (34). For marriages within a three-mile radius the *binna/dīga* distinction is less critical, since a man can, without much difficulty, work land simultaneously both in his own natal village and in that of his wife. *Binna* marriages in close villages are not, therefore, confined to the landless poor. In Table 3 the fourteen *binna* marriages in this category include three with cross-cousins, four with 'heiresses' and three cases of 'exchange marriage'. The remaining four cases fall into no obvious special category.

No special characteristic distinguishes the marriages in which both spouses came from Pul Eliya itself. That the total proportion of such marriages is high is not surprising. Given the inheritance system which I have described (pp. 83–4), most young men have everything to gain by marrying a local girl if a suitable candidate is available. Moreover, family and public opinion generally always approves of close endogamous marriages as tending to conserve property-holding within the local community.

If we now look at the distribution of *dīga* marriages in these tables, a different set of facts come to light. Although, all told, *dīga* marriages outnumber *binna* marriages the geographical spread is much less. In Table 3, in 82 per cent of *dīga* marriages (50 out of 62) the wife had been born within three miles of her husband; only in 8 per cent of cases (5 out of 62) had she come from more than six miles away. This is in striking contrast to the *binna* distribution. In only 54 per cent of *binna* marriages (21 out of 38) had the husband been born within three miles of the wife; no less than 42 per cent of *binna* husbands (16 out of 38) came from more than six miles away. Similarly in Table 2 23 per cent of *binna* husbands (3 out of 13) came from more than seven miles away, but only 4 per cent of *dīga* wives (1 case in 26) travelled so far. These figures are consistent with the view that two general types of bias are at work. On the one hand, poor men and men with a caste taint not only tend to marry *binna*, but also tend to seek wives far away from their natal homes. On the other hand 'respectable people', men and women alike, especially those who are likely to inherit property, tend (*a*) to marry *dīga*, (*b*) to marry a spouse from very close at hand, and (*c*) as a corollary, to marry some very close relative—that is, first, second or third cross-cousins. Here (*b*) and (*c*) are really two aspects of the same thing; a high incidence of closely localised marriage over several genera-

87

tions has the automatic consequence that all *variga* members within a narrow geographical range are closely related.

However, quite apart from these trends there is probably a negative correlation between family prosperity and first cousin marriage; though this last would be difficult to establish conclusively. The real *preference* is for *dīga* residence and a wife from a near locality; cross-cousin marriage is coincidental. Although the Sinhalese will assert that a man has a *right* to marry his true cross-cousin, this does not constitute a rule of preferred marriage. When a man wants to marry, the total number of unmarried girls who are near at hand, of the right age, and not classed as 'classificatory sisters', is not large. Nearly all such girls are likely to be quite close relatives, some may be true cross-cousins. Except where the man's poverty is a factor in the situation the latter have no special attraction. Of the extant Pul Eliya marriages shown in Table 2 only two were first-cousin marriages. S. Subasinghe (A 1:5), a man of moderate means, whose father gambled away the family assets, married his cross-cousin (*dīga*) from Wiralmurippu; P. Kalu Banda (Dx:Z), landless, came from far away to marry his cross-cousin in *binna* at a time when his father-in-law was entangled in a caste scandal. Considering the circumstances this incidence is low and suggests that, on the whole, marriage with first cousins is avoided.

It can be seen from all this that the principle of *variga* endogamy is not quite what it appears. On the face of it, the rule is a caste rule; *variga* endogamy is enforced because sexual relations outside the *variga* are considered polluting in a ritual sense. This certainly is how the villagers themselves think of the situation, and they react to *variga* offences with that special kind of horror which, in our society, is reserved for incest and sacrilege. Yet, objectively considered, the rule of *variga* endogamy is simply a formal justification of the state of affairs which exists. The systems of land and property rights being what they are, it is in any case convenient for these North Central Province villagers to marry near relatives from villages near at hand. Only the exceptional, underprivileged individual is going to go far afield to find a wife.

The rule of *variga* endogamy serves to canalise these special cases. The ordinary man of property has no incentive to look outside the local group for a wife; the *variga* rule is designed for the others. In effect, it says: 'If you *must* go outside the local group of near relatives to find a wife, then you must confine your attention to certain specified villages, the inhabitants of which shall be treated as if they were relatives, no matter whether any actual relationship is known or not.'

There is an interesting contrast here between the villager's analysis of the situation and that of the sociologist. The villager says: 'We marry with members of our own *variga*.' He takes the existence of the *variga* as given. The sociologist sees the situation in reverse. *Variga* membership is only definable in terms of marriage and of *variga* court decisions. The members of a man's own *variga* are the inhabitants of those villages from which members of his own natal village have obtained approved mates within recent times. A court decision could at any time alter the boundaries of the *variga*.

The 'caste' aspect of the *variga* is thus partly fictional. In the conventional picture of Indian caste organisation an individual's caste is determined absolutely and permanently by the circumstances of his birth. In the Sinhalese Nuvarakaläviya *variga* this is true only to a limited degree. The fact of territorial endogamy is really prior to the existence of the *variga* considered as an endogamous sub-caste.

THE NATURE OF MARRIAGE

I have so far referred to all kinds of heterosexual matings as 'marriage' without explaining just what kind of alliance is denoted by this term. It is in fact often difficult to discriminate in this society between marriage and promiscuous mating. There is a perfectly valid sense in which it can be said that, if a woman is seen publicly to be cooking food for a man, then she is considered, for the time being, to be his common-law wife.

Except in the course of a formal marriage rite, men and women never actually eat together in public, but the sharing of food is taken as symbolic of sexual intercourse which is barely distinguished from marriage itself.

Divorce may be effected as easily as common-law marriage. The couple simply separate and the marriage is at an end.

One consequence of this simplicity is that it is rare to come across any adult, either male or female, who does not admit to having been 'married' more than once. Individuals who have been 'married' five or six times are not thought in any way exceptional, though many long-lasting stable marriages do occur. Divorce becomes less frequent as individuals get older, but the existence of children seems scarcely to affect the situation. One young lady of Pul Eliya, whose prospects as an heiress were considerable, was, in 1954, about 22 years of age. She had already been 'married' seven times. Three of the 'marriages' had been with the same husband. She already had two children by two of her five husbands, but showed few signs of any early intention to settle down. This was no doubt an extreme case, but it cannot be considered unique.

In addition to this extremely casual form of common-law mating the Pul Eliya villagers recognised two other forms of marriage.

First, instead of simply setting up house with a lover, a man may go through a very elaborate marriage ceremonial which includes the use of formal matchmakers, expensive feasting for assembled kinsmen, and, in some cases, the formal bestowal of dowry on the bride by the bride's parents.

Marriages of this type are numerically in a minority, but they include most of those which are sociologically important. In general, the arrangement and the staging of such formal marriages are matters for the parents of the couple concerned, and it is they who bear the expense. Such marriages form part of the strategy of village politics, the main issues at stake being the transmission of property from one generation to another. Expensive formal marriages are confined to the relatively wealthy; they can be thought of as political alliances with the kinsmen on either side assembling *en masse* to witness the treaty of friendship. But the parties concerned are likely to be rivals and potential enemies rather than natural companions. It is significant that when such marriages end in divorce, as they sometimes do, the quarrel becomes a *cause célèbre* and a source of long-standing bitterness between whole groups of kin. In contrast, the more casual type of marriage can break up without anyone commenting on the matter at all.

In both types of union, marriage, if it can be called such, establishes the inheritance potential of the children. Every child is an heir to both its recognised parents individually, no matter what form of marriage they may have been through (see Leach, 1955). But the formal type of marriage does more than that, it establishes a relation of affinity between two sets of kinsmen, and it is this alliance aspect of the union which receives ritual emphasis.

The third possible marriage procedure is to go to an official registrar of marriages and take out a marriage certificate. Ever since 1860 this has been the only strictly 'legal' form of marriage. Although the administration has at various times put diverse forms of pressure on the villagers to persuade them to conform to the law, very few actually do so. In a strict legal sense most North Central Province villagers are born illegitimate. The 1946 Census tables show that, in the Anurādhapura District as a whole, less than half of all women claiming to be 'married' had actually registered their marriages. Since the Urban, Tamil and Moslem populations are thought to register a fairly high proportion of their marriages, the incidence of registered marriages among the Sinhalese peasantry is obviously very low indeed.

The Pul Eliya villagers had a theory that no one could get appointed to any kind of government office—such as Village Headman, Vel Vidāne, Village Committee Member—unless he had registered his marriage. Therefore those who thought that they might be in the running for such offices usually registered their marriages, but no one else was at all likely to do so.

The villagers' explanation of their reluctance to conform to the law was twofold. First, the marriage certificate cost a fee, without bringing any advantages; secondly, registration of marriage creates a legal distinction between legitimate children (born after registration) and illegitimate children (born before); it was suggested that if, after the death of a rich man who had registered his marriage, the 'legitimate' heirs chose to go to law, they would be able to disinherit their less legitimate brothers and sisters. The wording of the 'Report of the Kandyan Law Commission 1935' ('Report', 1935) certainly makes it appear that this might be the case, though whether this has ever actually happened I cannot say.

The villagers evidently prefer things as they are. What this amounts to is that nearly everyone indulges in a series of experimental relationships of a 'trial marriage' type, which may result in a woman bearing children to several different 'husbands'. A minority of individuals, chiefly selected children of relatively rich men, sooner or later get used as pawns in the game of village politics; their marriages are formally emphasised as symbols of alliance between rival factional groups. The larger the property holding the more likely it is to be treated as a strategic issue in this way, but it is not solely a matter of absolute wealth. A ceremonial marriage is rather a public proclamation of achieved status.

The most spectacular marriage that anyone could remember in Pul Eliya in recent years was that in which K. Dingiri Banda (A2:B2) (compound B2) married *dīga* the daughter of K. Murugathe (A2:3) (compound A2). Dingiri Banda comes of an almost property-less family while Murugathe's circle includes most of the richest men in the village. The marriage was probably arranged through the good offices of Dingiri Banda's 'father' (his father's mother's sister's son), W. Mudalihamy (B1:3) who was then Vel Vidāne of the village and Badderāla of the *variga* court. Pride compelled Dingiri Banda's father, U. Kapuruhamy (B2:5), to demonstrate to his new affines that he was as good a man as they. The result was a marriage party that has passed into Pul Eliya myth, and U. Kapuruhamy has been hopelessly in debt ever since!

This marriage took place around 1932. Although Murugathe's daughter died within three years and Dingiri Banda married again, the alliance was permanent. Dingiri Banda now looks after Murugathe, who is an old man, and Dingiri Banda's daughter by his first wife is Murugathe's heir. It is of interest that when Dingiri Banda's first wife died he changed his residence and went to live with his father-in-law, thus asserting in very positive fashion the value he placed on the affinal relationship.

But while ceremonial marriage demonstrates status, it does not in itself affect the legal potential of the offspring. The individual's inheritance potential is in every case determined by the circumstances of his birth rather than the circumstances of his parents' marriage. This point was nicely emphasised by the fact that, although Pul Eliya villagers very seldom went to the bother and expense of contracting a 'registered marriage', they were absolutely meticulous about registering the birth of children and recording in detail the names of both parents.

DESCENT, FILIATION, AFFINITY

These various behaviours with regard to 'marriage' and inheritance have a number of interesting theoretical implications.

Ever since Malinowski coined the phrase 'sociological paternity' to describe the relationship between a Trobriand boy and his mother's husband (Malinowski, 1927), it has been fashionable among anthropologists to make more and more precise category distinctions as between the various functions of parenthood. Briefly the point at issue is this. We now recognise that the 'father–son' relationship which we meet with in a patrilineal social structure ordinarily combines within itself a number of distinguishable rights and obligations which in other social situations can appear as distinct relationships. Several different types of role differentiation have been emphasised in the course of the anthropologists' theoretical discussions.

First, there is the distinction between *pater* and *genitor* which appears repeatedly in the recent Africanist literature, but which is most strikingly illustrated in the institution of ghost marriage as it appears for example among the Nuer. This distinction is one

93

which is already implicit in Malinowski's Trobriand analysis, and turns on the legal principle that, in most societies, a formal institution which we call *marriage* endows the husband with certain culturally defined rights over the children of the wife, but that these rights of the *pater*, whatever they may be, need have nothing to do with the fact of sexual intercourse. The *genitor* of the woman's children is conceptually a distinct social person. The argument then goes on to imply that in most societies the rights of the *genitor* as such are minimal and are in any case secondary to the rights of the *pater*.

From this point of view one of the striking features of the Sinhalese situation is that the role of *pater* is ordinarily indistinguishable from the role of *genitor*. Except in the case of adoption, the rights that a father has in his son, or the son in his father, stem exclusively from the acknowledged biological fact that the son is the result of his father's cohabitation with his mother.

The second category distinction which has been developed by the theorists is that between *filiation* and *descent*; this in turn is linked up with another Latin borrowing, the distinction between a man's rights over his wife *in uxorem* and *in genitricem*.

Here the core of the argument seems to be that in a unilineal descent structure we must distinguish the status that a child derives from one of his parents, by which he becomes a member of a particular lineage—this we call *descent*—from other statuses that he receives independently from each of his parents by virtue of the fact that his parents are married and he is their recognised legal son.

In this terminology the relationship of a Trobriand boy to his father (mother's husband) is one of 'complimentary filiation' (Fortes, 1953). I do not question the analytical importance of this distinction between *descent* and *filiation*, but it is one which lays all the stress upon the relationships between parents and children while pushing into the background the co-existent relationships between the parents themselves, both in their capacities as husband and wife and in their capacities as members of distinct kin corporations.

From this point of view the theoretical interest of the Sinhalese material is that, in this society, a clear cultural distinction is made between marriage regarded as an alliance between kin groups and 'marriage' as the sexual union of a man and a woman for the purpose of procreating children. Marriage in the first case establishes a relationship of *affinity*; 'marriage' in the second case establishes the *filiation* of the children; relationships of *descent* are not involved at all since there are no unilineal descent groups in which the individual automatically acquires a membership by virtue of his birth.

Finally, we may note one further implication of the 'ambiguity' of Sinhalese marriage in this part of Ceylon.

The fact that it is cohabitation rather than formal marriage which establishes the inheritance rights of the consequent children makes sense of the hypocritical actions of the *variga* court to which I have drawn attention. In practical operation the *variga* rules do not ensure the sexual exclusiveness of the *variga* but, formerly, the judgements of the *variga* court did ensure that all *variga* heirs were recognised as *variga* members, and, vice versa, that no one who was not recognised as a *variga* member could inherit any part of the *variga* land.

Thus, despite the ambiguity of its boundaries, it does seem that the *variga* 'as a whole' can usefully be thought of as a landholding corporation of which the *variga* court members are the representatives. These court members, by controlling recruitment to the *variga* from outside, are indirectly exercising control over the allocations of all lands held individually by *variga* members. But this '*variga* as a whole' only has a significance in relation to the North Central Province community as a whole. The '*variga* as a whole' is not an entity of which the ordinary Pul Eliya villager ever becomes aware; he simply takes its existence for granted.

Village politics are carried on within the framework of a single *variga*, in terms of its smaller sub-divisions. It is to these smaller units—the *pavula* ('families')—that the individual villager's immediate loyalties are attached. It is to these units that we must now turn our attention.

'VASAGAMA', 'GEDARA' AND 'PAVULA'

I must here again remind the reader that I am describing the customary behaviour of Sinhalese villagers in the North Central Province in 1954. I have no wish to imply that anything I say has validity for any other period or for any other part of the country.

In some parts of Ceylon, notably in the Kandyan highlands, the more respectable class of villager lays claim to two types of patronymic broadly comparable to the English surname. These names, the *vasagama* name, and the *gedara* name, are usually (though not always) transmitted from father to son and, because of this, some sociologists have described Sinhalese society as *patrilineal*. From an anthropological point of view this is quite misleading. When applied to whole societies the terms *patrilineal* and *matrilineal* have no meaning unless they are associated with a principle of unilineal descent. Sinhalese society resembles English society to the extent that the 'surnames' are transmitted patrilineally, but neither English nor Sinhalese society contains corporate groups of the clan-lineage type, recruitment to which is based on patrilineal descent exclusively.

In the Kandyan system the *vasagama* 'surname' is primarily an index of hereditary class status. A *vasagama* name such as 'Tennekoon Mudiyansēlāgē' asserts a claim to be descended from a particular Kandyan official—*mudiyānse* being originally a title in the gift of the Kandyan king vaguely equivalent to that of English knighthood (Pieris, 1956, p. 172). It is probable that in times past the use of such title names was strictly controlled. Today it is almost meaningless. Almost anyone with any kind of claim to 'respectability' is likely to assert that he is the possessor of a high-sounding *vasagama* name, and no historical significance attaches to the fact that *all* inhabitants of Pul Eliya called themselves Rāja Guru Mudiyansēlāgē. This name might be translated 'descendants of the *mudiyānse* who was teacher to the king'. Some cynics in the village maintained that it had been invented by the local village schoolmaster in about 1920! This cannot actually have been the case, for the name appears on a Pul Eliya marriage certificate dated 1895, but the only inference that can be drawn from the use of this name is that, in their own estimation, the Pul Eliya villagers are of the highest Goyigama respectability.

Gedara names are a Kandyan institution which has recently been well analysed by S. J. Tambiah (1958). Generally speaking the possession of a gedara name such as Migahakotuva Gedara asserts descent from a quite recent ancestor who was the owner of an estate named Migahakotuva. Maintenance of the gedara name implies a latent, though often remote, claim to be considered as one of the potential heirs to the estate. Those who share the same gedara name do not necessarily share anything else but all alike look upon the original estate as their 'family home'. If the estate is dissipated the gedara name ceases to serve any function and passes out of use. Gedara names are usually transmitted from father to son, but not necessarily exclusively so. The children of binna-married daughters, for example, are likely to assume their mother's gedara name rather than that of their father. Members of the gedara often live on or near the estate in question, but this is not necessarily so.

In Pul Eliya there were no gedara names. Where the word gedara was used it meant simply a house, that is a residential building. Nevertheless there existed in Pul Eliya an un-named social grouping which corresponded in structure to the Kandyan gedara. I shall refer to this social unit as a 'compound group'.

COMPOUND GROUPS

The compound (vatta—'garden') is in the first place an area of ground within the main village area (gamgoda) surrounded by a fence. Although fence positions are changed from time to time, there is good evidence that the general layout of the village has changed little over the last seventy years. On the whole, the compound, regarded as a piece of ground, is a continuing entity transmitted unchanged from generation to generation.

But each compound is associated with a particular group of

97

people, namely those who own the land in the compound and have the right to build houses there. With few exceptions the products cultivated in the *gamgoda* area are permanent plantation crops which endure beyond the life-span of single individuals, for example, jak trees, coconut palms, areca nut palms, plantains, betel vines. These fruit trees are individually owned and individually transmitted to individual heirs. It follows that not all the 'owners' of a compound necessarily reside there, but they have the right to do so.

I have already discussed in chapter III the list of thirty-nine household heads (Table 1, pp. 55–8) and the allocation of these thirty-nine domestic family heads to thirteen compound groups. We must now examine the relationship between elementary family and compound group in greater detail. The actual asset value of the house-sites and fruit trees within any particular compound is always very small and claims to ownership of such compound land are concerned with kinship rather than with property as such. The principle involved is rather a subtle one.

The primary economic requirement for a villager is not that he should be the owner of land, but that he should be a member of the village with rights to a share in the water of the tank. All members of the village (provided they do not transgress against caste rules) transmit to all their children this first essential right to membership of the village. Pul Eliya villagers do not use *gedara* names or detailed genealogies to specify this membership transmission, they simply employ the much vaguer notion that house compounds are continuing units. For example, it is remembered that one Kadira Velathe Mohottāla (D 1 : 2) occupied a house close to house-site VI (Map *C*, p. 45) when the present oldest inhabitant, Punchirala Gamarāla (D 2 : C), was a small boy. It is believed that all the individuals shown in the small genealogy opposite compounds D 1 and Dx (Table 1, p. 56) are descendants of this man or possibly of his wife. The exact details of the pedigree are uncertain, but because the descent is admitted all these individuals are 'members of the village'—they are *Pul Eliya*

98

minissu—Pul Eliya people, even though some of them live out-side the main *gamgoda* area.

A contrary instance is that of R. Punchirala (X:4), compound X, whose case is described in some detail in Appendix 2. It will there be seen that although R. Punchirala himself claims to be a member of the local *variga* because he has paid the fine imposed on him by the *variga* court, most Pul Eliya villagers deny him this status. One of the crucial facts which they cite as evidence is that R. Punchirala has no rights in any compound within the village *gamgoda* area, nor is he the owner of any plot in the Pul Eliya Old Field.

Although the Pul Eliya villagers do not have any verbal expression precisely corresponding to the term 'compound group' as I have here defined it, they are acutely sensitive to the fact that fences within the main *gamgoda* are not only boundaries to pro-perty, but symptoms of barriers to social relations.

The erection of a new fence separating two houses marks the occurrence of fission within what was formerly a single com-pound group; in the same way the removal of a fence, or the construction of a new gate, has the opposite implication. During my stay a fence separating house-sites II and XVIII in com-pound B1 was ostentatiously removed to mark the end of a 25-year-old quarrel, while at much the same time a gap in the fence separating compounds A1 and A2 was carefully blocked up.

There was a general complaint that today there are far more fences than before. 'In the good old days', I was told, 'everyone could pass freely from one garden to the next without let or hindrance.' I very much doubt whether this was really the case.

The village is bigger now. There has been some segmentation and a number of new house compounds have been established. Some compounds have been growing; others shrinking. But most of these changes were explained to me on the ground with meticulous attention to detail, so that the state of affairs around 1890 could be reconstructed with confidence (see Map *D*). Compounds were separate in the past just as they are today. The real change is related to the switch-over from *paravēni* to *sinakkara* and *badu* land ownership. So long as the villagers' sole interests were concentrated on the land of the Old Field there were factors at work which tended to make the residential arrangements in the *gamgoda* constantly revert to the same overall plan—for ownership of house-sites is directly related to ownership of the *paravēni* plots

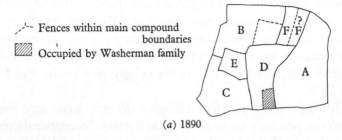

(a) 1890

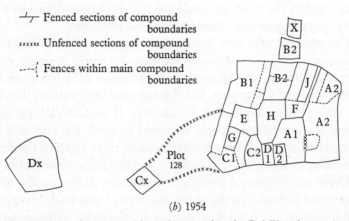

(b) 1954

Map *D*. Changes of compound boundaries within the Pul Eliya house-site area from 1890 to 1954. Cx is linked with C1, Dx with D1.

in the Old Field. But the possession of *sinakkara* and *badu* plots does not bind a man to his neighbours in the same way and this has very probably been reflected in a greater emphasis on the separation of residential areas.

The villagers certainly had a very strong feeling that the physical layout of the village was permanent. In October 1954 S. Subasinghe (A1:5), a member of compound A1, demolished his house in order to rebuild it. Though built of sun-dried clay and thatch it turned out that the house rested on cut stone foundations which had every appearance of tenth-century work. The stones might of course have been brought there from elsewhere, but their presence gave a certain air of authenticity to Subasinghe's own comment, which was: 'My ancestors were rich men, we have lived here since the days of Parākrama Bāhu'!

We can see then that the compound group has certain corporate aspects. It is not a 'corporate group' (*verband*) in Weber's sense (1947, p. 133), since, for one thing, it has no representative leaders, but it is, I think, a 'corporation aggregate' in Maine's sense (1883, p. 187); the estate is a continuing entity, certain types of ownership right relate to the estate as a whole rather than to any particular part of it, and are vested equally in all individuals who acquire rights in the estate.

At the same time I think I should emphasise that neither the compound group (nor its prototype the *gedara*) can properly be described as a descent group.

Membership of the compound group (or *gedara*) is established by successfully asserting a claim based on pedigree, but recruitment to compound groups is not automatic. There is no single descent principle in terms of which compound group membership can be exclusively defined.

There are parallels no doubt with the Maori *hapu* which Firth describes (1929, p. 98) as based in 'ambilateral descent' and with the Iban *bilek* group which Freeman has described (1958) as based in 'utrolateral filiation'. But such terminologies suggest a degree of mechanical regularity which is absent in the empirical facts of the Sinhalese case. The essence of the matter seems really to be this. A married man must live somewhere and that ordinarily means that he must assert a claim to a house-site either on the basis of his own pedigree or on that of his wife's. By establishing such a claim he puts himself in relationship with other men who are simultaneously asserting claims to associated house-sites. But the identification with a single particular estate is not really a final irrevocable commitment, nor does the use of pedigree make

THE KINSHIP SYSTEM

the compound group a 'descent group'. Some members of Pul Eliya had in fact acquired their house-sites by cash purchase and not by filiation at all. Some examples will illustrate this point.

Case 1: The formation of compounds C 1 and Cx[1]

This case illustrates the assimilation of a group of wrong *variga* origin, through adoption and house purchase.

Kadirathe Gamarāla (C 3) had a legitimate family by his first wife C:Z 3. Late in life he married a girl (C:Z 1), known as 'Kirihamy', of wrong *variga* from Wewelketiya. This 'Kirihamy' already had a son Mudalihamy (C:Z 2), who was brought up as a member of Kadirathe Gamarāla's household. On the death of Kadirathe Gamarāla, house-site XIX was occupied jointly by his son Appurala Vedarāla (C:6), a legitimate member of the Pul Eliya *variga*, and the latter's step-brother Mudalihamy (C:Z 2), who was wrong *variga*. Appurala and Mudalihamy were close friends, but Mudalihamy had no land rights; however, he had been allowed to marry within the *variga*—his wife came from Palugollewa (36) about four miles north of Pul Eliya.

A.V. Bandathe (Z:C), son of Appurala Vedarāla (C:6), married *binna* in Syambalagaswewa (18) and, on the death of Appurala Vedarāla, Mudalihamy (C:Z 2) was left in effective possession of the house-site. The then Vel Vidāne, U. Kadirathe (A 2:4), wished to provide his son-in-law, B. Hetuhamy (Y:1), with a house-site; he therefore per-suaded A.V. Bandathe (Z:C) to start a lawsuit designed to oust Mudalihamy and his heirs from house-site XIX, which Bandathe would then sell to Hetuhamy.

Litigation was protracted. In the end Bandathe was forced to sell the house-site to Mudalihamy's four children, C 1:1, C 1:2, C 1:3 and Cx:1, for cash. It is only since this transaction was completed—about 1950—that the members of compounds C 1 and Cx have been treated as full members of the Pul Eliya community; this despite the fact that they have lived in Pul Eliya all their lives. It will be observed that two of the house-sites of this group (house-sites XVI and XVI A) lie outside the main *gamgoda* area (Map C, p. 45).

It was asserted by the Vel Vidāne (B 1:7) that, in selling his house-

[1] Except where special charts are provided the kinship status of individuals mentioned in this and later case histories is most readily seen by reference to the large kinship chart *i* (at end of book).

site, A.V. Bandathe had renounced all further claim to be considered a member of the Pul Eliya community; I am not certain whether this view could be considered strictly orthodox, but it is consistent with the principle that only those with actual or potential property rights within the *gamgoda* area can properly be regarded as Pul Eliya citizens (Pul Eliya *minissu*).

Case 2: *Danapala of Marutamadu* (52)

This case makes the further point that property rights in the *gamgoda* area and in the Old Field are linked. Punchirala Gamarāla (D 2: C), house-site V, is elder brother of Appurala Vedarāla (C: 6). His first wife, R. Kiri Etani (D 2: Z), came from Tammane Elawaka (54) and was of 'wrong *variga*'. B. Danapala, a prosperous and ambitious man from Marutamadu (52), is of the same *variga* as R. Kiri Etani and has also married a woman from Tammane Elawaka. Tammane Elawaka is in the same *tulāna* as Pul Eliya and Danapala, who has a number of influential friends, has aspirations to become *tulāna* Headman. Around 1943 Punchirala Gamarāla (D 2: C) went bankrupt and sold his *gamvasama* lands to a trader Antoni (T: 3); in 1952 Antoni's widow sold the property to Danapala; it seems likely that Punchirala Gamarāla connived at this arrangement. This sale had the implication that Danapala, a man of 'wrong *variga*', could consider himself a Pul Eliya Gamarāla. Very bitter hostilities were aroused; the near relatives of the *tulāna* Headman, K.V. Appuhamy (A 2: 7), were particularly incensed.

Danapala now claimed that he was a Pul Eliya citizen and should be given a house-site. The interesting point is that he could readily have acquired a site by taking up a leasehold (*badu*) or freehold (*sinakkara*) plot from the Crown, but what he needed was an 'ancestral' (*purāna, paravēni*) plot located in the *gamgoda* area. In 1954 manœuvres to this end were still proceeding. Danapala was alleged to have offered the impoverished members of compound B 2 a substantial sum of money for a small house plot, but the *tulāna* Headman (A 2: 7) and his *massinā*, the Vel Vidāne (B 1: 7), were said to have threatened the most drastic reprisals if the offer was accepted.

The villagers in general were clearly on the side of the Headman and the Vel Vidāne in this matter. The thesis was that Danapala was of the wrong *variga*, therefore he *ought* not to have a house-site.

Of course if Danapala had been prepared to repudiate his own relatives in Marutamadu and Tammane Elawaka and marry a girl from Pul

Eliya he would have been readily accepted, but that would have put him in an inferior position.

In 1954 the policy of the Pul Eliya leaders was simply to make things so awkward for Danapala that he would finally agree to sell the land back to one of themselves. Meanwhile they charged him the cost of his ritual duties as Gamarāla but they did not invite him to their village festivities.

Case 3: The formation of compound G

This case is more straightforward since the 'wrong *variga*' issue is not at stake. It represents the normal method of incorporating a remote relative into the local group. Compound G (house-site XX) was formerly part of compound C. Around 1907 Appurala Vidāne (A1 : W) purchased the land from Ukkurala Vidāne (H : 1) and then gave it as a gift to A. Bandathe (G : Z 2). Bandathe was the husband of Dingiri Etani II (G : Z 1) who had been adopted in infancy as a foster child by Appurala Vidāne. G : Z 1 and G : Z 2 were both of the correct *variga* (the first came from Yakawewa (43), the second from Walpola (63)), but neither had any hereditary status in Pul Eliya. However, Bandathe's 'ancestral title' to compound G is now acknowledged by all.

At the same time as he gave Bandathe a house-site, Appurala Vidāne also gave him a considerable area of land including a plot in the Old Field (plot 17) (see pp. 132, 198, 226).

All three cases bring out the point that while, ideally, rights in any particular compound are based in a theory of descent, descent is an idea which can be adapted to circumstances. Provided that a man has full title to 'ancestral' land (*paravēni*), it will very quickly come to be asserted that the title itself is 'ancestral'. Contrariwise the best way to maintain the purity of descent is to prevent interlopers of wrong *variga* from encroaching upon the 'ancestral' land.

'PAVULA'

I have gone to some length to explain the sociological nature of the compound group (*gedara*) because this is important for an understanding of the Pul Eliya social system. But Pul Eliya villagers themselves do not think of their society as being composed of compound groups in quite this way. When they discuss aggregates of people the term they ordinarily use is *pavula*, and this is a somewhat different notion.

Pavula has much the same range of meanings as the English word 'family'. At the smallest scale it could mean simply one woman and her children or even simply 'my wife'; at the other extreme it might mean 'kinsmen' in the widest sense. For example, on one occasion I was explicitly told that 'all of us in our *variga* are of one *pavula*'.

But apart from the elasticity of scale there are also two variant *types* of meaning. When an Englishman speaks of 'my family' he may be referring to a small domestic group comprising his wife and children or perhaps to a rather larger circle of relatives which includes uncles and aunts and cousins and which can actually be observed to assemble together as a corporation for such occasions as 'family' weddings, and 'family' funerals. Such a collectivity we might reasonably describe as a man's 'effective' family. On the other hand this same Englishman, particularly if he has pretensions to gentility, will use the term 'family' to denote (a rather vaguely defined) descent group sharing a common pedigree—for example, 'the Cavendish family'. Certainly for the readers of *Burke's Landed Gentry* 'family' is something determined by genealogy. This we might call an 'ideal' family.

In the Sinhalese case it is worth while making a comparable distinction between an 'ideal' *pavula* which comprises the direct biological descendants of one woman and an 'effective' *pavula* which is a group of kinsmen allied together for some specific political purpose.

'Ideal' pavula

The importance of the 'ideal' *pavula* concept is particularly marked in the context of step-sibling and half-sibling relationships. For example, where a man marries two women in succession and raises a separate family by each, the descendants of the first wife are said to comprise one *pavula* and the descendants of the second wife another *pavula*. Such a distinction can be very important where legal rights to property and succession are concerned, but we should not assume that the *pavula* in this 'ideal' sense is an effective solidary social group.

In its composition such an 'ideal' *pavula* is very similar to that of the compound group (*gedara*), but whereas the latter is linked to the existence of a particular landed estate, *pavula*, in all its senses, is a concept of kinship *per se*.

Recruitment to a compound group is primarily through pedigree. But pedigree alone provides only a latent right which is asserted through the fact of common residence. For example, in terms of pedigree the members of sub-compounds D1 and Dx (see Table 1, p. 56) are all latent members of compound D. In 1954 N. Punchi Banda (Dx:4), who had been reared in house-site XVII outside the *gamgoda* area, had asserted his rights by building a house in compound D six feet away from that of S. Jaymanhamy (D1:9), occupant of house-site VI. But while these two men are recognised as being of the same compound group by virtue of their descent from a common ancestor three generations back, they are *not* ordinarily regarded as being of the same *pavula*, even in an 'ideal' sense.

The grouping that is emphasised in the compound group notion is that of shareholding in a common estate; in contrast, the term *pavula* stresses kin relationship rather than shared title. The two ideas are not wholly distinct, but they are by no means identical.

This becomes very clear when we turn to consider the 'effective' *pavula*, by which I mean those groups of kinsmen who can be seen to co-operate together and who express their co-operation by saying 'We are of one *pavula*'.

'Effective' pavula

A characteristic feature of this society is that the bond between a man and his wife's brother is an extremely close one. Brothers-in-law address one another as *massinā*—cross-cousin—and are often in a pronounced joking relationship. The feeling that brothers-in-law have a *right* to claim one another's assistance in all circumstances is very strong indeed. 'My brother-in-law' seems to be almost invariably included in 'my *pavula*' and if Ego and his brother-in-law are living in the same community the relationship is a most powerful and effective one.

Equally characteristic is the fact that the relationship between full brothers is marked with strain. The use of the differential terms *ayiyā* (elder brother), *malli* (younger brother) emphasises the fact that the relation is never one of equality. Often it is so reserved as to approximate to an avoidance relationship.

Full brothers are necessarily of the same 'ideal' *pavula*, but this does not imply that they are at all likely to co-operate together. In this society the 'solidarity of the sibling group' upon which Radcliffe-Brown laid so much stress is a matter of formality and ritual rather than of everyday fact.

In life crisis ceremonials and other situations which call for polite visiting, brothers will be seen to stand together. But full brothers are seldom close friends and they do not ordinarily co-operate in their economic activities.

The 'pavula' status of half-siblings and step-siblings

I have already remarked that the 'ideal' *pavula* concept serves in particular to distinguish full siblings from half-siblings. In contrast the 'effective' *pavula* is more likely to embrace half-siblings than full siblings.

There are a number of variations here which deserve careful analysis. One of the consequences of the instability of the marriage tie is that half-sibling and step-sibling relationships are exceptionally frequent. Foster-siblings are also common.

By *half-siblings* I mean two individuals having one common parent.

By *step-siblings* I mean two individuals of quite separate parentage, but of whom the father of one has later married the mother of the other.

By *foster-siblings* I mean a case where a woman's child dies in infancy and she then adopts and rears the unwanted infant of some other family. Such a child is treated as a sibling of the mother's other children, but is not her legal heir.

The part-sibling relationship varies in the ways described in the following pages.

Half-siblings

The half-sibling relationship alone has several variants depending on whether the common parent is the father or the mother and on whether or not the two half-siblings share a common residential home.

In the case of half-siblings who share a common father and reside with him, the general pattern is to treat the common father as if he were two separate legal personalities. For example, if a man X marries a woman A and has children by her Aa, Ab, Ac, then A, Aa, Ab, Ac together form 'one *pavula*' (*eka pavula*); if X then marries another wife B and has children by her Ba, Bb, then B, Ba, Bb also constitute 'one *pavula*', distinct from the first. In our terminology Aa, Ab, Ac are 'half-siblings' of Ba, Bb.

Normal Sinhalese custom is that when Aa, Ab, Ac achieve adult status, X will divide up among them that part of his estate which is theirs by virtue of their rights of filiation. After that they are no longer his heirs and the residue of his estate will be inherited by his second family Ba, Bb.

The consequent relationship between half-brothers of the same father seems to be one of indifference which lacks the respect and animosity built into the full brother relationship.

In the case of half-siblings of the same mother the position is different for, while all are of 'one family' (*eka pavula*), there is a difference of status between the sibling who is by birth a member of the local household (*gedara*) and the sibling who is not.

For example, a man X marries a woman B who already has a child Bp by another man. B then bears another child Bq, having X as father. X, B, Bp, Bq all live together in the same household, the marriage being a *dīga* (virilocal) marriage. Then Bp and Bq are half-siblings, but of one *pavula*. Bq has status in the local *gedara*, but Bp has not. If Bp and Bq are both boys, Bq should respect Bp as his 'elder brother', but Bq is heir to X and Bp is not. In such a case the formula is that 'X rears (*äthikaranavā*) Bp'. It seems that very commonly considerable affection may grow up both between X and Bp and between Bp and Bq. I met with a whole series of cases in which Bp, with the connivance of Bq, had been given a share in X's estate, but I met with no instance where the relation between Bp and Bq was one of hostility.

Still another variety of the half-sibling relationship arises when a woman B has a child Bl by X and then marries *binna* a man Y by whom she has further children—Bm, Bn. This situation contains all the elements of strain inherent in the normal full sibling relationship. This is because household (*gedara*) membership and family (*pavula*) membership are again coincident. However, in practice, the issue is usually avoided. With half-siblings of this kind Bl is reared either by X or some other relative and not by Bl's own mother B. I cannot identify in my records any instance of a *binna*-married wife attempting to rear, as one family, a set of her own children who are in half-sibling relationship to one another.

Step-siblings

This relationship is created when a man X has a child Aa by a woman A and then marries B who already has a child Ba by some other husband. Aa and Ba are step-siblings.

The mutual status of Aa and Ba will depend upon the status of A and B with regard to X. For instance, in the example given in case 1 (p. 102), B was an outsider; in consequence the status of Ba was very inferior, being entirely dependent on the generosity of X and Aa. But there are other possibilities. For example, B. Ausadahamy (A 2 : Y) and B. Hetuhamy (Y : 1) were step-brothers, but since both Ausadahamy's parents and both Hetuhamy's parents came from Yakawewa and all four had been quite closely related to one another from birth, the step-brothers were able to treat one another as equals. Possibly if Hetuhamy had resided in Pul Eliya instead of in Yakawewa the situation might not have been so comfortable.

Foster-siblings

This relationship is similar to that of step-sibling, but is full of latent hostilities. If a woman A has a child which dies in infancy she may adopt as foster-child another child Bp of the same age which for one reason or another cannot be properly nursed by its own mother. Such a child is not properly speaking of the same *pavula* as A's other children

109

Al and *Am*. Nor has it any legal standing in the local *gedara* of the mother. Available case histories suggest that *Bp* is likely to be specially favoured by his or her foster-parents but treated as an outsider by the foster-siblings *Al* and *Am*.

In sum, these case variants illustrate the fact that, in this society, the sibling bond between brothers combines several separable relational factors. Recognition of 'brotherhood' entails the moral obligation of respect from the younger brother to the older, but such respect may be modified according to whether or not the brothers are born of one mother and also by whether or not both brothers have, by birth, the same degree of territorial right in the household and compound (*gedara, vatta*) in which they are co-residents.

Some specific case histories illustrating these variants are given below in the section dealing with gift-giving and inheritance (pp. 132 ff.).

This detailed discussion of part-sibling relationships is of theoretical interest since it demonstrates that the kind of distinction to which Malinowski first drew attention when he coined the phrase 'sociological paternity' to describe the relationship between a Trobriand father and a Trobriand son is not confined to societies with unilineal descent systems.

In the Trobriand case Malinowski's point was that although, in this matrilineal system, a son is not deemed to be the 'descendant' of his father (*genitor*), nevertheless an elaborate set of social bonds link a boy to his mother's husband (*pater*). In the Sinhalese case the roles of *pater* and *genitor* are indistinguishable, yet even so there are several variant social relationships which may link a man to the children who are growing up in his house.

The apparent elasticity of the *pavula* concept springs from the fact that the social relationships implied by the use of the terms *appa* (father), *ammā* (mother), *ayiyā* (elder brother), *malli* (younger brother) and so on can be stretched or constricted in various ways according to the weight which particular individuals choose to place on the circumstances of birth and residence of their relatives.

In practice, for each individual 'my (effective) *pavula*' is that group of my near kinsmen with whom I am effectively in good and amicable relationship. It is that group of kinsmen from whom I expect support in the particular context I have in mind; it will usually include kinsmen from other villages besides my own; it will nearly always include my brothers-in-law and my cross-cousins, but it may or may not include my 'brothers'—for example, full brothers, half-brothers, step-brothers and parallel cousins. My *full* siblings are always members of 'my (ideal) *pavula*' for formal purposes, but this need not be the case in informal situations.

The importance of affinal relationship for the structure of the effective *pavula* can be seen in the villagers' attitude to formal marriage.

'*Pavula*' membership and marriage

As we have seen already the majority of marriages are informal. Broadly speaking such informal marriages are of two types.

(*a*) There are marriages in which the *dīga*-married wife or the *binna*-married husband is a rather remote relative who comes from far away and is, through the operation of marriage, fully incorporated into the local group. Such a marriage establishes an affinal link between the local household and the original household of the incoming spouse, but this is not a tie to which anyone attaches much importance.

(*b*) There are marriages in which the *dīga*-married wife or the *binna*-married husband is already a close relative from close at hand, a cross-cousin for example. In such cases husband and wife are already members of the same *pavula* and the marriage merely reinforces an existing political solidarity.

In contrast, in most of the marriages which are accompanied by elaborate ceremonial the parties come from different 'ideal' *pavula*. They are already related to one another, but not as first cousins. The parents of bride and bridegroom stand as representatives of opposed factions which become allied together by virtue of the marriage.

Such marriages are arranged by the parents of the individuals concerned and the marriage ceremony involves the assembly of large numbers of kin from both sides. The villagers themselves refer to such marriages as linking the two *pavula*, and the strategy behind the negotiations leading up to such an alliance is explicitly designed to strengthen the position of 'our *pavula*'. To emphasise the equality of status of the two contracting parties it is usual to arrange two marriages at the same time, so that there shall be an exchange of personnel, even though there may be an interval of several years between the two marriages.

Formal marriage links of this kind do not result in the complete merging of the two *pavula*, the two groups are simply 'bound together' (*bandi*).

This notion of an alliance between two separate groups is an idealist concept. In theory, the guests at a wedding belong either to the *pavula* of the bridegroom or to the *pavula* of the bride, but since nearly everyone is likely to be quite closely related to both sides any allegiance to one party rather than to the other will be on grounds of political interest rather than biological descent.

In practice, the *pavula* groups which manifest themselves on the occasions of weddings and other life crisis ceremonials are something of a compromise between 'ideal' *pavula* (that is, kindreds defined as descendants of a common ancestress) and 'effective' *pavula* (that is, political factions clustered around a leader). In such formal *pavula* full brothers may sit side by side, and fathers and sons may be of the same party, but relationships of affinity are given recognition besides those of biological descent (see case 6, pp. 121 f.).

The 'ideal' *pavula* is a kind of Chinese box concept. Since all members of the *variga* are relatives, any two of them can always represent themselves as being of the same 'ideal' *pavula* by making an appropriate choice of common ancestor. The 'effective' *pavula* is much more selective; affinal ties are here as important, or even more important, than links of common descent. An 'effective' *pavula*, like its 'ideal' counterpart, consists of individuals who are in the last analysis members of one kindred descended from a common ancestress. But in the 'effective' *pavula* kinship serves as an explanation rather than as a cause of political alliance. One cannot infer from a study of genealogy alone just which of a man's kinsmen will be treated as belonging to his 'effective' *pavula*.

A man's 'effective' *pavula* comprises those of his kinsmen who *at any particular time* can be relied upon to act as allies; the time element is crucial. The composition of an 'effective' *pavula* is not determined once and for all by the accident of birth; as with a political party, its size, its membership and its effectiveness all depend upon the initiative of its leading members.

Examples of 'pavula' composition

So much for the theory. I shall now provide the evidence. My first example illustrates a large number of the points we have been discussing. It shows clearly that the principle of recruitment to an effective *pavula* is quite different from that to a 'compound group'; it demonstrates the importance of brother-in-law and cross-cousin links as mechanisms for enlarging the range of the individual's effective *pavula*, and it exemplifies such matters as foster relationships and exchange marriages.

Case 4: The 'effective' pavula of V. Menikrala (B 1:7)

Chart *a* is designed to show the 'effective' *pavula* clustered about the personality of V. Menikrala (B 1:7), the Pul Eliya Vel Vidāne. I have omitted certain residents of Wiralmurippu whom V. Menikrala considered to be his close relatives, since they do not play any other part in this story.

V. Menikrala's uncle U. Kadirathe (A 2:4) was his predecessor as Vel Vidāne; Kadirathe's son K.V. Appuhamy (A 2:7) was the *tulāna* Headman. Some years previously Kadirathe had arranged an important exchange marriage with a wealthy, and politically very influential, family in Yakawewa. His own daughter had been married to B. Hetuhamy (Y:1), the Yakawewa Vel Vidāne, and B. Hetuhamy's stepbrother, B. Ausadahamy (A 2:Y), had been married to (A 2:H) the daughter of Kadirathe's elder brother, U.G. Pinhamy (H:A 2).

K. Kapuruhamy was an adopted son of V. Menikrala's father. He had inherited nothing from the latter and stood in a kind of servant relationship to his 'younger brother', V. Menikrala.

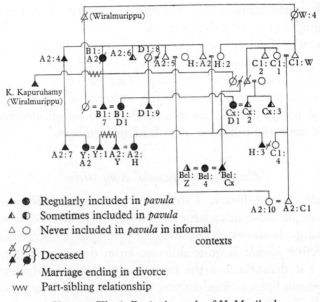

▲ ● Regularly included in *pavula*
△ ◐ Sometimes included in *pavula*
△ ○ Never included in *pavula* in informal contexts
⚥ ⚥} Deceased
≠ Marriage ending in divorce
www Part-sibling relationship

Chart *a*. The 'effective' *pavula* of V. Menikrala
(B 1 : 7), summer 1954.

When V. Menikrala referred to 'our *pavula*' (*apē pavula*), he was usually referring to a group which he also spoke of as *apē sahōdara* (lit.: 'we siblings'). This comprised:

(i) V. Menikrala himself (B 1 : 7);
(ii) K.V. Appuhamy (A 2 : 7) and Ukku Banda (H : 3)—his cross-cousins;
(iii) S. Jaymanhamy (D 1 : 9)—his cross-cousin and brother-in-law;
(iv) B. Hetuhamy (Y : 1) and B. Ausadahamy (A 2 : Y)—his 'classificatory brothers';
(v) (sometimes) K. Kapuruhamy—his foster brother.

V. Menikrala's statements about members of the senior generation were much less definite. Since he consistently claimed close ties with his influential mother's brother, U. Kadirathe (A 2 : 4), he could not but admit that Kadirathe's three full brothers, U. Sirala (A 2 : 5), U.G.

Pinhamy (H:A2) and U. Wannihamy (A2:6) were also members of *apē pavula*, but he only did so when pressed. He did not treat any of these three men as close kin, and with U. Sirala and U.G. Pinhamy he was not on speaking terms at all.

I have distinguished on the chart the individuals whom V. Meni-krala regularly treated as close kin, certain others whom he sometimes treated as close kin, and also a number of people whom he did not treat as relatives at all. Let us see if we can understand the principles of inclusion and exclusion which operate here.

In the next chapter I show that there has been a century-long hostility between the members of compound C and the members of compound B which apparently originated in a dispute over the *gamvasama* lands of the Meda bāga. V. Menikrala's father's mother's father was Punchirala Badderāla (B1:1) who was Gamarāla of the Meda bāga sometime around 1855. For reasons now unknown the succession later passed to the heirs of Punchirala Badderāla's sister (C:B) whose son's son U.V. Pinhamy (C1:W) at present holds the lands in question; Punchirala Badderāla's own heirs have never accepted this diversion of their 'rights' (see Chart *i* at the end of the book and p. 201).

It is evident that this basic quarrel has repeatedly found new outlets for expression. In 1954 factional feeling in the village was so intense that it was quite impossible for anyone to claim close relationship with both V. Menikrala (B1:7) and U.V. Pinhamy (C1:W) at the same time. The individuals shown on Chart *a*, whom V. Menikrala did *not* recognise as close kin, are those who, for one reason or another, were, at this date, closely allied to U.V. Pinhamy (C1:W).

The most recent source of animosity lay in the following circum-stances. In 1953 U.V. Pinhamy had negotiated an exchange marriage with the *pavula* of U. Kadirathe (A2:4). U.V. Pinhamy's daughter (C1:4) was to marry Ukku Banda (H:3), son of U.G. Pinhamy (H:A2), while U.V. Pinhamy's son, P. Herathamy (A2:C1), was to marry S. Punchi Menika (A2:10), daughter of U. Sirala (A2:5).

The first of these marriages actually took place in 1953 but in the spring of 1954 Ukku Banda had abandoned his pregnant wife and dis-appeared from Pul Eliya. He had last been seen making his departure on the carrier of V. Menikrala's bicycle, V. Menikrala being Ukku Banda's cross-cousin. U.G. Pinhamy (H:A2) put all the blame on V. Menikrala, and even accused him of murdering Ukku Banda and burying his corpse in the jungle!

Now V. Menikrala was already on bad terms with his father-in-law, U. Sirala (A2:5), for Sirala had long ago divorced his first wife, Ukkuhamy (D1:8) and had endeavoured to disinherit Ukkuhamy's children, including Menikrala's wife (B1:D1). The break-up of Ukku Banda's marriage made it likely that the betrothal of Sirala's daughter to P. Herathamy would also be broken off. It was, therefore, generally assumed that Menikrala had aided and abetted Ukku Banda's departure so as to spite both U. Sirala and U.V. Pinhamy at the same time.

Actually, after a good deal of bickering, P. Herathamy did marry Sirala's daughter. As a consequence of this marriage U. Sirala and U.V. Pinhamy became 'close *massinā*' and throughout the autumn of 1954 they co-operated together most ostentatiously. It was at this point that V. Menikrala and U. Sirala finally ceased to be on speaking terms.

Of the other individuals shown on the diagram, M. Kirala (C1:2) was brother-in-law to U.V. Pinhamy and in U.V. Pinhamy's effective *pavula*, but Kirala's deceased brother M. Kirihamy II (Cx:1) had once been V. Menikrala's brother-in-law and was spoken of as having belonged to Menikrala's *pavula*. On this account Menikrala sometimes claimed to be closely related to Kirihamy's two sons (by a different wife), K. Tikiri Banda (Cx:2) and K. Nanghamy (Cx:3). Since Tikiri Banda was married to V. Menikrala's wife's sister, he was fairly effectively a member of V. Menikrala's group, but his younger brother Nanghamy was in a marginal position and was frequently to be found working for U.V. Pinhamy who was his *māmā* (father's sister's husband). The optional nature of *pavula* recognition is well illustrated by the fact that V. Menikrala (B1:7) regularly treated Bel:4 and her husband Bel:Z as if they were quite close kinsmen. The only genuine connection was that Bel:4 had formerly been married to Menikrala's deceased nephew Bel:Cx; the reason for recognition in this case being that Bel:Z, a resident of Bellankadawala, worked land in that village belonging to Menikrala.

This account makes a long story, but if the reader will follow through the argument carefully he will find that it shows up very clearly how the 'effective' *pavula* grouping, although very elastic in size and indefinite in its boundaries, is nevertheless structured according to perfectly definite principles. An element of choice exists as to who is or is not treated as a close kinsman, but the choice is not arbitrary.

The leadership of 'effective' pavula

One further aspect of the *pavula* needs to be stressed. The fore-going analysis makes it clear that the effective *pavula*, from some points of view, is simply a small-scale political faction in which the ties to the leader are expressed in kinship terms. The total number of such factional leaders in a community at any one time is obviously limited. The Pul Eliya villagers' accounts of the recent past showed that formerly the three Gamarāla (that is, the owners of the three *gamvasama* plots in the Old Field (see p. 166)) invariably became leaders of *pavula* factions, and even in 1954, although the Gamarāla title had ceased to be of practical signifi-cance, the three individuals who, by birth, should have been Gamarāla (that is, S. Subasinghe (A 1 : 5), U.V. Pinhamy (C 1 : W), and Punchirala Gamarāla (D 2 : C)), were still treated as *pavula* leaders. It is also clear that the office of Vel Vidāne, because of its economic and political advantages, automatically makes the holder a *pavula* leader whether or not he is also by birth a Gama-rāla. Otherwise, the only individuals who are likely to become the focal point of *pavula* links are social climbers, energetic men who seem to be favoured by a lucky horoscope and who are, there-fore, worthwhile kinsmen. M. Naidurala (Dx:Y) is a case in point. Although at an earlier stage in his life he had been shunned because of entanglement in a caste scandal (see Appendix 2) he was, in 1954, prospering exceedingly and was clearly a man with many relatives.

The poorer, less influential members of the community need not be seriously committed to any one effective *pavula*. All the members of compounds B 2 and Cx (Table 1, p. 57) made rather a point of the fact that they were related (but not too closely related) to at least two different *pavula* leaders.

As in all 'kindred' systems, the fact that two men both say 'we are of the *same pavula*' does not necessarily mean that both belong to *identical pavula*. Thus K.V. Appuhamy (A 2 : 7) would invariably describe himself as of the same *pavula* as his cross-cousin V. Menikrala (B 1 : 7), but a gathering of V. Menikrala's close kinsmen would not have had exactly the same composition as a gathering of K.V. Appuhamy's close kinsmen. An 'effective' *pavula* is always, to some extent, personal to the individual on whom it is focused.

The relationship between brothers-in-law

'Brothers' are always in elder-brother/younger-brother relationship. It is a relationship of inequality and polite respect. In contrast, 'brothers-in-law' (*massinā*) are in a standing of equality and may joke together.

The reason for this difference in expected behaviours is plain. Brothers are expected to be co-resident; brothers-in-law are not. Co-residence implies joint-heirship to a common estate; joint-heirship is a relationship of restrained rivalry. Although brothers in this society are often seen to be rivals this does not derive from any intrinsic principle of kinship; the rivalry is manifest only in so far as they are competitors for managerial control of the same piece of parental property. It is only because brothers are expected to reside virilocally (*dīga*) that personal relations between them are expected to be difficult.

Brothers-in-law do not ordinarily have managerial interest in the same piece of land, and it is for this reason that they are able to co-operate on a basis of equality without strain. This is not simply a theoretical ideal, it is readily observable as a fact. A labour team of any sort is far more likely to contain individuals related as *massinā* than it is to contain full brothers. Specific examples are given in chapter VII.

Brothers-in-law will only be co-resident if one of them has married *binna* (uxorilocally). In that event there is a contradiction between the rivalry for managerial control and the expectation of close co-operation between equals. It is precisely the kind of situation in which, according to Radcliffe-Brown's well-known theory (1952, chs. IV and V), we should expect a stereotyped joking relationship to develop.

In fact, as we have seen already, a *binna*-married husband is

often a man who has come from far away and is in very inferior
dependent status *vis-à-vis* his affinal relatives. Such a case is not
likely to produce a situation of rivalry and formal joking. The
difficulties only arise when the *binna*-married husband is a man
from close at hand, a man with property rights of his own, a man
perhaps of the same 'ideal' *pavula*, even a cross-cousin.

*Case 5: The joking relationship between J. Punchirala
and M. Naidurala*

The outstanding Pul Eliya example of a joking relationship between
co-resident *massinā* was that between J. Punchirala (Dx:2) and
M. Naidurala (Dx:Y). Although these two men were not closely
related at birth, the case illustrates most of the points I have just
mentioned.

Compound Dx is located on *badu* land outside the *gamgoda* area.
Residence in this compound does not in itself imply Pul Eliya citizenship. The compound was first established by M. Naidurala (Dx:Y)
after he had been driven out of Yakawewa on account of a caste
dispute (see Appendix 2).

J. Punchirala (Dx:2), brother-in-law to Naidurala, was reared in
Pul Eliya in compound D1. He later lived *binna* with his affines at
Watarekkewa (21). Naidurala prospered and in 1954 J. Punchirala
returned from Watarekkewa to reside with Naidurala in compound Dx.
At the same time N. Punchi Banda (Dx:4), son of Naidurala and sister's
son of J. Punchirala, asserted the claims of the Dx compound group to
Pul Eliya citizenship by building a house in compound D1 within the
gamgoda area.

Properly speaking, it was J. Punchirala who had the standing of local
resident while Naidurala's position was that of *binna*-married husband,
yet it was Naidurala who was the elder and wealthier man. The stereotyped joking between them corresponded to these contradictions.
While Punchirala was economically dependent upon Naidurala,
Naidurala's own status as a Pul Eliya citizen derived from Punchirala,
or rather from the fact that Punchirala and Naidurala's wife were of
'one *pavula*'.

In 1954 it was notable that all members of compound Dx were
particularly emphatic in stressing their common *pavula* membership.
The importance for Naidurala of his alliance with J. Punchirala may be

gauged from the fact that when Naidurala's first wife, J. Guni Etani (Dx: 1), died, he immediately married her younger sister, J. Kiri Etani (Dx: 3). Both these women were J. Punchirala's full sisters.

I shall not elaborate the details of the 'joking' behaviour itself. Briefly it took the form that both parties repeatedly performed elaborate and highly obscene 'practical jokes' at each other's expense. They also made a point of recounting the history of past jokes in each other's presence. The pair were obviously close friends.

This long discussion of *pavula* composition may be summarised thus:

When one encounters a group which purports to be a *pavula*, it is likely to be a combination of two distinguishable structures. On the one hand the 'ideal' *pavula* (Rivers's *kindred*) lays emphasis upon the 'solidarity of siblings', more particularly of full siblings. On the other hand the 'effective' *pavula* ('personal kindred': 'kin-based political faction') lays particular emphasis on the mutual obligations of *massinā*, that is of brothers-in-law and the children of brothers-in-law.

In practical affairs the relationship *ayiyā/malli* (elder brother/ younger brother) always carries an implication of restraint and inequality, whereas the *massinā/massinā* relationship has the opposite implication of equality, alliance and co-operation.

It is consistent with this contradiction between the ideal and the actual that whereas true cross-cousins, like brothers-in-law, are commonly close friends, parallel cousins, even when they live next door in the same compound, may be almost ignored except on formal occasions.

In theory, both the *massinā* and the *ayiyā/malli* cousins should be members of 'my *pavula*', but for most practical purposes it is only the former who count.

The formal expression of 'pavula' membership

Almost the only occasions when *pavula* membership becomes explicitly formalised are those of life crisis ceremonials, for example, girls' puberty ceremonies, formal marriages, funerals.

'PAVULA'

To such festivals a householder is likely to invite (*a*) all the members of the local community except those whom he positively dislikes, and (*b*) certain highly selected members of outside communities whom he looks upon as near kin. The total assemblage of people is considerably larger than that which anyone would ordinarily think of describing as 'our *pavula*', but the persons excluded from invitations mark the outer limit of ordinary *pavula* relationships. Furthermore, since those who accept the invitations arrive in parties rather than as individuals, the anthropological observer can see directly just where the lines of social cleavage really lie.

Case 6: *The puberty ceremonial of V. Menikrala's daughter*

While I was resident in Pul Eliya, V. Menikrala (B1:7), whose 'effective' *pavula* has already been described, held a puberty ceremonial for his daughter to which he invited most of Pul Eliya village and also a number of relatives from Wiralmurippu (57) and Bellankadawala (55). At this party the Pul Eliya household heads listed in Tables 1 and 2 (pp. 55, 82) grouped themselves into the following *pavula*:

Pavula a   Relationship to leader

U. Kadirathe (A2:4)   Leader
K.V. Appuhamy (A2:7)   Son (by first wife)
U.G. Pinhamy (H:A2)   Brother (elder) (resident in different compound)
B. Ausadahamy (A2:Y)   'Son-in-law'

Pavula b

K. Murugathe (A2:3)   Leader
K. Dingiri Banda (A2:B2)   Son-in-law
B. Siriwardena (A2:Z5)   Granddaughter's husband
K. Menikrala (B2:6)   Son-in-law's brother
K. Wannihamy (B2:7)   Son-in-law's brother
U. Kuda Pinhamy (B2:E3)   'Half-brother': mother's half-sister's son
U. Wannihamy (A2:6)   'Younger brother': adopted son (see p. 225 n.)

Pavula c

S. Subasinghe (A1:5)   Leader
A.V. Punchi Etani (B1:A1)   Father's sister
P. Ran Banda (A1:6)   Cross-cousin

121

Pavula d

Punchirala Gamarāla (D2:C)	Leader
P. Kapuruhamy (C2:D2)	Son (by first wife)
P. Kirala (D2:1)	Son (by second wife)
K. Tikiri Banda (Cx:2)	Step-brother's grandson
K. Nanghamy (Cx:3)	Step-brother's grandson
J. Punchirala (Dx:2)	Second wife's sister's son
M. Naidurala (Dx:Y)	Second wife's sister's son-in-law
N. Punchi Banda (Dx:4)	Second wife's sister's grandson
N. Ran Manika (Dx:5)	Second wife's sister's granddaughter
K. Punchi Etani (D1:6)	Grandfather's half-brother's daughter
A. Sitti Etani (D1:Z3)	Remote: sister-in-law of D1:6
A. Ranhamy (Cx:Y)	Step-brother's daughter-in-law
A. Bandathe (G:Z2)	Remote
B. Appuhamy (G:1)	Remote: son of G:Z2

Pavula e

S. Jaymanhamy (D1:9)	Arrived at the party by himself. He was brother-in-law to the host and mother's brother to the girl who was being celebrated

The following Pul Eliya householders were not invited:

	Reason for exclusion
U.V. Pinhamy (C1:W)	Core members of U.V. Pinhamy's effective
P. Herathamy (A2:C1)	*pavula* forming a faction group in opposition
U. Sirala (A2:5)	to V. Menikrala (B1:7) (see Chart *a* and
M. Kirala (C1:2)	pp. 113–16)
K.V. Kapuruhamy (F:Dw)	Personal economic rivalry to V. Menikrala (B1:7) (see pp. 245 ff.)
M. Herathamy (B1:Dw)	Had just quarrelled with his wife (B1:8) and returned to Diwulwewa
U. Kapuruhamy (B2:5)	Uncertain; perhaps because considered wrong *variga* (see p. 196)
K. Ukkurala (H(S))	Wrong *variga*
R. Punchirala (X:4)	Wrong *variga*

This again makes it clear that, while there is some connection between compound group membership and *pavula* allegiance, the correlation is nowhere very close.

It will be observed that the occupants of compounds A, B and H are associated in the *pavula* groups *a*, *b*, *c*, while the occupants of compounds C, D and G are associated in *pavula* group *d*. It will be found that this is just what we might expect from the analysis of the land tenure situation given in the next chapter.

It is of particular interest that the members of compound G associated themselves with their neighbours in compounds C and D and *not* with their foster relatives in *pavula c*. This is an example of the general principle that, in this society, kinship is allowed to lapse if it does not correspond to the territorial facts of the case. The large number of people who put themselves under Punchirala Gamarāla's leadership on this occasion exaggerates his true influence. At least half of *pavula d* in the above list would have formed a *pavula* with U.V. Pinhamy (C 1 : W) as leader if the latter had gone to the party at all.

Such ambiguity is characteristic of the whole system. Let me repeat: although recruitment to a *pavula* is based in kinship alone, a *pavula* is in essence a political faction. Every individual is free to align himself with any leader of any *pavula* faction throughout the community. He then turns this allegiance into a kinship tie by 'activating' an appropriate series of kinship links. The whole system thus presupposes the existence of the overall *variga* organisation by which everyone in the village is necessarily a kinsman of everyone else.

For example, M. Naidurala (Dx:Y) and his family arrived as followers of Punchirala Gamarāla (D 2 : C). Questioned on this, Naidurala immediately replied 'But I am Punchirala Gamarāla's *bānā* (son-in-law)'. The actual relationship is that Naidurala's wife's mother was sister to Punchirala Gamarāla's second wife.

Now for this particular occasion it was apparently quite obvious to everyone in the village that Naidurala was a member of Punchirala Gamarāla's *pavula*, but this was not his permanent status. As a wealthy, though somewhat marginal, member of the community, he could, and did, adjust his status in various ways. For example, on different occasions during my stay he was at pains to explain: (*a*) That he was V. Menikrala (B 1 : 7)'s *massinā*—on the ground that he is 'brother' to Menikrala's Wiralmurippu cross-cousin Hetuhamy (see Chart *d*, p. 140), the facts being that Naidurala's wife and Hetuhamy's wife are full sisters. (*b*) That he was 'brother' to S. Subasinghe (A 1 : 5)—the relationship in this case being that

Naidurala's wife's mother's sister's daughter is married to Subasinghe.

The significant point about these two claims is that Subasinghe is one of the hereditary Gamarāla and Menikrala is the Vel Vidāne. The two men are leaders of different *pavula* groups, but Naidurala owns freehold acre land (Map *B*, plots 121–3) which abuts on to Menikrala's land (plot 120) on one side and on to Subasinghe's land (plots 125–7) on the other. The three men together control one of the main irrigation channels in the village (p. 233). In elaborating these rather fanciful claims of close kinship with Menikrala and Subasinghe, Naidurala is simply expressing in a kinship frame the observable fact that these three men, for certain purposes, form a co-operative team. They own adjacent plots of land, therefore they *must* be kin.

Claims of this kind may sometimes seem as far fetched to villagers as they do to us, especially when they result in palpable inconsistencies, but it is a fundamental feature of the system that everyone should possess alternative *pavula* possibilities.

When a new formal marriage takes place, then, for a while, the *pavula* link established by that marriage is very firm; the brothers-in-law co-operate publicly on all possible occasions. The relationship *may* be an enduring one; but *if* the ties weaken, each of the individuals concerned can always link himself up with someone else.

But while I must stress the elasticity of the *pavula* concept I do not want to give the impression of a system of total fluidity. Political interests are closely linked with property interests and though the relative economic status of individuals is changing all the time it is not completely fluid. The practical application of the *pavula* concept to the factual situation will only become apparent when we have fully analysed the distribution of landholdings among different individuals and ascertained how these individuals are aligned into factional groups, but a part of the pattern can be explained at once.

The villagers conceive of their village as made up of three *bāga*, each the holding of a single man—a Gamarāla; but in turn each

Gamarāla has sub-let numerous portions of his *bāga* to tenants. This is an ideal construction which, as we see in chapter v, differs widely from the present facts of the case. But what is relevant here is that when the Pul Eliya villagers were explaining their system to me they consistently used a certain form of phraseology. The village consists of three *bāga*; the villagers are members of three *pavula*; formerly the head of each *bāga* was a Gamarāla; formerly each Gamarāla was head of one of the three *pavula*. This displays very clearly the principle though not the facts.

Members of one *pavula* are persons bound together under a leader by debts of social obligation—this is true in the minimal sense where *pavula* used by a man means 'my wife' and also in the maximal sense where it means 'all the members of our *variga*' and also in all intermediate usages of the term. Clearly *pavula* is close to, and overlaps with, the notion of compound group (*gedara*). It is always highly probable that 'my *pavula*' will include many members of 'my *gedara*', but the two concepts do not coincide; *gedara* membership is established by the existence of legal rights, which may be potential rather than actual; *pavula* membership is manifested in the effective operation of social obligations.

KINSHIP TERMINOLOGY

Anthropological accounts of kinship systems usually start with a description of the terminology of kinship. I have left all reference to this matter to the end, and it is with some reluctance that I embark upon it now. The general form of Sinhalese kinship terminology is of the type which Murdock describes as Iroquois. This is a well-known fact and has been the basis for the mistaken assumption made by Rivers, Hocart, Pieris and other writers that the Sinhalese system is 'patrilineal'.[1] The facts can be briefly stated as follows.

The term system is classificatory in the widest sense. There is

[1] Murdock, 1949; for extended descriptions of Sinhalese kinship terminology see Hocart, 1924–8; Lewis, 1884–6; Mendis-Gunasekera, 1914; Pieris, 1956; and Ariyapala, 1956.

complete discrimination as to sex—and also as to generation. Men and women use the same terms. The generations that are distinguished are five in number—I, grandparents, II, parents, III, own, IV, children's, V, grandchildren's. In generations II, III and IV (but not in I and V) Ego makes a term distinction between father's relatives and mother's relatives. In particular father's brother is distinguished from mother's brother, and father's brother's child (who is classed as Ego's sibling) is distinguished from mother's brother's child (the cross-cousin). There are the usual 'logical extensions'; mother's sister's husband rates as a 'father's brother' and her children as Ego's siblings; father's sister's husband rates as a 'mother's brother' and her children as cross-cousins.

The formal marriage rule is that a man should marry a girl of his own generation who is classificatory cross-cousin (*nāna*). Hence father-in-law is classed as mother's brother (*māmā*).

Present-day application of this terminology varies considerably in different parts of Ceylon. In Pul Eliya the behaviours expected between pairs of males were roughly as follows—

Kiriāttā/miniburā (grandfather-grandson): friendly informality.

Appā/putā (father-son): extreme respect tending to avoidance.

Loku appā/putā (father's elder brother/younger brother's son): respect relationship rather lacking in feeling on both sides.

Bāppa/putā (father's younger brother/elder brother's son): as above.

Ayiyā/malli (elder brother-younger brother): marked respect, formality.

Māmā (māmandi)/bānā (mother's brother-sister's son): respect, but much less than between father and son (except in case of *binna*-married son-in-law towards his father-in-law, when restraint is extreme).

Massinā/massinā (cross-cousins, including brothers-in-law): familiarity tending to joking relation.

—but these should not be thought of as rigid stereotypes.

The extent to which these formally expected behaviours play a significant part in day-to-day relationships has to some extent emerged in the foregoing discussion. We have seen for example that both the cross-cousin and the brother-in-law relationships form crucial links in the articulation of *pavula* groupings. The degree to which any particular specimen of such a relationship is in fact treated as a joking relationship serves as an index of its importance for the individuals concerned, and of the extent to which the social situation presents inconsistent obligations.

Again we have seen that the *ayiyā/malli* relationship between full brothers is often a cloak for strain and jealousy; in such cases *ayiyā/malli* behaviour is likely to be very formal. But the relationship between classificatory brothers may be easy-going and friendly. The use of *ayiyā/malli* terminology lacks the implication of claim which is inherent in *massinā/massinā* (cross-cousin) terminology, and there is a fairly general tendency to use *ayiyā/malli* for all males of one's own generation with whom no specially close kinship is asserted.

Similarly *bāppa*—('father's younger brother')—is very widely used for males of the senior generation, while *māmā* ('mother's brother'), because of the implication of claim, is applied much more cautiously. The term *māmandi* which is an intensified form of *māmā* is commonly used for all 'important' *māmā*. Between a *māmandi* and his *bāna* there is always a relationship of marked restraint and marked obligation on both sides.

We may summarise the situation thus. Owing to the fact that, within the *variga*, everyone is related to everyone else in a variety of different ways, Ego is generally faced with some degree of choice as to how a particular individual should be classed. The general practice is that, if kinship categories are used at all, a relative will be classed on the 'paternal' side unless there is special reason to do otherwise. Thus any male of the father's generation tends to be *loku appā* or *bāppa* (father's elder or younger brother) unless there is some quite specific reason for rating him as *māmā* (mother's brother). Similarly, in Ego's own generation, males are *ayiyā* or *malli* (elder or younger brother) unless there is special reason for classing them as *massinā* (cross-cousin).

The 'paternal' terms *loku appā, bāppa, ayiyā, malli* may be quite unstressed though as the relationship becomes close they carry with them an implication of rivalry, and consequent jealousy, between the speaker and the referrent; in contrast, the terms *māmā* and *massinā* contain an element of claim. A *māmā* is expected to help his *bāna* in various ways; *massinā* are expected to co-operate with one another over the whole range of economic and social activities.

A little consideration will show that these usages fit with the previous distinctions that I have drawn between *variga*, 'compound group' (*gedara*), and *pavula*. The *māmā*, *massinā*, *bāna* terms are primarily categories of affines to whom Ego is bound by ties of obligation. In contrast the *loku appā, bāppa, ayiyā, malli, putā* terms are categories of persons whose common link is descent from a common ancestor. The latter categories express a recognition of relationship but carry very limited implication of mutual obligation (cf. Dumont, 1957).

It is in line with this analysis that marriage, which is a crucial element in the structure of obligations, is supposed to be confined only to 'cross-cousins' (*massinā/nāna*). In practice many marriages are between individuals who are 'classificatory siblings', but it is significant that in such cases the 'affinal' terminology always supersedes the 'patrilineal descent' terminology. By that I mean that if a man marries a girl who is a 'classificatory sister' her brothers will cease to be classed as *ayiyā* or *malli* and will become *massinā*; likewise her father will become *mamandi* instead of *bāppa*. Expressed in another way we may say that the 'patrilineal descent' terminology, in its wider ramifications, does little more than specify the recognition of kinship in the most general sense; the affinal terminology on the other hand delimits the boundaries of the effective *pavula* and is, therefore, a matter of crucial structural significance.

Now that I have analysed in detail the various verbal categories in terms of which the Pul Eliya villagers conceive their kinship system, we can proceed to examine the application of these categories to the social processes involved in the transmission of property from one generation to another.

PROPERTY TRANSMISSION

The *variga*, *gedara* and *pavula* groupings which I have described in the earlier sections of this chapter provide the social framework within which and through which land and other property is transmitted from generation to generation. *Variga*, *gedara* and *pavula* are not, in any strict sense, property-owning corporate groups, but they are, in varying degrees, groups which endure through time independently of the life-span of particular individuals. The groups endure because the estates endure, but the groups have no corporate existence which could survive a dispersal of their landed property. In this respect they differ from 'lineages' which, in theory at least, owe their continued existence to a charter of common descent rather than of common property.

It seems reasonable to say that the present Pul Eliya *variga* is 'the same' *variga* as it was fifty years ago even though its membership has entirely changed. In a similar way at least some of the 1954 Pul Eliya *gedara* may be said to be 'the same' *gedara* as existed in 1890. *Pavula* certainly are more flexible, but even here there is continuity. The earliest Pul Eliya land dispute on record in the administration files is in an entry for 25 March 1861. This refers to a quarrel between Kadira Velathe Mohottāla (D 1:2), who was probably mother's mother's mother's mother's father to the S. Jaymanhamy (D 1:9) in Chart *a* (p. 114) and Naidu (rāla) Gamarāla (C:2) who was father's father to the U.V. Pinhamy (C 1:W) in the same chart.[1] The membership of factional groupings within the village keeps changing all the time, but, since the issues over which factional disputes tend to arise are recurrent, there is a tendency for opposition between families (*pavula*) to assume a more or less stereotyped pattern. The factional disputes of this generation are, by and large, between the heirs of those who indulged in similar factional disputes a generation ago.

But who are these 'heirs'? Land and other property may be transmitted from individual to individual in a variety of different

[1] The skewing of generations in this case is discussed at pp. 203–4.

It is thus the case that, as a result of mortgage sales, land does regularly pass into the hands of non-*variga* members; but only for a while. Since the 'outside' buyers of land are traders rather than cultivators they are likely, at the first opportunity, to sell the land back again to a local villager. Mortgaging procedure does not ordinarily result in the permanent loss of land to the *variga* as a whole; it simply provides a mechanism for transferring land from one compound group to another. We shall be able to follow up some detailed examples of this process in the next chapter.

Gifts

Whereas most sales of land are brought about by economic compulsion, gifts are voluntary transactions. It is therefore most unlikely that land will be *given* to someone outside the *pavula*. Gifts of land may lead to factional disputes among the recipients, but they are not in themselves a mechanism for transferring land from one kinship corporation to another. Nevertheless it needs to be remembered that the ownership rights of individual Sinhalese are, in theory, almost unconditional. Any owner *may* give away his property to anyone he chooses.

Several varieties of land gift may usefully be distinguished. The types correspond to the distinctions between sibling, half-sibling, step-sibling and foster-sibling relationships analysed above at pp. 107–10.

(i) A man may adopt a child of which he is not the acknowledged father. Such a child has no standing as an heir, but if the adopted father chooses to make a gift of land during his own lifetime his proper heirs cannot later dispute the claim.

One such case is that of A. Bandathe (G : Z 2), who is married to a foster-daughter of Appurala Vidāne (A 1 : W). Neither Bandathe nor his wife had any hereditary rights in Pul Eliya land, but Appurala during his own lifetime gave various lands to Bandathe together with full documentary title (see also pp. 104, 198, 226).

A similar case was that of Mudalihamy (C : Z 2) who was son of a wife of Kadirathe Gamarāla (C : 3), but had no other status in Pul

Eliya. Kadirathe Gamarāla had a son Appurala Vedarāla (C:6) who has no direct descendants resident in Pul Eliya. Most of the land now owned by members of compound Cx originated as a gift from Appurala Vederāla to his half-brother Mudalihamy (see pp. 102, 206).

It is worth noting that gifts of land on this pattern are among the most frequent sources of factional quarrels. In the above cases S. Subasinghe (A1:5) and his 'foster-cousin' B. Appuhamy (G:1) are bitter enemies; so also are M. Kirala (C1:2) and A.V. Bandathe (Z:C) (see Chart b, p. 134).

(ii) A quite different type of gift-giving *inter vivos* occurs when a man (or more rarely a woman) decides to divide up his property among his ordinary potential heirs while he himself is still alive. There are two main causes for this kind of action. First, a man who feels near the end of his life may decide to adopt the life of a saint (*upāsakarāla*). He then begins to behave according to the 'eight precepts' of the Buddhist canon in a rigorous way. He becomes a sort of lay monk, abstains from all 'temptations of the flesh' and generally prepares himself for the life to come. In Pul Eliya, in 1954, Punchirala Gamarāla (D2:C) and U. Kapuruhamy (B2:5) were both in this category. The former lived on the verandah of his son's (P. Kirala (D2:1)) house, the latter lived in a separate hut erected on a plot of freehold acre land adjacent to compound B2 where his sons K. Menikrala (B2:6) and K. Wannihamy (B2:7) continued to live. These old men, both over 70 years of age, were leading very saintly lives. Although they still engaged in agricultural work, they had already given away their property to their heirs and both were landless. Both, it may be remarked, had had very little land to give.

The other occasion for this kind of behaviour is when a man of mature years marries a new wife at a time when he already has an adult family by an earlier marriage. He is then likely to hand out as a gift to the children of his first marriage that part of his estate which is their total due. It is then clearly understood that when the parent finally dies only the heirs to the new marriage will have claims. In Pul Eliya, in 1954, U. Kadirathe (A2:4) and M. Naidurala (Dx:Y) had both already given shares of their estate to their

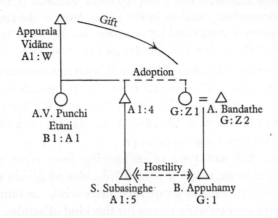

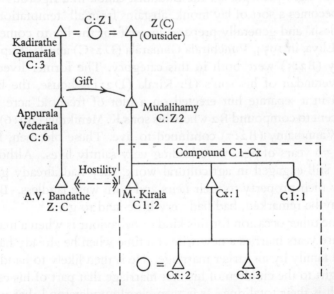

Chart *b*. Transmission of land by gift instead of inheritance. (i) Cases of gifts to adopted daughter and step-sibling leading to hostility between heirs in next generation.

adult children by earlier marriages. The property which remained in their personal control was to be inherited by the children of their existing marriages (see Chart *c*).

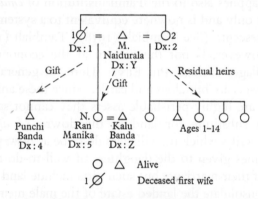

Chart *c*. Transmission of land by gift instead of inheritance. (ii) Gifts to adult children of a first marriage leaving children of a later marriage as residual heirs.

(iii) A third type of gift-giving is closely associated with the notion of dowry (*dävädda*). In Kandyan Ceylon dowry-giving is an institution which increases in importance as we move up the social-economic scale. Girls of wealthy and/or high-status parents often receive dowries of quite staggering dimensions, but among the rural peasantry dowry is not an important matter. The theory behind dowry-giving is that a daughter rates with her brothers as an heir to the parental estates but, if a *dīga*-married daughter can be given her potential share of the inheritance in the form of cash or jewellery or other movables, then she will have no further

135

claim on the parental land. Ideally, land should be transmitted to male heirs only. Dowry-giving, as an important institution, tends therefore to be confined to those social classes which are sufficiently affluent to be able to hold a part of their assets in ready cash and other movables.

It is a consequence of this that in those social classes where dowry-giving is associated with the existence of landed estates the localised *gedara* grouping has a fairly markedly patrilocal composition. The men of the society are domiciled on the land; the women, married in *diga*, take with them movable assets which are later used to provide dowries for their own daughters. This pattern has recently been described for villages in the vicinity of Kandy; it applies also to the Tamil institution of *chidenam*. It is a tendency only and is nowhere equivalent to a system of double unilineal descent. (See Tambiah (1958); Tambiah (1956).)

This, however, is not the pattern at the economic level of N.C.P. villages such as Pul Eliya. Here, in general, the only movable assets are buffaloes and cattle. Since these animals range freely and are highly perishable assets they cannot satisfactorily serve as a substitute for land in the dowry of *diga*-married daughters. Gifts which the villagers describe as dowry (*dāvädda*) are sometimes given to the daughters of well-to-do men on the occasion of their marriage, but such gifts include land and do not serve to consolidate the landed estate of the male members of the *gedara* as in the instances cited by Tambiah. When this 'so-called dowry' is given in Pul Eliya it is indistinguishable in kind from an advance share of the inheritance.

A case will illustrate the point. Tables 5 and 6 (pp. 184-9) show that B. Hetuhamy (Y:1) is the registered holder of several tracts of land. This man, resident in Yakawewa, is son of one of the richest and most influential men in the district. When B. Hetuhamy married the daughter of U. Kadirathe (A 2:4) (Chart *c*), the latter was delighted to bestow on his daughter a large dowry, and it is this land which now appears in the official records as belonging to B. Hetuhamy (Y:1). However, at much the same time, U. Kadirathe gave his son K.V. Appuhamy (A 2:7) a similar share of land. Kadirathe has now married again and it is clearly understood that neither Appuhamy nor Hetuhamy nor Hetuhamy's wife will share in the residue of Kadirathe's estate when the latter dies. The question of whether the land registered in Hetuhamy's name is to be considered as his wife's dowry or his wife's inheritance or as a personal gift to Hetuhamy is thus simply a matter of terminology.[1]

Binna-married husbands are in much the same position. Such a man ordinarily lives off his father-in-law's land in the hope and expectation that the land will ultimately be inherited by his wife. If relations between father-in-law and son-in-law are good then the elder man may formally transfer the property to his daughter during his own lifetime.

Examples: M. Naidurala (Dx:Y) had given land to his daughter N. Ran Manika (Dx:5) for the use of her *binna* husband, P. Kalu Banda (Dx:Z) (see Chart *c*). On the other hand U.G. Pinhamy (H:A2) had pointedly refused to transfer any land title to his *binna*-married daughter (A2:H), wife of B. Ausadahamy (A2:Y). The practical difference between the two cases did not seem to be very great since in both cases the father-in-law continued to manage the estate; but the implied difference in the status of the two sons-in-law was clearly understood. Ausadahamy was constantly complaining.

Direct inheritance

Order of birth or sex does not affect the inheritance potential of a child and *other things being equal* every member of a group of full siblings will inherit equally from both parents. In practice it seldom works out quite like that.

Of any group of siblings, some are likely to move, at marriage, to villages other than that in which they were born and in which they are most likely to inherit land. If the new village is close to the old one an heir may be able to retain his land and work it himself, but anyone whose residence is remote from the land which

---

[1] If this marriage ended in divorce there would probably be a lawsuit. The land is properly speaking the property of Hetuhamy's wife; it was registered in Hetuhamy's name so as to get round certain inconvenient government regulations.

pound group. Subasinghe owns land in Pul Eliya inherited from his father (A 1 : 4); he also owns land in Wiralmurippu inherited in part from his father and in part from his mother. A portion of his Pul Eliya land has been mortgaged to Herathamy V.V. for Rs. 200. Herathamy V.V. has leased this land back to Subasinghe *ande*, so Subasinghe works the land and gives half the proceeds to Herathamy V.V. as

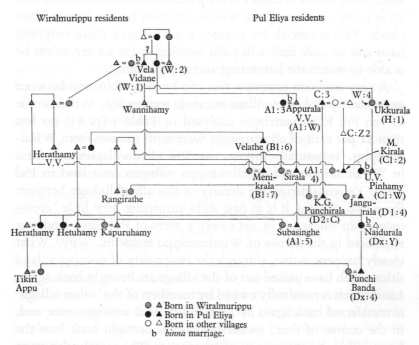

Chart *d*. Specimen of 'affinal network' between Pul Eliya and Wiralmurippu.

interest on his loan. But the land which Subasinghe owns in Wiralmurippu is not worked by him. It is given on *ande* to one of his mother's relatives; so some if not all of the paddy which Subasinghe gives to Herathamy V.V. is given back again by some of the latter's subordinates.

When *ukas* and *ande* contracts are examined individually the terms often seem excessively onerous; how can the cultivator possibly afford to pay such rates of interest? But seen in the larger context of contractual relations between affinal kin we see that the economic burdens of indebtedness tend to cancel out. What Peter owes to Paul, Paul, for some quite different reason, owes to Peter. The residue of the total pattern is not an impossible burden of debt, but an extremely dense mesh of reciprocal indebtedness which binds together not merely the members of a single village, but all the members of a single *variga* living within a few miles of one another.

The pattern of marriage discussed earlier in the analysis of Tables 2 and 3 (pp. 81–9) is closely related to these factors. The marriages of the relatively wealthy tend to be confined within the local 'close contact' area because the wealth involved constitutes the capital on which the elaborate inter-village debt structure is built up. Poorer members of the community are allowed to marry further away because the shares of land they can possibly inherit are so small as to make no difference one way or the other.

Land sales to kinsmen

The structure is not, however, entirely maintained as a system of debts. Outright sales of land to relatives do occur, as in the following case.

The Kadirathe Vederāla (Dw: F) mentioned above (p. 138) had two sisters (F: 2 and another), both of whom resided with their husbands in Bellankadawala (55). Their share in the original Pul Eliya estate of their father, Kappurala Vederāla (F: 1), has mostly been retained and has now devolved upon their heirs, most of whom continue to work the Pul Eliya land while living in Bellankadawala. One of the second-generation heirs (a girl, Y: Bel) has married *dīga* in Yakawewa (43). Her husband, finding it inconvenient to work his small share of the land when living so far away, sold it outright to his classificatory younger brother, M. Naidurala (Dx: Y), who is resident in Pul Eliya.

A factor in this case is that Naidurala's family were at one time entangled in a caste scandal (Appendix 2). From the point of view of the sellers of the land it was at that time probably considered better to sell the land outright, and then break connection with Naidurala, rather than engage in an *ukas* or *andē* contract with its implication of enduring relationship. An outright sale of land usually implies that the two parties to the transaction do not wish to recognise any continuing relationship.

The question of whether, at any particular time, an inheritance is retained or sold or mortgaged and leased may be of the very greatest importance for the owner's future, for in the long run it may determine whether the heir goes on to become a wealthy 'capitalist', like the various Vel Vidāne in my story, or whether he sinks gradually into a position of permanent serfdom in relation to some mortgage-holding overlord. Intelligence, industry and general business flair all come into it, but chance too plays a hand. Consider the case of the present Pul Eliya Vel Vidāne, V. Menikrala (B 1:7), son of Velathe (B 1:6).

Although Velathe was a man of means and brother-in-law of the former Vel Vidāne, U. Kadirathe (A 2:4), his son Menikrala was only one of seven children. Menikrala's original inheritance potential was thus poor. But Menikrala's three brothers all died without leaving children. Selling part of their land for cash, Menikrala used the proceeds to buy out the rights of his three *dīga*-married sisters and also to purchase support at the Vel Vidāne election which followed his uncle's retirement. Today Menikrala is the sole heir to his parents' property and, as Vel Vidāne of the village, his economic position is impregnable.

The 'fragmentation' of holdings

These various cases illustrate a variety of themes, but there are two in particular to which I wish to draw attention. First, as to 'fragmentation'. For many years Ceylon government officials have held the view that the traditional system of inheritance was intrinsically bad because it must lead to extreme fragmentation of holdings. Many features of land legislation—such as the rules incorporated in the Land Development Ordinance of 1935—are expressly designed to prevent this supposed fragmentation. But is it really the case that there is a fragmentation problem at all?

Of course it is perfectly obvious that if the Sinhalese villagers applied their bilateral rules of inheritance with legal precision then the property rights in any particular plot would rapidly become very widely dispersed. But we must also remember that whenever the total population of an agricultural area is increasing at a greater rate than the area of land under cultivation, then the average possible holding per individual must always decrease. These two logical inferences are quite distinct and should not be confused.

It is perfectly true that in the North Central Province the average size of holdings has tended to decrease over the last fifty years, but this is due to the increase in population and not to the operations of the bilateral rule of inheritance. There is no evidence at all that the inheritance system as such tends to excessive fragmentation. North Central Province villagers are sensible practical farmers; they are perfectly well aware as to what is the minimum size of plot which, given present cultivation techniques, it is practical to farm. They do not operate their inheritance rules in such a way as to make the whole system uneconomic. In the ordinary way bilateral inheritance serves as an effective mechanism for breaking up large estates, but it is not used in a legalistic way. If a legalistic claim leads to ridiculous conclusions the claim is abandoned.

Statistical order and individual 'luck'

The second theme which my cases illustrate is that the 'order' which my analysis reveals is of a general, statistical, structural type. When we examine the system as a whole we can see that it has a certain regularity of pattern. But at the level of individual cases this is not so. The individual's inheritance prospects are at all times wildly unpredictable. Inheritance rights are not pre-determined by sex or birth order and they can be radically altered from time to time by the marital behaviour of one or other parent or by such accidents as the number of siblings that are born and that survive, or the place of residence which these siblings happen to adopt at the time of marriage. Inheritance is thus to an extreme degree a matter of luck. It is then hardly surprising that the casting of horoscopes is considered by all Sinhalese to be a matter of supreme importance. Indeed throughout Ceylon fortune-telling in a wide variety of forms is an extremely highly developed 'science'.

That the outcome of inheritance is, in the last analysis, a matter of luck is well understood by all concerned. It is a point that is given an institutionalised emphasis in the special rules governing the ownership of livestock.

All animals, although they roam wild, are branded with the names of individual owners. Very commonly the owners are young children. When a calf is born it is likely to be branded with the name of a child of the owner of the cow. Calves born in succession are marked in turn in the name of each child of the family. In this way a boy of ten years old, if he is lucky, may be the owner of an expanding herd of half-a-dozen animals; if he is unlucky his calves all died in their first year of life. This intriguing system has two important implications. First, livestock are usually of very minor importance in 'inheritance', properly so called. When a rich man dies most of his animals already belong to his heirs. But secondly, the principle of luck is here frankly allowed to override the principle of equality. Two children of the same parents may end up with entirely different shares in the livestock portion of their total estate.

In passing, I would remark that these livestock transactions are relevant for our assessment of the absence of formal dowry-giving. A girl who is to receive no dowry may nevertheless be the owner of a number of valuable cows and buffaloes. In the strategy of arranged marriages this is a factor which is taken into account, though as an anthropological investigator it was a line of inquiry that I found impossible to pursue very far. Cattle were not ordinarily described as dowry (*dāvädda*) but clearly a girl's attractiveness could be notably enhanced by the simple process of giving her several extra animals. On one occasion I learned that U. Sirala (A2:5) was branding animals in his daughter's name. My informant immediately drew the correct inference: 'I suppose that the girl will very shortly be married.'

CHAPTER V

TRADITIONAL LAND TENURE

INTRODUCTION

This chapter contains an analysis of the present tenure system in the Pul Eliya Old Field and also an analysis of the tenure of land within the house-site and garden areas (*gamgoda*). It shows in detail how the principles of ownership and inheritance described in chapter IV actually work out in practice.

In the latter part of the chapter this detail is carried to the point of unreadability, so let me start by explaining my intentions.

The Pul Eliya villagers usually asserted that this part of their landed property is held and transmitted according to 'traditional' (*purāna*) rules. These traditional rules are complicated, but it is not too difficult to understand what they are. Accordingly, in the first part of the chapter I shall describe the precise nature of this 'traditional' system and I shall explain also in just what way existing published accounts are inaccurate or incomplete. But even when I have done all this I shall still have described only an ideal order —a model system. Moreover, this particular model is so complex that it invites scepticism. The professional anthropologist is bound to ask: How can such a system possibly work out in practice?

The only way to answer such questions and to demonstrate that the ideal theory is genuinely related to actual behaviour is to describe exactly what happens. But the details are indeed formidable, and only the most enthusiastic and patient reader can be expected to pursue all the permutations and combinations in such a maze. The precise analysis of 'who owns what and why' has therefore been collected together into the second half of the chapter (section B) as a kind of appendix. I have done my best to arrange and cross-reference this latter section so that those who have the patience can in fact follow the maze through from beginning to end; but I cannot pretend that it is easy.

The detail is presented not for its own sake, but because I need to justify my thesis. I am offering to my anthropological colleagues the awkward doctrine that, in this society, the kinship system is not a 'thing in itself', but rather a way of thinking about rights and usages with respect to land. The land is fixed, the people change. Ownership is not determined by simple rules; it evolves and fragments by the processes of gift, sale, and inheritance, but all the time the land is in the same place and the 'owners' must adjust their relationships to conform to this inescapable fact.

At no point in time is there ever a perfect functional fit between the facts of the kinship system and the facts of the land tenure system; both are always in process of modification. Land tenure and kinship structure are both 'patterns of jural relationship', but they are relative ideas which cannot be viewed separately and both are aspects of something else. The continuity of the society does not depend upon any continuing pattern of jural relationships; within certain limits the pattern can vary rapidly and quite drastically. The limits in question are not jural but topographical, the size of the tank and the shape of the field.

My overall thesis is that Pul Eliya society is not governed by any general structural principles such as have been claimed to prevail in various types of society possessing unilineal descent systems. Pul Eliya society is an ordered society, but the order is of a statistical not a legal kind. If I am to demonstrate this, I must show both that the individual facts are chaotic and that, taken *en masse*, they have a pattern. Such a demonstration can hardly be designed to make comfortable reading; I have done my best.

The less enthusiastic reader who does not pretend to any special interest in the professional subtleties of anthropologists will probably feel that he has had enough when he gets to the end of section A.

This preliminary account of the 'theory' of traditional land tenure in Pul Eliya should be of interest to students of Ceylon history as well as to anthropologists. It is, therefore, important that there should be no ambiguity about what I am describing.

SECTION A: THE THEORY OF
TRADITIONAL TENURE

THE CLASSICAL SYSTEM AS DESCRIBED BY
IEVERS AND CODRINGTON

I have already explained in chapter II that Ievers, in his *Manual of the North Central Province* (1899), describes an idealised type of land tenure which he represents as being the typical traditional system operating in all villages of the North Central Province. Codrington (1938) and Pieris (1956) have both accepted Ievers's account as an accurate historical reconstruction. All three authors seem to suppose that at one time this kind of tenure prevailed throughout Dry Zone Ceylon.

There is documentary evidence that tenures approximating to that described by Ievers existed over much of the northern part of the North Central Province in the latter part of the nineteenth century. This area has, even today, a consistent ecological pattern which is best summarised by the phrase 'one tank—one village'. But this ecological pattern is not general to the whole of the Ceylon Dry Zone, nor even to the whole of the two Northern Provinces, nor even to the whole of the Nuvarakalāviya District. It therefore seems to me unlikely that Ievers's tenure system ever prevailed over any very wide area. The system is certainly extremely interesting and it *may be* of considerable antiquity, but certainly, in part, it is a peculiarity of this particular region.

I shall start by giving a summary of the ideal type as it has been previously described. Codrington, relying on information obtained at Vavuniya in 1909, records a tradition concerning the correct procedure for re-establishing a new village on the site of an old one. The story should probably be regarded as providing validation for a particular type of tenure rather than an account of any actual series of historical events. The account serves to explain how the village field is supposed to be laid out.

The following is a quotation from Codrington's text which

10-2

assumes that a new community is to be established by colonists from an existing village:

The people who propose to found a new village go to the site and sleep on the tank bund to see if there are devils or dreams (hine, sopne). If any devil appears they abandon the proposal. The appearance of a tusker or of a white horse or of a man riding is the best omen. They then report to the (old) village, and the names of applicants and the amount of paddy land to be assigned to each are written on a talkola or slip of palmyra leaf. Two gamarālas are then elected, one for the ihala bāgē, one for the pahala bāgē. The amount of money each man will contribute towards the repair of the breach in the bund is decided, and pangu apportioned accordingly. They then clear the breach of jungle and call in the Tamil kulankatti people and bargain with them as to the earthwork.... After the breach is closed the new settlers come together and pay the money agreed upon according to pangu. No money is paid for the gamvasama, älapata or kurulupāluva; the älapat panguva, however, pays. They then go to divide the field (vela), looking in the jungle for good land and sending men to various spots in the jungle and on the bund to cry 'hoo'. They then come to one place, sit down and call upon the Gods.... Then one rises with a kätta (billhook) and cries 'hā-purā' and cuts a tree once; this is näkata-ta val allanavā, 'taking (possession of) the jungle at a lucky time'. After cutting boundaries in the jungle in three places, i.e. three lines at right angles to the bund, they measure the ihala bāgē lengthwise with kirivāl creepers in bamba or fathoms, leaving the kurulupāluva, älapata and älapat panguva and dividing the rest crosswise into pangu and gamvasama. There should be ten pangu in all, but if there be many people and several bāgēs there may be seven pangu in each bāgē.... Then the pahala bāgē is measured in the same way. Afterwards the jungle is felled and the mūndukiriyal rice sown. After reaping, mūndu-kiriyal is sown again, and after the tree stumps have rotted and have been burnt the field ridges (niyara) are made.

After sowing the first mūndukiriyal the villagers clear round the vādiya or temporary camping place and build small houses of branches (kalal geval) without pila (verandah) or fence, close to one another for fear of wild beasts. Then the women come with dogs and fowls, the dogs to keep watch and to give alarm of wild animals, the fowls to give notice of daybreak and to frighten away beasts. The land is then divided into gardens according to the pangu and proper houses built. The old custom was to build them in a row with a common pila in order that when the men went to Kandy and elsewhere on rājakāriya or service their families might not be exposed to danger. The collection of houses (gamgoda) lies close to the tank bund and is surrounded by a ring fence. The tis-bamba or 'thirty fathom' clearing round this fence to let in light and air is due to the British Administration, and not so long ago the jungle came right up to the fence and leopards carried off the cattle tied in the pila. (Codrington, 1938, pp. 63–65.)

This ideal scheme specifies a very precise relationship between: (a) the tank, (b) the field, and (c) the village. It further implies that the field shall be roughly rectangular with its longest side lying at right angles to the bund of the tank. The field is in major sections, bāga (bāgē).[1] Maps B and E may be taken as illustrative of this account.

As Codrington recognised, this description fits very nicely with the ideal pattern previously described by Ievers who wrote:

Each tract or pota is divided into two or three portions called bāgē, viz. ihalabāgē, medabāgē and pahalabāgē. Each pota has two small strips, one at the tank end and the other at the opposite end which are called kurulupālu meaning 'an allowance of extra land as compensation for damage by birds'. Two larger strips at each end next the kurulu-pālu are called elapat. These are the property of the gamarāla who is the hereditary chief cultivator of the village. The other portion in the middle of the pota is divided equally among the shareholders, including the gamarāla and the divisions are called pangu. A panguwa is an original share but as the family increases it may become subdivided.... The pangu are divided across the field by ridges parallel to the bund of the tank and each contains one or two strips called issarawal. One issara is a range of beds between two of these ridges.... The gamarāla put up two watch huts one at each elapata and the other pangukārayō (shareholders) jointly build a watch hut for every three or four pangu and watch by turns. (Ievers, 1899, p. 172.)

[1] Following Pieris I write bāga throughout; Codrington and Ievers both write bāgē which corresponds to the pronunciation. My elapata follows Ievers's spelling and is the same as the more correct älapata of Codrington and Pieris. My pangu is the same as Codrington's pangu, Ievers's pangu and Pieris's pamgu.

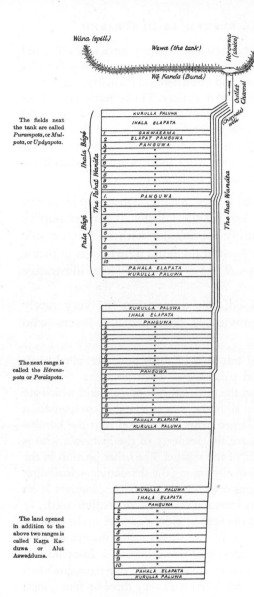

The fields next the tank are called *Purampota*, or *Mulpota*, or *Upáyapota*.

The next range is called the *Hérenapota* or *Peralapota*.

The land opened in addition to the above two ranges is called Kaṭṭa Kaduwa or Alut Asweduma.

EXPLANATION OF TERMS

IT is supposed that in this village there are ten pangu (shares) and a gaṇwasama held by a Gamarála. There may be any number of shares, but the division is in this manner shown. Some villages contain only one field called Purampota, &c., and this, if small, is not divided into bágé. If large there may be three bágé: Ihalabágé, Medabágé, Pahalabágé. Each bágé contains an equal number of pangu; and the reason of the division in this manner is so that good and bad land may be equally distributed.

The *gaṇwasama* panguwa belongs to the Gamarála, and for this he has no duty to perform (such as earthwork on bund, clearing channels, fencing, &c.).

The *kurulla páluwa* belongs to the Gamarála as an allowance for damage by birds, beasts, &c. It means literally "bird-damage."

Elapata means "a side." This belongs to the Gamarála panguwa, and is free of rájakáriya (either earthwork, pinpara, &c.), as in the case of the gaṇwasama; but the Gamarála must put up and keep the fence all round.

The *elapat paṇguwa* belongs to the Gamarála, but, unlike the elapata and gaṇwasama, the ordinary rájakáriya must be done for it.

Betma = any portion of any field equally divided according to pangu, and cultivated by all the shareholders when the water in the tank is not sufficient to irrigate a whole field (pota).

Ihat = the channel side of a field.

Pahat = the side of the field opposite to the channels.

Wanata = the line of jungle yearly cleared on ihat and pahat sides for protection of the crop from damage by wild animals.

Issara = a panguwa, or, if it is divided in two by a ridge in the middle, half a panguwa.

Aññyama = a pahala elapata in a betma cultivation, i.e., the lowest panguwa when only a portion of a field is cultivated. It is given to the Gamarála.

Tatta máru, *Kara máru*, *Sóra máru*. In this Province (North-Central Province) these words have no difference of meaning. When a panguwa belongs to several shareholders, or becomes too much subdivided, it is taken for cultivation turnabout as may be agreed upon according to the number of the shareholders. It is not a common practice.

Diagram 2. Ievers's schematic diagram of an ideal *bāga* system (for comparison with Map *E*).

By way of illustration Ievers published a diagram which is here reproduced (Diagram 2). The letterpress in the margin of the diagram has led to some confusion.[1] Ievers states that his hypothetical field contains only 10 *pangu*,[2] but adds that 'each *bāgē* contains an equal number of *pangu*'. Most readers would infer that his diagram shows 5 *bāga* in all, each with 10 *pangu* but with all 5 *bāga* controlled by one Gamarāla. I can only remark that such a field layout is in the highest degree improbable.

Since the Sinhalese term *gama* (pl.: *gam*) is commonly translated as 'village', many writers have thought that a Gamarāla was simply a village headman; Ievers himself writes as if this were so. But, in this region, the normal holding of a Gamarāla is not a village but a *bāga*. The Sinhalese think of a village tank and its associated lands as constituting a single unified estate. The ultimate landlord of this estate is either the Crown, or an absentee landlord, or the priest of some local temple. Under the traditional system this ultimate landlord would always have sublet the estate to *one or more* primary grant-holders—the Gamarāla. The position was accurately described by Codrington:

The Sinhalese gama, plural gam, normally signifies a village but the word is applied to an estate or even to one field. . . . Of the gama, whether village or estate, the centre is the paddy land, of which the high land is considered to be the appurtenance. . . . The gama normally consists of paddy fields, gardens, and miscellaneous fruit trees and chena (hēna, pl. hēn) that is jungle land, cleared, burnt and cultivated periodically. . . . In the country where paddy cultivation is carried on by means of tanks, the houses are gathered together in the neighbourhood of the tank bund. Such a village until recent times consisted of a number of families of the same caste and related to one another, presided over by one or two hereditary Gamaralas—whose holding was the gamvasama.

The classes known in India as the village servants, the blacksmith, the washerman, the potter and others (tovilkārayō) live in separate villages of their own similarly organised. (Codrington, 1938, p. 1.)

[1] See, for example, Pieris, 1956, pp. 236 f. where Ievers's diagram (modified) has been reproduced without the marginal notes.

[2] Properly *paṃguva* (sing.); *paṃgu* (pl.).

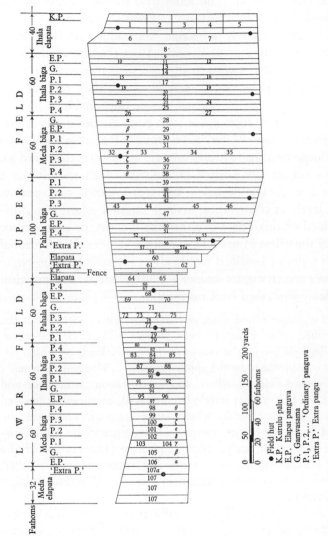

Map *E.* Pul Eliya Old Field. Details of field strips (*issaraval*) drawn to scale showing the relation of the strips to the *bāga* system. For comparison with Table 4 and Diagram 2. The 'fathoms' (*bamba*) of this map are normal arm-spans and are approximately 2 in. short of the English 6 ft. measure.

● Field hut
K.P. Kurulu palu
E.P. Elapat panguva
G. Gamvasama
P.1, P.2,... 'Ordinary' panguva
'Extra P.' Extra pangu

As may be gathered from chapter II this description correctly outlines the general state of affairs prevailing even now in the vicinity of Pul Eliya. The unit estate associated with one particular tank may sometimes consist of one *gama* and sometimes of several. In the latter case each sub-unit is called a *bāga*. In any one village there are as many Gamarāla offices as there are *bāga*, though on occasion one individual may hold more than one such office at one time. The number of *bāga* in a village and hence the number of Gamarāla offices is permanent and unalterable.

THE FORMAL THEORY AS APPLIED TO
PUL ELIYA

In Pul Eliya and in all the neighbouring villages the estates of the different Gamarāla are immediately adjacent to one another and are ordinarily fed from the same irrigation channel. The different Gamarāla must, therefore, co-operate.

The different Gamarāla who control a single field are not thought of as close kinsmen. They are heads of different *pavula* and essentially of exactly equal status. They may then be *massinā* —brothers-in-law—but cannot properly be brothers, since *ayiyā/malli* are always of unequal status. It is true that, on one occasion, I was given the hazy outline of a myth which started by saying that Pul Eliya was founded by three *sahōdara* ('brothers'), but when I pursued this and asked whether one of the brothers was senior to the others, my informant quickly changed the subject. The term *sahōdara* may, as a matter of fact, include persons standing in *massinā* relationship (see p. 114).

The Gamarāla was a grant-holder, not an owner. In accepting a grant of land he also undertook a number of service responsibilities associated with the grant. The nature of the service depended on the grant-holder's caste and various other factors. According to local tradition, the original service obligation undertaken by all three Pul Eliya Gamarāla was to provide annually a certain weight of water lily flowers for the use of the temples in Anurādhapura (see p. 76). This story is probably simply

153

a rationalisation from the village name 'Pul Eliya' which means 'flowery open space', but some service tenures of this kind are authentic. (See Tennent, 1859, vol. I, p. 367.)

The inhabitants of Pul Eliya are all members of the cultivator caste (Goyigama) which stands at the head of the caste hierarchy. The various grant-holders in non-Goyigama villages took on much more menial service duties than that of picking flowers.

In addition to this traditional feudal service, the Gamarāla had an obligation to collect taxes, to entertain government officials and to maintain the tank in good working order. Most of these latter obligations remained even after the coming of the British and the abolition of Kandyan feudalism. Some of these duties were carried out by the several Gamarāla jointly while others were worked on a roster basis. In the outcome there was no clearly defined Village Headman and it was this fact which led the exasperated British administrators to institute the dictatorial office of Vel Vidāne.

During the latter part of the British period the Vel Vidāne was the sole channel of communication between village and government while the rights and duties of the Gamarāla were of no practical account, but the independent authority of the Vel Vidāne was only gradually established. In Pul Eliya, down to 1926, the office of Vel Vidāne was always held by someone who was simultaneously entitled to call himself Gamarāla, and the relationship between successive Vel Vidāne has commonly been that of *māmā* to *bāna* rather than father to son. The initial postulate that authority should be distributed among the different *pavula* of the village rather than concentrated in one place seems to have survived throughout.

But the traditional Gamarāla did not act on his own; he had feudal duties to perform and this implied that he must have tenants.

In every community each traditional *bāga* is subdivided into a certain specific number of traditionally established equal shares (*pangu*). There might, for example, be two *bāga* each of ten shares, or three *bāga* each of twenty shares. In Pul Eliya there were

154

originally three *bāga* each of six shares, making eighteen shares in all.

A share is primarily a share in tank water. The *gamgoda* land on which the house-sites stand was originally laid out in parallel strips, *bāga* by *bāga*, in such a way that each *bāga* block had equal access to the irrigation channel running through it. Even today the house-sites and their associated gardens conform approximately to this initial gridded plan (see Map *C*, p. 45).[1] It is an arrangement of this kind that Codrington's informants were referring to when they told him that in a new village the house-sites should be laid out 'according to the *pangu*'.

A similar arrangement prevailed in the irrigated field itself. The main irrigation channel was laid out in a single straight line which was then divided up into major segments 'according to the *bāga*'. Then, within each *bāga* block, the subsections were divided up 'according to each *panguva*'. The details of this subdivision are complicated and will presently be described, but the net result is that each *panguva* has allocated to it an exactly equivalent portion of the main irrigation channel. Certain sections of the channel were not allocated to the *pangu* in this way, but were reserved as the perquisites of the various Gamarāla.

Once the sections of the main irrigation channel had been laid out and divided, each shareholder then proceeded to develop the land at right angles to the irrigation channel. How much land a particular man opened up in this way would depend partly on the lay of the ground, partly on the individual's energy, partly on the amount of water available. There were, however, no set limits. The shape of the Pul Eliya Old Field today simply represents the approximate shape it happened to have in the year 1900 when the government survey was made. Diagram 3 (p. 162) shows how the main irrigation channel runs in a straight line along the northern side of the field. The various strips are then extended at right angles from this channel towards the south (Map *E*, p. 152). But

---

[1] Cf. Map *D* (p. 100); compound A is linked with the Ihala bāga, compounds C and D with the Pahala bāga and compounds B and D with the Meda bāga (see below, pp. 200, 204, 210).

they vary considerably in length, and the irregularities were formerly even greater than they are now. In 1890 the strips embracing plots nos. 39–53 extended considerably further to the south into a piece of ground that has now been abandoned.[1]

Since 1900 the shape of the field has been 'frozen'. Land tenure, as the British authorities understood it, necessarily consisted of rights to a particular piece of land rather than rights to a particular quantity of water. Consequently all *land* not actually under cultivation at the time of the survey was treated as Crown property. But it is the emphasis on rights in *water*, as opposed to rights in *land*, which explains the many peculiarities of the traditional system which are already apparent in Ievers's account.

It will be immediately obvious that in times of scarcity those parts of the irrigation channel which are close to the tank will receive a more regular supply of water than parts further away. For the same reason, although the field is very nearly flat, and the field strips are supplied with water at both ends and in the middle,[2] the northern end of each strip, adjacent to the main channel, is slightly better placed than the southern end.

As an adjustment against these discrepancies we find that, within the field as a whole and also within each *bāga* as a section of the field, the land is subdivided into small allocations which are designed to minimise, as far as possible, the consequences of unavoidable inequalities in the distribution of water. In Pul Eliya this equalisation principle has been carried to extremes.

From here on the reader should follow the description by reference to Map *E* (p. 152) and Table 4 (between pp. 144 and 145).

In the first place the field as a whole is divided into two sections, the Upper Field and the Lower Field. These are the units which Ievers describes as tracts (*pota*). The Lower Field has roughly half the area of the Upper Field. The three *bāga* are made up from sections in each field. Each field is divided into three main sections but if we count the sections of the Upper

---

[1] See Map *B*, empty area between plots 129 and 137. The ground was given up because of irrigation difficulties and poor soil.

[2] This applies only to the strips in the Upper Field. For details, see p. 162.

Field as Ihala (A), Meda (B) and Pahala (C), then the corresponding sections in the Lower Field are arranged C, A, B. Each *bāga* also comprises an 'end piece' (*elapata*). Thus the *bāga* are as follows:

A. Ihala *bāga*: Upper end of Upper Field plus upper section of Upper Field plus middle section of Lower Field.

B. Meda *bāga*: Lower end of Lower Field plus middle section of Upper Field plus lower section of Lower Field.

C. Pahala *bāga*: End piece made up of lower end of Upper Field plus upper end of Lower Field plus lower section of Upper Field plus upper section of Lower Field.

The general effect is that shareholders who own land in the lowest and least advantageous portion of the Upper Field also own land in the highest and most advantageous portion of the Lower Field.

'PANGU'

Here it is necessary to digress and say something further about the exact nature of a *panguva* holding.

The translation of the word *panguva* as 'share' is very appropriate, for it corresponds closely to the notion of share as it is used in the parlance of English company law. A *bāga* contains a fixed number of *pangu* just as the ordinary capital of an English commercial company consists of a fixed number of 'shares'. It is possible for one individual to own several shares or alternatively for one share to be owned by several distinct individuals. Moreover, within one village community one particular individual may own parts of a number of different shares in different *bāga*. In theory, the number of shares is fixed from the start and should never change. But the number of individual shareholders is varying all the time. It follows that there is no precise correspondence between the number of strips (*issaraval*) in the field and the division into shares (Rhys-Davids, 1871). On this point Ievers's original diagram and his written account are both misleading.

If we examine Map *E* (p. 152) in detail and consider only the central part of each field, we can see that each *bāga* consists of

60 fathoms in the Upper Field, plus 60 fathoms in the Lower Field. Now there were originally six *pangu* in each *bāga*. Thus the original arrangement was that each *panguva* had 10 fathoms in the Upper Field and 10 fathoms in the Lower Field. Very probably, when the field was first laid out, the strips were actually laid out in this way so that they were regularly at 10-fathom intervals all the way down the field. At the present day, however, the width of the strips varies considerably. There are strips of 4, 4½, 5, 7, 8 and 10 fathoms. This variation is shown to scale on Map *E*. Even so, apart from minor discrepancies, the original general layout into 60-fathom major blocks has never been lost sight of. The *bāga* blocks as wholes have remained almost unchanged (see Table 4).

For every strip in the *pangu* portion of the Upper Field, there is a corresponding strip of corresponding width in the Lower Field. This pairing is an essential feature of the system. It is not possible to own *pangu* land in the Upper Field without also owning a corresponding piece of land in the Lower Field. Land can be bought and sold or alienated in other ways, but if an owner wishes to dispose of one-third of his *pangu* land he cannot simply dispose of that worst portion of it which is in the Lower Field. He will have to divide off one-third of his Upper Field strip and also one-third of his Lower Field strip. This fragmentation makes very good sense if it is remembered that what is being disposed of here is not really land at all, but rights to a proportion of the total water supply. The 'fragmentation' that results is not an economic vice but a moral virtue!

The final detail which completes the logical perfection of the Pul Eliya system of equalised shares is that the order of the strips in the Upper and Lower Fields is reversed. What I mean by this can be seen from reference to Map *E* where the details of Meda bāga are given for both fields. If the strips in the Meda bāga in the Upper Field are numbered α, β, γ, δ, etc., starting from the top of the *bāga*, then in the Lower Field they would have to be numbered in the reverse order starting from the bottom of the *bāga*. This feature, though not peculiar to Pul Eliya, is not found in all the villages round about, though in other respects the Old

Field tenure in all communities is very similar. It seems evident
that it is a feature which derives from an early phase in Pul Eliya
history, for the present generation of villagers appear to be quite
unaware that their strips are arranged in this fashion; all they
know is that every Upper Field strip has its counterpart in the
Lower Field.

Strips are sometimes shared by more than one owner. For
example, K. Dingiri Banda (A2:B2) and A.V. Punchi Etani
(B1:A1) are the owners of plot nos. 15 and 16.[1] This holding
amounts to half a *panguva* in the Ihala bāga. The total holding
consists of one strip in the Upper Field (plots 15 and 16) and
another strip in the Lower Field (plots 91 and 92). Each strip is
shared by the two owners. Division is effected by cutting each
strip in half and reversing the holding in alternate years. Each
owner works the northern half of each strip every other year.

All this sounds most improbable but, in fact, this part of the
ideal scheme is adhered to closely. Table 4 has been drawn up
in such a way that the six right-hand columns show the correspondence between the 1954 ownership of *pangu* strips in the
Upper Field and Lower Field respectively. The generalisation
that 'every *pangu* plot in the Upper Field has a counterpart plot
in the Lower Field owned by the same individual' is very nearly
true. Such small discrepancies as exist are due to the existence of
'undivided holdings'—for example, plots 9–12 plus 95–7 make
up a single holding shared by the heirs of a common estate; the
same is true of plots 33–5 plus 103. Two genuine 'exceptions'
occur; the Lower Field plots 106 and 66 are *not* owned in the
same way as their Upper Field counterparts plots 28 and 52–3.
Explanations for these two cases are given elsewhere (p. 207).

This table confirms unambiguously that down to 1954 it was
still the general practice in Pul Eliya that no one could acquire a
holding in the Upper Field without simultaneously acquiring a
corresponding plot in the Lower Field.

[1] Plot numbers refer to the numbers in the Vel Vidāne's paddy census return
for 1954. The corresponding numbers appear on Maps *B* and *E* and in Table 6.

THE ALLOCATION OF WATER

Finally we need to consider the arrangement by which proportionately equal amounts of water are fed into the field strips through the irrigation channels. There is only one main water channel leading from the *gamgoda* area to the Old Field (see Map *C*, p. 45). This channel is then divided into branches which feed into the Upper Field on the north and south sides and in the middle; the northern branch also extends along the northern edge of the Lower Field. These various ditches are not single channels, but multiple parallel channels which branch off and rejoin one another in a seemingly very complicated manner. However, once the principles involved are understood these permutations and combinations turn out to be quite straightforward.

The distribution of the water is the responsibility of the Vel Vidāne. In theory he should make use of a traditionally established set of numerical ratios which relate to the relative sizes of the different sections of the Old Field. The 1954 Vel Vidāne (V. Menikrala (B 1:7)) seemed scarcely to understand the rationale of the system and much of my information on this point came from his predecessor, U. Kadirathe (A 2:4).

The essence of the system of water allocation is that the flow of water in any particular channel can be subdivided into numerical proportions by making the water flow over a device called a *karahankota*. This is, in effect, a miniature weir consisting of a log of wood into which two or more flat-bottomed grooves of equal depth have been cut. The length of the grooves is proportional to the required ratio of division. For example, suppose the Vel Vidāne wishes to divide a moderate flow of water in proportions 2:1, he might make a *karahankota* with grooves of 12 in. and 6 in. breadth respectively; the flow of water over the 12-in. 'weir' is then assumed to be twice the flow of water over the 6-in. 'weir'. The fact that the Vel Vidāne today makes his calculations in English inches does not necessarily mean that the system itself is recent. In pre-British times the Sinhalese possessed a carpenter's rule, *vadu riyana*, which was a cubit measure divided into 24 *angula* (finger joints). This could have been used in the same way, and even with the same numerical values, as the modern footrule.[1]

The traditional reckoning is that, if Upper and Lower Fields are both being cultivated, then each 60 fathoms of *pangu* land in the Lower Field is only entitled to one-third as much water as each 60 fathoms of *pangu* land in the Upper Field. The water rights of the three *elapata* seem to have been less precisely defined though each was, in theory, 40 fathoms deep. The proportions of the different sections of the field are supposed to be as follows:

Field section	Fathoms	Numerical proportion of water allocation	
Upper Field			
Ihala elapata	40	?3	
Ihala bāga pangu	60	6	
Meda bāga pangu	60	6	
Pahala bāga pangu	60	6	
Pahala elapata	40	?3	— 24
Lower Field			
Pahala bāga pangu	60	2	
Ihala bāga pangu	60	2	
Meda bāga pangu	60	2	
Meda elapata	40	?2	— 8

When filling in 'acreage' figures in the annual paddy census return for plots in the Lower Field the Vel Vidāne adjusts his figures so that the total acreage for the Lower Field (16 acres) is just one-third of that for the whole Upper Field (48 acres) (see Table 4, 1954 columns). Since the areas are quite fictitious it seems obvious that this computation must have originated in the traditional rule about water allocation.

A complication results from the fact that the Upper Field is fed with water by three channels—one down each side and one down the middle, whereas the Lower Field is fed from one side only. If we distinguish the channels by letters as in Diagram 3 then the proportions of water flowing in each channel are supposed to be as follows:

Karahankota 1 (K 1):
Channel A direct to Lower Field, $\frac{1}{4}$ total supply.
Channel B to Upper Field, $\frac{3}{4}$ total supply.

[1] Pieris, 1956, p. 89.

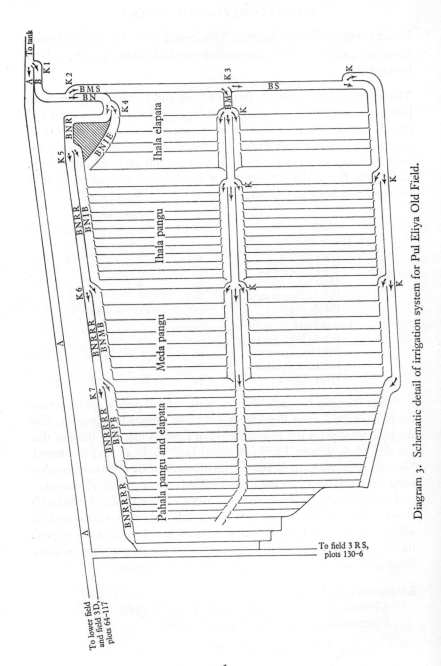

Diagram 3. Schematic detail of irrigation system for Pul Eliya Old Field.

To tank

K1

K2

BMS
BN

BNR

BNIE

K4

K5

Ihala elapata

BNRR
BNIB

Ihala pangu

K6

BNRRR
BNMB

Meda pangu

K7

BNRRRR
BNPB

Pahala pangu and elapata

BNRRR

A

A

BS

K3

BMS

K

K

K

K

K

K

To field 3 R S,
plots 130–6

To lower field
and field 3 D,
plots 64–117

Channel B is then further divided as follows:
Karahankota 2 (K 2):
 Channel BN to northern side of Upper Field, $\frac{1}{4}$ of channel B.
 Channel BMS to middle and southern side of Upper Field, $\frac{3}{4}$ of
 channel B.

Further along its course channel BMS
is again divided:
Karahankota 3 (K 3):
 Channel BM to middle of Upper
 Field, $\frac{1}{2}$ of channel B (i.e. $\frac{2}{3}$ of
 BMS).
 Channel BS to southern side of
 Upper Field, $\frac{1}{4}$ of channel B (i.e.
 $\frac{1}{3}$ of BMS).

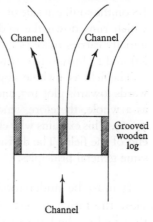

Channels BN and BS are then each
treated in the same way, as follows:
 BN is first divided:
Karahankota 4 (K 4):
 BNIE to Ihala elapata, $\frac{1}{8}$ of channel
 BN.
 BNR to remainder, $\frac{7}{8}$ of channel
 BN.

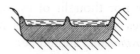

Diagram 4. *Karahankota.*

BNR is then ducted as far as the
beginning of the Ihala bāga and divided:
Karahankota 5 (K 5):
 BNIB to Ihala bāga, $\frac{1}{4}$ of channel BN.
 BNRR remainder, $\frac{5}{8}$ of channel BN.

BNRR is then ducted to the beginning of the Meda bāga and divided:
Karahankota 6 (K 6):
 BNMB to Meda bāga, $\frac{1}{4}$ of channel BN.
 BNRRR remainder, $\frac{3}{8}$ of channel BN.

BNRRR is then ducted to the beginning of the Pahala bagā and
divided:
Karahankota 7 (K 7):
 BNPB to Pahala bāga, $\frac{1}{4}$ of channel BN.
 BNRRRR remainder, $\frac{1}{8}$ of channel BN.

This channel BNRRRR then feeds the Pahala elapata. Within each *elapata* and each *bāga* block the water is ducted separately into each strip (*issara*) but at this stage no special precautions are introduced to ensure equal distribution between each strip.

The subdivisions of channel BN on the north side of the field and of BS on the southern side of the field are virtually the same. Channel BM which runs down the middle of the field is somewhat different. It initially carries twice as much water as the other two, but feeds water left and right into the strips on either side.

The field as a whole slopes very slightly (*a*) from plot no. 1 downwards towards plot 107, and (*b*) from north to south. The Upper Field as a whole, therefore, tends to drain off on the lower side of strips 55–63. This explains why channel BS is not carried on right to the lower end of the field. The division of water in the Lower Field follows the same general principles.

It must be understood that from the Vel Vidāne's point of view the ratios are established by tradition; they are not something which he has to work out for himself. Moreover the ratios are not thought of as fractions but as *karahankota* of different sizes with the grooves measured in inches. The above seven *karahankota* should be:

	Lengths in inches	
Karahankota	Groove *a*	Groove *b*
1	6	18
2	6	18
3	12	6
4	3	21
5	6	15
6	4	12
7	12	6

In 1954 several of the *karahankota* were missing but those that existed were consistent with the possibility that some recent Vel Vidāne had worked to the above numerical formula or at any rate had copied older *karahankota* which were constructed on this principle.

The complexity of the arrangement is itself relevant to my theme since such a system is virtually unalterable. Although the present generation of Pul Eliya villagers are not at all clear about the inner logic of it all they are keenly aware that the numerical formulae handed down from ancient times are very important. The general view seemed to be: 'We don't understand why things are arranged like this, but this is how they are, and we had better leave them alone.'

The recent great extension of 'acre land' cultivation—*sinak-kara* and *badu*—has reduced the crucial importance of the Old Field holdings and the owners are doubtless a good deal less fussy about the mathematical accuracy of their water rights than formerly. Nevertheless it was quite clear that blocking or tapping a neighbour's water channel was still by far the most common cause of village quarrels and inter-compound litigation. In the 1954 *Yala* season water was fairly plentiful. Had there been a critical scarcity I might have observed the formal rules in much more rigid application.

'RĀJAKĀRIYA' DUTIES

We see then that the use of both land and water in the Old Field is very elaborately enmeshed in a variety of institutional devices all serving the same general purpose. The emphasis throughout this tenure system is on the principle that each *panguva* within each *bāga* shall have exactly equal rights to the total available water.

As against these equal rights, each *panguva* carries also exactly equal obligations with regard to the maintenance of the tank bund, maintenance of field fencing, etc. The precise obligations attaching to a *pangu* holding are today defined by government regulation; their substance has not changed since 1850. The duties are collectively known as king's work (*rājakāriya*). Briefly they are:

(1) Each shareholder shall carry out a certain amount of repair work on the bund annually, proportional to the amount of his holding.

(2) Each shareholder shall build and maintain that portion of the main field fence which is opposite the ends of any strip which he works.

165

(3) Each shareholder shall maintain in good condition any irrigation ditches which go past or through the land which he works.

(4) Each shareholder shall take his turn to sit up all night in one of the field huts to ward off wild animals which are liable to attack the field.

This last obligation, which is an extremely onerous duty, applies to the whole season during which the crops are in ear. The enforcement of these *rājakāriya* obligations is a matter of some complexity and I shall postpone discussion until a later section.

PERQUISITES OF THE GAMARĀLA

So far we have been discussing only the rights and obligations of 'shareholders' in general, that is of all individuals who have rights to *pangu* within a particular *bāga*. We have not distinguished the Gamarāla's rights from those of his followers.

Today indeed there is no distinction. *All* shareholders, Gamarāla and tenant alike, are now presumed to hold their land freehold. But formerly the Gamarāla's legal status was quite distinct from that of the junior stockholders in his *bāga*. Ievers's original account here seems to be essentially accurate in all respects.

Of the total length of water channel allocated to a *bāga* only part was originally divided up among the various *pangu*. The remainder was allocated as an end piece (*ēlapata*)[1] and this was initially a perquisite of the Gamarāla. Moreover, out of the total *pangu* in any one *bāga* two had a special status. One, the *ēlapat panguva*, was supposed always to be owned by the holder of the *ēlapata* and was, therefore, initially a perquisite of the Gamarāla. The other, the *gamvasama*, must always be owned by the Gamarāla. This last is still the case. Always, within each *bāga*, there is one *panguva* which is described as the *gamvasama*, and the owner of this strip is automatically entitled to call himself Gamarāla, though today there is no advantage in doing so.

Formerly, as owner of the *gamvasama*, the Gamarāla had special obligations as well as special perquisites. Among other

[1] See note on p. 149.

things he had to contribute grain to the annual village feasts and he had various ritual duties at the associated religious ceremonies.[1] In Pul Eliya these obligations are still imposed upon the holder of any *gamvasama* plot whether or not he chooses to lay claim to the title of Gamarāla.

As shown in Map *E* (p. 152) each of three *bāga* has one *elapata*, one *elapat panguva*, one *gamvasama* and four ordinary *pangu*.

According to Ievers the *elapata*, the *elapat panguva* and the *gamvasama* should *all* belong to the Gamarāla, but this represents only an ideal initial situation. When detailed Pul Eliya records begin in 1886 the pattern had already diverged widely from this ideal. In that year, in each of the three *bāga*, the *gamvasama*, *elapat panguva* and *elapata* were in different hands.

Nevertheless the theoretical association of the *elapata* with the *elapat panguva* provides yet another example of the principle of 'fair shares'.

Since the *elapata* constitutes the end of the field it therefore carries with it the obligation to build and maintain the whole of the end fence. This is about ten times more fencing than attaches to any ordinary *panguva* strip. Because of this extra fencing obligation the owner of an *elapata* is excused from the duty of carrying out tank repair work. But the *elapat panguva* has no such privilege. Thus the idea behind the doctrine that the *elapata* and the *elapat panguva* should always be owned by the same individual is simply to ensure that no one wholly escapes from the unpleasant obligation of carrying out tank repair *rājakāriya* duty. This was felt to be particularly important since in the event of a breach in the bund all villagers must be equally responsible.

In a comparable way, while the owner of an *elapata* and the owner of a *gamvasama* must both pay for the building of watch huts, the latter, as Gamarāla, escapes the *rājakāriya* duty of night

[1] For example, at the annual ritual known as *mutti manggalaya*, one Gamarāla tends the lamps in the *vihāra* and in the *kōvil*; one Gamarāla supplies the ritual pots (*mutti*); one Gamarāla pays for two shot-gun cartridges, the firing of which forms part of the ceremony. The obligations rotate among the three Gamarāla in successive years.

watchman. But, unlike the owner of the *elapata*, the *gamvasama* owner must do his share of bund repair *rājakāriya* along with the other shareholders. In Pul Eliya this carefully differentiated system of rights and obligations has been rigorously maintained even though the status of the Gamarāla as a specialised class of individual is no longer formally recognised. The rights and duties attach to the land itself, not to the individuals who own it.

CONTEMPORARY PRACTICE IN PUL ELIYA

So much then for the theory behind the tenure of land in Pul Eliya Old Field. Now let us consider the actual state of affairs as it existed in 1954.

According to present-day Pul Eliya tradition the Old Field originally contained 18 *pangu*, six for each *bāga*, but at some un-specified date in the past two extra *pangu* were added to the Pahala bāga by reducing the amount of land allocated to the Pahala elapata.

The circumstances which brought this change about are not now remembered so I was fortunate that among the few nine-teenth-century documents relating to Pul Eliya which still survive there are two tax returns which appear to confirm the tradition.

The village Vel Vidāne still submits annually to the revenue administration a return[1] purporting to show the exact amount of land cultivated throughout the village and the precise ownership of each plot. Today this return is compiled for the purpose of crop statistics, but its form is just the same as that of the paddy tax census of the 1870–90 period. It is, therefore, easy to correlate surviving tax census documents with the layout of the modern field.

Table 4 has been drawn up from this documentary evidence to show the relationship between the 1954 Old Field holdings (Upper Field) and those of the years 1889, 1890. This table is analysed in detail in section B of the present chapter.

The detailed analysis shows that the 1889 list is drawn up

[1] The 'paddy census' (see Table 6).

according to a scheme of 18 *pangu*; the 1890 list on the other hand fits the present-day arrangement of 20 *pangu*. The story of the 'two extra *pangu*' must therefore be correct and the alteration must have occurred shortly before 1890.

Because of this satisfactory fit of documentary evidence with oral tradition I feel confident that Map *E* (which 'fits' the present-day arrangement of strips to an 'original' system of 18 *pangu* and three *elapata*) is justified and correct.

'Originally' the field consisted of 3 *bāga*; each *bāga* comprised a 40-fathom *elapata* and 6 *pangu*; each *panguva* comprised 10 fathoms in the Upper Field and 10 fathoms in the Lower Field. Such discrepancies as now exist result from the fact that shortly before 1890 two fathoms from *panguva* four of the Pahala bāga together with 22 fathoms from the Pahala elapata were re-classified as forming 'two extra *pangu*'. Since that date the Pahala bāga has been deemed to consist of 8 *pangu* as opposed to the 6 *pangu* in each of the other two *bāga*. The principal effect of this reclassification has been to alter the type of *rājakāriya* obligation falling on owners of these plots of land. Details are given at pp. 207 f.

'BETHMA'

The arrangement of the irrigation channels together with the Vel Vidāne's assumptions concerning water allocation for the different parts of the field have the following implications:

(1) The Upper Field consists of two equal parts—the north half of the field and the south half of the field.

(2) The Lower Field is half the area of the Upper Field.

Thus the field as a whole is divided into three supposedly equal areas, each of which contains the same number of strips of the same width, owned in the same way. One-third of every holding falls into each of the three main parts of the field. This symmetry has important consequences.

The North Central Province institution of *bethma* has received frequent comment. This is an arrangement whereby the shareholders in a field which is short of water may agree to cultivate only a proportion of that field and then share out the proceeds among themselves. The theoretical procedure, as recently described by Farmer, is as follows:

The village has an admirable system, known as *bethma*, under which, if the whole extent of the paddy field cannot be cultivated for lack of water, as many of the tracts as can be irrigated are divided, regardless of their ownership, between the peasants in proportion to their several holdings, and thus cultivated as a compact block with minimum waste of water (Farmer, 1957, p. 558).

The earliest reference to *bethma* in this form is in administration documents of the 1861–4 period.

I have studied these entries with care, but they are unfortunately ambiguous. It is evident that the Government Agent of that date imagined that the system was supposed to work in the way that Farmer has described, and he on several occasions records the fact that he had ordered reluctant villagers to carry out *bethma* division in this way. But it seems to me probable that this form of *bethma* was the unintended invention of the British Government Agent himself!

At the present time different villages seem to work *bethma* in different ways, and there is no means of ascertaining which, if any, of these methods is the ancient traditional system. But what is quite clear is that the Pul Eliya method is very much simpler than that described by Farmer. Furthermore it is *bethma* which provides the ultimate justification for fragmenting each individual holding in the complicated way I have described. For Pul Eliya the system is as follows.

If the villagers are to cultivate rice in the Old Field during the *Yala* (April/September) season they will decide from the start either to cultivate the whole of the field or two-thirds of the field (that is, the whole of the Upper Field only) or just one-third of the field (that is, the northern half of the Upper Field only). No pooling of proceeds or reallocation of holdings is necessary since the land is already divided up in such a way that each shareholder works the whole or two-thirds of one-third of his total holding as the case may be.

In my limited experience this is the most common form of *bethma* in all this area. The ideal scheme described by Ievers, in which the total field is divided into two or more tracts (*pota*), corresponds to the actual facts for all the villages in the Pul Eliya area. It is invariably the case that every strip or holding in the upper tract has a corresponding strip or holding in the lower tract, though the precise manner in which this is effected is not always the same. This fragmentation of individual holdings is always directly associated with the local practices regarding *bethma*. The relative size of the different tracts (*pota*) is such that when the water is scarce cultivation of the upper tract only, or of half the upper tract divided longitudinally, serves as a *bethma*.

Farmer's description, which is the orthodox one, implies that individual Sinhalese farmers get on so well together that they can readily agree to a reallocation of land in times of water scarcity. I can only say that this does not correspond to my experience!

CULTIVATION AREAS

Before proceeding, we may note one further feature of the Tax Lists (Table 4). For the years 1889 and 1890 the areas of each individual holding are given *in seed quantities* (P = *pāla*; L = *lāha*: where 1 *pāla* = 10 *lāha*). But in the 1954 Plot List areas are given in *acres*. The numerical totals at the bottom of the table are in each case nearly the same; the 1889/90 Tax Lists show that the upper part of the Old Field had a *sowing area* of about 48 *pāla*, the 1954 returns show the same field as having an *area* of just short of 48 acres. This latter figure exaggerates the facts by about 50 per cent. The coincidence of numbers is no accident.

The administration's requirement that the Vel Vidāne's crop returns should show cultivation areas in acres rather than in seed quantity dates from the early days of this century. The villagers, however, still reckon land areas in terms of seed sown and have no satisfactory method of converting one scale into the other. In making out his annual returns the Vel Vidāne now works to a simple rule of thumb.

Sinakkara land and *badu* land has been surveyed by government officials and hence the true acreage of such holdings is known and is entered accordingly. For the Old Field on the other hand, all that is really known is that it contains 20 *pangu*. Now when the Old Field was originally surveyed in 1900, the *whole field* was shown to be just over 40 acres. It thus became established that in Pul Eliya '1 *panguva* "equals" 2 acres' and this tradition has stayed. Today when working out the allocation of labour obligations for the purpose of *rājakāriya* duty every 2 acres of *sinakkara* land and *badu* land counts as 1 *panguva*.

In this way it was argued that at the beginning of 1954 there were 52 *pangu* in Pul Eliya in all. Of these 20 were the Old Field *pangu* and 32 were represented by 64 acres of *sinakkara* and *badu* land. (Cf. 48 *pangu* (Table 5) plus plots 124, 151–2 (Table 6).)

The quite erroneous acreages shown in the 1954 Plot List for the plots in the Old Field were arrived at by reversing this argument. Every 6 *pangu* in the upper tract of the Old Field are reckoned as 12 acres. This leaves out of account both the *elapata* of the Upper Field and the whole of the Lower Field. Consequently by the time the Vel Vidāne has completed his returns so as to show an acreage figure for each plot he has about 20 acres too many. Pul Eliya village, like all other villages in the area, has been submitting these bogus crop returns annually ever since the beginning of the century, and the same type of error has persisted throughout.

For Pul Eliya the return for 'area cultivated' has never been less than 15 per cent in excess and has often been over 50 per cent in excess. It seems likely that similar errors exist in the crop returns of every other village in the area. One important consequence is that the administration believes that the total area under cultivation is substantially larger than is really the case. It has therefore been inferred that crop yields per acre are much lower than is really the case.

It must be admitted that, judged by the standards attained in countries such as China, Japan and Italy, the paddy yields achieved by Sinhalese peasants are unimpressive, but they are nothing like so poor as the official statistics might suggest.

SUMMARY: IDEAL AND ACTUAL
TRANSMISSION OF LAND

I have now analysed fairly completely the theory behind the complicated partitioned layout of the Pul Eliya Old Field. We have also seen that, so far as the distribution of holdings is concerned, 1954 practice corresponded fairly closely with the ideal theory.

When we come to examine the various legal processes by which ownership rights are transmitted from generation to generation the correspondence between theory and practice is much less close.

We have already seen in chapter IV that individual holdings can be acquired either by purchase, or by gift, or by inheritance. Despite this the Old Field is commonly spoken of as being *paravēni*—'heirloom property' or *purāna*—'ancient traditional' and it is a matter of prestige for every owner to claim that he inherited his holding from his own ancestors. Such claims are very largely fictional. In section B of this chapter, I provide a nearly complete analysis of the history of every plot in the Old Field since 1890. One fact which emerges from this analysis is that out of the 107 numbered plots no less than 45 have changed hands by sale at least once between 1890 and 1954. A number of these have been sold several times over.

But this deviation from theory does not imply a breakdown of traditional custom. The essence of traditional custom is, as we have seen, that all land should be retained in the hands of members of the local *variga*. In 1890 only one of the recorded plot-holders was an 'outsider' in this sense; he owned, according to the record, 7½ acres. In 1954 it was likewise the case that only one of the recorded plot-holders was an outsider; he owned 3½ acres.[1] From the *variga* point of view the 1954 situation was a great improvement on the 1890 position.

---

[1] These acres are notional acres, see above, p. 171, but the two figures are strictly comparable. The 1890 'outsider' was Alisandini Nikala Pulle; the 1954 'outsider' was B. Danapala.

Most sales of land are between members of the local *variga* and traders, who are outside the *variga* system, but as a rule land which is sold away to an 'outsider' is, within a short while, bought back again by some other member of the local *variga*.

When this happens the close network of kinship existing between all local *variga* members can be used to obscure the sale transaction. Because the Old Field is thought of as *paravēni*, it is felt to be slightly discreditable either to be a seller or a purchaser of such land. Purchasers hold their land by virtue of documentary titles made out by Anurādhapura lawyers, but the details of sale are not formally entered in any government record and it is fairly easy to pretend that the title is really hereditary. When I inquired of the present owners how they had acquired their holdings, I was almost invariably told that the land had been inherited from an ancestor. Only careful cross-checking would reveal a case of purchase.

An actual case will illustrate the type of disguise that takes place:

Table 4 shows that the land now represented by the 1954 plot numbers 6, 7, 8 and 14 was, in 1890, in the hands of Alisandini Nikala Pulle (T:1), a well known trader. It is quite certain that this trader sold all these strips to Appurala Vidāne (A1:W), the common ancestor of the present listed owners. But since plot 14 is part of the Ihala bāga *gamvasama* and carries with it the title of Gamarāla, it is particularly discreditable that this land should have been in the hands of a trader. Accordingly, while I was living in Pul Eliya, I was told nothing of this episode. Instead it was pretended that Appurala Vidāne had acquired his title to these plots by marrying the legitimate heiress of the previous Gamarāla. Later, documentary evidence from the government archives showed what had really happened. Appurala Vidāne undoubtedly married the lady in question (A1:3), but he did so some years after her father had sold her birthright to the trader. In this kind of way the Pul Eliya villagers are able to persuade themselves that their system is much more nearly traditionally 'correct' than is really the case.

CHANGES IN THE ECONOMIC STATUS
OF HOUSEHOLDS

Another feature which may be inferred from the detailed analysis of plot transmission is that it is the property of the relatively wealthy which tends to get sold rather than the property of the poor. With scarcely any exceptions it is the lands of the gentlemen of title (Vel Vidāne, Gamarāla, Mohottāla, Badderāla, Vederāla) which have passed through the hands of the traders. Undistinguished households with no great pretensions have mostly kept their lands intact throughout. This reflects an important feature of the social dynamics of the Pul Eliya community considered as a whole.

This is a society which gives prestige to the man of property. But in return, any high-status individual is expected to indulge in lavish expenditure. *Rites de passage* can prove a formidable expense, even for men of moderate means, but among those who are reputed to be wealthy such festivals are liable to be quite wildly extravagant. It is never sufficient to be simply an owner of capital; the successful high-status individual must demonstrate openly that he is a person of good fortune favoured by the planetary deities. He must demonstrate his luck (*näkat*). For such a man gambling is not a vice, it is a social necessity. Consequently it is the 'wealthy' rather than the 'poor' who need cash loans, just as it is the wealthy rather than the poor who have the credit to raise them. Every story of financial disaster starts in the same way. The rich man took his first step on the downward path toward bankruptcy by mortgaging part of his land to a trader at an impossible rate of interest.

The potential profits of land ownership in Pul Eliya are very high and the discrepancies of wealth between the rich and the poor are, at any one time, considerable, but households cannot be permanently distinguished in terms of economic class. During the period studied some households stayed permanently at one economic level, but others changed their position very rapidly several times within a generation.

In 1890 the richest man in the village was Kadirathe Gamarāla (C:3), Gamarāla of the Pahala bāga. His son Punchirala Gamarāla (D2:C) was still alive in 1954. By that date the latter owned no land at all, and had not been able to give any land to his dependents. The converse is also true. The great majority of those who were relatively well off in 1954 owed their position to 'luck' and enterprise rather than to inheritance. The wealthy men of 1954 had all had ancestors in the village in 1890 but, in general, these ancestors were among the poorer members of the community.

The allegedly baneful and extortionate activities of the village trader are an important factor in bringing about this constant change in the economic status of particular households. From a social point of view this must be considered a positive function. Without some such equalising mechanism the community would quickly cease to be homogeneous in terms of economic class, and would probably disintegrate altogether.

So much then for the general implications of the processes of property transmission. The details are given in section B which now follows. It may seem absurd to go into such intricate detail about the holdings and subdivision of title in such a small area. After all, the whole of the Old Field is only 40 odd acres in extent, while the house-site *gamgoda* zone covers a mere 6 acres. But in the ideology of the villagers themselves, it is the holdings in this traditional *paravēni* land which really matter. It is a *paravēni* holding which gives a man membership of his village and status in his village. Administration files are crammed with generation-long legal disputes concerning plots of a quarter-acre or less. It is the titular appurtenances rather than the economic value of the land that is in dispute. In 1954 Pul Eliya villagers still had extremely strong feelings about these titles. It is only in the light of such values that we can understand the pattern of land succession and the overall social structure of the associated community.

CONCLUSION

The main point that I have sought to establish in section A of this chapter is that the Old Field is laid out according to an extremely intricate yet absolutely logical ideal pattern. The actual arrangement is not identical with the ideal arrangement, and the villagers themselves have no clear understanding as to what the ideal arrangement is. The *ideal* system is functionally perfect. Everything fits together like a jig-saw puzzle, the technology of irrigation, the technology of rice-growing and the egalitarian ideology of village politics.

In the *actual* system the fit is imperfect, nevertheless the functional interrelationships of the different aspects of the ideal system are such that the system as a whole can scarcely be tampered with. Between 1890 and 1954 the *only* change in the layout of the field was that the fence between the Upper and Lower fields (which in any case is taken down every year) was moved 10 fathoms 'Up Field'. The point I want to stress is that, in so far as Pul Eliya society is focused on the tenure of land in the Old Field, it *must* adjust itself to the facts of the Old Field layout; it cannot alter the field to suit the convenience of society.

SECTION B: PLOT SUCCESSION IN THE OLD FIELD, 1890–1954

INTRODUCTION

The following pages contain a nearly complete analysis of the transmission of all holdings of land in the Upper Old Field between 1889 and 1954. The purpose of the analysis is to demonstrate:

(*a*) The practical application of the principles of inheritance.

(*b*) The relationship between this actual system of land holding and the idealised *pangu* system described by Ievers.

177

(c) The importance of 'compound groups' for the understanding of property distribution.

(d) Some of the more ordinary procedures by which the inconveniences of customary law can, if need be, be circumvented.

Various types of evidence have been utilised in making the analysis, in particular:

(a) A very carefully recorded map of the holdings existing in 1954.

(b) The Pul Eliya Vel Vidāne's 'pangu list' and 'paddy census' returns for 1953 and 1954 (Tables 5 and 6, pp. 184–189).

(c) Various incomplete tax records for the period 1860–93, but notably two nearly complete lists for the years 1889–90. This documentary evidence comes from the Government Archives in Nuwara Eliya.

(d) A synthesis of remembered genealogies given by various members of the 1954 Pul Eliya population.

(e) A detailed residence map of Pul Eliya in 1954.

(f) Statements by the 1954 Pul Eliya population concerning the previous occupants of various house-sites, and about the history of particular land plots.

(g) Miscellaneous evidence derived from the files of the Land Office, Anurādhapura.

Each of these different types of evidence may individually be considered liable to error, but the synthesis of all of them into a single consistent pattern implies a high probability of overall accuracy. Inaccuracies where they occur are likely to be mainly in the genealogical record. Male members of the present generation often remember of their predecessors simply that they were related as 'brothers' (ayiyā/malli) or as cross-cousins (massinā/massinā). But 'brothers' may be half-brothers or ortho-cousins, and massinā may be brothers-in-law. Thus, while it is certain that the intensity of endogamy within the total community has at all times been high, it is probable that the remembered genealogies tend to exaggerate this endogamy. The genealogies make it appear that the frequency of first cross-cousin marriage was higher in the past than it is today; I do not consider that there is reliable evidence that this was really the case.

FORM OF ANALYSIS

Cross-reference

The acrostic-minded reader who wants to pursue the following analysis to its limits will find it useful to refer to the various maps and tabulations listed below. Of these the most basic are items 1, 2 and 6, without which the listed details will hardly be comprehensible.

(1) Map *E* (p. 152). This is a schematic map of the Old Field as it existed in 1954. The widths and the lengths of the strips (*issaraval*) are drawn to scale and the allocation of strips to the different *bāga, pangu* and *elapata* is also shown. The small numerals 1–107 marked in the strips themselves are the plot numbers of the Vel Vidāne's 1954 'paddy census' (Table 6).

(2) Table 4 (between p. 144 and p. 145). This shows, in parallel columns, the officially recorded names of the owners of holdings in the Upper Old Field in the years 1889, 1890 and 1954. The chart has been so arranged that, so far as possible, the arrangement of names on the chart corresponds to the arrangement of strips in the field.

(3) Map *C* (p. 45). The layout of the residential portion of the village as it existed in 1954.

(4) Map *D* (p. 100). (*a*) and (*b*). These two diagram maps show the changes in compound boundaries within the main house-site area (*gamgoda*) between the years 1889 and 1954. Map *D* (*b*) was as directly observed; Map *D* (*a*) is to some extent inferential, but is consistent with the verbal statements of the 1954 inhabitants. Three members of the 1954 population had personal recollection of the 1889 period.

(5) Table 1 (pp. 55–8). This shows the allocation of the thirty-nine household heads (of 1954) to house-sites and compound groups.

(6) Chart *i* (at the end of the book). This large and complex genealogy, in which individuals are shown by numbers, records the kinship position of nearly every Pul Eliya inhabitant mentioned in this book who was of adult status by 1954.[1] The kinship connections shown are those which appear to be relevant for a proper understanding of the transmission of property in land. Other kinship connections, where known, are not shown. This genealogy gives emphasis, therefore, to

---

[1] Certain individuals of 'wrong *variga*' status are omitted.

lines of descent at the expense of links of affinity. With the links as shown the level of overall endogamy is extremely high; if all affinal links were recorded in addition, the pattern would be generally similar but a number of additional 'compound groups', mainly located in Wiralmurippu, would be found to be integral with the system.

The chart is designed so as to show not only descent links but also residential grouping and 'compound group' affiliation.

Name forms

Where Table 4 gives a name in the form Kapurala ge Ukkurala, this means Ukkurala *son of* Kapurala. In the Tax Lists of the 1890 period all the names are those of men; where land was owned by a woman, tax was paid by her husband or by her brother. The Vel Vidāne's paddy census return for 1954 also showed a bias in favour of males, though some female owners are included.

Certain personal names, for example, Naidurala, Ukkurala, Wannihamy, Kirihamy, Pinhamy, Velathe, Kadirathe, Punchi Etani, Tikiri Etani, etc., occur very frequently. Confusion between different individuals easily occurs, and this confusion is by no means confined to the anthropological observer. Genealogies are undoubtedly adjusted retrospectively and from this point of view the lack of individuality in personal names is very convenient. To avoid confusing the reader I have used distinguishing initials. Thus, among the Pul Eliya family heads of 1954, there were three different men called Ukkurala ge Pinhamy; I have distinguished them as U.G. Pinhamy, U.V. Pinhamy, and U. Kuda Pinhamy. Similarly I have made such distinctions as Tikiri Etani I and Tikiri Etani II. In the various charts and name lists recorded here no two individuals are represented by exactly the same name. An index to personal names is given in Appendix 3 (pp. 321–31).

Correlation between Map E and Table 4

The Vel Vidāne's paddy census for 1954 (Table 6, p. 185) distinguished sixty-three plots in the Upper Old Field. Of these the first five were more or less square holdings distributed among

180

the top three strips of the field, while the remaining fifty-eight plots were distributed among the remaining thirty-nine strips of the field in the manner shown on Map *E* (p. 150). There are good grounds for supposing that formerly the top strip of the 1954 Lower Field (plots 64–5) was rated as part of the Pahala elapata.

That being so the relation of plots to strips and *bāga* in the Upper Old Field may be summarised as follows:

Original field sections	1954 plot nos.	No. of strips	No. of fathoms
Ihala elapata	1–8	5	40
Ihala bāga	9–27	12 (6 *pangu*)	60
Meda bāga	28–38	8 (6 *pangu*)	60
Pahala bāga	39–55	12 (6 *pangu*)	60
Pahala elapata	56–65	6	40

Including plots 64–5, the Ihala elapata and the Pahala elapata are each 40 fathoms deep, and each of the three bāga is 60 fathoms deep. The strips vary in width as indicated on the map.

The Lower Old Field (excluding plots 64, 65) consists of:

Original field sections	1954 plot nos.	No. of strips	No. of fathoms
Pahala bāga	66–79	11	60
Ihala bāga	80–97	12	60
Meda bāga	98–106	8	60
Meda elapata	107	4	40

As previously explained (p. 158) there is a complicated one-to-one correspondence between the ownership of strips in the Upper Field and the ownership of strips in the Lower Field. The precise details of this correspondence are shown in Table 4. The present analysis, therefore, concerns itself *only* with the transmission of holdings in the Upper Field. The transmission of holdings in the Lower Field has been virtually the same. There is a seeming discrepancy in the fact that the Upper Field Pahala bāga contains seventeen plots (twelve strips) while the Lower Field Pahala bāga contains only fifteen plots (eleven strips); this is explained below (pp. 207–8).

The ownership and transmission of plots 1–65 is discussed in sequence. This amounts to an analysis of the Upper Old Field proceeding from the top downwards, both on Map *E* and on Table 4.

The 1954 Vel Vidāne's paddy census (Table 6) included an acreage figure for each plot. These figures are very inaccurate, but they are based on a long-established computation which assumes that '1 *panguva* equals 2 acres' (see p. 172).

The 1889 and 1890 Tax Lists also show area figures against each owner's name. These latter are computed in 'seed sown'. The 1890 list is drawn up on a scheme of '1 *panguva* equals 2 *pāla*'. Consequently in most cases, 1 acre in the 1954 list is equivalent to 1 *pāla* in the 1890 list, and this provides a useful check on my correlation between the two tabulations. In contrast, most, though not all, of the 1889 list is drawn up on a scheme of '1 *panguva* equals 2·2 *pāla*'. No great significance need be attached to this difference. Strictly speaking a *panguva* is not a fixed area at all; it is simply the amount of land watered by a particular length of irrigation channel. Each *panguva* comprises 10 fathoms of irrigation channel in the Upper Field and 10 fathoms of irrigation channel in the Lower Field. But *pangu* are divided up into strips (*issaraval*) in a variety of ways and the strips are of varying lengths. Consequently, although each *panguva* is entitled to the same amount of water, the *pangu* do not all cover the same area of ground. Prior to the cadastral survey of 1900 *pangu* might vary in area from year to year (see p. 155).

All bureaucratic attempts to compute *pangu* areas according to a fixed scale produce fictitious results no matter whether the scale is in *pāla* (seed quantity) or in land area (acres). On the other hand it is evident that the acre figures of 1954 are, in the main, derived from the *pāla* figures of 1890.

The 1954 area figures for the whole of the Upper Field total nearly 48 acres. The corresponding total for 1890 was 48·5 *pāla*. It has clearly needed a good deal of arithmetic manipulation to keep this total constant, but this consistency provides yet further evidence that all the Vel Vidāne's figures are based on traditional convention rather than on measurement. The actual area of the Upper Field is slightly less than 30 acres.

The traditional arrangement of the Old Field was that it contained 3 *bāga* each of 6 *pangu*; each *bāga* having its own elapata. The 1889 list was drawn up according to this ideal scheme. No Meda elapata is shown because this lies at the bottom of the Lower Field and was not cultivated in the season in question. In contrast, the 1890 list with its irregular area figures—which in general correspond to those of the 1954 list—was evidently an attempt to record the ownership of the field strip by strip. We need not assume that there was any drastic rearrangement of the field between 1889 and 1890. The *strip* arrangement in 1889 was probably identical to that shown on the 1890 list, just as the theoretical *pangu* arrangement in 1890 was identical to that shown on the 1889 list.

For example, in 1954 it was said that the Meda bāga contained 6 *pangu*, that is, as shown in the 1889 list. In actual fact the Meda bāga *pangu* land in 1954 was made up of eight strips, the two upper strips being wider than the others, that is, as shown in the 1890 list. Furthermore a court case record dated 1861 happens to mention that the Meda bāga then contained eight strips. Accordingly we should not infer from the 1889 list that in that year the Meda bāga contained only six strips.

In contrast, it is evident that the additional complications of the 1890 Pahala bāga list as compared with that for 1889 reflect, among other things, an increase in the number of *pangu* from six to eight (see pp. 169; 207 f.).

General changes in the village; changes
in compound boundaries

(See Appendix 4, p. 332, and Map *D*)

The 1954 village contained thirty-nine family heads resident in thirteen compounds of which ten were within the original

Table 5. *Pul Eliya pangu list, season* 1953–54

Total *pangu*:	48	*Rājakāriya* duty	
Bund (ft.):	2438	Bund:	25½ ft. per acre
Spillway (ft.):	480	Spillway:	5 ft. per acre

Name	Acres: Old Field	Acres: Other	Total	*Pangu*	Bund (ft.)
V. Menikrala (B1:7)	2¼	4	6¼	3⅛	159½
K.V. Appuhamy (A2:7)	1	2	3	1½	76½
U. Kadirathe (A2:4)	2	3	5	2½	127½
M. Naidurala (Dx:Y)	½	1½	2	1	51
S. Subasinghe (A1:5)	2	2	4	2	102
U.G. Pinhamy (H:A2)	2½	4	6½	3¼	165¾
U. Sirala (A2:5)	¼	8	8¼	4⅛	210½
U. Wannihamy (A2:6)	¼	4	4¼	2⅛	108½
A.V. Punchi Etani (B1:A1) } P. Ran Banda (A1:6) }	3¼	4	7¼	3⅝	185
P. Kapuruhamy (C2:D2)	1½	—	1½	¾	38¼
K. Punchi Etani (D1:6)	1¾	—	1¾	⅞	44½
U. Kuda Pinhamy (B2:E3)	1	3	4	2	102
K. Muragathe (A2:3)	3½	—	3½	1¾	89¼
K. Tikiri Banda (Cx:2)	¼	2	2¼	1⅛	57⅓
U.V. Pinhamy (C1:W)	2	—	2	1	51
A. Bandathe (G:Z2)	1½	3	4½	2¼	114¾
M. Kirala (C1:2)	¼	—	¼	⅛	6⅓
M. Herathamy (C1:3)	¼	—	¼	⅛	6⅓
M. Sinni Etani (C1:1)	¼	—	¼	⅛	6⅓
K. Dingiri Banda (A2:B2)	¾	4	4¾	2⅜	121
B. Hetuhamy (Y:1)	—	4	4	2	102
R. Punchirala (X:4)	—	2	2	1	51
N. Punchi Banda (Dx:4)	½	½	1	½	25½
N. Ran Manika (Dx:5)	½	½	1	½	25½
K. Menikrala (B2:6)	¼	½	¾	⅜	19
K. Appuhamy (W:B2)	¼	½	¾	⅜	19
K. Wannihamy (B2:7)	¼	½	¾	⅜	19
K.V. Sirala (Z:Dw)	½	—	½	¼	12¾
K.V. Kapuruhamy (F:Dw)	1	—	1	½	25½
K.V. Punchi Etani (Dw:1)	1	—	1	½	25½
W. Punchi Etani (Dw:W)	1½	—	1½	¾	38¼
U.V. Menikrala (Bel:1)	½	—	½	¼	12¾
W. Nanghamy (Bel:5)	¼	—	¼	⅛	6⅓
M. Ran Manika (Bel:4)	¼	—	¼	⅛	6⅓
B. Danapala (——)	2	—	2	1	51
P. Ran Etani (W:J)	1½	—	1½	¾	38¼
R. Mudalihamy (X3)	—	1	1	½	25½
A.V. Bandathe (Z:C)	¾	—	¾	⅜	19
J. Punchirala (Dx:2)	2	2	4	2	102
Totals	40	56	96	48	2438

NOTE. Old Field *elapata* land is not liable to *rājakāriya* and is, therefore, excluded from this list. The original table was computed in *amuna*. I have substituted acre figures on the basis 1 *amuna* = 4 *pāla* = 4 acres. The 'acres' of Table 5 and the 'nominal acres' of Tables 4 and 6 are not mutually consistent (see pp. 172, 182).

Table 6. '*Paddy census*'. *Pul Eliya Vel Vidāne's plot list*, 1954

This list, which is submitted to the V.C.O. for the purposes of a paddy census, includes plot 'acreage'. In the case of Old Field plots these acreages are wildly inaccurate. The original list also included the names of *andē* tenants but these have been omitted here since the inaccuracies were very numerous. The plot numbers correspond to those shown on Maps *B*, *E* and *F*, but field names and numbers were not specified in the list.

Plot no.	Name of owner	Nominal acreage	Field section (these details not in original list)
			OLD FIELD
1	U. Wannihamy (A2:6)	1	
2	U. Kadirathe (A2:4)	$\frac{1}{2}$	
3	U. Sirala (A2:5)	$\frac{1}{2}$	
4	U.G. Pinhamy (H:A2)	$\frac{1}{4}$	
5	V. Menikrala (B1:7)	$\frac{1}{4}$	
6	S. Subasinghe (A1:5)	1	IHALA ELAPATA
7	A.V. Punchi Etani (B1:A1)	1	
8	P. Ran Banda (A1:8)	2	
9	U. Kadirathe (A2:4)	1	
10	U.G. Pinhamy (H:A2)	$\frac{1}{3}$	
11	V. Menikrala (B1:7)	$\frac{1}{3}$	
12	U. Sirala (A2:5)	$\frac{1}{3}$	
13	W. Punchi Etani (W:Dw)	1 ⎫	Gamvasama
14	S. Subasinghe (A1:5)	1 ⎭	
15	K. Dingiri Banda (A2:B2)	$\frac{1}{2}$	
16	A.V. Punchi Etani (B1:A1)	$\frac{1}{2}$	
17	A. Bandathe (G:Z2)	1	
18	J. Punchirala (Dx:2)	$\frac{2}{3}$	
19	M. Naidurala (Dx:Y)	$\frac{1}{3}$	
20	U.G. Pinhamy (H:A2)	1	
21	U.G. Pinhamy (H:A2)	1	IHALA BĀGA
22	K. Menikrala (B2:6)	$\frac{1}{4}$	
23	K. Appuhamy (W:B2)	$\frac{1}{4}$	
24	K. Wannihamy (B2:7)	$\frac{1}{4}$	
25	A.V. Punchi Etani (B1:A1)	1	
26	U. Kadirathe (A2:4)	$\frac{1}{4}$	
27	U. Wannihamy (A2:6)	$\frac{2}{3}$	
28	U.V. Pinhamy (C1:W)	$1\frac{1}{2}$	Gamvasama
29	K.V. Appuhamy (A2:7)	$1\frac{1}{2}$	
30	P. Kapuruhamy (C2:D2)	$1\frac{1}{2}$	
31	U. Kuda Pinhamy (B2:E3)	$1\frac{1}{2}$	
32	U. Kadirathe (A2:4)	$\frac{3}{4}$	MEDA BĀGA
33	S. Subasinghe (A1:5)	$\frac{1}{4}$	

Table 6 (cont.)

Plot no.	Name of owner	Nominal acreage	Field section (these details not in original list)
34	A.V. Punchi Etani (B 1:A 1)	¼	
35	P. Ran Banda (A 1:6)	¼	
36	K. Punchi Etani (D 1:6)	1½	MEDA BĀGA (cont.)
37	M. Naidurala (Dx:Y)	1½	
38	A.V. Punchi Etani (B 1:A 1)	1½	
39	K. Muragathe (A 2:3)	2	
40	V. Menikrala (B 1:7)	1	
41	P. Ran Etani (W:J)	1	
42	B. Hetuhamy (Y:1)	1	
43	K. Tikiri Banda (Cx:2)	¼	PAHALA BĀGA
44	M. Sinni Etani (C 1:1)	¼	
45	M. Kirala (C 1:2)	¼	
46	M. Herathamy (C 1:3)	¼	
47	B. Danapala (—)	2	Gamvasama
48	P. Ran Etani (W:J)	½	
49	V. Menikrala (B 1:7)	½	
50	U. Kuda Pinhamy (B 2:E 3)	1	....
51	U.V. Menikrala (Bel:1)	¾	
52	N. Punchi Banda (Dx:4)	⅜	
53	M. Naidurala (Dx:4)	⅜	....
54	K. Tikiri Banda (Cx:2)	¼	
55	N. Ran Manika (Dx:5)	¼	
56	K.V. Punchi Etani (Dw:1)	½	
57	M.V. Ran Manika (Bel:4)	½	'Extra *pangu*'
57a	W. Nanghamy (Bel:5)		
58	V. Menikrala (B 1:7)	¼	
59	P. Ran Etani (W:J)	¼	
60	B. Danapala (—)	1¼	PAHALA ELAPATA
61	K.V. Punchi Etani (Dw:1)	½	'Extra *pangu*'
62	M.K. Sobittu (Priest)	⅛	....
63	B. Danapala (—)	¼	Kurulu pāluva

See chapter v, pp. 207f. and Table 4

Upper Field

————————————————————————————FENCE————

Lower Field

64	U.V. Menikrala (Bel:1)	¼	PAHALA ELAPATA
65	K. Punchi Etani (D 1:6)	¼	
66	K.V. Punchi Etani (Dw:1)	¼	
67	U.V. Menikrala (Bel:1)	¼	
68	U. Kuda Pinhamy	½	PAHALA BĀGA
69	V. Menikrala (B 1:7)	¼	
70	P. Ran Etani (W:J)	¼	

Table 6 (*cont.*)

Plot no.	Name of owner	Nominal acreage	Field section (these details not in original list)
71	B. Danapala (—)	1	
72	M. Kirala (C1:2)	$\frac{1}{8}$	
73	M. Sinni Etani (C1:1)	$\frac{1}{8}$	
74	K. Tikiri Banda (Cx:2)	$\frac{1}{8}$	
75	M. Herathamy (C1:3)	$\frac{1}{8}$	PAHALA BĀGA (*cont.*)
76	B. Hetuhamy (Y:1)	$\frac{1}{2}$	
77	P. Ran Etani (W:J)	$\frac{1}{2}$	
78	V. Menikrala (B1:7)	$\frac{1}{2}$	
79	K. Murugathe (A2:3)	1	
80	U. Kadirathe (A2:4)	$\frac{1}{8}$	
81	U. Sirala (A2:5)	$\frac{1}{8}$	
82	S. Subasinghe (A1:5)	$\frac{1}{4}$	
83	K. Menikrala (B2:6)	$\frac{1}{8}$	
84	K. Appuhamy (W:B2)	$\frac{1}{8}$	
85	K. Wannihamy (B2:7)	$\frac{1}{8}$	
86	U.G. Pinhamy (H:A2)	$\frac{1}{4}$	
87	N. Punchi Banda (Dx:4)	$\frac{1}{8}$	
88	N. Ran Manika (Dx:5)	$\frac{1}{8}$	IHALA BĀGA
89	U.G. Pinhamy (H:A2)	$\frac{1}{4}$	
90	A. Bandathe (G:Z2)	$\frac{1}{4}$	
91	K. Dingiri Banda (A2:B2)	$\frac{1}{8}$	
92	A.V. Punchi Etani (B1:A1)	$\frac{1}{8}$	
93	W. Punchi Etani (W:Dw)	$\frac{1}{4}$	
94	A.V. Punchi Etani (B1:A1)	$\frac{1}{4}$	
95	V. Menikrala (B1:7)	$\frac{1}{8}$	
96	U.G. Pinhamy (H:A2)	$\frac{1}{8}$	
97	U. Wannihamy (A2:6)	$\frac{1}{8}$	
98	M. Naidurala (Dx:Y)	$\frac{1}{2}$	
99	K. Punchi Etani (D1:6)	$\frac{1}{2}$	
100	A.V. Punchi Etani (B1:A1)	$\frac{1}{2}$	
101	P. Kapuruhamy (C2:D2)	$\frac{1}{2}$	
102	U. Kuda Pinhamy (B2:E3)	$\frac{1}{2}$	MEDA BĀGA
103	P. Ran Banda (A1:6)	$\frac{1}{4}$	
104	U. Kadirathe (A2:4)	$\frac{1}{4}$	
105	K.V. Appuhamy (A2:7)	$\frac{3}{4}$	
106	K. Tikiri Banda (Cx:2)	$\frac{3}{4}$	
{107 / 107a	U.V. Pinhamy (C1:W)	3	'Extra *pangu*' and MEDA ELAPATA see p. 207 n.

END OF OLD FIELD

Table 6 (*cont.*)

Plot no.	Name of owner	Nominal acreage	Field section (these details not in original list)
			FIELD 3D
108	S. Subasinghe (A1:5)	$\frac{1}{2}$	
109	A.V. Punchi Etani (B1:A1)	$\frac{1}{2}$	
110	P. Ran Banda (A1:6)	$\frac{1}{2}$	
111	R. Mudalihamy (X:3)	$\frac{3}{4}$	
112	J. Punchirala (Dx:2)	$\frac{3}{8}$	See chapter VI, pp. 220 f.
113	N. Punchi Banda (Dx:4)	$\frac{3}{8}$	
114	N. Ran Manika (Dx:5)	$\frac{3}{8}$	
115	M. Naidurala (Dx:Y)	$\frac{3}{8}$	
116	V. Menikrala (B1:7)	$1\frac{3}{4}$	
117	A.V. Punchi Etani (B1:A1)	$\frac{1}{4}$	
			FIELD 'GALKANDA'
118	R. Punchirala (X:4)	$2\frac{1}{2}$	See Appendix 2
			FIELD 3L
119	A. Bandathe (G:Z2)	3	See p. 226
			FIELD 3 AC
120	V. Menikrala (B1:7)	2	
121	M. Naidurala (Dx:Y)	1	See pp. 225 f.
122	N. Punchi Banda (Dx:4)	$\frac{1}{2}$	
123	N. Ran Manika (Dx:5)	$\frac{1}{2}$	
124	M. Naidurala (Dx:Y)	4	Encroached land (see p. 235)
			FIELD 3 AA
125	S. Subasinghe (A1:5)	$\frac{2}{3}$	
126	P. Ran Banda (A1:6)	$\frac{2}{3}$	See pp. 225 f.
127	A.V. Punchi Etani (B1:A1)	$\frac{2}{3}$	
			FIELD 14 R/S
128	A. Ranhamy (Cx:Y)	2	See p. 226
			FIELD 14 J
129	J. Punchirala (Dx:2)	$1\frac{1}{2}$	See p. 226
			FIELD 3 T/Q
130	U. Kuda Pinhamy (B2:E3)	$1\frac{1}{4}$	See p. 226

Table 6 (*cont.*)

Plot no.	Name of owner	Nominal acreage	Field section (these details not in original list)
			FIELD 3 R/S
131	K. Menikrala (B2:6)	$\frac{1}{2}$	
132	K. Appuhamy (W:B2)	$\frac{1}{2}$	
133	K. Wannihamy (B2:7)	$\frac{1}{2}$	See p. 223
134	S. Subasinghe (A1:5)	$1\frac{1}{2}$	
135	P. Ran Banda (A1:6)	$\frac{1}{4}$	
136	A.V. Punchi Etani (B1:A1)	$1\frac{1}{2}$	

			FIELD 14 Y
137	U. Wannihamy (A2:6)	3	See p. 225

			FIELD 14 I/H
138	U.G. Pinhamy (H:A2)	1	
139	K.V. Appuhamy (A2:7)	2	
140	U. Sirala (A2:5)	$1\frac{1}{2}$	
140*a*	U. Wannihamy (A2:6)	$\frac{1}{4}$	
141	U. Kadirathe (A2:4)	1	
142	U. Wannihamy (A2:6)	$\frac{1}{2}$	See pp. 224 f.
143	U.G. Pinhamy (H:A2)	1	
144	U. Sirala (A2:5)	2	
145	U. Kadirathe (A2:4)	2	
146	U. Wannihamy (A2:6)	$\frac{1}{2}$	
147	U.G. Pinhamy (H:A2)	2	

148	B. Hetuhamy (Y:1)	5	
149	K. Dingiri Banda (A2:B2)	4	See p. 228
150	U. Sirala (A2:5)	5	
151	U. Kuda Pinhamy (B2:E3)	2	See p. 230
152	K. Wannihamy (B2:7)	2	

	LAND UNDER KUMBUKWEWA TANK		
153	Punchirala Gamarāla (D2:C)	3	
154	P. Kapuruhamy (C2:D2)	3	
155	K. Tikiri Banda (Cx:2)	2	
156	M. Kirala (C1:2)	3	See pp. 230 f.
157	U.V. Pinhamy (C1:W)	3	
158	S. Jaymanhamy (D1:9)	3	
159	A. Sitti Etani (D1:Z3)	$\frac{1}{2}$	

gamgoda area. The 1954 oldest inhabitant Punchirala Gamarāla (D2:C) was, by his own reckoning, aged 73, which would have made him 9 years old in 1890. He alleged that in his extreme youth there were only five or six 'houses' (i.e. compounds) in the whole village. This is consistent with other evidence. Punchirala Gamarāla also provided a list of the principal villagers at the time he could first remember, and this fits well with the 1890 tax list. He also claimed that the Pul Eliya villagers of those days led a life of leisured ease. All the work in the fields was done by serf labour from the Vāddā village of Tulawelliya (59) and there was no necessity to cultivate chena. The historical facts are that the nineteenth century was a period of almost continuous famine and pestilence. That such a terrible epoch should now be remembered as a golden age reflects the very high evaluation set on the traditional way of life, especially by the older members of the present-day population.

The thirteen compounds of 1954 may be distinguished under three heads:

(i) Compounds which are continuations of compounds already in existence in 1890.

(ii) Compounds which have fragmented off as separate segments of these 'original' compounds.

(iii) Entirely new compounds.

The continuity, expansion, shrinkage, fragmentation or innovation of compound groups has been closely linked with the varying fortunes of the owners of land in the Old Field.

At first glance Map *D* and Chart *i* suggest that the overall process has been one of ever-increasing fragmentation. This impression is not illusory, but needs to be considered in relation to the demographic situation, which has been one of rising population.

It is in the nature of the case that genealogies as collected by anthropologists tend to assume a pyramidal form. In past generations it is only the ancestors who are remembered; other characters who died without heirs or who were in any way disreputable tend to be forgotten. This has certainly happened in the Pul Eliya case. The genealogy (Chart *i*) is complete for the adults of the present generation; it is not complete for previous generations. However, since we know that sixty years ago the population was very much smaller, the genealogical gaps may not be very numerous.

Name code

Because of the ambiguity of personal names I have throughout this book used a letter and number code to identify and distinguish the different characters of my story. The code is more particularly designed to relate individuals to the large genealogy (Chart *i*) and to the compounds as distinguished on Map *D* (p. 100).

The individual's code number specifies at a glance both the locality in which he or she was ordinarily resident after marriage and the locality of birth; certain exceptions to this rule are noted below.

In general, the first part of the code number specifies the place of adult residence. Thus, of the present generation, all individuals resident in compound A2 have a code number starting with A2 and will be found in the A2 section at the right-hand end of the genealogy. Children under marriageable age are not included in the genealogy and have not been given code numbers. The second part of the code number consists of either a simple digit as in A1:5 or else of a letter-digit combination as in B1:A1. Code numbers of the first type have been given to individuals who are closely associated with only one compound, namely that in which they are or were resident as adults. Code numbers of the second type apply to individuals who have close links with two different compounds, namely that in which they were born and that in which they are or were resident as adults. An index to the code numbers is given in Appendix 3 where the individuals are grouped according to their compound membership.

In detail the code numbers include the following forms:

(1) Numbers of the type A1:5. The individual concerned is located in the A1 section of the genealogy. Compounds distinguished in this

way are: Pul Eliya compounds—A, A1, A2; B, B1, B2; C, C1, C2, Cx; D, D1, D2, Dx; E; F; G; H; J.

Compounds in other villages—Bellankadawala (Bel); Diwulwewa (Dw); Nawana (N); Periyakkulam (P); Wiralmurippu (W); Yakawewa (Y); miscellaneous (Z).

(2) Numbers of the type B1:A1. The individual concerned is ordinarily located in the B1 section of the genealogy, but in some cases may appear in the A1 section also. Exceptionally, individuals with code numbers beginning with P, Y, or Z are located in the section of the genealogy with which they are most closely associated, thus P:B2 is in section B2; Y:1, son-in-law of A2:4 is in section A2; Z:Z1, first husband of B2:D1, is in section B2.

(3) The numbers H(S) and Z(C) are two special cases, being individuals of 'wrong *variga*' status associated with compounds H and C respectively.

All code numbers are indexed according to compound group in Appendix 3.

It may be remarked that when a man has a code number of the form A1:5 this implies *dīga* residence, while a number of the form B1:A1 implies *binna* residence. For a woman the converse is true, *dīga*-married women have numbers of the form B1:A1 and *binna*-married women have numbers of the form A1:5.

ANALYSIS

The analysis falls into two parts. The first part (pp. 194–211) describes in sequence of plot numbers, strip by strip, the changes of ownership for each *bāga* of the Upper Old Field between 1889 and 1954. This section of the analysis includes references to the concomitant changes in the boundaries of the *gamgoda* compounds, but, to avoid ambiguity, the evidence concerning the *gamgoda* compounds is again summarised in the second part of the analysis (pp. 211–216).

I will state here certain inferences which may, in my view, be drawn from the evidence and which should help the reader to understand why the material has been presented in this particular way.

(i) Throughout the period under review the village was dominated by the holder, for the time being, of the office of Vel Vidāne. This individual was responsible for all returns made to the government. In certain instances this gave him the power to manipulate the processes of property succession in his own favour.

(ii) Although the office of Gamarāla was not recognised by the government, the villagers continued to attach importance to the title and they continued to maintain that the village had three Gamarāla, one for each *bāga*. The Gamarāla is properly the holder of the *gamvasama* plot in the Upper Field. Where this plot happened to fall into the hands of an individual of the wrong *variga*, the villagers have been inclined to compromise and say that the holder of the *elapat panguva* can rate as a Gamarāla.

(iii) To be a full member of the community, a man of Pul Eliya (*Pul Eliya miniha*) it is necessary (*a*) to be of the right *variga*, (*b*) to have a holding of land in the Old Field, and (*c*) to have rights in a compound in the Pul Eliya *gamgoda*.

Since, in theory, title to land in the Old Field is always *paravēni*, that is, by right of inheritance, (*c*) should logically follow as a consequence of (*b*). In practice there is not this one-to-one correspondence. Where there is discrepancy, greater importance is attached to (*b*) than to (*c*). Thus, those who reside in the village but do not own land there are *not* Pul Eliya *minissu*. This applies not only to R. Punchirala (X:4) and K. Ukkurala H:((S)), who have a wrong *variga* taint, but also to *binna*-married husbands dependent exclusively on the bounty of their father-in-law, for example, B. Siriwardena (A2:Z5) and B. Ausadahamy (A2:Y), and even to the wealthy shopkeeper K.V. Kapuruhamy (F:Dw).

In contrast, those who own land in Pul Eliya Old Field, but do not own a house-site, almost invariably have some kind of latent claim on a Pul Eliya *gamgoda* compound and can assert it if they choose to do so.

(iv) The natural processes of inheritance tend to fragment individual holdings. Marriage to near kin tends to consolidate holdings. At the end of the period 1890–1954 the Pul Eliya *minissu*, as a group, had at least as much control over their village lands as they had at the beginning. This outcome is the result of appropriate marriages. In most cases the marriages are *not* planned with any such end in view, but it is the *statistical* outcome of the total marriage pattern that land rights are conserved within the local group to a very high degree.

(v) The economic necessity to counteract inheritance fragmentation by marriage is reflected in the general characteristic already observed that heirs to the same property tend to be opposed, while affines tend to associate. The relations between brothers-in-law (*massinā*) and between father-in-law and son-in-law (*māmā-bānā*) are solidary alliance relationships; relations between father and son or between full brothers are strained relationships.

It is my thesis that this pattern of behaviours is the correlate of the pattern of land holding as linked with the inheritance rules. Given a different contextual situation, for example, one in which rights to inherited property were *not* at stake, quite different behaviour patterns would prevail. In later chapters we shall see that this is in fact the case.

Here my purpose is simply to describe the facts about land-holding succession and marriage so as to demonstrate that although any individual series of marriages is lacking in pattern, the total pattern of marriage is adapted to the unchanging territorial arrangements of the village and of the village field.

I. PLOT OWNERSHIP 1889–1954

Ihala bāga

Elapata (*plots* 1–8)
Elapat panguva (*plots* 9–12)
Gamvasama (*plots* 13–14)

In the traditional system, as described by Ievers, these plots should be a special perquisite of the Gamarāla (see p. 149). The whole of this property was in fact in the possession of the Gamarāla of the Ihala bāga down to about 1875. I record him as Naidurala Gamarāla I (A:1). He had two children, a son Kadirathe 'former Vel Vidāne' (A1:1), and a daughter Ranhamy (A2:1), who married *binna* a husband (A2:Z1) from Punewa (25). The two children inherited in equal shares. Kadirathe (A1:1) obtained **plots 6–8, 13, 14**; Ranhamy (A2:1) obtained **plots 1–5, 9–12**. Ranhamy's share mostly passed to her daughter, Tikiri Etani I (A2:2) who married *binna* Kapurala ge Ukkurala (A2:Z2) from Ambagahawewa (86). **Plot 9**, however, was inherited by Ranhamy's other daughter Dingiri Etani I (Z:A2) who married *dīga* away from Pul Eliya.

The *binna* marriage of Tikiri Etani I (A2:2) resulted from a lack of male heirs. Her husband (A2:Z2) was a man of high status, and he was induced to make a *binna* marriage by the 'heiress' qualifications of his bride. It will be observed that Tikiri Etani I (A2:2) received a much larger share than did her sister Dingiri Etani I (Z:A2), who left the village. In 1954 **plots 1–5, 10–12** belonged to the children and grandchildren of Tikiri Etani I (A2:2) and Ukkurala (A2:Z2). Of these, U. Kadirathe (A2:4), K.V. Appuhamy (A2:7), U. Sirala (A2:5) and U. Wannihamy (A2:6) lived in compound A2. U.G. Pinhamy (H:A2) was living in compound H and V. Menikrala (B1:7) in compound B1. **Plot 9** was at some point sold by Dingiri Etani I (Z:A2) to her sister's son, U. Kadirathe (A2:4).

Kadirathe (A1:1) who inherited **plots 6–8, 13, 14**, became Gamarāla and later Vel Vidāne, but then went bankrupt. He sold all his land except **plot 13** to Alisandini Nikala Pulle (T:1), a Low Country Sinhalese trader. Kadirathe (A1:1) gave **plot 13** to his son (A1:2), but the latter also went bankrupt, sold his holding to the same trader, and left the district.

The trader sold the land he had acquired from Kadirathe (A1:1) to Appurala Vidāne (A1:W), then a resident of Wiralmurippu (57). Some time *after* this Appurala (A1:W) married *binna* Tikiri Etani II (A1:3), daughter of Kadirathe (A1:1). Appurala became Vel Vidāne of Pul Eliya around 1908 and was thereafter the dominant figure in Pul Eliya affairs down to about 1926. In 1954 Appurala's descendants ignored the fact of Kadirathe's bankruptcy and claimed that they had inherited their lands direct from Naidurala Gamarāla I (A:1). Of these descendants, S. Subasinghe (A1:5) and P. Ran Banda (A1:6) lived in compound A1; A.V. Punchi Etani (B1:A1) who had married *dīga* into compound B1 still lived there as a widow. Subasinghe ranked as Gamarāla by virtue of his ownership of **plot 14**.

Plot 13 which the trader (T:1) had acquired from Kadirathe's son

13-2

was sold to Kirihamy (W:3), another resident of Wiralmurippu. In 1954 it was registered in the name of W. Punchi Etani (Dw:W) (deceased) of Diwulwewa (56), who was Kirihamy's daughter's daughter. M. Herathamy (B1:Dw), the *de facto* owner of this land, was in 1954 married *binna* to A.V. Punchi Etani's daughter M. Ran Manika (B1:5). This marriage was a failure, but it represented a clear attempt to recover control of the fragmented *gamvasama* **plot 13** (see pp. 138, 247–8). If M. Herathamy had been shown as the registered owner he might have claimed the rank of Gamarāla.

Ihala bāga panguva 1 (*plots 15–17*)

At a date prior to 1886 the whole *panguva* was shared by two sisters from compound B. Their titled brother, Punchirala Badderāla (B1:1), was already deceased. One sister (C:B) was married to Naidurala Gamarāla II (C:2), the other (B2:1) was wife to Appurala (B2:Z1). Appurala by this marriage had a son Menikrala (B2:2), who died without heirs, and three daughters. One daughter Maniki Etani (B1:B2) married her cross-cousin Punchirala Badderāla ge Wannihamy (B1:2). The second daughter Puli Etani (B2:3) married *binna* a man of low status named M. Ukkurala (B2:Z3). The third daughter (P:B2) married *dīga* in Periyakkulam (33). M. Ukkurala was probably of 'wrong *variga*'.

Appurala's wife, Dingiri Munika (B2:1), later married *binna* one Kawrala (B2:Z2), whose origins are obscure; by this second marriage she had a son K. Ukkurala II (B2:4). The latter married *dīga* K. Walli Etani (B2:E2) who was heiress to compound E.

This compound contains a large Bo tree and the site is said to be haunted by the spirit guardian of a former shrine that is supposed to have existed there. The owners have not actually lived in the compound for several generations though they carefully maintain the fences. In 1954 compound E belonged to U. Kuda Pinhamy (B2:E3) who lived with his *bāna* in compound B2.

Puli Etani (B2:3) and M. Ukkurala (B2:Z3) had a son U. Kapuruhamy (B2:5), who in 1954 was an old man of about 70. Because of the circumstances of his birth he was still treated as of marginal *variga* status, and seldom appeared at family functions. Significantly this Kapuruhamy in recounting his genealogy tried to make out that his father Ukkurala (B2:Z3) had come from Ambagahawewa (86). This served to confuse him with his father-in-law's brother, Kapurala ge Ukkurala (A 2 : Z 2), a man of high status, who really did come from Ambagahawewa.

It was consistent with this that Kapuruhamy should have laid great stress on his own 'correct' marriage with K. Punchi Etani II (B 2 : A 2) and with the fact that his son K. Dingiri Banda (A 2 : B 2) had consolidated this alliance by marrying K. Punchi Etani's brother's daughter (see p. 92).

Maniki Etani (B 1 : B 2) and Wannihamy (B 1 : 2) had a son W. Mudalihamy (B 1 : 3) who married *dīga* A.V. Punchi Etani (B 1 : A 1). This Mudalihamy became Vel Vidāne on the retirement of his father-in-law Appurala Vidāne (A 1 : W) around 1926. He also acquired the title of Badderāla. In 1954 A.V. Punchi Etani (B 1 : A 1) was living as a widow in compound B 1 together with her daughter M. Ran Manika (B 1 : 8) who, at this time, was married *binna* to M. Herathamy (B 1 : Dw), heir to the *gamvasama* plot 13 (see above).

The plot succession in Panguva I was as follows:

Plot 15: Appurala's wife (B 2 : 1) to Menikrala (B 2 : 2) to Puli Etani (B 2 : 3) to U. Kapuruhamy (B 2 : 5) to his son K. Dingiri Banda (A 2 : B 2). K. Dingiri Banda (A 2 : B 2) originally married *dīga* the daughter (A 2 : 8) of K. Murugathe (A 2 : 3). Murugathe's wife Kumari Etani (A 2 : P), who came from Periyakkulam (33), was a granddaughter of Appurala (B 2 : Z 1) and already had a certain residual claim in this plot. The affinal link with Periyakkulam has been maintained by the *binna* marriage of M. Dingiri Banda (P : B 1), son of W. Mudalihamy (B 1 : 3) and A.V. Punchi Etani (B 1 : A 1). M. Dingiri Banda (P : B 1) lives in Periyakkulam in the compound in which Kumari Etani (A 2 : P) was born.

K. Dingiri Banda's affinal linkage with K. Murugathe (A 2 : 3) was strategically important for the impoverished members of Compound B 2 (see p. 92), and consequently, on the death of his wife (A 2 : 8), K. Dingiri Banda (A 2 : B 2) himself went to live with his father-in-law in compound A 2 so as to maintain the relationship. In 1954 the position was that K. Dingiri Banda (A 2 : B 2) had remarried and was living in a separate house in compound A 2. His daughter by his first marriage (A 2 : 9) had married *binna* B. Siriwardena (A 2 : Z 5) from Watarekkewa (21) and was keeping house for her grandfather, K. Murugathe (A 2 : 3).

Plot 16: Appurala's wife (B 2 : 1) to Menikrala (B 2 : 2) to Maniki

Etani (B 1 : B 2), to Mudalihamy (B 1 : 3) to Mudalihamy's widow A.V. Punchi Etani (B 1 : A 1). It was a matter of adverse comment in the village that A.V. Punchi Etani had so far refused either to remarry or to divide up her property among her children.

Plot 17: the wife (C : B) of Naidurala Gamarāla II (C : 2) to their son Naidurala Gamarāla ge Ukkurala (H : 1). In 1890 this man's full brother Velathe (C : 4) was Vel Vidāne; on Velathe's death Ukkurala (H : 1) became Vel Vidāne. At this time Ukkurala (H : 1) probably resided in compound G; he later moved to Wiralmurippu and finally to Ulukkulema (3).

On leaving Pul Eliya, Ukkurala (H : 1) wanted to endow his adopted daughter Banda Etani (H : 2) with a house and property; at the same time Appurala Vidāne (A 1 : W) similarly wished to endow his adopted daughter Dingiri Etani II (G : Z 1). A complicated transaction ensued.

Ukkurala (H : 1) 'sold' to Appurala Vidāne (A 1 : W) the house-site area represented by **compound G** together with **plot 17**; Appurala Vidāne (A 1 : W) 'sold' to Ukkurala (H : 1) the house-site area represented by **compound H** together with **plot 21**. It is unlikely that any cash changed hands, but it is probable that both sales were supported by legal documents which might, if necessary, be produced in court as evidence of possession.

Appurala Vidāne (A 1 : W) finally gave **compound G** and **plot 17** to A. Bandathe (G : Z 2), husband of Dingiri Etani II (G : Z 1); Ukkurala (H : 1) gave **compound H** and **plot 21** to U.G. Pinhamy (H : A 2), husband of Banda Etani (H : 2).

The explanation of all this is as follows: Holding the office of Vel Vidāne, Ukkurala (H : 1) and Appurala Vidāne (A 1 : W) were both in a position to manipulate orthodox custom to their own advantage. Both Ukkurala (H : 1) and Appurala Vidāne (A 1 : W) wished to transfer land of the *paravēni* 'heirloom' category to their *adopted* daughters. By customary law an adopted child has no right of inheritance. Any owner can make a gift of land to anyone he chooses simply by verbal declaration but, in the absence of legal documents, such gifts are liable to litigation after the death of the donor.

The effect of the transactions I have described was to provide the adopted children of Ukkurala (H : 1) and Appurala Vidāne (A 1 : W) with a permanent status in the Pul Eliya community which could be backed up if need be by legal documents. The transactions thus had the effect of creating two entirely new compound groups, G and H.

Ihala bāga panguva 2 (*plots* 18–20)

Kadira Velathe Mohottāla (D 1:2) lived in compound D. He was already a prominent Pul Eliya owner in 1861. In 1954 Punchirala Gamarāla (D 2:C), aged about 70, remembered that as a small boy he had known Kadira Velathe Mohottāla as an old man and that he had addressed him as *māmā*. It is consistent with other evidence that Kadirathe Gamarāla (C:3) and Kadira Velathe Mohottāla (D 1:2) were first cousins, though the latter must have been much the older man.

The present members of compounds D 1 and Dx claim direct descent from Kadira Velathe Mohottāla. Although there are difficulties about accepting this claim, it is not impossible (see plots 36 and 37 below).

According to the present owners, the whole *panguva* passed from Kadira Velathe Mohottāla to his daughter (D 1:3). **Plots 18–19** then passed to her son Jangurala (D 1:4) and **plot 20** to Jangurala's full sister (D 1:5), wife of M. Kirihamy (D 1:C). In 1954, **plot 18** belonged to Jangurala's son J. Punchirala (Dx:2) and **plot 19** to Jangurala's daughter (Dx:1), wife of M. Naidurala (Dx:Y). **Plot 20** was inherited by M. Kirihamy's daughter, K. Punchi Etani (D 1:6), aged about 60 in 1954, and then formed the dowry of her daughter Ukkuhamy (D 1:8) when the latter married U. Sirala (A 2:5) of compound A 2.

The marriage of Ukkuhamy (D 1:8) and U. Sirala (A 2:5) ended in a celebrated divorce (see p. 316). Sirala, in order to prevent his wife's relatives from recovering their land, 'sold' **plot 20** to his full brother, U.G. Pinhamy (H:A 2). In the course of subsequent litigation U. Sirala spent a period in gaol, but U.G. Pinhamy's title was proved good. U.G. Pinhamy (H:A 2) compensated his brother by buying him out of prison.

It may be remarked that it is, in a sense, appropriate that U.G. Pinhamy should be the owner of land which was originally the heirloom property of members of compound D. U.G. Pinhamy's compound H occupies ground of which a part was at one time within the boundaries of compound D (see Map *D*).

Ihala bāga panguva 3 (*plots* 21–4)

In 1890 the whole *panguva* was owned by the trader Alisandini Nikala Pulle (T:1). Previous ownership is not known. Later the whole was purchased by Appurala Vidāne (A1:W), who exchanged it with Ukkurala (H:1) for plot 17. Ukkurala gave **plot 21** to his adopted daughter's husband, U.G. Pinhamy (H:A2) (see above: Ihala bāga panguva 1). **Plots 22–4** were given by Appurala Vidāne (A1:W) to U. Kapuruhamy (B2:5), resident in compound B2. U. Kapuruhamy, a poor man, was a 'brother' of Appurala Vidāne's son-in-law, W. Mudalihamy (B1:3). The gift put Kapuruhamy in a sort of servant status *vis-à-vis* Appurala (A1:W). The present owners of these plots, Menikrala (B2:6), Appuhamy (W:B2) and Wannihamy (B2:7) are U. Kapuruhamy's sons. Menikrala and Wannihamy live in compound B2. Appuhamy is married *binna* in Wiralmurippu. It is primarily the ownership of these plots which entitles these men to call themselves Pul Eliya *minissu*.

Ihala bāga panguva 4 (*plots* 25–7)

The history of the *panguva* is the same as that for plots 1–14 (see above). The present owners are the descendants of Ranhamy (A2:1) and Kadirathe 'former Vel Vidāne' (A1:1). **Plot 25** was at one stage sold to Alisandini Nikala Pulle (T:1) and then purchased by Appurala Vidāne (A1:W).

Summary

Traditionally the ownership of the Ihala bāga is associated with the ownership of compound A. This compound was nearly bankrupt at the beginning of the period, but by 1954, as a result of satisfactory marriage alliances with wealthy *pavula* in Wiralmurippu (57) and Yakawewa (43) and also with the Pul Eliya compound B, most of the land was again owned by the theoretically correct households.

Since 1870 two members of compound B1 have held the title Badderāla and two have been Vel Vidāne; in compound A, three men have been Vel Vidāne and one is now *tulāna* Headman. At the present time (1954) compounds A1, A2 and B1 between them control most of the wealth and political influence in the village.

MEDA BĀGA

Gamvasama (*plot* 28)
Elapat panguva (*plot* 29)
Elapata (*at bottom of lower field*) (*plot* 107)

Naidurala Gamarāla II (C:2) is mentioned in a document dated 1861 as Gamarāla of the Meda bāga. He was an active man in 1886. In 1890 he was still alive, but had divided most of his property among his heirs. By his first wife (C:D) he had a son Kadirathe Gamarāla (C:3). He later married the sister (C:B) of Punchirala Badderāla (B1:1) and by her had two further children, Velathe (C:4) and Ukkurala (H:1). This Velathe was Pul Eliya Vel Vidāne in 1890 and had the title Mohottāla. He died around 1898 and was succeeded as Vel Vidāne by his full brother Ukkurala (H:1). The latter later moved to Wiralmurippu where his son U.V. Pinhamy (C1:W), the present owner of **plots 28 and 107**, was born.

In his own right Naidurala Gamarāla II (C:2) was Gamarāla of the Pahala bāga; he acquired rights to the Meda bāga *gamvasama* only through his second marriage. Hence on the division of his property his rights in the Pahala bāga *gamvasama* went to the child of his first marriage, Kadirathe Gamarāla (C:3); similarly his rights in the Meda bāga *gamvasama* (**plot 28**) went to the children of his second marriage, Velathe (C:4) and Ukkurala (H:1).

It is important to note that neither of these men ever married back into compound B1. From the point of view of the latter the Meda bāga *gamvasama* is the traditional estate of compound B1 and the fact that it is now held by U.V. Pinhamy (C1:W) instead of by V. Menikrala (B1:7) is one of the primary bases for the very marked hostility between these two men.

In 1889/90 Velathe (C:4) as Vel Vidāne treated **plots 28-9** as an undivided holding. In 1889 he shows himself as owner of **plot 28** and his brother and his son as joint owners with himself of **plot 29**. In the following year he reversed the procedure and put himself down for **plot 29** while entering his brother's name against **plot 28**. There are grounds for supposing that Velathe and Ukkurala maintained a polyandrous household at this time, but as Ukkurala was credited with fathering children on five different 'wives' in four different localities, this scandal has to be treated with reserve.

Velathe's mentally defective son V. Kirihamy (C: 5) (died *c*. 1925) inherited a half-share in the joint holding and called himself Kirihamy Gamarāla on that account. Kirihamy's share was sold to a trader Alvis (T: 2) who resold it to U. Kadirathe (A 2: 4). This **plot 29** is now owned by Kadirathe's son, the *tulāna* Headman (A 2: 7).

Ukkurala's share, **plots 28, 107**, was inherited by U.V. Pinhamy (C 1: W) who was reared by his mother (W: 4) in Wiralmurippu. The latter was a daughter of Vela Vidāne (W: 1) and a cross-cousin of Appurala Vidāne (A 2: W). U.V. Pinhamy only came to live in Pul Eliya after his marriage to Sinni Etani (C 1: 1).

Meda bāga ordinary pangu (plots 30–8)

Although the 1889 list shows only four holdings here, each of equal size, it is certain that as early as 1861 these four *pangu* were already, as now, divided in six equal strips. It would seem that *pangu* 1, 2 and 3 of the 1889 list correspond to the five strips covered by **plots 30–7** in the 1954 list, while *panguva* 4 corresponds to **plot 38**. I have no evidence regarding the identity of Velathe 'former Vel Vidāne' shown as holding *panguva* 3 in 1889. Vela Vidāne (W: 1) shown in the 1889 list as holding Meda bāga *panguva* 2 and also Pahala bāga *panguva* 4 was head of a wealthy compound in Wiralmurippu. He was *māmā* to Appurala Vel Vidāne (A 1: W) (see above, plots 6–8, 14). Vela Vidāne was at one point married to a younger sister (W: C) of Naidurala Gamarāla II (C: 2). She seems to have died without heirs around 1889, whereupon her property reverted to her brother, who divided it among his heirs. The Meda bāga land went to Kadirathe (C: 3), the child of his first wife (C: D); the Pahala bāga land went to Velathe (C: 4) and Ukkurala (H: 1), the children of his second wife (C: B) (see also plot 47).

Kadira Velathe Mohottāla (D 1: 2) is mentioned in a document dated 1861 as holding four out of the eight strips of the Meda bāga of that time. He appears to have been *bāna* to Naidurala Gamarāla II (C: 2), although of much the same age. **Plots 30–7** were the hereditary property of compound D. By 1890 Kadirathe Gamarāla (C: 3) had inherited a substantial share of this property through his mother.

Plot succession. **Plot 30**, held by Kadirathe Gamarāla in 1890, passed to his daughter Walli Etani (C: 7), who died without heirs; her property passed to her adopted son, P. Kapuruhamy (C 2: D 2), the actual son of her brother Punchirala Gamarāla (D 2: C) by his first marriage.

Plot 31 belonged to Dingiri Etani (B2:D1), a sister of Kadira Velathe Mohottāla (D1:2). In 1890 she was married outside Pul Eliya to Kiri Naidurala ge Naidurala (Z:Z1), supposedly a *bāna* of Naidurala Gamarāla I (A:1). By this marriage she had children, of whom a daughter, Tutti Etani (A2:Z4), married Kapurala ge Kandathe (A2:Z3), compound A2. Dingiri Etani (B2:D1) later married the heir (B2:E1) to the abandoned garden E, by whom she had a daughter K. Walli Etani (B2:E2), mother of the present owner U. Kuda Pinhamy (B2:E3) (see Ihala bāga panguva 1 above).

Plots 32–7 were apparently held undivided by Kadira Velathe Mohottāla (D1:2) and Kadirathe Gamarāla (C:3). In 1890 Kadirathe Gamarāla (C:3) is shown as holding two-thirds and his *massinā* one-third. In 1954 the successors to Kadirathe Gamarāla (C:3) held one-third and the successors to his *massinā* two-thirds. I do not know the reason for this switch.

Plots 32–5 passed to Appurala Vedarāla (C:6), a son of Kadirathe Gamarāla (C:3). This Appurala (C:6) sold half his holding (**plots 33, 35**) outright to Appurala Vidāne (A1:W). The 1954 holders (A1:5), (A1:6) and (B1:A1), were Appurala Vidāne's heirs. Appurala Vedarāla (C:6) mortgaged the other half of his holding, **plot 32**, to a trader Antoni (T:3). Appurala Vedarāla's son, A.V. Bandathe (Z:C), inherited the mortgage deed; he married *binna* outside Pul Eliya and sold the deed to U. Kadirathe (A2:4). Kadirathe (A2:4) has redeemed the mortgage and is now full owner of the land.

The present owners of **plots 36** and **37** are K. Punchi Etani (D1:6) and Kiri Etani (Dx:3), second wife of M. Naidurala (Dx:Y). The former is resident in compound D1. The latter is resident outside the *gamgoda* area in compound Dx, but her sister's son N. Punchi Banda (Dx:4) in 1954 built a house in compound D1. To validate ownership of these plots and house-sites both owners claim to be great-grand-daughters of Kadira Velathe Mohottāla (D1:2). At first sight this appears highly unlikely. In 1954 K. Punchi Etani (D1:6), had a grandson, S. Jaymanhamy (D1:9), already aged 30, while Kadira Velathe Mohottāla's cousin (*massinā*), Kadirathe Gamarāla (C:3), had a grandson P. Kirala (D2:1), only aged 22.

The discrepancy raises some points of interest. Because women begin to bear children soon after puberty, while middle-aged men often marry very young wives, a line of descent traced exclusively through females may quickly become chronologically out of step with a similar line traced through males. In the above instance, for example, P. Kirala (D2:1) was fifty years younger than his father Punchirala Gamarāla (D2:C), but Jaymanhamy (D1:9) was only thirty years younger than his mother's mother (D1:6). Thus the skewed generations shown on the genealogy, though dubious, are quite possible.

Discrepancies of this sort are probably quite common but are not easily noticed. The Sinhalese rule is that a man should marry a *nǟnā*— that is a girl of his own generation. Even if the rule is broken, terminology tends to disguise the error. 'My sister's husband' is always my *massinā* (cousin) even when, according to strict genealogy, he might properly be addressed as *māmā* (uncle) or *bǟnā* (nephew).

Plot 38 belonged in 1890 to Badderāla ge Wannihamy (B1:2), it was inherited by Wannihamy's son, Mudalihamy (B1:3), who also became a Badderāla and whose widow A.V. Punchi Etani (B1:A1) is now the registered holder. She has not remarried and still lives in compound B1.

Summary

It appears from this analysis that 'originally' (that is, around 1850) most of the land of the Meda bāga belonged to members of compounds B and D. The head of compound B was a Badderāla and the head of compound D a Mohottāla. There followed a phase from about 1860 to 1900 when, as a result of appropriate marriages, most of the property was controlled by compound C. However, since 1900, as a result of the alliance between compounds A and B, the compound C interests have mostly been eroded away again. Compound D, which around 1938 was almost completely extinguished, is now once more in the ascendant owing to the energy of M. Naidurala (Dx:Y).

V. Menikrala (B1:7), the present head of compound B, does not personally own any land in the bāga but U. Kadirathe (A2:4) is his *māmā* and K.V. Appuhamy (A2:7) his *massinā*.

It is perhaps significant that Velathe Vidāne (C:4) was made a Mohottāla soon after he became part owner of plots 28–9 and that K.V. Appuhamy (A2:7) became *tulāna* Headman just after he had become owner of plot 29. Such ranks are not supposed to be hereditary but it is clear that formerly *variga* court titles tended to stay with particular compound groups. The prestige necessary for the assumption of such an office derives from wealth and 'good family', but it is visibly manifested in the ownership of *gamvasama* plots. And this is true even today.

Pahala bāga

Pahala panguva 1 (*plot* 39)

In 1886 the whole *panguva* belonged to Dingiri Etani (B2:D1), (cf. plot 31 Meda bāga). Later it was owned by her two sons, Pinhamy (Z:Z2) and Wannihamy (Z:Z3) who lived outside Pul Eliya, and by her daughter Tutti Etani (A2:Z4), wife of Kapurala ge Kandathe (A2:Z3). The latter 'bought out' the rights of Pinhamy and Wannihamy. The 1954 owner, K. Murugathe (A2:3) is son of Tutti Etani and Kandathe.

Pahala panguva 2 (*plots* 40, 41)

In 1889 Badderāla ge Wannihamy (B1:2) lived in compound B1. He had a sister (B1:4) married *binna* to Badderāla ge Kirihamy (B1:Z2) from Vilava, 40 miles away. The Vilava people are very 'high' Goyigama and the Pul Eliya villagers overlooked the breach of *variga* endogamy. Today, on account of this marriage, they claim that Vilava is part of the Pul Eliya *variga*. Badderāla ge Kirihamy (B1:Z2) (usually remembered as Vilo-Kirihamy on account of his origins) had no descendants. The 1886 tax list gives his name as Vilava Kirihami. The 1954 holder of **plot 40**, V. Menikrala (B1:7), is Vilo-Kirihamy's wife's sister's daughter's son.

The 1954 holder of **plot 42** is P. Ran Etani (W:J), resident in Wiralmurippu, who is daughter's daughter to Badderāla ge Wannihamy (B1:2) and step-daughter to Velathe (B1:6).

Pahala panguva 3 (*plots* 42–6)

The names shown against this panguva in 1889 and 1890 are not identifiable.

Around 1890 **plot 42** belonged to K. Pulingurala (J:1). It was inherited by his son Punchirala Anumātirāla (J:2), who left the village and went to live with his 'brother' (his mother's sister's son), U.V. Menikrala (Bel:1) in Bellankadawala. The latter sold the plot to U. Kadirathe (A2:4), who gave it by way of dowry to his daughter (Y:A2) on the occasion of her marriage to B. Hetuhamy (Y:1) of Yakawewa.

This last gesture had been accompanied by an attempt to purchase

House XIX in compound C for Hetuhamy's use; a manœuvre which had been resisted only by lawsuit.

About 1895 **plots 43–6** were held by Kadirathe Gamarāla (C:3). They were later inherited along with house XIX in compound C by Appurala Vedarāla (C:6). The latter gave both the plots and the house to his step-brother Mudalihamy (C:Z2) (see p. 133). Later Appurala's *binna*-married son A.V. Banda (Z:C1), claimed that Mudalihamy's heirs had no title, and tried to sell the estate to B. Hetuhamy (Y:1) (see p. 214). In 1954 M. Kirala (C1:2) owned the house. The four Old Field **plots 43–6** form a single strip (*issara*) with multiple ownership. Seven individuals claimed a share in the holding, namely K. Tikiri Banda (Cx:2), K. Nanghamy (Cx:3), M. Sinni Etani (C1:1), M. Kirala (C1:2), K. Pemawathie (B2:Cx), M. Herathamy (C1:3), K. Ran Manika (Z1:Cx). Since their ancestor Mudalihamy (C:Z2) was an outsider, and possibly even of the wrong *variga*, this land is the only thing which entitles his descendants to claim the status of Pul Eliya *minissu*. In 1954 the entire holding was actually worked by the eldest male, M. Kirala (C1:2). I do not know how the crop was divided.

Pahala gamvasama (plot 47)
Pahala elapat panguva (plots 48–50)
Pahala panguva 4 (plots 51–5)
Pahala elapata (plots 56–65)

Documents show that Kadirathe Gamarāla (C:3) assumed the title of Gamarāla some time between 1886 and 1889, which must mark the date at which Naidurala Gamarāla II (C:2) divided up his property among his heirs.

Naidurala Gamarāla II was Gamarāla of the Meda bāga only by virtue of his marriage to Punchirala Badderāla's sister (C:B) and his rights in the Meda bāga *gamvasama* were transmitted to his children by that wife, namely Velathe (C:4), and Ukkurala (H:1). Of these Velathe was Vel Vidāne in 1889/90.

Naidurala Gamarāla II was Gamarāla of the Pahala bāga in his own right by inheritance, but he shared undivided property rights in the Pahala elapata with his half-brother M. Kirihamy I (D1:C) and his half-sister (F:C), wife of Kapurala Vederala (F:1). Naidurala's share of the rights in the Pahala *gamvasama* and in the Pahala elapata was transmitted to his son Kadirathe Gamarāla (C:3). At this point the undivided Pahala elapata holding was divided.

For reasons unknown the unorthodox procedure was adopted of creating two 'extra *pangu*'.

The procedure adopted was intricate and entailed relaying a whole series of field strips (*issaraval*) at 4-fathom intervals instead of at the more usual 5-fathom spacing.

As laid out today, *pangu* 1–3 of the Pahala bāga together with the *gamvasama* (**plot 47**) and the *elapat panguva* (**plots 48–50**) have a total depth of 50 fathoms, leaving a further 50 fathoms for the remaining *pangu* and the *elapata* (including **plots 64–5**).

This 50 fathoms is divided into

(*a*) six strips of 4 fathoms = 24 fathoms (plots 51–62)

(*b*) one strip of 10 fathoms = 10 fathoms (plot 60)

(*c*) one irregular strip (*kurulu pāluva*) (plot 63)

(*d*) two strips of 8 fathoms = 16 fathoms (plots 61–2 and 64–5).

Of these (*a*) rate as *pangu* land and the remainder as *elapata* land and the *rājakāriya* duty varies accordingly (see pp. 167–8).

The *pangu* now are:

Panguva no. 4, plots 51–3	8 fathoms (originally 10 fathoms)
Extra panguva 'A', plots 54–7a	12 fathoms
Extra panguva 'B', plots 58–9 and 61–2	12 fathoms
Pahala elapata, plots 60, 64, 65	18 fathoms
Total	50 fathoms

The Lower Field counterpart to *panguva* 4 is represented by **plots 67** and **66** as before. The counterpart to the two 'extra *pangu*', taken together, is represented by **plot 107a**[1] of 8 fathoms depth. Thus, whereas

[1] The strip marked on Map *E* as 107*a* is the top strip of the original Meda bāga *elapata*. Plot 106, which is the same width (8 fathoms), is the counterpart strip to plot 28. In 1954 plot 107*a* was owned undivided by Jaymanhamy (D1:9), S. Ran Manika (B1:D1) and Podi Menika (Cx:D1), but was worked by K. Tikiri Banda (Cx:2), husband of Podi Menika. Since U.V. Pinhamy (C1:W) was the owner of both plot 106 and of plot 107, his *bāna* K. Tikiri Banda had arranged for a permanent exchange of plot 107*a* for plot 106 so that the whole of U.V. Pinhamy's holding should here be contiguous.

The whole of the Meda bāga *elapata*, including plot 107*a*, has a depth of about 32 fathoms as against the 'theoretical' figure of 40 fathoms. This was apparently due to the fact that in the year 1900 when the cadastral survey was made an additional 8-fathom strip at the bottom of the field was lying fallow and was not reckoned as part of the Old Field.

each ordinary *panguva* comprises 10 fathoms of the Upper Field plus 10 fathoms of the Lower Field, these three *pangu* are now unorthodox:

	Fathoms Upper Field	Fathoms Lower Field	Fathoms total
Pahala panguva 4	8	10	18
Extra panguva 'A'	12	4	16
Extra panguva 'B'	12	4	16

However, although the fathom symmetry of the arrangement is imperfect the division did have the effect of giving Kadirathe (C:3), Kirihamy (D 1:C) and Kapurala's wife (F:C) equal shares in notional acres, thus:

						Total acres
Kirihamy	Plots	54–5	58–9	65	107*a*[1]	
	Acres	$\frac{1}{2}$	$\frac{1}{2}$	$\frac{1}{4}$	$\frac{3}{4}$	2
Kapurala's	Plots	56–7	61–2	64	—	
wife	Acres	1	$\frac{3}{4}$	$\frac{1}{4}$	—	2
Kadirathe	Plots	—	—	60	—	
	Acres	—	—	2	—	2

To achieve this result the Vel Vidāne (Velathe (C:4)) himself contributed to the pool a total of $1\frac{1}{4}$ notional acres, namely **plots 54, 55, 107a,** all of which went to Kirihamy and his heirs. Although Kirihamy was Velathe's father's half-brother there is no obvious reason why Velathe should have had this fit of generosity.

I think the most likely explanation is that a succession dispute arose which was finally settled by the British administrator. Only a British official would reckon out equal shares in terms of acres rather than fathoms.

It may also be relevant that Kirihamy's son Pulingurala (J:1) was the recognised husband of his cross-cousin Ukki Etani (F:2), daughter of Kapurala Vedarāla (F:1), but that Ukki Etani's son Menikrala (Bel:1) was reputedly fathered by Naidurala ge Ukkurala (H:1), full brother to Velathe Vidāne (C:5) and not by Pulingurala. Alternatively, U.V. Pinhamy (C 1:W), another son of the same Ukkurala, asserted that Menikrala's father was unknown and that Ukkurala had only acknowledged his responsibility to save Ukki Etani's reputation. Nothing definite can be inferred from such scandal, though it is remarkable that **plots 50–3,** which in 1890 were registered in the name of

[1] *Ibid.*

Velathe Vidāne and his brother Ukkurala, later passed into the hands of Ukki Etani's descendants.

A striking feature of this unorthodox attempt to restructure the traditionally established territorial arrangements was that within a very few years all the persons concerned, except Kadirathe Gamarāla (C:3), had ceased to reside in Pul Eliya and were living scattered around in Diwulwewa (55), Bellankadawala (56) and Wiralmurippu (57). Whatever the precise circumstances of the case they were evidently accompanied by a great deal of social friction.

Plot succession. **Plots 47, 60, 63,** which represented Kadirathe Gamarāla's share as Gamarāla, were passed on intact by him to his son Punchirala Gamarāla (D 2 : C). The latter went bankrupt following unsuccessful ventures in shopkeeping. The lands were mortgaged to a Tamil trader from Wiralmurippu, Antoni (T:3), who foreclosed. The land was later sold by the trader's widow to Danapala of Marutumadu without giving the Pul Eliya villagers a chance to buy it back (see pp. 252 f.). In 1954 Danapala was alleged to be using his possession of these plots as a justification for claiming (*a*) that he was a Pul Eliya resident, (*b*) that it gave him the status to serve as *tulāna* Headman.

Plot 48 was inherited by M. Kirihamy's son's son's daughter, P. Ran Etani (W:J), resident in Wiralmurippu. **Plot 49** was inherited by her father Punchirala Anumätirāla (J:2), who sold up to Velathe (B 1:6), compound B 1, father of the 1954 holder V. Menikrala (B 1:7). At much the same time Velathe (B 1:6) married his cross-cousin Sitti Etani (J:B 1), who had been Punchirala Anumätirāla's wife. Thus P. Ran Etani (W:J) and V. Menikrala (B 1:7) are step-siblings. **Plot 50** also passed to Punchirala Anumätirāla (J:2), but through his mother Ukki Etani (F 2), daughter of Kapurala Vedarāla (F:1). Punchirala Anumätirāla sold up to the present holder U. Kuda Pinhamy (B 2:E 3).

Kirihamy (C:5), son and heir to Velathe (C:4), was imbecile. **Plots 51–3** seems to have passed undivided to Velathe's cross-cousins, Kadirathe Vedarāla (Dw:F) and his sister Ukki Etani (F:2). The circumstances are obscure. The holding then passed, still undivided, to the multiple heirs of Kadirathe Vedarāla (Dw:F), now represented by the person of K.V. Punchi Etani (Dw:1), jointly with two children of Ukki Etani who were registered as having been fathered by Ukkurala (H:1) (see p. 208). Ukki Etani's daughter's daughter (Y:Bel) later married *dīga* in Yakawewa and she then sold her share of the combined holding to M. Naidurala (Dx:Y) who is a distant *malli* ('younger brother') of her husband. In the Vel Vidāne's record Naidurala (Dx:Y) and his son N. Punchi Banda (Dx:4) are shown as holding plots 52–3, while K.V. Punchi Etani (Dw:1) is given as owner of the counterpart plot 66 in the Lower Field. In fact, however, they take turn and turn about; Naidurala and his son work the Lower Field plot 66 in every alternate year. U.V. Menikrala (Bel:1), shown as owner of plot 51 in 1954, is Ukki Etani's son.

Plots 54, 55 were shared between M. Kirihamy's (D1:C) son Pulingurala (J:1) and his daughter K. Punchi Etani (D1:6). Pulingurala's son Punchirala (J:2), sold his share to M. Naidurala (Dx:Y) whose daughter, N. Ran Manika (Dx:5), was 1954 owner of plot 55. The minute plot 54 belongs like plot 106 to the wife (Cx:D1) of K. Tikiri Banda (Cx:2), who is K. Punchi Etani's daughter's daughter. Strictly speaking it is shared with her siblings (D1:9 and B1:D1) but these, being relatively well off, do not assert their claim.

In 1954 plots 56 and 61 were held by K.V. Punchi Etani (Dw:1), son's daughter of Kapurala Vedarāla (F:1), resident in Diwulwewa (56).

Plots 57 and 64 were held by descendants of Kapurala Vederāla (F:1) resident in Bellankadawala (55), namely: U.V. Menikrala (Bel:1), M.V. Ran Manika (Bel:4), W. Nanghamy (Bel:5).

Plots 58 and 59 were transmitted in the same way as plots 48, 49 above.

Plot 65 was transmitted from M. Kirihamy I (D1:C) to his daughter K. Punchi Etani (D1:6).

Plot 62, which is a single square plot (liyädda) in the corner of the field, belongs to the temple priest. Its history is not now remembered.

Summary

Traditionally the Pahala bāga had been the domain of compound group C. At the end of the nineteenth century an inheritance dispute coupled with caste scandal led to the fragmentation of the compound group. By 1954 all the direct descendants of the original owners had ceased to reside in compound C. The Gamarāla line itself, in the persons of Punchirala Gamarāla (D2:C) and his descendants, was bankrupt and landless. Significantly, Punchirala Gamarāla and his residual heir P. Kirala (D2:1) now reside in the birth compound of Punchirala Gamarāla's father's mother, compound D.

The present residents in compound C have only tenuous claims on

Pul Eliya land of any sort. The rather special case of U.V. Pinhamy (C1:W) is discussed below (p. 214).

While the direct descendants of Kadirathe Gamarāla (C:3) have gone bankrupt, some of the heirs of his cross-cousin Kadirathe Vedarāla (Dw:F) have prospered, notably the shopkeeper K.V. Kapuruhamy (F:Dw) who has now returned to Pul Eliya. In theory, the land-holdings of Kadirathe Vedarāla's heirs in the Pahala bāga are widely distributed, but they are all registered in the name of K.V. Punchi Etani (Dw:1) who is married to P. Menikrala (Dw:D2), a son of Punchirala Gamarāla (D2:C). Hence the bankrupt Gamarāla's family still have a stake in the ancestral holding.

Parts of the Pahala bāga are held by a compound group resident in Bellankadawala (55) (also affinally related to Punchirala Gamarāla). Bellankadawala itself is a poor tank with an unsatisfactory sluice, and these people maintain their hereditary links with Pul Eliya as a kind of insurance policy. One day they might find it an advantage to resume full membership of the Pul Eliya community.

This completes the analysis of the devolution of plot-holdings in the Old Field, but some features of the succession of compound group membership have still to be mentioned. I shall therefore reconsider the compounds in alphabetical order.

II. COMPOUNDS

(See Maps C and D and Table 1)

Compound A

The original compound A has segmented into two parts, A1, containing house-sites VIII and X, and A2, containing house-sites XI, XIA, XII, XIII, XIV, XV; each part is separately linked by affinal ties with compound B1. In 1954 a section of the boundary between A1 and A2 was unfenced (Map D (b)); garden plot a (Map C) forms part of compound A2, it is the property of K.V. Appuhamy (A2:7).

S. Subasinghe (A1:7), as owner of plot 14, was entitled to call himself Gamarāla. He did not in fact do so but performed the appropriate duties at village festivals. In 1954 K.V. Appuhamy (A2:7) was *tulāna* Headman and lived in the same house (house-site XII) as his father, U. Kadirathe (A2:4), the retired Vel Vidāne.

Membership of compound A2 has not been established exclusively through right of descent. When Ukkurala (A2:Z2) of Ambagaha-wewa came to Pul Eliya as *binna* husband of Tikiri Etani I (A2:2) he was accompanied by his younger brother Kandathe (A2:Z3). In the first instance this may have been a polyandrous marriage, but Kandathe later married Tutti Etani (A2:Z4) a step-daughter of Kirihamy (B2:E1). Kandathe and his wife resided in compound A2 in the same house as Kandathe's brother Ukkurala (A2:Z2); their marriage was registered in 1895, perhaps because at that date Kandathe was a candidate for the office of Vel Vidāne. In 1954 K. Murugathe (A2:3), a child of this marriage, was aged about 70; he lived in house-site XIA next door to his former son-in-law K. Dingiri Banda (A2:B2) and in the same house as B. Siriwardena (A2:Z5) from Watarekkewa (21) married *binna* to Murugathe's daughter's daughter (A2:9). None of these people is directly descended from the original owners of compound A.

The residence arrangements in compound A2 are of interest. The householders U. Kadirathe (A2:4) (house-site XII), U. Sirala (A2:5) (house-site XIV) and U. Wannihamy (A2:6) (house-site XV) are full brothers. They live in three separate houses as far apart as possible. In contrast, U. Kadirathe (A2:4) and K. Murugathe (A2:3), who also address one another as 'brother' (*ayiyā/malli*), are parallel cousins and live in different sections of the same building (house-site XI/XII). B. Ausadahamy (A2:Y) lives in compound A2 by virtue of the fact that his *binna*-married wife, P. Sumanawathie (A2:H), has rights in this compound through her father's mother (A2:2). Furthermore this marriage was regarded as an exchange marriage paired with the marriage of B. Hetuhamy (Y:1) to U. Kadirathe's daughter K. Ran Manika (Y:A2); it was largely on this account that B. Ausadahamy's house (house-site XIII) was built on land which belonged to his brother-in-law K.V. Appuhamy (A2:7). This pair of exchange marriages linked the Pul Eliya ruling clique with the compound of Badderāla Arachchi of Yakawewa. The latter had affinal links with various local politicians and government officials. B. Hetuhamy (Y:1) was true son of Badderāla Arachchi and was Vel Vidāne of Yakawewa. Ausadahamy had no close blood connection with Hetu-hamy, but his mother had at one time been wife to Badderāla Arachchi and this was sufficient to make Ausadahamy and Hetuhamy into 'brothers'. It was originally intended that Hetuhamy's marriage should be *binna* and Ausadahamy's marriage *dīga*, but when Hetuhamy's efforts to purchase compound C1 were frustrated (see p. 206) he settled in Yakawewa in *dīga* status while Ausadahamy came to live *binna* in Pul Eliya.

Compound B

It was claimed that in times past members of this compound regularly provided the Gamarāla of the Meda bāga. Documentary evidence shows that ever since 1860 the actual title was always held elsewhere; on the other hand two recent members of compound B have held the title Badderāla. The compound has now split into two parts. B1 comprises house-sites II and XVIII and garden plots τ and Ω; B2 comprises house-sites III, IIIA, IIIB and IIIX, the last being a small shop. House-site IIIC can be considered an adjunct to this compound but is, strictly speaking, an encroachment on Crown land. Garden plot δ, which was formerly part of compound B1, was inherited by P. Ran Etani (W:J) from her mother W. Sithi Etani (J:B1), and then sold to U. Kuda Pinhamy (B2:E3). It is, therefore, now part of compound B2. The B1 group are wealthy and influential (V. Menikrala (B1:7) is the Vel Vidāne); the B2 group are poor. The latter originally came to Pul Eliya as clients of the B1 group; they now tend to regard themselves as clients of compound A2, stressing the affinal link represented by K. Dingiri Banda (A2:B2).

Compound C

This was the most influential group during the period 1860–1900, but with the death of Kadirathe Gamarāla (C:3) its fortunes declined rapidly. Kadirathe Gamarāla (C:3) had two sons Punchirala Gamarāla (D2:C) and Appurala Vedarāla (C:6) and one daughter Walli Etani (C:7). When the last named married *binna* the priest's cousin, Ranhamy (C:N) of Nawana, they set up house on a site which has now become a separate compound C2 (house-site VII). Kadirathe Gamarāla (C:3) also reared Mudalihamy (C:Z2) a son of his second wife by another father Z(C), a man of 'wrong *variga*'. At marriage, Punchirala Gamarāla (D2:C) set up house in compound D2 (see below). Also living in compound C at this time was Kadirathe Gamarāla's half-brother, Ukkurala Vidāne (H:1), who was Vel Vidāne of Pul Eliya, 1896–1907. Ukkurala occupied house-site XX, but as a result of a complex deal with Appurala Vidāne (A1:W) this house-site became separated off to form a new compound (compound G) (see p. 198). Thus, on the death of Kadirathe Gamarāla (C:3), and after the departure of Ukkurala (H:1), the remnant of compound C consisted of the present compound C1 (Map D (b)) embracing house-sites XIX and XXI and a block of garden land in between. In possession were the step-brothers Appurala Vedarāla (C:6) and Mudalihamy (C:Z2); Mudalihamy died first and then Appurala Vedarāla. At Appurala's death three of Mudalihamy's children were resident in the compound, M. Kirala (C1:2), M. Kirihamy II (Cx:1), M. Sinni Etani (C1:1) and the compound grounds had been extended westwards outside the *gamgoda* area to include plot 128 and house-sites XVI, XVIA (that is compound Cx). Appurala Vedarāla's legitimate heir was his son A.V. Bandathe (Z:C) who lived outside Pul Eliya. U. Kadirathe (A2:4), the then Vel Vidāne, offered to buy the property from A.V. Bandathe for cash, intending to give it to his son-in-law B. Hetuhamy (Y:1) (see p. 102), but the children of Mudalihamy (C:Z2) refused to be dispossessed. After a lawsuit the children of Mudalihamy obtained title deeds but had to pay A.V. Bandathe cash compensation.

It follows that the present occupant of house-site XXI (U.V. Pinhamy (C1:W)) lives in compound C1, not because he is a son's son of Naidurala Gamarāla II (C:2), but because he is married to a daughter of Mudalihamy (C:Z2). U.V. Pinhamy (C1:W) was reared by his mother in Wiralmurippu. In 1954 the Vel Vidāne (B1:7) took the line that, because of A.V. Bandathe's forced sale, *all* U.V. Pinhamy's hereditary rights in compound C had lapsed, but on this rather tricky point of law the Vel Vidāne was clearly a prejudiced witness.

Walli Etani (C:7) who inherited house-site VII was childless, but on the death (or divorce?) of Punchirala Gamarāla's first wife, the younger child of that marriage, P. Kapuruhamy (C2:D2), was adopted by Walli Etani (C:7) his aunt. P. Kapuruhamy has now inherited the house-site (that is compound C2).

Compound D

In 1886 the head of this compound was Kadira Velathe Mohottāla (D1:2) (see above, plots 18–20, 30–8). At this time the compound boundaries evidently included the present compounds D1 and H and parts of F and A1 (that is house-sites IV, VI and IX). Compound D2 (house-site V) was then a separate enclave occupied by a family of Washerman (Hēnayā) caste. This family either died out or moved away before 1890 and since then the ritual duties of washermen have been performed by a Hēnayā family from Lindahitidamana (62). After compound D 2 thus fell vacant it was occupied by Punchirala Gamarāla (D 2: C) who moved into it from compound C (see above).

It would appear that Kadira Velathe Mohottāla (D 1:2), or else his immediate heirs, must have gone bankrupt, for a large part of the compound was acquired by Appurala Vidāne (A 1:W). Part of this has been incorporated in compound A 1 and part now forms compound H.

The portion of land now remaining to the descendants of Kadira Velathe Mohottāla is very small; it comprises only compound D 1 (house-site VI), but the rights in question are jealously preserved. The members of compound Dx (see Table 1), though mostly residing outside the *gamgoda* area, are, by succession, members of compound D 1 and they assert their claims there. As will be seen from Appendix 2, the collapse in the fortunes of compound D has been linked with diverse accusations of caste scandal and witchcraft.

In most *pavula* contexts the present-day members of compound D are usually to be found allied with compound C, even though the kinship basis for such alliance is relatively weak. The political solidarity of these two compounds appears to date back to the middle of the nineteenth century.

Compound E

This compound (plot η on Map C), owned by U. Kuda Pinhamy (B 2:E 3), has not been occupied for many years; the owner refuses to live there on the ground that the land is haunted. The garden in question contains a Bo tree, which suggests that there may once have been a temple on this site. The last individual actually to reside in compound E was U. Kuda Pinhamy's mother's father's father (E: 1), whose name is not now remembered. Kuda Pinhamy's anxiety not to reside in compound E is difficult to justify on any rational grounds, but his feelings on the matter were strong. When his *bānā* Menikrala (B 2:6) and Wannihamy (B 2:7) tried to get him to move out of compound B 2 he managed to purchase the garden plot δ (Map C) from P. Ran Etani (W: J) and thus consolidated his status as a rightful member of compound B.

215

Compound F

At present the site of the main village shop (house-site IX). The owner, K.V. Kapuruhamy (F:Dw) claimed that he has the land by inheritance from his grandfather Kapurala Vedarāla (F:1). His brother-in-law, P. Kapuruhamy (C:D2), claimed that he gave the land to his sister as dowry. The true facts are obscure. The compound today includes the garden plot γ on Map C.

Compound G

See remarks concerning plot 17 and compound C. Compound contains house-site XX.

Compound H

See remarks concerning plot 17 and compound D. Ukkurala Vidāne (H:1), who originally lived in compound G, then a part of compound C, probably lived in compound H for a period before leaving Pul Eliya in 1907. The compound now contains house-sites IV and IVA. The latter is a shed housing K. Ukkurala (H(S)), client of U.G. Pinhamy (H:A2).

Compound J

It would seem that this ground (garden plot β, Map C) was originally part of compound F and that Kirihamy ge Pulingurala (J:1) resided there with his wife Ukki Etani (F:2). However, when the village was surveyed in 1900, the area was unoccupied and was treated as Crown land. It was later purchased by Ukki Etani's son, Punchirala Anumātirāla (J:2), who erected a house there. He later sold the land to a Tamil trader (T:3) whose daughter, resident in Medawachchiya (66), is still the owner.

Compound X (house-site I)

The ordinary villagers do not admit that this is part of the village at all. The name given to it (p. 54, n. 1) which can be translated 'the house perched on the other side' is equivalent to the American 'on the wrong side of the tracks'. For explanation of this prejudice see Appendix 2.

CHAPTER VI

NON-TRADITIONAL LAND TENURE

This chapter, like the last, is largely taken up with factual evidence, but I am concerned here to validate a different proposition. In chapter v I sought to show that the formal elaboration and symmetry of the *bāga* system in the traditional-style land tenure of the Old Field has the effect of constraining the kinship organisation of the community which owns the land. In Pul Eliya, I argued, people adapt their kinship allegiances to fit the topographical facts of the Old Field rather than the other way about. I also showed that in the only recorded instance of a major change in the Old Field layout the immediate consequences for the associated kinship group were catastrophic.

But in this present chapter we are concerned with new forms of tenure introduced under the auspices of the British Colonial regime. How have these new tenures affected Pul Eliya social organisation? Alternatively, how far has the established structure of Pul Eliya society modified the impact of the new tenures?

Clearly the problem needs to be considered in historical perspective. In 1954 Pul Eliya villagers had had experience of freehold (*sinakkara*) tenures for more than a generation; they had come to terms with the system and even approved of it. But the Crown leasehold (*badu idam*) system introduced under the Land Development Ordinance of 1935 was still a novelty. All *badu* land in Pul Eliya was still in the hands of the original grantees and no one could envisage with any certainty just how the special rules of succession, which were intrinsic to this form of tenure, were going to work out in practice.

FREEHOLD TENURE ('SINAKKARA')

The term *sinakkara* refers to land purchased outright from the Crown. Although it has been possible to acquire land in this way ever since about 1834, Pul Eliya *sinakkara* all originated at dates later than 1900.

There are two main classes of such land: (*a*) Plots lying under the Pul Eliya main tank, but requiring the construction of new irrigation ditches before they can be put into use; (*b*) *olagama* (see p. 46) in which the land is fed from a separate tank and both the tank and the land beneath it become the property of the freehold landlord.

The procedure for acquiring the land was that would-be purchasers applied for a grant to the Anurādhapura land office. After a delay, commonly lasting several years, the land office sent a surveyor who checked the area of the proposed plot and its boundaries, and the land was then sold outright to the applicants. The price, though very modest by official standards, was such that only the very wealthiest villagers could afford to make individual applications. Mostly the applications were made by syndicates.

In theory, the purchasers had no rights in the land until the sale was completed; in practice, a great deal of preliminary agricultural work was done before the application for a grant was made at all. *Sinakkara* land is useless unless it can be irrigated and the irrigation ditches were usually laid out in advance of the official survey. Furthermore, before rough jungle can be used as rice land it must be 'asweddumised', that is, cleared of tree roots, levelled out into flat terraces and carefully graded so that the irrigation water will feed into all parts of the field in a controlled and even manner. This entails a great deal of hard physical labour and also considerable skill and experiment. There is often a gap of several years between the date at which an area is first cleared of trees and the date at which it is in a state to produce irrigated rice.

The dates mentioned in this chapter should therefore be treated with some reserve. Most of them are taken from documents originating in the Anurādhapura land office.

Table 7, which is based entirely on official documents, shows the date at which the land was purchased, the surveyed area, the

Table 7. *'Sinakkara' (freeholds): sequence of title registrations*

Date	Area, acres	Land office field no.	Original purchaser	1954 plot no.	Name of 1954 owner
Before 1910	9 (5⅜ under cultivation)	3 D	Appurala Vidāne (A1:W)	108	S. Subasinghe (A1:5)
				109	A.V. Punchi Etani (B1:A1)
				110	P. Ran Banda (A1:6)
				111	R. Mudalihamy (X:3)
				112	J. Punchirala (Dx:2)
				113	N. Punchi Banda (Dx:4)
				114	N. Ran Manika (Dx:5)
				115	M. Naidurala (Dx:Y)
				116	V. Menikrala (B1:7)
				117	A.V. Punchi Etani (B1:A1)
1919	4 (uncleared)	3 K	Kapuruhamy ge Kirihamy (?) Kadirathe Vedarāla (Dw:F)	—	Various heirs of Kadirathe Vedarala (Dw:F)
1921	4¾	3 R	U. Kapuruhamy (B2:5)	131	K. Menikrala (B2:6)
				132	K. Appuhamy (W:B2)
				133	K. Wannihamy (B2:7)
		3 S	W. Mudalihamy (B1:3) A.V. Sirala (A1:4)	134	S. Subasinghe (A1:5)
				135	P. Ran Banda (A1:6)
				136	A.V. Punchi Etani (B1:A1)
1921	1¼	3 Q	K. Ukkurala (B2:4)	130 pt	U. Kuda Pinhamy (B2:E3)
1921	—	3 WY	M. Ranhamy (X:1)	House-site	R. Punchirala (X:4)
1921	9	14 H	U. Kadirathe (A2:4) U. Sirala (A2:5) U.G. Pinhamy (H:A2) U. Wannihamy (A2:6) A. Mudalihamy (D1:Z2)	141	U. Kadirathe (A2:4)
				142	U. Wannihamy (A2:6)
				143	U.G. Pinhamy (H:A2)
				144	U. Sirala (A2:5)
				145	U. Kadirathe (A2:4)
				146	U. Wannihamy (A2:6)
				147	U.G. Pinhamy (H:A2)
1922	4¾	14 I	As 14H 'U Kadirathe and four others'	138	U.G. Pinhamy (H:A2)
				139	K.V. Appuhamy (A2:7)
				140	U. Sirala (A2:5)
				140a	U. Wannihamy (A2:6)
1922	2	3 AA	Appurala Vidāne (A1:W)	125	S. Subasinghe (A1:5)
				126	P. Ran Banda (A1:6)
				127	A.V. Punchi Etani (B1:A1)
1923	4	3 AC	K. Velathe (B1:6) P. Jangurala (D1:4)	120	V. Menikrala (B1:7)
				121	M. Naidurala (Dx:Y)
				122	N. Punchi Banda (Dx:4)
				123	N. Ran Manika (Dx:5)
	½	14 J	P. Jangurala (D1:4)	129 pt.	J. Punchirala (Dx:2)
1924		3 AE	A. Mudalihamy (D1:Z2)	Abandoned house-site	
1926	3	AG/AH	Sobittu Terunanse (Priest)	Extension to temple land	
1926	3	14 M	A. Bandathe (G:Z2)	119	A. Bandathe (G:Z2)
1928	½	3 T	U. Sirala (A2:5)	130 pt.	U. Kuda Pinhamy (B2:E3)
	½	3 U	U. Murugathe (A2:3)	137 pt.	U. Wannihamy (A2:6)
1930	2	3 AJ 3 AL	U. Kapuruhamy (B2:5)	Temple Tank Land	K. Menikrala (B2:6) (areas marked TR and TG on Map *B*)
1930	½	14 R	M. Kirihamy II (Cx:1)	128	K. Tikiri Banda (Cx:2)
1934	½			Compound Cx	K. Tikiri Banda (Cx:2)
1932	3	14 Y	U. Wannihamy (A2:6)	137 pt.	U. Wannihamy (A2:6)

plot numbers as recorded on Map *B* and Table 6 (pp. 188 f.), the plot number on the official land office map, the name of the original grantee, and finally the name of the present owner.

Apart from plot 3 K, which was purchased in 1919 but has never been cleared at all, the plots were regularly taken up in the order in which they might most easily be irrigated. In this way, by 1934 all the readily utilisable land in the immediate vicinity of the Pul Eliya Old Field had passed into private hands.

The government rules regarding *sinakkara* sales were designed to produce distinct farmsteads of viable size in independent ownership. To some extent the villagers circumvented this by forming themselves into syndicates and then dividing up the land into small parcels as soon as they had acquired it. To a quite surprising extent they managed to reproduce in the *sinakkara* fields the 'fragmented' pattern of holding which characterises the traditional Old Field system. This demonstration that the villagers value 'fragmentation' for its own sake is of great interest and calls for careful examination.

As might be expected, it is the earliest of the *sinakkara* holdings which most closely reproduce the traditional pattern.

Field 3 D (*plots* 108–17)

The first entry in the official register of freeholds is field 3 D, which is recorded without date under the name of Appurala Vel Vidāne (A 1: W). The purchase must have been completed around 1908. The field lies immediately below the Pul Eliya Old Field and is now irrigated by an extension of the main channel to that field. From another point of view it consists of land at the back of the abandoned tank Kumbukwewa and may once have formed part of the bed of that tank.

The field must have been at least partly asweddumised before the 1900 survey. Late nineteenth-century tax records for Pul Eliya refer periodically to a field of 8 *pāla* extent, described as *wew tawalla* (tank-bed cultivation) and to another field (or perhaps the same one) of similar size called *alut asswedduma* (newly terraced field). In 1886 this field was cultivated by thirteen different individuals including representatives of all three *bāga*, the trader Alisandini Nikala Pulle and even the washerman Kapura Pediya.

However, at the time of the 1900 survey, this area was treated as Crown land and not as a *purāna* holding.

Although the land office record shows Appurala Vidāne as sole purchaser, village tradition is that shares were also contributed by (*a*) Appurala's half-brother Kirihamy (W:5) (Wiralmurippu), (*b*) P. Jangurala (D 1:4), and (*c*) K. Velathe (B 1:6). It is worth noting that, though these people were *not* closely related at the time, their descendants have established fairly close affinal links. Appurala's son's son Subasinghe (A 1:5) is married to a sister's daughter of Jangurala's wife. Velathe's son Menikrala (B 1:7) is married to a daughter's daughter of Jangurala's sister. Appurala's daughter A.V. Punchi Etani (B 1:A 1) married Mudalihamy Badderāla (B 1:3), who was Velathe's cross-cousin.

After purchase the land was laid out strictly in traditional style. It was measured out lengthways into 10-fathom strips (*issaraval*) and found to be rather over 110 fathoms long. Sixty fathoms were allocated to the Upper *pota pangu*, 30 fathoms to the Lower *pota pangu* and 20 fathoms to the *elapata*. The strips were then allocated as follows (in sequence starting from the Old Field end, see Map *F*):

Upper pota	Fathoms	Original owner	1954 plot no.
Elapata	15+	Appurala	109; 110 pt.
Panguva no. 1	20	Appurala and Kirihamy	108; 111
Panguva no. 2	20	Jangurala	112–15
Panguva no. 3	20	Velathe	116
Elapata	5+	Appurala	110 pt.; 117
Lower pota			
Panguva no. 1	10	Appurala and Kirihamy	a, b
Panguva no. 2	10	Jangurala	c, d
Panguva no. 3	10	Velathe	e, f

The Lower *pota* has never been asweddumised so the fence at the bottom end of the field actually runs between plots 'a' and 'b'. This fence is the responsibility of the *pangu* holders as in the Old Field. The holdings have all been inherited in quite uncomplicated fashion by direct succession except for plot 111. Plot 115, which is listed as belonging to M. Naidurala (Dx:Y), really belongs to his wife, Jangurala's younger daughter (Dx:3).

The complex circumstances surrounding plot 111 are elaborated elsewhere (Appendix 2). Briefly, Kirihamy mortgaged the land to a

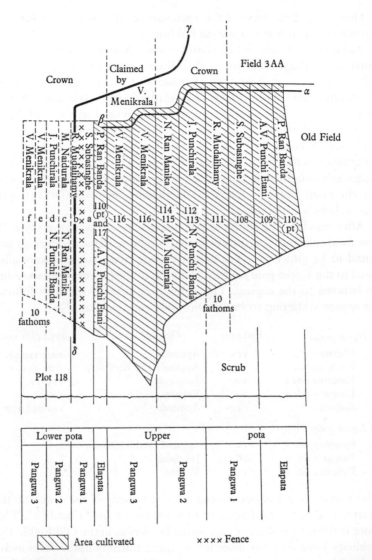

Map *F*. Pul Eliya *sinnakkara* Field 3 D. Details of strips and plot allocation. Shaded area under cultivation. Area included in dotted lines uncleared and unterraced. Black line γ–δ shows R. Punchirala's irrigation channel. Line α–β is extension of Old Field irrigation channel used to irrigate plots 108–17. For detailed discussion see pp. 221, 318.

trader and gave the deed to Kiri Etani, a foster-daughter of Appurala. The latter, through her husband P.V. Bandathe of Walpola (63), sold the deed to R. Mudalihamy (X:3) who redeemed the mortgage. Mudalihamy now lives in Syambalagaswewa (85) and regularly leases the holding on *andē* to his brother R. Punchirala (X:4).

It should be observed that, because the land has been divided up according to the traditional system which involves 'fragmentation' of individual holdings, each shareholder has got a usable piece of ground. If the land had been shared out according to English ideas at least one shareholder would have received a piece of land which he could not cultivate for want of water.

Field 3 K

The second plot to be purchased from the Crown was 3 K, which was acquired in 1919. It has never been cleared and the circumstances surrounding the purchase are now obscure. The present owners are the children of the original purchasers.

V. Menikrala (B 1:7), the present Vel Vidāne, controls the only irrigation channel from which this plot might be irrigated. He and the shopkeeper, K.V. Kapuruhamy (F:Dw), have both tried to persuade the other heirs to sell out their rights. In this competition, the fact that Menikrala controls the irrigation channel gives him an obvious advantage.

Field 3 RS (*plots* 130–6)

The third block to be acquired, 3 RS, was purchased in 1921.[1] The money for the purchase was again put up by Appurala Vidāne (A1:W), but the names of the purchasers are recorded as three, first, W. Mudalihamy (B1:3), Appurala's son-in-law, secondly, A.V. Sirala (A1:4), Appurala's own son, and thirdly U. Kapurala, which seems to be a mistake for U. Kapuruhamy (B2:5), who was foster-brother to Mudalihamy and stood in a client relationship with Appurala. The shares were $1\frac{3}{4}$ acres to Appurala, $1\frac{1}{2}$ acres to Mudalihamy, $1\frac{1}{2}$ acres to Kapuruhamy. The land is now held by immediate descendants of these three men in like proportions. As in the case of field 3 D it was irrigated by tapping into the main irrigation channel of the Old Field.

---

[1] Although the sale was confirmed only in 1921 the application for the land had gone in on 2 August 1919, that is a fortnight before the original application for block 3 K.

223

Fields 14 I, 14 H (plots 137-47)

The development of this land synchronised with two other more complicated projects. In order to develop the land to the north of the Old Field and to the south of the stream Wan Ela, two entirely new main irrigation channels had to be constructed. The northern channel was originally designed to feed fields AA and AC (plots 120–3, 125–7), the southern channel to feed fields 14 I and 14 H (plots 138–47). The southern area was tackled first by K.G. Punchirala Gamarāla (D 2 : C), but he failed to produce a satisfactory irrigation channel and abandoned his application for a grant. Soon afterwards U. Kadirathe (A 2 : 4), profiting by his elder's mistake, completed a satisfactory channel and then obtained Appurala Vidāne's support for financing the purchase of an area totalling nearly 14 acres. Some features of this acquisition are discussed further in Appendix 2.

Of the partners to the transaction Kadirathe (A 2 : 4), the leader, was Appurala Vidāne's '*bānā*' (Kadirathe's mother and Appurala's wife were cross-cousins); U.G. Pinhamy (H : A 2) was married to Appurala's adopted daughter and was brother to U. Kadirathe; U. Sirala (A 2 : 5), also a brother to U. Kadirathe, had just married A. Mudalihamy's daughter (D 1 : 8); U. Wannihamy (A 2 : 6), the fifth shareholder, was U. Kadirathe's youngest brother and a boy of 10 years old. The fact that this child was registered from the start as one of the original purchasers demonstrates the ease with which the villagers flouted the regulations and also the strong feeling that shareholdings must be widely distributed.

The present distribution of strip ownership makes it clear that the *combined* holding (14 H + 14 I) was laid out in the traditional fashion though the British administrators would certainly have been highly embarrassed if they had realised this. The field consists of regular 5-fathom strips except for plot 140 *a* which is an irregular corner-piece. The allocation is shown on the facing page.

The 'theory' of the layout is that the field is in three *pota* which have proportional sizes 1 : 2 : 4, the strips in *pota* 'a' being in the reverse order to the strips in the other two. Kadirathe, as leader, gets a special *gamvasama* allocation in the upper *pota* and U.G. Pinhamy as eldest brother gets an *elapata* which makes him responsible for the fencing at both ends of the field.

U. Wannihamy originally got a much smaller share than the others

Land office field no.	Field section (traditional)		1954 plot no.	Owner	Relative size (depth of holding in 5-fathom strips)
	ELAPATA		138 pt.	U.G. Pinhamy (H:A2)	1
	P	Panguva 1	138 pt.	U.G. Pinhamy (H:A2)	1
	O	Panguva 2	139 pt.	U. Kadirathe (A2:4)	1
14I	T	GAMVASAMA	139 pt.	U. Kadirathe (A2:4)	3
	A	Panguva 3	140 pt.	U. Sirala (A2:5)	1
	'A'	Panguva 4	140a	U. Wannihamy (A2:6)	Irregular*
	P	Panguva 3	140 pt.	U. Sirala (A2:5)	2
——————	O	Panguva 2	141	U. Kadirathe (A2:4)	2
	T	Panguva 4	142	U. Wannihamy (A2:6)	1*
	A	Panguva 1	143	U.G. Pinhamy (H:A2)	2
	'B'				
	P	Panguva 3	144	U. Sirala (A2:5)	4
14H	O	Panguva 2	145	U. Kadirathe (A2:4)	4
	T	Panguva 4	146	U. Wannihamy (A2:6)	1*
	A	Panguva 1	147	U.G. Pinhamy (H:A2)	4
	'C'				

* The holdings of U. Wannihamy are a kind of token. Field 14Y (Plot 137), which he acquired later, represents the 'missing portion' of *panguva* 4 in the above schema.

because of his age, but the partners carefully left the field block 14Y (plot 137) out of their initial application. Part of this was later purchased by K. Murugathe (A2:3) on U. Wannihamy's behalf, and the rest was acquired by Wannihamy himself in 1932.[1] In terms of the original layout of this field area, plot 137 represents the missing portion of *panguva* 4.

Fields 3 AA, 3 AC (plots 120–8)

The arrangement on the north side of the Old Field followed similar lines. Here Appurala Vidāne teamed up with the same partners as had assisted him in the purchase of field 3 D though this time his half-brother Kirihamy (W:5) was not brought in.

As in the previous case the cultivators ignored the land office

[1] U. Wannihamy (A2:6) is full brother to U. Kadirathe, but ten years younger. His parents died while he was an infant and he was brought up in the family of K. Murugathe, his classificatory elder brother, but thirty years his senior.

distinction between field 3 AA and field 3 AC. The combined block was irrigated from one channel, 2 acres being allocated to each of the principal partners, Appurala Vidāne (A 1 : W), Jangurala (D 1 : 4) and Velathe (B 1 : 6). This time, however, the land was not broken up into *pota* and *pangu*. As a result, the holders of plots 125–7 are at a disadvantage compared with the holders of plots 120–3; in fact parts of the former block have not been fully asweddumised because of lack of water.

Individually held freeholds

The only other parcels of freehold rice land are:

(*a*) Plot 130, acquired by U. Kuda Pinhamy (B 2 : E 3), partly by inheritance from his father and partly by purchase from U. Sirala (A 2 : 5), but never properly developed.

(*b*) Plot 129, the property of J. Punchirala (Dx : 2), which lies to the rear of compound Dx where Punchirala now lives. Irrigated from the Old Field waste flow.

(*c*) Plot 119, land purchased by Appurala Vidāne (A 1 : W) and given to A. Bandathe (G : 22), who had married his adopted daughter (see p. 198, remarks concerning plot 17 and compound G). No regular irrigation; relies on rain-water and waste water from the Old Field.

(*d*) Land register plots 3 AJ, 3 AL purchased by U. Kapuruhamy (B 2 : 5). No regular irrigation; can draw water from the Temple Tank in some conditions. The plots are marked TR, TG on Map *B*.

(*e*) Plot 128 lying between compound C and compound Cx. This is excellent land belonging to the owners of compound Cx. Prior to 1930 a government regulation had forbidden cultivation within 30 fathoms (*tis bamba*) of the tank bund, which explains why this ground was not taken up before.

The common feature about the plots in this list is that (i) they are held by single individuals and not by shareholding syndicates, and (ii) they are not linked with any of the main irrigation channels. The reason for this is that, generally speaking, a single individual is not capable of constructing and maintaining a large irrigation channel, and land based on such a channel has to be worked as a co-operative venture from the start.

Conclusions

There are two features of the *sinakkara* land development which seem to me most striking. The first is the manner in which Appurala Vidāne (A 1 : W), who was Vel Vidāne of Pul Eliya during most of the relevant period, managed to give himself and his friends a completely dominating economic position in the village. The descendants of Appurala (A 1 : W), Jangurala (D 1 : 4), Velathe (B 1 : 6) and U. Kadirathe (A 2 : 4) have almost completely squeezed out the opposition groups associated with compound C. The second is the remarkable ingenuity with which the villagers got round the letter of government regulations so as to reproduce in the earlier *sinakkara* holdings a pattern plainly modelled on the traditional *bāga-pota* system. That the villagers did this is relevant to my thesis for it confirms my argument that, in this society, structural continuity is to be found in the arrangements of the field system rather than in the ordering of kinship relations.

'BADU IDAM'

I shall postpone discussion of the *olagama* type of freehold and proceed direct to an examination of *badu idam*. This category of land, created by the Land Development Ordinance of 1935,[1] was designed to protect from exploitation the class of poor peasants which the inequitable rules of *sinakkara* freehold tenure had created. The formal rules of the system were roughly as follows:

Plots of Crown land, usually 2 acres in extent, were leased in perpetuity to a single title-holder at a nominal annual rent. The title-holder was required to 'asweddumise' the land (for which improvement he received a cash grant) and to maintain the land in cultivation. The title could be transmitted intact to a single heir whose name was specified in the deed of lease. The Crown retained the right to evict the tenant if the latter transgressed the rules of the lease. Since title could not be transferred without the consent of the Crown mortgaging in any form was impossible.

[1] Some leases date from 1933. It is not clear how this came about.

15-2

In theory, tenancies were to be allotted only to the landless, and the identity of these landless individuals was to be certified by the *tulāna* Headman. But the framers of the regulations seem to have been remarkably obscure in their definition of 'landlessness'.

An official document dated 1941 records that there were twenty-eight adult males in Pul Eliya entitled to *badu* leases on the grounds that they 'owned 1 acre of land or less'. It also records that at this date there were twenty 'families' (? married couples) in the village and that the total population was only eighty-two. I was not able to discover just how these figures had been computed, but it is quite obvious that the 'twenty-eight landless adult males' must have included the sons of relatively wealthy men. They were 'landless' simply because they had not yet inherited from their parents.

Quite a number of such men seem to have acquired *badu* leases in due course. It would be indiscreet to investigate too closely as to how this came about. Perhaps the scheme was unworkable from the start or perhaps the villagers simply outwitted the administration.

The approximate sequence of *badu* leases is shown in Table 8. It will be seen that although nine *badu* leases had been issued by 1945 not one of these had been allocated to a poor peasant. In every case the *badu* holding was simply an extension to land already held on *sinakkara* freehold.

Plots 148–50

Plots 148, 149, 150, which were opened up between 1950–2, were entirely new holdings but they are irrigated by an extension of a channel belonging to compound A 2. As might have been expected, we find that the *badu* holders of these plots also turn out to be members of compound A 2.

The case of **plot 148** is particularly revealing. It is registered in the name of B. Hetuhamy (Y: 1) and since the only other land with which he is credited is plot 76—half an acre in the Old Field—he was presumably represented to the authorities as a 'poor peasant of Pul Eliya'. As has been remarked before, this man is son-in-law to the wealthy

Table 8. *Badu idam* (*Crown leaseholds*):
sequence of title registrations

Date* of lease	1954 plot no.	Name
1933	129 extension	J. Punchirala (Dx:2)
1936	Land under Temple Tank	U. Kapuruhamy (B2:5)
1936	128 extension	K. Kirihamy (Cx:1)
1941	House-site XVII	M. Naidurala (Dx:Y)
1941	Land adjacent to XVII	R. Punchirala (X:4)
1941	119 extension	A. Bandathe (G:Z2)
1945	120 extension	V. Menikrala (B1:7)
1945	121–3 extension	M. Naidurala (Dx:7)
1945	125–7 extension	S. Subasinghe (A1:5) / A.V. Punchi Etani (B1:A1) / P. Ran Banda (A1:6)
1950	149	K. Dingiri Banda (A2:B2)
1950	118	R. Punchirala (X:4)
1952	148	B. Hetuhamy (Y:1)
1952	137 extension	U. Wannihamy (A2:6)
1952	150	U. Sirala (A2:5)
1952	151	U. Kuda Pinhamy (B2:E3)
1952	151A	K. Menikrala (B2:6)
1954	152	K. Wannihamy (B2:7)
1955?	153	Punchirala Gamarāla (D2:C)
—	154	P. Kapuruhamy (C2:D2)
—	155	K. Tikiri Banda (Cx:2)
—	156	M. Kirala (C1:2)
—	157	U.V. Pinhamy (C1:W)
—	158	S. Jaymanhamy (D1:9)
—	159	A. Sitti Etani (D1:Z3)

* Dates are those at which title was finally registered. Land was usually 'asweddumised' several years in advance of this date. Title deeds for plots 153 onwards had not been issued in November 1954.

and influential U. Kadirathe (A2:4), and son and heir of Badderāla Arachchi of Yakawewa (43), one of the wealthiest landowners of the district. In 1954 Hetuhamy was himself Vel Vidāne of Yakawewa. The owners of plots 149 and 150 are likewise very far from being 'poor peasants'.

Plot 118

Plot 118 (deed registered in 1950) was also new land, the holder being the 'outcaste' R. Punchirala (X:4). This case is such a complicated one that it deserves a special analysis (see Appendix 2). It illustrates very clearly a large number of the sociological principles which have emerged in the course of this monograph.

Plots 151–2

The owners of **plots 151** and **152** (developed between 1952 and 1954) were members of compound B2 and poor peasants in a genuine sense. In this case the necessary extension of the main irrigation channel from plot 137 to plot 151 (see Map *B*) received a special government subsidy, but even so it could only be supplied with water by the special favour of the members of compound A2. As emphasised previously, compound group B2 have been the dependent affines of compound group A2 for many years (see pp. 92, 213).

The analysis of *sinakkara* holdings has already shown how one result of Appurala Vidāne's operations at the beginning of the century was to split Pul Eliya into two economically differentiated factions. Compound groups A1, A2, B1 and Dx acquired all the wealth and influence, while compound groups C and D2 came to form an opposition faction which contained most of the genuine poor peasants in the community. It is remarkable that down to 1954, *despite the supposed purposes of the Land Development Ordinance*, not a single member of the underprivileged opposition had succeeded in getting a title to *badu* land.

The basic reason for this was not official corruption or inefficiency, but the more elementary fact that it was the Vel Vidāne's faction which controlled all the main irrigation channels. In these circumstances it was a waste of time for the opposition even to apply for land.

Kumbukwewa Field (plots 153–9)

In 1954 these underprivileged families were at last able to open up *badu* land, namely **plots 153–9** (Map *B*). They were able to do this because the government had intervened to recondition a small disused tank (Kumbukwewa) lying just to the west of plot 149. The government had also paid the cost of constructing a new main irrigation ditch which would serve these new *badu* plots.

Since, in theory, the claims of each individual applicant for *badu* land are considered on their merits, a factor such as 'kinship with neighbours' ought not to be relevant. But in this case, also, the villagers had successfully evaded the absurdities of the official regulations. I do not know quite how it was managed but the 'poor peasants' who were finally allocated holdings under the Kumbukwewa tank turned out to be a group of close kin. Thus:

Plot		Relation to leader
153	Punchirala Gamarāla (D2:C)	Leader
154	P. Kapuruhamy (C2:D2)	Son
155	K. Tikiri Banda (Cx:2)	Step-brother's grandson
156	M. Kirala (C1:2)	Step-brother's son
157	U.V. Pinhamy (C1:W)	Step-brother's son-in-law and classificatory half-brother
158	S. Jaymanhamy (D1:9)	Brother-in-law of Cx:2, holder of plot 155
159	A. Sitti Etani (D1:Z3)	Sister-in-law of K. Punchi Etani (D1:6) the grandmother of D1:9

The last-named might seem to be a rather marginal 'relative', but her presence in the list gives a clue to the villagers' technique for dealing with *badu* applications. A. Sitti Etani (D1:Z3), an elderly landless widow supporting a 9-year-old grandson, was clearly the strongest possible kind of applicant in terms of the government regulations, especially since the villagers could say, quite truthfully, that she had no *close* relatives living in Pul Eliya. But her land was actually worked by S. Jaymanhamy (D1:9) the holder of the adjacent plot 158, who, as her nearest local male relative (sister-in-law's grandson), would be expected to assist in her support in any case. Had Jaymanhamy applied for this extra holding in his own name, he would almost certainly have failed to get the grant.

Map *B*, plots 160–6 do not concern us. They were held under *badu* title by villagers from Tulawelliya (59). According to tradition the original Kumbukwewa tank had belonged to Tulawelliya in the first place.

IRRIGATION CONTROL AND THE DEVELOPMENTAL
SEQUENCE OF 'SINAKKARA' AND 'BADU' HOLDINGS

This total sequence of events demonstrates the truth of my earlier assertion that what really matters in the Pul Eliya situation is not the title to ground, but the rights over water and over irrigation ditches. Property in land is worthless unless it is linked with rights to draw water to irrigate the land. To irrigate land an owner must co-operate with others in the operation of an irrigation channel and the most likely group of people to do this effectively is a group of kinsmen.

In the Old Field, where the layout of the land was fixed, long-term kinship alliances were maintained so as to fit the facts of land tenure. In the new fields we can recognise two complementary processes. On the one hand, land is shared out among unrelated friends who thereafter establish kinship alliances; on the other, we note the syndication of kinsmen to work a common irrigation channel.

In the 'old days', all rice land under the Pul Eliya main tank was fed from a single main irrigation channel, the upkeep of which was the responsibility of all villagers alike. Irrigation thus served to consolidate the community. Whatever the cause and nature of factional strife might be, all must co-operate in the crucial matter of water allocation.

But today, if the Old Field and the various *sinakkara* and *badu* landholdings be considered together, there are in all four separate channels, each separately owned and managed. Thus:

Channel 1: the main feeder to the Old Field (plots 1–107) maintained by all villagers.

> 1 *a*.   Branch channel to plots 130–6 maintained by
>
> S. Subasinghe (A1:5) ⎫
> P. Ran Banda (A1:6) ⎬ Compound A1
> A.V. Punchi Etani (B1:A1) ⎭
> K. Menikrala (B2:6) ⎫
> K. Wannihamy (B2:7) ⎬ Compound B2
> U. Kuda Pinhamy (B2:E3) ⎭

1 *b*.   Branch channel to plots 108–17 maintained by

> S. Subasinghe (A 1 : 5)
> P. Ran Banda (A 1 : 6) ⎫ Compound A 1
> A.V. Punchi Etani (B 1 : A 1) ⎭⎫
> V. Menikrala (B 1 : 7) ⎬ Compound B 1
> J. Punchirala (Dx : 2) ⎫
> N. Punchi Banda (Dx : 4) ⎬ Compound Dx
> N. Ran Manika (Dx : 5) ⎭
> M. Naidurala (Dx : Y)

Channel 2: on the north side of Old Field leading to plots 120–7, maintained by same group which maintains channel 1 *b*.

Channel 3: on the south side of Old Field leading to plots 137–52, maintained by

> U. Kadirathe (A 2 : 4) ⎫
> U. Sirala (A 2 : 5) ⎪
> U. Wannihamy (A 2 : 6) ⎪
> K.V. Appuhamy (A 2 : 7) ⎬ Compound A 2
> U.G. Pinhamy (H : A 2) ⎪
> K. Dingiri Banda (A 2 : B 2) ⎪
> B. Hetuhamy (Y : 1) ⎭
> U. Kuda Pinhamy (B 2 : E 3) ⎫
> K. Menikrala (B 2 : 6) ⎬ Compound B 2
> K. Wannihamy (B 2 : 7) ⎭

Channel 4: Kumbukwewa restored tank, leading to plots 153–9, maintained by

> Punchirala Gamarāla (D 2 : C) ⎫
> P. Kapuruhamy (C 2 : D 2) ⎬ Compound D
> S. Jaymanhamy (D 1 : 9) ⎭
> U.V. Pinhamy (C 1 : W) ⎫
> M. Kirala (C 1 : 2) ⎬ Compound C 1
> K. Tikiri Banda (Cx : 2) ⎫
> K. Nanghamy (Cx : 3) ⎬ Compound Cx

The control of the channels corresponds very closely to the general pattern of factionalism which has repeatedly appeared in other parts of this book. The 'rich compounds' A 1, A 2, B 1 with

233

their dependent group B2, are allied together against the 'poor compounds' C and D, with the marginal compound Dx here ranged on the side of affluence.

It is not an absolutely clear-cut division for there are affinal ties which bridge the gap between the rival factions, but this ordering of the community in terms of their ownership of irrigation channels confirms my view that in this society the recognition of kinship is constantly being adjusted to fit the ground.

ENCROACHED LAND

Reference back to Map *B* will show that there are still certain parts of the cultivated area which have not so far been discussed. These areas are officially classified as 'encroached land'. They consist of (*a*) extensions to plots 120–8 in a northerly direction, (*b*) an extension westward of plot 118, (*c*) a southerly extension of plot 150.

The origin of these cultivated areas is as follows. Towards the end of the war the Ceylon administration was desperately anxious to increase paddy production by every means possible. For a brief period all restrictions on the use of Crown land were withdrawn. The villagers were told that if they would 'asweddumise' sections of Crown land they could do so without licence and that after the war was over they would be allocated proper *badu* titles for this land.

As might have been expected, the individuals who took advantage of this free licence were men possessed of substantial capital and enterprise. In Pul Eliya the three most active individuals were V. Menikrala (B1:7), M. Naidurala (Dx:Y), and U. Sirala (A2:5).

Unfortunately, by the time the land was ready to be brought into cultivation the war was over and Ceylon had become an independent country. The new administration felt that the promise to issue *badu* leases to relatively rich peasants was politically embarrassing, so the matter was simply left in abeyance.

In consequence by 1954 all those who had developed land under the wartime emergency regulations were legally at fault; they had encroached upon Crown land without licence or title, an offence which made them liable to heavy fines.

The attitude of the administration was ambiguous. For example U. Sirala (A2:5) had developed an 'encroachment' (plot 150) covering about 5 acres. After long dispute the Land Office gave him a *badu* title for 2 acres, thereby implying that the remaining 3 acres of 'encroachment' were illegal. But in 1954 another government department allowed Sirala to hire a government bulldozer to improve the levelling of his 'illegal' field.

Most other cases of 'encroachment' were similar. Fields which had originally been cleared and 'asweddumised' with the full approval of the Land Office were now being cultivated with the knowledge and approval of the V.C.O. but the cultivators had no legal title and in 1954 appeared to have no prospect of getting one.

Since the 'encroached' fields are cultivated only during the *Mahā* season direct observation of the irrigation was impossible. I remarked, however, that although I was assured that this land had to rely on rain-water only, the various channels were so disposed that the 'encroached' fields could quite easily be irrigated from the tank.

Two special cases deserve attention. The circumstances relating to plot 118 are described in Appendix 2. Plot 124, a 4-acre field cultivated by M. Naidurala (Dx:Y) was also exceptional in that although rated as encroached land it was listed in the Pangu list as liable for *rājakāriya* duty (see p. 172).

Now, in theory, since encroached land should receive no water from the tank the cultivator of encroached land should not be liable for *rājakāriya*. Plot 124 had in fact been under cultivation for a number of years, but down to 1953 it was genuinely denied access to tank water. Then, as the result of a special arrangement with the Vel Vidāne, the field was fed with water from the northern main channel. At this point Naidurala himself insisted that he be made liable for an extra stint of *rājakāriya* duty. He clearly felt that, even in the absence of a documentary title, the appearance of his 'encroachment' in the official Pangu list would give him a legitimately recognised vested interest.

It should be remembered that, in the traditional system, the fulfilment of *rājakāriya* served to reassert the existence of a *paravēni* title. The performance of *rājakāriya* was thus a right as well as a duty.

At the 1954 village meeting the V.C.O. asked no questions about Naidurala's sudden acquisition of 4 'non-existent' acres so I presume that he was privy to what had been done.

'OLAGAMA'

The term *olagama* has been briefly mentioned at the beginning of chapter II. Colloquially the term is now used in an indiscriminate fashion to describe any small disused tank capable of restoration. (Cf. Codrington, 1938, p. 4; Pieris, 1956, p. 39.) It has long been the policy of the government to offer such tanks and their associated land freehold to any investor who is prepared to restore the tank and keep the land in cultivation. At the beginning of this century a number of such tanks in the vicinity of Pul Eliya were purchased outright by some of the wealthier villagers. The enterprise evidently proved more costly than they had anticipated for today these tanks can hardly be said to be under cultivation at all. However, the nature of the associated land tenure presents a number of points of interest. In particular, Kudawewa and Ulpathgama which lie just to the east of Pul Eliya at the back of the Pul Eliya main tank are owned by Pul Eliya villagers and therefore deserve to be discussed in the context of the present chapter.

From the government point of view the two tanks are entirely separate entities. The records concerning them are entered in separate files on separate maps. However, as can be seen from Map *G*, although the two tanks are in fact separate, the land which they serve forms one continuous block. The Pul Eliya villagers regard this as part of the ancient land of Pul Eliya, much in the same way that they consider that field 3 D (Map *F*) is part of ancient Pul Eliya land, and there are indications that at one time this tract was divided up into *bāga* in much the same way as the Pul Eliya Old Field itself.

At the time of the survey in 1900 both tanks were in bad repair and the land was classed as Crown land. However, both tanks were worked for paddy during the *Mahā* season of 1907. I have not traced the date at which *sinakkara* title deeds were acquired from the Crown, but this appears to have been around 1910.

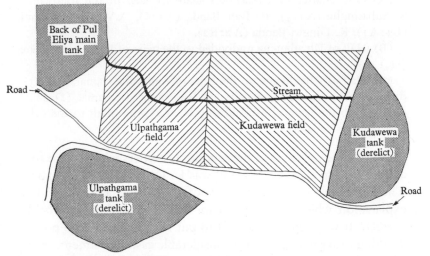

Map *G*. Ulpathgama and Kudawewa *olagama* tanks and fields.
For location, see Plate 1.

The initiative again came from Appurala Vidāne (A1:W). He allocated the land of Kudawewa to his own immediate heirs and to his dependent U. Kapuruhamy (B2:5), just as he did later in the case of plots 130–6. In contrast, the Ulpathgama land which lies just below that of Kudawewa was allocated to descendants of Naidurala Gamarāla II (C:2), who may well have had some traditionally established claim on the holding.

The net result was that around 1910 the total holding was held:

(A) Kudawewa by the Gamarāla of the Pul Eliya Ihala bāga and his associates.

(B) Half of Ulpathgama by the Gamarāla of the Pul Eliya Meda bāga and his associates.

(C) Half of Ulpathgama by the Gamarāla of the Pul Eliya Pahala bāga and his associates.

Although the three shares are not exactly equal the 'traditional pattern' is clearly evident.

By 1954 the distribution was:

(A) One quarter of Kudawewa share to each of the following: S. Subasinghe (A1:5), P. Ran Banda (A1:6), A.V. Punchi Etani (B1:A1), K. Dingiri Banda (A2:B2).

(B) Half of Ulpathgama undivided to the heirs of Ukkurala Vidāne (H:1).

(C) Half of Ulpathgama to the heirs of Kadirathe Gamarāla (C:3), divided: one-sixth to the heirs of Punchirala Gamarāla (D2:C); one-sixth to the heirs of Mudalihamy (C:Z2); one-sixth to the heirs of Appurala Vedarāla (C:6).

In 1954 the only one of these multiple owners who was making any attempt to cultivate his land was K. Dingiri Banda (A2:B2). The latter was working his share of Kudawewa as *vi hēna*. The explanation which I was given for this 'laziness' was probably correct. It was pointed out that to put the two tanks into proper working order would require considerable cash investment. Each of the numerous owners would have to subscribe a sum in proportion to the area of his holding. But no one individual exerted enough influence to be able to organise this. On the other hand, if one man had repaired the tank or tanks on his own initiative, then all the other shareholders would automatically benefit. In practice mutual jealousies effectively prevented anybody from doing anything.

Although this *sinakkara* holding was originally allocated in palpable imitation of the traditional *bāga* system, the 1910 owners of the three sections A, B, C had no Gamarāla standing in the eyes of the law, even though they had Gamarāla titles. Thus when the tracts were passed on by inheritance to the next generation all the heirs were of equal standing.

In a negative way this throws light on the crucial importance of the *gamvasama* holding in the traditional system. The fact that in the traditional system the owner of the *gamvasama* was *ipso facto* Gamarāla implied that every *bāga* always had a leader no matter how complex the fragmentation of individual holdings.

When the *sinakkara* titles to Kudawewa and Ulpathgama were first issued the Gamarāla owners of the land acted effectively as leaders and the land was cultivated. Now that the original leaders are dead, the land has been virtually abandoned, even though the economic rewards of rice cultivation are much greater than before. Today, because of the lack of leadership, each individual owner has to work his own particular share to the best of his own ability. This necessarily restricts the use of the land to chena cultivation, for proper paddy cultivation requires irrigation and that would mean collective enterprise under a leader.

CONCLUSION

In my analysis of the traditional system of tenure in the Old Field I emphasised the absolute equality of rights enjoyed by all the factional interests concerned. Each had exactly equal access to water and within each *bāga* every *panguva* was treated alike.

It is true that even under the old system the three Gamarāla and their immediate kin were privileged in comparison with other *pangu* holders, but, since every individual's land was necessarily distributed in different parts of the Old Field, all the villagers, rich and poor together, had a common interest in maintaining the efficiency of the irrigation system to all parts of the Old Field. There was no tendency at all for the rich to segregate themselves into the most advantageous sections of the field, leaving only the bad land to the poorer villagers.

The analysis of the *sinakkara* and *badu* holdings reveals a very different picture. Progressively the doctrine of 'fair shares for all' has disappeared.

Although the new fields were mostly laid out in a manner approximating to the traditional scheme, ownership was not distributed throughout the community, but only to the privileged friends of the Vel Vidāne. This had the effect that nearly all the new land came into the hands of compound groups A and B, while compound group C and their associates obtained hardly anything.

At first the favoured compound groups acted as if they were tenants under a Gamarāla. We have seen, for example, how plots 137–50 were developed with U. Kadirathe (A2:4) as 'Gamarāla', with equal *pangu* shares to each household in compound A2.

It was only at a much later stage that 'individualistic capitalism' emerged. When M. Naidurala (Dx:Y) and U. Sirala (A2:5) developed plots 124 and 150 from around 1945 onwards, they did so as private individuals without regard for their neighbours' rights and interests. It is probably significant that these two individuals were, in 1954, in trouble with their near kin. Naidurala, though still nominally a member of compound D, was for practical purposes mainly allied with compounds A and B (see pp. 123–4); Sirala, though properly a member of compound A2, was in a tangle of trouble over his past and present affinal alliances with compounds D and C (see p. 116).

Meanwhile the poor of the village, all members of compounds C and D, had been segregated off into the downstream plots 153–5, where they were *badu* tenants of what is, in effect, a State-subsidised farm. This new segregation of land into 'holdings of the rich' and 'holdings of the poor', with the rich controlling all the best land, is bound to have very drastic implications for the village considered as a social entity.

The principle of fair shares for all which permeated the traditional system did not simply reflect a static fact that the traditional village was a highly cohesive social unit. It is rather that the traditional system of tenure *imposed* social solidarity upon the village members.

The new English model systems of tenure fail to do this. The modern villager is economically better off than his predecessor; but the price of prosperity has been greater social dissension.

PLATE II

A   Pul Eliya tank looking from north to south along the bund. At this level the tank is about one-quarter full. The construction in the foreground is the 'modern' sluice (*horovva*).

B   A single *issara* (see p. 149) strip in the Pul Eliya Upper Old Field with *vatamalu* stacks (see p. 260) and unreaped paddy on the right.

PLATE III

A   Small single-roomed dwelling-house with cooking area on the left.
(Cf. Diagram 1, p. 60.)

B   Shrine to the elephant deity Pulleyar at Diwulwewa village. The base is of
cement 'borrowed' from a government contractor; the *lingam*-shaped phallic
stones are decorated with white paint. The largest stone represents Pulleyar
himself; the smaller ones denote lesser deities, his servants (see p. 35).

CHAPTER VII

THE ORGANISATION AND
REWARD OF LABOUR

INTRODUCTION

So far, in discussing the tenure under which Pul Eliya villagers hold their paddy land, I have been concerned only with the ownership of primary title. It is evident that property in this sense is very unevenly distributed among the various households of the community.

But the distribution of primary title gives a misleading indication of the way in which the economic benefits of cultivation ultimately accrue to different numbers of the population.

It has been my constant theme that while the heirs to a common estate (that is full brothers) tend to be opposed to one another, marriage results in a co-operative relationship between brothers-in-law, that is between individuals who are *not* potential owners of the same property.

Thus labour co-operation follows a pattern which is antithetic to that of land ownership, and the rewarding of labour has the effect of counterbalancing the unequal distribution of primary title.

I shall discuss this phenomenon in two phases. I shall first examine the organisation of labour in respect to cultivation in the Old Field, that is in a situation where hereditary property rights are at stake. We shall here find that, broadly speaking, a kinship pattern prevails; a man co-operates with his father-in-law and his brothers-in-law, but steers clear of his father and his full brothers. As a contrast I shall take much briefer note of two situations which call for labour co-operation, but do *not* relate to a context of hereditary right, namely tank fishing and shifting cultivation (*hēna*). Here we shall find, in both cases, that kinship is incidental; a man is just as likely to co-operate with his father or his brother or a casual friend as with a brother-in-law or a father-in-law.

This may seem trivial and negative evidence, but it seems to me to be of great significance. It demonstrates that the kinship behaviours which are quite clearly apparent in the Old Field situation are *not* determined by jural rules of a moral kind, they are simply a by-product of the economic facts of the situation. Change the economic context and the appropriate behaviour changes too. The non-anthropologist will find nothing surprising in this; but it runs counter to a good deal of recent anthropological theorising.

SECTION A: THE OLD FIELD

To understand the ultimate allocation of production from land held on either *paravēni* or *sinakkara* title we need to take into account three factors additional to the ownership of primary title. These are:

(1) Long-term mortgage (*ukas*).
(2) Short-term sharecropping lease (*andē*).
(3) Direct labour rewarded either by wages or in kind or by reciprocal work.

These factors are here considered in relation to the *Yala* paddy growing season of 1954. During this season only the Old Field area was cultivated but, had it been possible to present an analysis of the entire annual cycle including both the *Mahā* and *Yala* seasons, the general picture would certainly be the same.

Mortgage, share-cropping and hired labour are matters on which Ceylon sociologists and politicians are liable to hold highly prejudiced opinions. Recent legislation has been based on the assumption that the institutions concerned amount to economic exploitation of the poor tenant by the rich landlord.[1] I must here remind the reader again that what I write relates only to Pul Eliya; I do not claim to know what goes on elsewhere.

[1] I have in mind particularly Sarkar and Tambiah (1957) and the astonishing piece of Marxist legislation known as the Paddy Lands Act, 1958.

Under Pul Eliya conditions most landlords and most tenants are close kin and the economic implications of landlord-tenant relationships are clearly quite different from what they would be if the landlords and the tenants were different sets of people.

In Pul Eliya the effect of *ukas*, *andē*, and labour-sharing institutions was simply to distribute, among a wide group of kinsmen, the economic product of land which is 'owned' by a single individual. The kinship principles which are relevant are ones which we have already frequently encountered in earlier chapters. In summary these are:

(1) Co-resident members of a 'compound' have certain common hereditary interests which drive them towards mutual co-operation even in the face of much personal hostility.

(2) Marriage establishes an alliance between two households and in some cases between whole 'families' (*pavula*). The bond between brothers-in-law (*massinā*) is an extremely close one which is ideally perpetuated in the next generation by the analogous bond between the sons of brothers-in-law, who are also *massinā* (cf. Dumont, 1957, pp. 24 ff.).

A similar bond often exists between sisters-in-law (*nǟnā*) and the daughters of sisters-in-law, who are also *nǟnā*.

(3) In contrast, the relationship between full brothers is often one of marked strain, though a half-brother or step-brother relationship can be a close bond, especially if the two individuals are not both co-resident in the birth compound of their common parent. 'Classificatory' brothers whose common link is affinal—for example the husbands of two sisters—can also co-operate without strain (see pp. 108–9).

(4) As extensions of these primary ties we find that the tie between a man and his *massinā*'s son (*bǟnā*) is one of co-operation, as is also the tie with the son of a 'friendly' half-brother, or of an affinal classificatory brother. But relations between a man and his own married sons tend to be difficult until he has disposed of all his property; similar though milder difficulties often separate a man from his full brother's children.

(5) As an outcome of this complex of relationships every individual feels himself to be a member of a widely ramifying 'family' (*pavula*), to the members of which he is linked either by ties of common descent

or by ties of affinity. Some members of an individual's *pavula* are resident within his own compound, others are outside his compound within the same village, and others again reside in neighbouring villages.

(6) *Pavula*, thus described, are the effective kin groups of the society and it is groupings of this kind which act together corporately to achieve political ends. In this book we are concerned primarily with the allocation of rights in land and we therefore meet with *pavula* as corporate factions engaged in rivalry concerning rights to land and to the produce of land. Since the membership of compound groups is closely bound up with the possession of hereditary rights in land, we find that *pavula* rivalries can also be regarded as rivalries between competing compound groups, or parts of compound groups, but the membership of a man's *pavula* and of his compound group do not coincide.

With this summary of principles in mind we can proceed.

MORTGAGE ('UKAS')

Mortgage and share-cropping transactions have already been briefly discussed in chapter IV, where the interdependence of the two institutions has been stressed.

Mortgage is a technique for raising ready money against a pledge of either jewellery or land. It is not in itself an outright sale but, since the interest charges on the original loan are very high, the chances of a mortgager redeeming his pledge are usually small. But, inasmuch as mortgage delays the transfer of ultimate title, it serves an important social function. It slows down the rate at which particular household groups change their economic status. The high incidence of 'gambling bankruptcy' among the wealthier members of the community has already been discussed (p. 175). The institution of mortgage serves to cushion the social consequences of such personal disasters.

Whenever land is mortgaged against a cash loan it is the normal expectation that the mortgagee, whether he be a kinsman or not, will lease the land back on *andē* to the original owner. If the owner then chooses to be reticent, as is usually the case, the anthropological observer has no immediate evidence that anything has happened at all. Although my notebooks contain details of a number of *ukas* cases the list is almost certainly incomplete. The Vel Vidāne was no doubt well aware of all the relevant facts but since he himself was often a principal, his statements on this topic were quite unreliable.

The extreme complexity of the network of economic obligation which may develop out of mortgage contracts and the manner in which these tie in with kin relationships can be illustrated from the details of a single case which, though somewhat elaborate, seems quite typical of the general pattern.

Mortgage of the Ihala bāga 'gamvasama'

Background

Plots 13 and 14 together comprise the Ihala bāga *gamvasama* (see p. 185). In terms of tradition, ownership of these plots carries with it the highest status in the village, that of Gamarāla of the Ihala bāga, but, quite apart from this, the situation of this land in relation to the village tank makes it the most desirable section of the entire Old Field. The land is not shaded by trees, it is exceptionally well watered, it carries a relatively light *rājakāriya* obligation and, owing to its position close to the village, it is unlikely to suffer attack from wild animals.

Since the beginning of the century ownership of this land has been divided. Plot 14 has belonged to members of compound A1, who are still regarded by many Pul Eliya people as interlopers from Wiralmurippu. Plot 13 has belonged to a household in Wiralmurippu related by marriage to the members of compound A1, though not closely. In Pul Eliya the economic fortunes of compound A1 have been declining for many years, but their affinal relatives in compound B1 are now the wealthiest sector of the whole community.

The leading member of compound B1 is the Vel Vidāne (V. Menikrala (B1:7)). The economic advantages of his office enable him to act as 'banker' for all his close associates whom he rates as his *pavula*. This brings him into natural opposition with K.V. Kapuruhamy (F:Dw), the trader shopkeeper, who is 'banker' for the rest of the community.

This Kapuruhamy had recently come to Pul Eliya from Diwulwewa (56). He is the grandson of Kapurala Vedarāla (F:1) who in 1890 was co-owner, together with his *bāna* Kadirathe Gamarāla (C:3) of the Pahala bāga *gamvasama* lands (p. 206). For reasons unknown (p. 209) Kapurala Vedarāla's family left Pul Eliya; they resided nearby, first on an *olagama* called Konwewa and then at Diwulwewa, but they retained their original interest in the Pahala bāga lands and also in the associated *gamgoda* area, compound F. Very close affinal ties were maintained with Pul Eliya. By 1950 K.V. Kapuruhamy (F:Dw), then resident in Diwulwewa, was double brother-in-law (by sister-exchange marriage) to P.G. Menikrala (Dw:D2) son of Punchirala Gamarāla (D2:C) and grandson of Kadirathe Gamarāla (C:3). With the bankruptcy of Punchirala Gamarāla, K.V. Kapuruhamy (F:Dw) had been left the most influential member of this whole group and he had then moved back to Pul Eliya. His interests often coincided with those of U.V. Pinhamy (C1:W), another *bānā* of Punchirala Gamarāla, though the two men were not very directly related.

The passionate hostility between V. Menikrala (B1:7) and U.V. Pinhamy (C1:W) has already been noted. This was matched by similar hostility between V. Menikrala and K.V. Kapuruhamy. Pinhamy and Kapuruhamy were close friends and when I left the village they were my joint hosts to a party from which all members of V. Menikrala's *pavula* were excluded.

These facts are all relevant to what follows. In 1954 both plots 13 and 14 were under mortgage.

Plot 14

The circumstances here have already been described at p. 140. The owner, S. Subasinghe (A1:5), had mortgaged the land to the Vel Vidāne of his home village of Wiralmurippu. The latter had leased the land back *andē* to Subasinghe while Subasinghe had in turn leased land which he owned in Wiralmurippu to a near relative of his mortgagee. Only Wiralmurippu interests were involved, and as far as Pul Eliya was concerned no compound group other than that of A1 had any stake in the land.

246

Plot 13

Here the situation is very much more complicated. In the official Vel Vidāne's return the land was shown as belonging to W. Punchi Etani (Dw:W) of Diwulwewa, a lady who had been dead for the past two years. She had been born in Wiralmurippu and had been married *dīga* in Diwulwewa to Mudalihamy (Dw:2), a brother of K.V. Kapuruhamy (F:Dw). She had had seven children, of whom five were married and two were infants.

The Pul Eliya Vel Vidāne maintained that division of the property in these circumstances was difficult, and that he was holding it undivided in the interests of the infants; meanwhile he considered the land to be held on *andē* by M. Herathamy (B1:Dw), W. Punchi Etani's eldest son, who must give an appropriate share of the crop to his siblings or to their guardians.

When I arrived in Pul Eliya this Herathamy was living *binna* in house II as the husband of M. Ran Manika (B1:8), second cousin (*nānā*) to the Vel Vidāne.

It transpired later that the Vel Vidāne had some years previously made an advance of Rs 25 to Mudalihamy (Dw:2), father of Herathamy; this was secured by a mortgage on plot 13. The Rs 25 was probably given on the understanding that Herathamy should marry Ran Manika and that Herathamy should inherit plot 13, thus bringing the ownership of the land back to Pul Eliya. After the death of Mudalihamy, Herathamy, as owner *de facto* (though not *de jure*) had extracted a further loan of Rs 50 from his father's brother, the trader K.V. Kapuruhamy (F:Dw), against *ukas* of plot 13.

After I had unearthed these facts the Vel Vidāne changed his argument and claimed that the position was that:

(*a*) The plot was owned by (the deceased) W. Punchi Etani (Dw:W);

(*b*) her heirs had let it on *andē* to their (deceased) father, M. Mudalihamy (Dw:2);

(*c*) Mudalihamy had given the land on *ukas* to himself, the Vel Vidāne (B1:7);

(*d*) he, the Vel Vidāne, had given the land back on *andē* to M. Herathamy (B1:Dw);

(*e*) M. Herathamy had given the land on *ukas* to K.V. Kapuruhamy (F:Dw);

(f) K.V. Kapuruhamy had given the land back on *andē* to M. Herathamy.

At harvest time, to my astonishment, I discovered that the crop was in fact divided up according to this elaborate set of fictions.

It was admitted that the case was complicated but, to make matters worse, K.V. Kapuruhamy had now persuaded M. Herathamy to sell him the land outright, and he was in possession of a lawyer's document to this effect. V. Menikrala, the Vel Vidāne, promptly countered by pointing out that this document had no standing since it was not Herathamy's land in the first place. The sale could not be recognised unless K.V. Kapuruhamy obtained the consent of all Herathamy's siblings. Since these included two children aged 5 and 6 living at a remote village under the guardianship of Kapuruhamy's eldest brother, with whom he, Kapuruhamy, was on notoriously bad terms, V. Menikrala seemed to be fairly safe! When I left the village a lawsuit on the subject appeared to be in the offing.

In working the land Herathamy received the assistance of his father's sister's husband, P.G. Menikrala (Dw:D2), K.V. Kapuruhamy's double brother-in-law. This man lived *binna* in Diwulwewa and worked land there which was owned by Kapuruhamy. In respect to Pul Eliya plot 13 P.G. Menikrala provided buffaloes for ploughing and threshing but he did so as part of his debt relationship with his brother-in-law; the buffaloes were not paid for directly out of the plot 13 crop.

When the crop had been threshed it was divided up as follows:

(i) Four per cent to the Vel Vidāne, as fee for his professional services.[1]

(ii) One-third of balance to W. Punchi Etani (deceased), that is to Herathamy and his siblings.

(iii) One-third of the then remaining balance to V. Menikrala, as *ukas* holder.

(iv) One-half of the then remaining balance to K.V. Kapuruhamy, as *ukas* holder.

(v) Residue to Herathamy personally.

Herathamy's personal share was bagged and taken to the house of his mother-in-law, A.V. Punchi Etani (B1:A1). A week or so later Ran Manika (B1:8) gave birth to a son and duly declared that Herathamy was the father, a fact which Herathamy acknowledged by signing

---

[1] See footnote, p. 266.

the birth certificate. Thus, provided Herathamy could be prevented from selling the land, this child might ultimately inherit the plot.

A week later Ran Manika's mother threw Herathamy out of the house and the 'marriage' was at an end. This event would not prejudice the inheritance prospects of the new-born infant. I do not know what happened to Herathamy's share of the crop at this stage, but I fancy that his ex-wife and ex-mother-in-law kept most of it!

These elaborate details show very well how *ukas* and *andē* and kinship connections dovetail in together. It will also be obvious that the issue was being fought out between factions rather than between individuals. Herathamy himself was a mere pawn in proceedings which were part of a long-term struggle between the members of compound B1 and their Wiralmurippu relatives, on the one hand, and the members of compound D2 and their Diwulwewa relatives on the other.

SHARE-CROPPING TENANCY ('ANDĒ')

Since a mortgage lease often endures for years before it is redeemed or foreclosed and since a mortgage is normally reciprocated by an *andē* lease to the mortgager, some *andē* leases have the appearance of long-term contracts. In principle, however, an *andē* contract (in the sense that the term was used in Pul Eliya) was always very short term. It was properly a contract to cultivate a piece of land on behalf of the owner (or of the mortgagee as the case might be) for one crop season only. Once the harvest was over the contract was at an end; the owner was then under no obligation whatever to renew the contract to the same tenant in the following season. Indeed to speak of the share-cropping cultivator as a 'tenant' of the landlord is misleading. The Pul Eliya people themselves thought of the relationship as one in which the share-cropper worked on behalf of the owner, and the crop at all stages was referred to as the owner's crop. Only when the harvest was finally threshed and the grain divided up among the various interested parties did the 'tenant' take his share.

While mortgage (*ukas*) was something most people were

inclined to be ashamed of, there was nothing in any way embarrassing about letting land out on *andē*, nor was it considered
humiliating to be the recipient of *andē*. *Andē* was the standard
technique whereby landowners suffering from some temporary or
permanent disability could keep their land in cultivation. To accept
an *andē* lease in such circumstances was an act of friendship; the
'tenant' was helping the landlord with his cultivation.

The main reasons for letting land out on *andē* can be enumer-
ated as follows:

(1) Widows who are landlords invariably let out *all* their land.

(2) Male landlords who are old, or sick at the time of sowing, are
also likely to let out most, if not all, of their land.

(3) Landlords who are resident outside the village in question
usually lease their land to a local resident. It is inconvenient to work
land more than two miles from the cultivator's home.

(4) Very rich landlords, of whom there are very few, are likely to
lease away most of their land simply because they cannot go to the
trouble of arranging the cultivation directly themselves.

(5) Where a holding has been inherited 'undivided' by a number of
co-heirs one of the heirs may work the whole plot. He will then stand
in *andē* relationship to his co-owners.

The scale on which *andē* leasing takes place is indicated by the
statement that in the *Yala* harvest of 1954, out of 64 nominal
acres, no less than 33¾ acres were let on *andē*.

In general the recipients of *andē* leases are poor men who
cannot support themselves from their own private plots. Often
the leaseholder is a close relative of the owner. In Pul Eliya sons-
in-law held land on *andē* from their fathers-in-law, sons from
their fathers, brothers from brothers, and in one case, a *binna*-
married husband was deemed to be holding land on *andē* from his
wife. Indeed, wherever the leaseholder is of the same *variga* as
the owner, some principle of kinship is likely to be invoked by the
leaseholder so as to procure beneficial terms from the landlord.
In nearly all the cases which I recorded the nature of this kinship
link was obvious; examples are provided by Table 11 (p. 277).

On the other hand, *andē* leases are not necessarily between members of the same *variga*. In a number of instances Pul Eliya landlords had leased land to members of the Vanni-Väddā village of Tulawelliya. According to Pul Eliya tradition, the members of this village were formerly hereditary serfs of the Goyigama villagers of Pul Eliya. Today the people of Tulawelliya own land freehold but, since they have very little of it, most of them need to go outside to earn an additional income. The Goyigama of Pul Eliya still consider that they have the right to force the people of Tulawelliya to work for them, but in actual fact the situation is now reversed. The peasants of Tulawelliya maintain that they have the right to work on the Pul Eliya fields; they exploit the fact that they are the traditional servants of Pul Eliya in order to obtain *andē* leases from the richer members of the Pul Eliya community.

DIRECT LABOUR REWARDED BY WAGES OR IN KIND

It is evident that this reliance on traditional rights carries considerable moral force. Pul Eliya landlords who wish to have their land cultivated by others have three alternatives before them:

(1) They can let the land on lease (*andē*).
(2) They can hire casual labour on a payment-in-kind basis.
(3) They can hire casual labour on a cash-wage basis.

In 1954 there was still an emphatic feeling that the payment of cash wages is not compatible with a transaction between friends or kinsmen. Services between members of the same *variga* should never be paid for outright in cash. All service should properly be reciprocated in kind on some other occasion. If this was impracticable, then any debt between friends should be settled by the gift of goods, not money.

Although the Vanni-Väddā people of Tulawelliya are not of the same *variga* as the Goyigama of Pul Eliya, nevertheless they belong to the same traditional social system, and services provided by the Tulawelliya people should, therefore, be paid for in kind at traditionally established rates.

I inquired into the details of such transactions with some care and I verified that it was actually cheaper for Pul Eliya landlords to employ Tamil labourers for cash wages than to employ Tula-welliya labourers on a payment-in-kind basis. This was because the Tulawelliya people always insisted on being paid in rice 'at traditional rates', and the current monetary value of rice was very high. Yet even so the employment of casual Tamil labourers for cash wages was rare, whereas the employment of Tulawelliya people both as labourers and as share-cropping tenants was very common.

Both sides appreciated the moral virtue of this procedure. The Pul Eliya people said they *ought* to employ the Tulawelliya people because they were their established friends from ancient times. In Tulawelliya, the particular Pul Eliya landlords who employed Tulawelliya labourers were singled out by name as individuals of especial merit.

'ANDĒ' TENANCIES FROM 'OUTSIDER' LANDLORDS

The converse of this employment of 'outside' labourers by Pul Eliya landlords is the employment of Pul Eliya labourers by 'outsider' landlords. The position here is somewhat intricate and is relevant for our understanding of *variga* solidarity.

The complications of *rājakāriya* obligations—such as those en-tailing a roster of night watchmen—and the necessity for the whole village to synchronise its use of the irrigation system, imply that it is almost impossible for a non-resident 'outsider' to work land in Pul Eliya unless he can count on the assistance of some kind of local agent. When land falls into the hands of Tamil traders the villagers habitually exploit this fact so as to compel the trader to sell the land back on reasonable terms. The *andē* institu-tion in such circumstances provides a means of compromise. The village leaders are not necessarily averse to land being owned by an 'outsider' provided he is one of their friends who will lease the land back to one of their close relatives. If, however, the 'out-sider' owner is deemed to be an enemy, the village leaders will endeavour to deny him *andē* assistance.

In 1954 the only Old Field landlord who was not a member of the Pul Eliya *variga* was Danapala of Marutamadu (see p. 209), and the leaders of the village were attempting to apply the usual sanctions against him. Unfortunately, from their point of view, there were several 'blacklegs'. In 1953 R. Punchirala (X:4), the 'outcaste', had worked the land *andē*, and in 1954 the 'scoundrel' K. Menikrala (B2:6) did the same. Both these men were marginal to the *variga* and neither could be induced to act in the interests of *variga* solidarity.

Menikrala's case is particularly interesting. Although his father's father, Ukkurala (B2:Z3), had been of 'wrong *variga*' Menikrala and his siblings were accepted as full Pul Eliya citizens for most purposes. But Menikrala himself was considered to be unmarried and he therefore had no brother-in-law within the *variga*. This made Menikrala's *variga* status inferior to that of his two married brothers K. Dingiri Banda (A2:B2) and K. Wannihamy (B2:7). This case illustrates how the effective boundaries to *variga* membership are established through the recognition of affinal ties rather than through the validation of a status established at birth (see also Appendix 1).

Discussion of the rewards accruing to *andē* tenants as distinct from the manner of their selection will be held over; this aspect of the matter is considered at pp. 266 f.

CALENDAR OF WORK

The pattern of labour organisation varies greatly at different parts of the agricultural season according to the technical activity involved. The total sequence can best be considered in phases, but first I should say something about the work calendar as a whole which is shown in schematic form in Table 9.

The Sinhalese, with their almost obsessional interest in horoscopes, have long been accustomed to reckon time by two alternative calendars—one solar and the other lunar[1]—the 'luck' of any particular day being dependent upon the conjunction of the two systems. Although the European 'solar' calendar is not quite the same as the traditional zodiacal cycle, it is very similar, and the peculiar way in which the 1954 Pul Eliya villagers managed to

[1] Pieris, 1956, p. 92.

Table 9. Approximate calendar of activities, 1954–5

Lunar month	Date of full moon (new moon)	Season	Rites	Paddy-growing activity	Chena activity	Other activities
BAK	18 April	(Season between two years)	—		**RAIN**	—
WESAK	(2 May) 17 May	U	NEW YEAR	*Yala* ploughing	—	—
POSON	16 June	S	—	18 May: *Yala* sown	—	—
ASĀLA	15 July (31 July)	N A	—		**HOT**	—
NIKINI	14 Aug.	A ⎫ V A S	Mutti Mangalaya	18 Aug.: *Yala* reaped / Stack shifting / Stacks fenced	**DRY** / Chena clearing starts	Ploughing by tractor / Tank low: cattle on *mahā* stubble and at back of tank
BINARA	13 Sept.	S A	18 Sept.: New Rice festival	18 Sept.: Threshing / Granaries filled	Chena burning / *Vi hēna* sown	—
VAP	11 Oct.	M A S I T A	—	*Mahā* ploughing by buffalo when rain starts / Temple Field sown	*Kurakkan hēna* sown	Tank repair work / Tank fishing / House thatching and building
IL	9 Nov.	A	—	**HEAVY**	—	V.C.O.'s meeting 5 Nov.
UNDUVAP	8 Dec.	—	—	**RAIN**	—	—
DURUTU	6 Jan.	S I T A	—		*Kurakkan* harvest	—
NAVAM	5 Feb.		—	*Mahā* harvest	*Vi hēna* harvest	—
MĀDIN	7 March	(Season between two years)	—	(*Mada* sown if *Mahā* fails)	**RAIN**	—
BAK	6 April		—			—

Note on the Sinhalese months and seasons.

The Sinhalese lunar year is usually held to begin with the month Bak (cf. Pieris, 1956, p. 92). Pul Eliya villagers seemed to regard Wesak as the first month. The three seasons are not precisely defined. Usna (hot) covers the *Yala* crop growing and harvest; Samasita (cool) is the period of preparing the land and sowing the seed for both shifting cultivation (*hēna*) and for the *Mahā* crop; Sita (cold) extends over the main period of the *Mahā* growing season up to the *hēna* and *Mahā* harvests. The interval between the end of the *Mahā* harvest and the start of the *Yala* ploughing is 'the season between two years' and covers parts of the months Mädin and Bak.

Vas is a three-month period of Buddhist ritual significance. It ends at the full moon of the month Binara which here synchronises closely with the Yala combine lunar and calendar dates is very probably part of ancient tradition.

Whenever the Old Field is to be cultivated it is essential for the whole village to adhere closely to a predetermined programme of work, for when the tank sluices are open the whole field can take water and when the sluices are shut the whole field must run dry. No ploughing can be done on a dry field, but once the water has been let in to soften the earth work must proceed everywhere simultaneously. Thereafter, to avoid loss by evaporation, the ploughed field must be sown, and the crops carried through to harvest with the least possible delay.

There must, therefore, be agreement about the dates on which the sluice will be open, the date at which sowing will be completed, the varieties of rice that will be sown, and the dates at which it is planned to have harvest ready and the field drained. Under rules in force in 1954 the Village Cultivation Officer held a village meeting at the beginning of each cultivation season and formally agreed these various dates with the assembled villagers. Although this particular form of bureaucracy is a recent innovation it has always been necessary for the villagers to agree among themselves upon such matters.

Since the prospect of rain during the *Yala* season is substantially worse than that for the *Mahā*, the usual practice is to grow low-yielding rapid-maturing varieties during the *Yala* season and rather slower-maturing varieties during the *Mahā*. The *Yala* varieties are known as 'three month rice' and the *Mahā* varieties as 'four and a half month rice'. In the *Mahā* season some land is cultivated from direct rain-water only and in such cases the cultivator can use his own discretion. But a gambling element is always present. The higher-yielding varieties all take longer to mature and therefore run greater risk of being destroyed by drought.

The key dates to which the villagers agree with the approval of the V.C.O. are 'lucky days' conventionally spaced. For example, in 1954 the first day of the month *Wesak* in the lunar calendar fell on 2 May. The Pul Eliya villagers considered this to be the

New Year. The *Wesak* full moon fell on 17 May and they agreed with the V.C.O. that the *Yala* sowing should be completed by 18 May.

Since they were growing 'three month rice' they planned to start reaping on 18 August, and in fact did so. They then held the New Rice festival on 18 September and threshing was allowed to start that evening.

A similar programme required the *Mahā* season to be fitted in between the full moon of the month *Vap* (11 October) and the end of the lunar year (beginning of April), though as it turned out the winter rains that year were very erratic and the crop probably failed.

A similar mixed calendar applied to the chena cultivation. The clearing of chenas started around the full moon of the month *Nikini* (14 August) and proceeded spasmodically. The *vi hēna* (rice chenas) were sown around the middle of the month *Vap* (11 October) and the *kurakkan* chenas one month later. The rice in the *vi hēna* case was a variety called *dik vi*, a 'four and a half month paddy' which was expected to be harvested at the end of February at the same time as the *kurakkan*.

Since chenas are not dependent upon a public water supply the various cultivators have discretion about their precise time-tabling. But there seemed to be a general tendency to pick sowing dates according to the moon while predicting harvesting dates according to the civil calendar. The reason for this is quite simple. In general, these villagers thought in terms of the months of the ordinary European calendar; but for any specific action in which luck might be concerned, or for religious festivals, they consulted an astrologer, who usually provided them with a date taken from the lunar calendar. Different astrologers seem to have different systems of calculation and neighbouring villages did not all adhere to exactly the same time-table.

PLATE IV

A   Harrowing by buffalo (*poru-gānavā*).

B   Stack shifting. Building a *kola goda* stack (see p. 261) at the edge of a threshing floor (*kamata*). The smaller stacks in the distance are *vatamalu*.

PLATE V

A   Stack owner going through a threshing-floor ritual immediately before
commencing threshing operations (see p. 262).

B   Threshing (see p. 263). The structure to the rear of the stacks is a
field watch hut.

Phases of the agricultural cycle

With this general background in mind, we can now proceed to consider the sequence of activities during the *Yala* agricultural season, phase by phase.

Phase I: ploughing; preparation of the field; sowing

This initial sequence of activities has the following component parts:

(*a*) First ploughing (*bim naginavā*).

(*b*) Bund repairs (*niyara kotanavā*). (As is usual with rice cultivation the total plot is divided up into flat rectangular sections (*liyädda*) surrounded by low banks about 6 in. wide and 8 in. high (*niyara*). These have to be repaired each season.)

(*c*) Second ploughing (*dehi hānavā*).

(*d*) Harrowing by buffalo (*poru-gānavā*) (Plate IV A).

(*e*) Making of water channels within the square plots (*liyädda*) (*äla mang adinavā*).

(*f*) Smoothing of ground with hand leveller (*vapuranavā*).

(*g*) Broadcast sowing of seed (*vi ihinava*).

It is of some interest that a thirteenth-century account divides the agricultural process into exactly similar categories, and in some instances uses the same terminology (Ariyapala, 1956, pp. 331–2).

The labour requirements for this initial phase of the cultivation cycle are partly determined by the weather. Field work is only possible after rain or at times when the field has been flooded with water drawn from the village tank under order from the Vel Vidāne. Sometimes, therefore, there is a rush to get the whole process completed within a short period, and in this case there may be competition to employ outside labour. Ideally, however, the first ploughing and the bund repairs are carried out at leisure by the plot-holder himself some time in advance of sowing. The remaining five stages of the sequence are ordinarily carried out in quick succession and require the organisation of a labour team; stages (*d*) to (*g*) should generally all be completed within one day.

The plot-holder who owns his own plough buffaloes will naturally use them; poorer men may have to hire buffaloes, ploughs and harrows.

It is one of the advantages of working land on *andē* that, as a rule, it is the owner rather than the 'tenant' who has to provide the seed, the animals and the implements.

Phase II: the growing crop

Once the seed is in the ground the demand for labour is slack. The only work is that of irrigation control, which is easily managed by the plot-holder personally. It is an index of the sensitive technical attention which must be paid to the irrigation at different stages of the plant growth that of the thirteen different 'conditions' of rice recognised by the Sinhalese, eight concern the growing crop. These are:

1. *goyam pala*—sprouted seed.
2. *isnam pala*—sprouts standing in 4–6 in. of water.
3. *hin bandi*—ear first visible in the stalk.
4. *mahā bandi*—ear about to break.
5. *pudinanā*—ear clear of its sheath.
6. *goyam kalu randanavā*—ear with grains separated but still green.
7. *kiri vadinavā*—grain changing colour; milky state.
8. *pahuna*—ripe and ready for reaping.
9. *vi karala*—cut paddy on the straw while still in field.
10. *mäduvam*—cut paddy on the threshing floor.
11. *vi*—threshed paddy.
12. *hal*—dehusked rice.
13. *bat*—cooked rice.

The irrigation technique is that, immediately after sowing, the water supply is cut off from the muddy *liyädda* for about 7 days, by which time the rice will be sprouting. After that the level of the water is slowly raised so that the tips of the shoots continue to show above water. When the water is about 6 in. deep it will be kept at this level until harvest.

In this part of Ceylon the rice seedlings are not transplanted. Transplanting is advocated by government agricultural officers, but it is unlikely that any such procedure would be economic. In drought years—which are frequent—the whole crop is bound to be lost anyway and, although transplanting certainly increases the yield per acre, it also increases costs and slows up the rate of maturity of the crop. The villagers here showed themselves highly resistant to official propaganda, but it did not seem that their refusal to experiment was due merely to conservatism or laziness.

Since the irrigation arrangements are such that all the villagers must follow the same agreed cultivation programme, they naturally prefer to play safe with technical procedures which they know and understand. Moreover, although the work in the irrigated fields slacks off as soon as sowing is completed, this does not imply that the villagers have nothing to do. It is precisely at these seasons when labour demand is slack in the main paddy fields that supplementary economic activities, such as chena cultivation or tank fishing, are likely to be at their height. A major technical innovation such as the introduction of transplanting would have complicated and largely unpredictable repercussions on the labour supply available for a whole host of minor, though none the less essential, village activities.

Phase III: harvest

At harvest the whole available man- (and woman-) power of the village is simultaneously fully employed. Under these conditions the basic social structure of the community is manifested in labour group formation. Since we are dealing with a society in which 'everyone is related to everyone else', kinship principles alone do not suffice to divide up the population into significant structural groups. But the strength of kinship obligation is not evenly distributed. Under conditions of maximum labour demand, each individual is endeavouring to obtain from his friends, neighbours and relatives the maximum amount of labour assistance. The actual labour teams which then emerge provide a measure of where the stress of social obligation is greatest. The argument of previous chapters has already provided a theoretical indication of what sort of groups these are likely to be; the empirical data which follow provide, in some respects, a validation of the theory.

In the first place it needs to be understood that, although the village as a whole adheres to a single irrigation time-table, this does not result in absolute synchronism of harvest work. Different varieties of rice have different maturation periods so that even if sowing has been completed within the space of a few days, reaping may still be spread over several weeks. For the *Yala* harvest of 1954 all the seed sown was classed as 'three month paddy' but it actually included three varieties—*kirimurunga, monelvari* and *ilangamatta*—and maturation ranged from 90 to 115 days.

The first of these varieties produces a glutinous rice which was used in the New Rice ceremonies preceding the main threshing, but I think other rapid-growing soft-kernel varieties can also be used for this purpose.

The stages of harvest work are as follows:

(*a*) Rice is cut by sickle, properly with the left hand. An *upidda* is 'one sickle cut', that is about six hand clutches. The straw is cut to the base. Each *upidda* is laid on the ground, normally to the rear and to the left of the reaper. It lies there all day in the sun. If rain comes it will have to be turned.

(*b*) Preparatory to stacking, the *upidda* are clumped together in loose sheaves (*mapidda*).

(*c*) The sheaves are then built up into stacks (*vatamalu*) constructed at the corner of the *liyädda* plot on the top of the ridge (*tunata*). Ordinarily one such stack contains the rice from three or four *liyädda*, but this will depend on the distribution of landholding. Each *vatamalu* belongs to one individual owner. Where weather conditions are satisfactory this preliminary stacking will be completed on the same day as the initial reaping. At this stage in the Pul Eliya Old Field in 1954 there were about 420 *vatamalu* stacks distributed over the 40 acres.

(*d*) Each of the principal plot-holders now prepares a threshing floor (*kamata*). This ordinarily consists of a single square *liyädda* cleared of stubble and scraped smooth. Although the field has only been fully drained for a few days the ground has already an almost brick-like hardness and the plain scraped surface needs little treatment. It receives an occasional sprinkling of water designed to lay the dust. In all, twenty such *kamata* were constructed. Their position and ownership is discussed below.

(*e*) As the *kamata* are completed work teams are organised to shift the crop from the small *vatamalu* stacks to the threshing floor. Here the sheaves are built up into much larger stacks referred to as *kola goda*. The process of collection is intricate since, owing to the complex pattern of primary tenure and subsequent *ukas* and *andē* contracts, each individual cultivator is likely to have a stake in a variety of different *vatamalu* distributed in different parts of the field. The crop owner must, therefore, not only assemble his crop at a convenient threshing floor, he (or she) must also ensure that it is appropriately stacked (see Plate IV B).

At the end of stack shifting there might be eight or more *kola* stacks by the side of a single threshing floor. The contents of each such stack was in some way unique, either because it contained grain of some special variety or because the shared ownership was in some way different from that of any other stack. For example, A.V. Punchi Etani (B 1 : A 1) had leased land to (*a*) P. Kapurala (Bel:2), (*b*) P. Kirala (D 2:1), (*c*) M. Kirala (Cx:1), (*d*) M.V. Tikiri Appu (Bel:3). Her crop originally stood in roughly 40 *vatamalu* stacks in different parts of the field. This was later conveyed partly to *kamata* no. 3 and partly to *kamata* no. 15 (Diagram 5, p. 272). It was stacked in four *kola* stacks corresponding to the four different *andē* leases.

Ideally a carrying team (*kayiya*) would consist of seven individuals. Of these two would be dismantling the *vatamalu* and making the sheaves up into man-loads (*kolamittiya*) which are carried on the back in a specially designed hide sling (*gōnahamma*); three would be running a shuttle system, carrying the loads from the *vatamalu* to the threshing floor; two would be building the threshing-floor stacks.

Very few teams were in fact of this optimum size. In one case the cultivator himself carried out the whole of the work alone except for the part-time assistance of his wife; this was P. Ran Banda (A 1:6) working at *kamata* no. 1. Naturally his work programme got badly behindhand.

261

Once the *kola* stacks have been built the owners of cattle have the right to admit their animals to graze on the stubble. The stacks must therefore be fenced off. In a number of cases the threshing floors had purposely been sited close together so that one fence could be put around a whole group of stacks. The precise manner of this grouping proved to be very revealing and will be discussed presently.

Phase IV: threshing

Threshing itself was traditionally associated with an elaborate complex of ritual,[1] and in 1954 the older Pul Eliya inhabitants still seemed to believe that the final yield would depend upon an adequate adherence to religious and magical procedures (see Plate V A). The ritual bears on the problems of the organisation of labour in the following respects:

(1) There is still a strong taboo on the participation of women in any part of the work of threshing.

(2) No household threshing rice from the Upper Old Field may commence threshing before the New Rice festival, which is an all-village rite.[2]

(3) Since work on all threshing floors starts on the same night, and can only be undertaken by men, and since each floor requires a minimum team of two men, and the village contains only thirty-four adult males, there is here a state of full employment. The numbers are made up by workers from Diwulwewa, Bellankadawala, Wiralmurippu and Tulawelliya.

The sequence of technical operations on the threshing floor is as follows. The contents of each *kola* stack are threshed separately. The work is always carried out at night so as to take advantage of the cool air and avoid exhausting the buffaloes (see Plate V B).

---

[1] Cf. Lewis (1884), Ievers (1880), Coomaraswamy (1905).

[2] *Sinakkara* and *badu* lands and even the lands of the Lower Old Field were deemed to be free of this overriding ritual restriction. Rice from such land could be threshed whenever the owner thought fit, though a private offering to the deities was felt to be advisable by many.

Stage 1. The straw to be threshed is heaped in the middle of the *kamata*, leaving a circle on the outside empty. (*vata dana*—'the divided circle.) The team of buffaloes (usually four in number) is now led in and made to walk around on top of the heap. The inside, right, buffalo is *muduna* (the top) and the outside, left, buffalo is *kalavatiya* (the maker of the circle). These two buffaloes need to be specially trained.

Stage 2. The threshers toss the corn and straw from the centre towards the circumference, which was previously empty. (*muduna kadanavā*—'breaking the top'.)

Stage 3. The buffaloes are made to tread out the straw at the circumference. (*vata kadanavā*—'breaking the circle'.)

Stage 4. The threshers toss the centre corn to the edge and the edge corn to the centre, gradually heaping the straw back into the centre and then repeating stage 1. (*pala peridenava*—'shaking out the fruit'.)

Stage 5. The straw has now been fully separated from the grain and chaff. This empty straw is thrown back on to the stacks outside the *kamata*. (*mäda bānavā*—'unloading the middle'.)

Stage 6. The grain and chaff is swept together into a heap. (*nelanavā*—'gather fruit'.)

Stage 7. The grain and chaff is winnowed by tossing into the breeze and fanning. (*hulan kerenavā*.)

Stage 8. On the completion of winnowing the threshed grain has to be measured out into the proper shares of the various owners. It is then removed to the granaries by the women. It is only when the grain has already been measured that the women may set foot on the threshing floor.

Stage 9. When threshing is completed the straw must be baled up and shifted to store. It is partly used as cattle food but also as thatching material. The process of straw baling is considered to be very arduous and unrewarding work and outside labour is often hired for cash.

LABOUR ORGANISATION

At each stage of the harvest there are several alternative types of labour organisation which may be brought into operation. These are four in number, namely:

(i) A plot-holder may do the work himself with the aid of other members of his household. The only theoretical restriction here is the exclusion of women from the work of threshing, but in practice two other factors are relevant. The actual work of threshing is an intricate technique, so that the principal member of a threshing team must always be a man of some maturity. Furthermore, since the buffaloes have to be trained buffaloes, and buffaloes seldom take kindly to strangers, the organisation of threshing teams is affected by the pattern of buffalo ownership, which is complex. In Pul Eliya there were more than enough buffaloes to go round, but there was a scarcity of trained buffaloes and competent buffalo drivers.

(ii) Reapers may be employed on the basis that they receive one bushel of grain for each bushel area of land which they reap. Thus, if the field reaped has been sown with one bushel of seed the reaper will earn one bushel of grain.

(iii) Individual coolies may be hired on a daily basis for cash. The standard rate of pay in 1954 was 3 Rupees per day for men and 2 Rupees per day for women. As explained above, such employment was very seldom given to fellow Sinhalese. Tamil labourers were quite often employed in this way, particularly for unpleasant jobs such as straw baling. The hired labourer received no food, though sometimes he obtained tea.

(iv) The cultivator may organise a *kayiya* (i.e. labour team). The general principle is that the plot-holder collects a group of his friends and relatives to assist him on the understanding that on some other occasion he will give reciprocal service to each of the individuals concerned.

Choice as to the form of labour to be employed will depend upon the type of task and the particular circumstances of the cultivator. From a sociological point of view the *kayiya* system is of especial interest since the membership of such labour teams provides an index of the significant groupings in the community.

'KAYIYA' (LABOUR TEAMS)

Analysis showed that in nearly all cases the main principle of recruitment was that of affinal kinship. The organiser of the team was ordinarily a *māmā* ('mother's brother') or a *massinā* ('brother-in-law', 'cross-cousin') to each of the individuals whom he summoned. Adult full brothers were very seldom seen working in the same *kayiya* though half-brothers, step-brothers and brothers by adoption sometimes did so.

I noted two exceptions here, both of which were special cases:

(i) On one occasion K. Tikiri Banda (Cx:2) and K. Nanghamy (Cx:3) teamed up to work together on behalf of their *dīga*-married sister K. Ran Manika (Z:Cx) of Karapikkada. She had undertaken an *andē* responsibility for harvesting plot 29, the property of the village headman K.V. Appuhamy (A2:7). She reaped the field herself, but threshing, which is exclusively a male task, was done by her brothers working together.

(ii) K. Wannihamy (B2:7) and his 'bachelor' brother K. Menikrala (B2:6) regularly worked together. These two men lived together in the same house (house III) and, although I was given specific assurances to the contrary, it is difficult to avoid the conclusion that to some extent this was a case of polyandry. Behaviours here were not fully consistent. While Wannihamy was 'close' to his brother Menikrala, he was also notably 'close' to his brothers-in-law, Tikiri Banda (Cx:2) and Nanghamy (Cx:3). The latter were not, however, on friendly terms with Menikrala, and certainly did not recognise him as a husband of their sister.

Fathers and sons are likely to work together in one team so long as the sons are unmarried, but once the son becomes an individual householder they are likely to appear in different labour teams, especially if the son marries *binna*. On the other hand, an old man who has already divided his property can work in comfort with his sons on whom he has become dependent.

Generally speaking, consistency between the residence pattern and work behaviour was striking. Individuals who lived under the same roof nearly always worked in the same team; but individuals who lived in the same compound in different houses very seldom worked in the same team. The exceptional case again came from compound B2, house III. K. Menikrala (B2:6) and K. Wannihamy (B2:7) did not co-operate with their co-resident *māmā*, U. Kuda Pinhamy (B2:E3). Wannihamy clearly recognised that this was an unnatural state of affairs, for he kept telling me that Kuda Pinhamy 'ought' to build a house for himself in his own compound (compound E, see p. 215).

Before I discuss the empirical details of individual *kayiya* I must say a little more about the 'landlord-tenant' relationship expressed in the term *andē*. Part of nearly every *kayiya* team was made up of pairs of individuals who were already associated by an *andē* contract. We need to understand how this comes about.

'ANDĒ': THE REWARDS OF LANDLORD AND TENANT

The simple theory of *andē* is that, after the payment of sundry expenses—such as fees to the Vel Vidāne[1]—the leaseholder will take half the residue of the crop and the landlord the other half. It is, however, up to the landlord to make sure that he is not cheated. As the Pul Eliya people worked the system, the owners of *andē* holdings were expected to provide one unit of labour on each of three occasions, namely: (i) at sowing, (ii) at stack shifting, and (iii) at threshing, these being the occasions when an ill-disposed tenant might indulge in fraudulent procedure. The presence of the landlord, or of his representative, on these occasions is not, however, simply that of witness. He is there as a labourer. This was made quite clear by the fact that elderly widows, such as A.V. Punchi Etani (B1:A1), who had let out their land on *andē* lease, but were not able to be present themselves, actually went so far as to hire outside labourers to act as their 'witnesses' on the specified occasions.

Now the labour force which the leaseholder can provide directly from the members of his own household is likely to number only two or three persons—say the man, his wife and one child—so that the labour provided by the landlord's witnesses

[1] The Paddy Lands Act 1958 has abolished the right of the Vel Vidāne to claim a fee for his services. The consequences of this could be remarkable. In 1954 the Vel Vidāne took a commission of 24 *sēru* per 100 *lāha*, which, on the face of it, meant a commission of 4 per cent. Unfortunately I did not check the relative sizes of the measures in question. Regulations appeared to allow the Vel Vidāne only 1½ per cent.

totals up to something between a quarter and a third of the whole. It is thus very much an over-simplification to say that, in an ordinary share-cropping arrangement, the rent received by the landlord amounts to 'one-half the residue of the crop'. A substantial part of this 'rent' must be considered as a reward for the labour contributed by the landlord or his agents. The Pul Eliya people themselves fully appreciated the economic value of the labour contributed by the landlord, for in circumstances in which the landlord was unable to provide his labourer-witness the landlord's share would be cut down from one-half to one-third.

It did not prove possible to verify in full detail the precise shares accruing to all the different landlords and tenants. Particular *andē* leases were subject to various kinds of special contract, depending upon whether the landlord or the tenant provided the buffaloes, the ploughs and the seed and also upon the nature of other debt relationships already existing between the contracting parties. The mortgage case described above (pp. 245 ff.) provides an instance of this.

The Pul Eliya people themselves seemed to think of the *andē* relationship as one of mutual service rather than of tenancy.

It was said that if a poor man wished to obtain land on *andē* from a rich landlord he would offer him a ritual gift of oil cakes (*kavum petaya*). The landlord, as a matter of prestige, would always offer his client the best land at his disposal. But this 'poor client' element only applied to a small proportion of all *andē* transactions; in most cases it was rather that the *andē* tenant was a man (usually a near relative) who as a matter of mutual convenience had undertaken to cultivate the land *on behalf of* the landlord. Up to the point at which the grain had been threshed the crop was consistently spoken of as belonging to the landlord and not to the tenant. At the final division of the crop the Vel Vidāne's commission is divided off first, then the owner's share, and finally the tenant takes the residue. But the ideology is that the tenant's share is a gift from the landlord as reward for labour services; it is not felt that the landlord receives a payment of 'rent' from the tenant.

The case of 'undivided estates' makes it particularly clear that the 'rent' terminology is largely inappropriate. Where a holding is inherited by a large number of heirs so that subdivision of the plot is inconvenient, it is quite usual to retain the plot intact and lease it *andē* to one or other of the heirs. For example, plot 43 represents one-eighth share of one *panguva*. It is one-quarter of a strip of land originally given to Mudalihamy (C:Z2) and inherited by his four children. Plot 43 was the share of M. Kirihamy (Cx:1), deceased. In 1954 Kirihamy's estate was undivided. The product of the land accrued to his widow and four children, all of whom were adult. The four children comprised two girls, married *dīga* away from Pul Eliya, and two boys, Tikiri Banda (Cx:2) and Nanghamy (Cx:3). The manner of working the strip was to consider that the estate as a whole was leased *andē* to Tikiri Banda and Nanghamy in turn. The 'owner's share' of the crop then accrued to Kirihamy's widow, who lived with Nanghamy, and this was in turn reallocated into five parts among the heirs.

In 1954, Tikiri Banda held the *andē* of the land, but he in turn had sublet to his uncle M. Kirala (C1:2), who was also working the three neighbouring portions of the strip on behalf of himself and his two siblings. I did not observe the actual division of the crop, but I have no reason to suppose that the correct fractions were not worked out. Pul Eliya farmers were prepared to take a lot of time and trouble on such matters.

The principle on which different *andē* contracts were based derived from the economic doctrine that the landlord, the labourer, the seed and the buffaloes constitute the four main factors of production, each of which is separately entitled to its own reward.

Thus the following ideal categories of *andē* lease were distinguished:

(*a*) Normal *andē*—owner contributes seed, buffaloes, ploughs and one unit of labour at sowing, stacking and threshing.
Shares: 50 per cent to owner; 50 per cent to tenant.
(*b*) *tunen andē* ('third' *andē*)—owner contributes seed, buffaloes, ploughs, but no labour.
Shares: $33\frac{1}{3}$ per cent to owner; $66\frac{2}{3}$ per cent to tenant.

(c) *hataren andē* ('quartered' *andē*)—owner contributes labour as above, but no seed, buffaloes or ploughs.

Shares: 25 per cent to owner; 75 per cent to tenant.

(d) *andē havula* ('partnership' *andē*)—owner contributes half seed, half buffaloes, and half the *total* labour force.

Shares: owner takes an initial share of paddy equal to whole of the seed (that is twice his contribution) and thereafter 50 per cent of the residue. *Example*: Suppose a 2-bushel field gives a nett crop of 30 bushels; owner and tenant each contribute 1 bushel of seed. At the division, after the Vel Vidāne's fee has been paid, owner takes 2 bushels, leaving 28 bushels; then 14 bushels go to owner and 14 to tenant.

Partnership *andē* of this last category included a number of cases where close kin were working as a farming group. For example, plots 107 in the Lower Field were owned by U.V. Pinhamy (C1:W) and were worked by him jointly with his son P. Herathamy (A2:C1) and his nephew (*bānā*) K. Nanghamy (Cx:3). The buffaloes were contributed by U.V. Pinhamy, but Nanghamy had contributed 2 bushels of seed. Nanghamy was entitled to 4 bushels of grain before calculating the residue, which was then allocated 50 per cent to Pinhamy, 25 per cent to Herathamy and 25 per cent to Nanghamy.

The hire of buffaloes and ploughs against payment in kind, as against direct payment in cash wages, is part of this same pattern. For example, the village schoolmaster leased the Temple Field for the *Mahā* season of 1954/5 from the High Priest of Kadawatgama (39). He employed labourers from Diwulwewa (56) and paid them in cash at Rs 3 per day. Since neither the schoolmaster himself, nor his labourers, nor the High Priest, were members of the Pul Eliya *variga*, it was quite proper to make payment in cash. In a similar way, the schoolmaster hired plough cattle, ploughs and harrows at Rs 2 per day. But comparable transactions between members of the Pul Eliya *variga* were nearly always conducted on a delayed 'payment in kind' basis. U. Kuda Pinhamy (B2:E3) hired plough cattle from V. Menikrala (B1:7); the contract was that for one bushel of land he would pay one

bushel of grain at harvest. In return for this hire Kuda Pinhamy
was to have the use of buffaloes for ploughing (twice), harrowing
and threshing.

The variety of detail in such cases makes it impossible to
generalise at all precisely about the rewards accruing to 'tenants'
and 'hired labourers', but what is relevant here is that all *andē*
contracts establish debt relationships which are ultimately settled
by payments in kind rather than in cash. In this sense *andē*
arrangements between members of the same *variga* can be seen
as part of the general system of reciprocities between kin.

The facts which I have been discussing here have some bearing
on the definition of marriage given in chapter IV (pp. 89 ff.).

When a young man establishes *binna* domestic relations with a
woman and she begins to cook for him, she is provided with a
separate hearth and the couple are treated as a distinct economic
unit within the compound of the girl's parents. The young man
will be dependent for his livelihood mainly on the grain which he
obtains either from his father-in-law or from his own father. In
either case he is likely to be treated as being in *andē* relationship
with the parental landlord. Only if he actually shares a granary
with a member of the senior generation will be be regarded as
fully incorporated into the household of the granary owner.
A young *binna*-married husband is very unlikely to be in this
position. In contrast, a *dīga*-married youth is quite likely to share
in the granary of his father. In this case marriage does not
separate the husband from his parental household in the way that
binna marriage does. Even so, the wife of a *dīga*-married youth
will cook for her husband on a hearth which is separate from that
of her mother-in-law, so that here too marriage initiates a process
of fission in the domestic group which is completed when the
young husband begins to store his grain separately from that of
his parents.

DETAILED ORGANISATION OF THE LABOUR TEAMS

Having outlined the general principles through which *kayiya* teams are recruited and shown the very close interconnection between ties of kinship and ties of economic obligation as manifested in the *andē* system, I shall now examine in detail some of the actual labour groupings which emerged during the course of the Pul Eliya *Yala* harvest of 1954.

There were, in all, twenty threshing floors. I was told that threshing floors could be sited anywhere according to the owner's convenience, and that they were located in such a way that the labour of shifting stacks, etc. was reduced to a minimum. As it turned out thirteen of the threshing floors were located in the Ihala elapata. This was a convenient place from which to carry the threshed grain and straw back home into the village compound. For each exceptional case there was a rational explanation. For example, M. Naidurala (Dx:Y), made a threshing floor in compound Dx itself and carried his sheaves there directly, but in this particular case this was the easiest thing to do. B. Danapala, the outsider landlord, was going to remove his grain ultimately by cart so he made his threshing floor on his own land in the Pahala elapata. U.V. Pinhamy (C1:W) owned two main blocks of land which were far apart, so he made two threshing floors, one in the Ihala elapata and the other at the far end of the field on plot 107. So far as I could judge, there was no conscious intention on the part of the villagers that the threshing floors should be arranged in any special way. Nevertheless, when the stacking arrangements were mapped out, it was clear that a very definite pattern had emerged.

Since choice was free, each individual teamed up with his closest bond friend to share in the construction of a threshing floor and in the building of *kola* stacks. The final arrangement is summarised in Diagram 5 and Table 10.

What we may call the 'in group'—those who reside in the main village and have well-established hereditary status there—have all sited their *kamata* in the Ihala elapata and have further

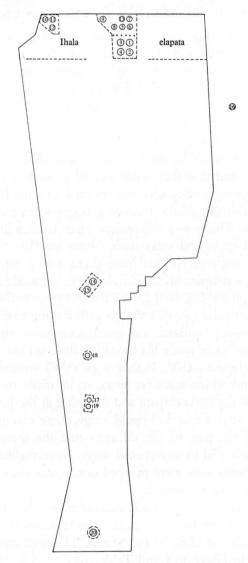

Diagram 5. Relative position of threshing floors (*kamata*) at the *Yala* harvest of 1954.

272

Table 10. *Distribution of threshing floors ('kamata')*

Kamata no.	Where located: plot no.	Principal owners	Remarks
		Group A. *Kamata* located in the Ihala elapata	
1	7	*S. Subasinghe (A1:5)	Four adjacent *kamata*.
2	8	*P. Ran Banda (A1:6)	Composition of group
3	6	*U.V. Menikrala (Bel:1)	fully analysed in text
4	8	*M. Herathamy (B1:Dw)	
5	3	*U. Sirala (A2:5)	Four adjacent *kamata*. Co-
		U.V. Pinhamy (C1:W)	owners of no. 5 are
6	3	P. Kapuruhamy (C2:D2)	brothers-in-law. Re-
7	3	S. Jaymanhamy (D1:9)	mainder of group associ-
8	3	A. Bandathe (G2:Z2)	ated as neighbours in
			compounds G, C1, C2
			D1
9	2	*U. Kadirathe (A2:4)	The retired Vel Vidāne
		K.V. Appuhamy (A2:7)	and his son the *tulāna*
			Headman. Note the
			central position
10	1	*U. Wannihamy (A2:6)	Three adjacent *kamata*.
11	1	K. Dingiri Banda (A2:B2)	Though owners all from
12	1	B. Siriwardena (A2:Z5)	compound A2, no two
			are blood relatives
13	3	U. Kuda Pinhamy (B2:E3)	See pp. 265, 275. No other
			member of compound
			B2 assisted here
		Group B. *Kamata* located in 'outside' positions	
14	60	*B. Danapala (—)	Wrong *variga*
15	61	*K.V. Punchi Etani (Dw:1)	Resident in Diwulwewa
		M. Kirala (C1:2)	Wrong *variga* origins
16	Compound Dx	*M. Naidurala (Dx:Y)	Caste taint (Appendix 2)
17	87	*N. Punchi Banda (Dx:4)	Caste taint but avoids his father at *kamata* 16
18	77	*U. Kapuruhamy (B2:5)	Wrong *variga* origins, an *upāsakarāla*
19	89	B. Ausadahamy (A2:Y)	*Binna*-married husband working land of father-in-law
20	107	*U.V. Pinhamy (C1:W)	*Kamata* additional to no. 5

* Owner of ground on which *kamata* located.

roughly sorted themselves out according to their compound group filiation. This accounts for thirteen of the twenty *kamata*.

The principal owners of six of the other seven *kamata* are all in one way or another 'outsiders'. *Kamata* 14 belongs to a non-resident of 'wrong *variga*' status; *kamata* 15 to a man whose *variga* standing is marginal (see p. 282); 16 and 17 to members of the 'outside' compound Dx; *kamata* 18 is that of an *upāsakarāla* (see p. 133)—a man who has voluntarily left the world; *kamata* 19 is that of a *binna*-married husband on bad terms with his father-in-law; *kamata* 20 was simply a supplementary threshing floor belonging to the owner of *kamata* 5—significantly, the usual rituals associated with the construction and use of *kamata* were omitted in this case.

So far, the 'structural pattern' is clear, but my use of the expression 'principal owner' in the tabulation oversimplifies the facts. Each *kamata* was used by a number of different cultivators, namely those who built their *kola* stacks alongside it. The group of people who co-operated in this way in the use of one *kamata* ordinarily constituted a single *kayiya* (work team). They had worked together reciprocally to help each other in the task of stack-shifting, and it was roughly the same people who later worked together in teams of two or three in the work of threshing. But these threshing-floor groups were not absolutely exclusive, for some individuals worked in turn on several different floors; either in order to fulfil conflicting obligations or else with the specific purpose of accumulating claims on other people.

For example, P. Kapurala (Bel:Z) of Bellankadawala sometimes worked with his father-in-law U.V. Menikrala (Bel:1) on *kamata* 3, but he threshed the paddy from the plots which he was working for M. Dingiri Banda (P:B 1)[1] on *kamata* 6, which put him in a team with P. Kapuruhamy (C2:D2). He explained this switch in terms of convenience—there was more space at *kamata* 6—but there was an element of reciprocity also. P. Kirala (D2:1), half-brother to P. Kapuruhamy, was working on *kamata* 3.

---

[1] Resident in Periyakkulam (33), son of A.V. Punchi Etani (B1:A1) in whose name the plots in question were registered.

Another case of 'mixed allegiance' was that of U. Kuda Pinhamy (B2:E3), whose *kamata* (no. 13) was the last to be constructed. Kuda Pinhamy himself had first of all worked in six different *kayiya* and then summoned to his assistance an entirely mixed group consisting of K. Ukkurala (H:(S)), Punchirala Gamarāla (D2:C), U. Sirala (A2:5), K. Murugathe (A2:3) and M. Naidurala (Dx:Y). This last, however, was a unique case. The great majority of *kayiya* were focused around a core of close kinsmen, especially affinal kinsmen.

To appreciate the full pattern the reader needs to understand that the *kayiya* team may derive from either of two nuclei.

On the one hand there is the fact that around each *kamata* are constructed a set of *kola* stacks, the contents of which will in due course be threshed out on that *kamata*. Each *kola* is in some way distinct, either because of the type of rice or because of the ownership. In cases of *ukas* and *andē* several different people may have some kind of ownership to a single *kola* stack. The total number of 'owners' associated with a single *kamata* may thus be quite considerable. Such groups of 'owners' turned out to be mainly kin-based.

But on the other hand the responsibility for getting the crop shifted from the small *vatamalu* in the field to the large *kola* stack at the *kamata* is the primary responsibility of the original culti-vator, and he will ordinarily have to organise a *kayiya* to help him with the work. Here again the composition of the *kayiya* has a basis in affinal kinship but a 'stack-shifting team' may consist of different individuals from those who act together as co-owners of the associated *kamata*. This distinction will become clear if I cite two cases in detail.

THRESHING-FLOOR ORGANISATION

Case 1 gives the composition of a stack-*owning* team associated with a cluster of four adjacent *kamata*; Case 1 *a* gives the composi-tion of the stack-*shifting* team employed in building certain of the stacks mentioned in case 1. Case 2 provides comparable informa-tion for two other *kamata* in another part of the field.

Case 1. Ownership of 'kola' stacks at 'kamata' 1–4

Table 11 gives the full details of the ownership of the individual *kola* stacks erected around *kamata* nos. 1–4 as listed above on Table 10. There were fourteen such stacks in all and they comprised paddy from twenty-three different plots. In the 'ownership' column I have placed the cultivator's name first, followed by the superior landlord's name, if any.

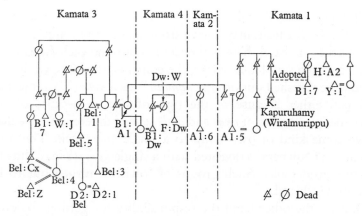

Chart *e*. Kinship and *kayiya* organisation. (i) Kinship links between individuals listed in Table 11.

Chart *e* shows the close mesh of affinal kinship which links all these individuals together. It will be observed that, while 'half-sibling' and 'foster-sibling' connections are often relevant, ties of direct filiation and full siblingship are seldom given much weight. The reasons for this have been discussed at length in chapter IV.

It will be seen that P. Kirala (D 2:1) was the cultivator initially responsible for *kola* stacks 3 *c*, 3 *d*, 3 *e*. In order to shift the crop from the *vatamalu* stacks in the open field to the *kola* stacks at *kamata* 3, P. Kirala organised a full-scale *kayiya* team of seven persons. It will be seen from case 1 *a* that the principle of team formation is the same as before, even though the membership is different.

Table 11. *Ownership of 'kola' stacks at 'kamata' 1–4*

Kamata no.	Kola stack no.	Paddy from plot nos.	Details of ownership
1			S. Subasinghe (A1:5)
	1a	6	ukas/andē with Herathamy V.V. (Wiral-murippu) (see p. 140)
	1b	14, 33, 82	Subasinghe alone
	1c	40, 69, 95	K. Kapuruhamy (Wiralmurippu) andē from V. Menikrala (B1:7)
	1d	86, 96	K. Kapuruhamy (Wiralmurippu) andē from U.G. Pinhamy (H:A2)
2			P. Ran Banda (A1:6)
	2a 2b	8, 35, 103	P. Ran Banda alone. Probably two varieties of rice
3			U.V. Menikrala (Bel:1)
	3a	51	U.V. Menikrala alone
	3b	42	U.V. Menikrala andē from B. Hetuhamy (Y:1)
	3c	64, 67	P. Kirala (D2:1) andē from U.V. Menikrala (Bel:1)
	3d	25	P. Kirala andē from U.V. Menikrala andē from A.V. Punchi Etani (B1:A1)
	3e	70	P. Kirala andē from V. Menikrala (B1:7) andē from P. Ran Etani (W:J)
	3f	38, 94	M.V. Tikiri Appu (Bel:3) andē from U.V. Menikrala (Bel:1) andē from A.V. Punchi Etani (B1:A1)
	3g	57	P. Kapurala (Bel:Z) andē from M.V. Ran Manika (Bel:4) and W. Nanghamy (Bel:5) (jointly)
4			M. Herathamy (B1:Dw)
	4a	13, 93	M. Herathamy ukas/andē from K.V. Kapuruhamy (F:Dw), V. Menikrala (B1:7) and W. Punchi Etani (Dw:W) (see p. 266)

277

Case 1a. Membership of 'kayiya' team which assisted P. Kirala (D2:1) for the stack shifting of 'kola' stacks 3c, 3d and 3e in case 1

	Name	Relationship to leader and remarks
A	P. Kirala (D2:1)	Leader
B	Punchirala Gamarāla (D2:C)	Father (old man), co-resident
C	P. Kapuruhamy (C2:D2)	Half-brother by same father—not co-resident; deputised as representative of V. Menikrala (B1:7)
D	P. Herathamy (A2:C1)	*Bānā*—father's step-brother's daughter's son—also *massinā*—wife's father's half-brother's son
E	B. Hetuhamy (Y:1)	Distant. In the team because he was assistant to U.V. Menikrala (Bel:1) on *kola* stack 3b. U.V. Menikrala was P. Kirala's father-in-law
F	M.V. Ranhamy (D2:Bel)	Wife
G	A.V. Punchi Etani (B1:A1)	*Nānā* to mother-in-law. First owner of *kola* stack 3d

In this team B. Hetuhamy (Y:2) was really deputising for U.V. Menikrala. The latter was on rather bad terms with his son-in-law, P. Kirala. Kirala had no land of his own, but Menikrala had promised to transfer the title in plots 64 and 67 to his wife, M.V. Ranhamy, if Kirala would agree to live *binna* in Bellankadawala. As Kirala refused to do this he only had the plots on *andē* (*kola* stack 3c), and received relatively little labour assistance from his father-in-law.

P. Herathamy (A2:C1) seems to have joined this team mainly so as to avoid working with his father and father-in-law on *kamata* 5.

Case 2. Stack ownership and labour organisation at 'kamata' 14 and 15

By way of contrast we may consider the situation at *kamata* 14 and 15, which were located in the Pahala elapata and which were largely owned and worked by 'outsiders'.

The facts are best understood if it be noted that the principal cultivator is K. Menikrala (B2:6) acting as *andē* tenant to the 'outsider' B. Danapala (see p. 253). All the individuals named, except two, have marginal status with respect to the Pul Eliya *variga*. The two exceptions are K.V. Appuhamy (A2:7) and A.V. Punchi Etani (B1:A1) and it is thus very revealing that these two superior landlords

Table 12. *Ownership of 'kola' stacks at 'kamata' 14–15*

Kamata no.	Kola stack	Paddy from plot nos.	Stack ownership
14	14a 14b 14c	47 60, 71 63	K. Menikrala (B2:6) *andē* from B. Danapala (Marutamadu)
15	15a	105	M. Kirala (C1:2) *andē* from K.V. Appuhamy (A2:7)
	15b	100	M. Kirala (C1:2) *andē* from A.V. Punchi Etani (B1:A1)
	15c	54	K. Tikiri Banda (Cx:2) *andē* from his wife and his wife's siblings (Cx:D1); (D1:9); (B1:D1)
	15d	24, 85	K. Wannihamy (B2:7)
	15e	23	K. Wannihamy (B2:7) *andē* from K. Appuhamy (W:B2)
	15f	22, 83	K. Menikrala (B2:6)
	15g	84	K. Menikrala (B2:6) *andē* from K. Appuhamy (W:B2)
	15h	56, 61	P. Menikrala (Dw:D2) *andē* from his wife K.V. Punchi Etani (Dw:1) and from his brother-in-law K.V. Kapuruhamy (F:Dw)

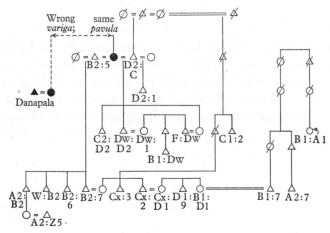

Chart *f*. Kinship and *kayiya* organisation. (ii) Kinship links between individuals listed in Table 12.

both sent hired labourers as representatives instead of attending in person.

K. Appuhamy (W: B2), landlord of plot 23, and full brother to both K. Menikrala (B2:6) and K. Wannihamy (B2:7) did not attend the *kayiya* at all; neither did the fourth brother K. Dingiri Banda (A2:B2). K. Nanghamy (Cx:3) assisted his brother-in-law, K. Wannihamy (B2:7) at *kola* stacks 15*e* and *d*, but did not assist his own brother (Cx:2) on *kola* stack 15*c*.

The two landless old men Punchirala Gamarāla (D2:C) and U. Kapuruhamy (B2:5) assisted their respective sons; P. Kirala (D2:1) assisted his half-brother, P. Menikrala (Dw:D2), on one occasion. B. Siriwardena (A2:Z5), *bǟnā* to K. Menikrala (B2:6) and K. Wannihamy (B2:7), helped with stacks 15*d*–15*g*.

P. Kapuruhamy (C2:D2) assisted M. Kirala (C1:2) at stacks 15*a*–15*b*, apparently as reciprocity for work done by Kirala at *kamata* 6. P. Kapuruhamy did not work with his full brother (Dw:D2) at *kola* stack 15*h*.

At threshing time M. Herathamy (B1:Dw) assisted at stack 15*h*, and in return received help at *kamata* 4 from both P. Herathamy (A2:C1) and K.V. Kapuruhamy (F:Dw).

DISCUSSION OF 'KAYIYA' EXAMPLES

These examples illustrate the general principles of labour-group formation. Kinship alone does not *determine* who shall join in a common work team. People work together because of economic relationships, that is because of debt obligations of the *ukas* and *andē* types or because of obligations of reciprocity. Nevertheless we find, on actual inspection, that the people who work together are bodies of kinsmen linked together by *pavula* ties such as have been described in earlier chapters.

The nature of the kinship obligation is made particularly clear in the last case. Here K.V. Appuhamy (A2:7) and A.V. Punchi Etani (B1:A1) were not members of the *pavula* concerned—indeed both of them were in a distinctly hostile relationship with several of the individuals shown in the chart. By failing to attend personally at the *kayiya* they avoided any expression of kinship, but they did not thereby escape the economic obligation; both

sent hired representatives to contribute their appropriate share of
the appropriate labour.

Above all I would emphasise the element of choice that is
present. There is no clear-cut jural obligation that a particular
individual should contribute his labour to one group rather than
to another. On the contrary, every individual is subject to a
variety of such obligations and he chooses that course which
appears most advantageous or convenient to himself. The
structural pattern which emerges as the result of these multiple
choices is a 'social fact' in the Durkheimian sense; it is something
quite outside the immediate awareness of the participants, just as
the suicide rate is quite outside the conscious awareness of any
individual suicide.

Let us examine again just why the participants in *kamata* 15
(case 2) should have found it convenient to stack their *kola* at the
Pahala elapata instead of at the Ihala elapata. The reasons they
gave were simply those of convenience. B. Danapala wanted his
stacks on his own land; K. Menikrala (B2:6) was working the
land; therefore it was convenient for K. Menikrala to have his
own stacks next to Danapala's stacks. K. Wannihamy (B2:7) was
working land adjacent to that of his brother. P. Menikrala
(Dw:D2) was going to take his crop to Diwulwewa anyway, and
kamata 15 was immediately adjacent to the land (plots 56, 61)
which he had been cultivating. For M. Kirala (C1:2) and his
nephew K. Tikiri Banda (Cx:2), it was a matter of convenience.
Kola 15 *a, b* and *c* contained the crops from plots 54, 105 and 100,
and all these could much more easily be threshed at the Pahala
elapata than at the Ihala elapata.

All these arguments seem perfectly sensible, but M. Kirala
(C1:2) found equally good reasons for moving the product of
plots 44–6 and 72–8 to *kamata* no. 6 in the Ihala elapata, so 'convenience' cannot be only a matter of location.

Probably the real factors that influenced M. Kirala in this case
were something like this. He is a poor man with little land of his
own; it is not worth his while to make his own *kamata*, so he will
share with someone else. It is in fact 'obvious' that he should

share either with his 'step-brother', P. Kapuruhamy (C2:D2) at *kamata* no. 6, or with his brother-in-law, U.V. Pinhamy (C1:W), at the adjacent *kamata* no. 5, particularly since some of the land he is working, that is plots 44 and 73, actually belongs to U.V. Pinhamy's wife. But M. Kirala is also working land on lease from A.V. Punchi Etani (B1:A1) (plot 100) and from K.V. Appuhamy (A2:7) (plot 105), both of whom are on bad terms with U.V. Pinhamy (C1:W). Tact urges him to thresh this particular crop elsewhere, so he takes it to *kamata* no. 15, where his brother's son, Tikiri Banda (Cx:2), and the latter's brother-in-law, K. Wanni-hamy (B2:7), are already installed.

All this detail appears random and arbitrary, yet how beauti-fully appropriate it is from a 'structural' point of view! Each of the stack builders at *kamata* nos. 14 and 15 was in some degree an 'outsider'—or at least 'on the margin' of the Pul Eliya *variga*.

The dubious standing of U. Kapuruhamy (B2:5) and his sons has been noted already (p. 196); K. Menikrala (B2:6) had put himself further outside the pale by agreeing to work for the out-sider Danapala (cf. p. 253). In contrast, K. Dingiri Banda (A2:B2), whose wife's *variga* standing was impeccable, did *not* join this *kayiya* but made his own *kamata* no. 10 *inside* the Ihala elapata.

M. Kirala (C1:2) and his nephew, K. Tikiri Banda (Cx:2), likewise belong to a group of very imperfect hereditary status in Pul Eliya. They are descendants of Mudalihamy (C:Z2), who came from Wewalketiya. Though they reside on land which once belonged to Naidurala Gamarāla II (C2), this is the outcome of gift and purchase, not hereditary right (p. 214). It fits exactly with this ambiguous status that M. Kirala (C1:2) should have had one *kola* stack with the 'in group' on *kamata* no. 6 and two more with the 'out group' on *kamata* no. 14.

Again, P. Menikrala (Dw:D2), though born in Pul Eliya, resides in Diwulwewa as husband to a granddaughter of Kapurala Vedarāla (F:1), who seems to have been driven out of the village soon after 1890 (p. 209). The only 'in group' *kamata* on which he might have had any claims was no. 6, but this was owned by his full brother, P. Kapuruhamy (C2:D2), whom he must avoid.

He might perhaps have worked with his wife's brother's son, M. Herathamy (B1:Dw), on *kamata* no. 4, but this would have brought the *ukas/ande* dispute described on pp. 245 ff. right out into the open.

My point is that the positioning of individual stacks is the outcome of a combination of 'accidental' circumstances, but the total pattern which emerged at the end was a significant arrangement which represented the social structure in a quite valid way and in a manner which was consistent with the behaviour of the same individuals in much more formal situations such as village festivals and family festivals (that is, girls' puberty and marriage).

FENCING OF 'KAMATA'

There is ordinarily a considerable interval between the completion of the *kola* stack building and the commencement of threshing. During this period the cattle will be grazing in the stubble, so that the various groups of *kamata* standing within the paddy field area must be fenced.

The manner in which the fencing was accomplished provided another illustration of the way in which technical operations can display the relative strength and weakness of competing sets of social obligations.

The barbed wire which was used for the fencing was wire taken down from the fencing of the main field, which is jealously preserved individual property (see p. 167). Each of the 'out group' *kamata* within the *pangu* sections of the Old Field area was fenced off individually with wire taken from the ends of the *issara* strips in which it stood. On the other hand *kamata* 14 and 15 in the Pahala elapata were surrounded by a single fence made up of wire taken from the fence dividing the upper and lower fields. This wire actually belonged partly to B. Danapala, the owner of plot 63 (*kamata* 14), and partly to K.V. Punchi Etani (Dw:1), the owner of plot 61 (*kamata* 15).

In the case of the thirteen 'in group' *kamata* in the Ihala elapata the situation was more complex. *Kamata* 10, 11 and 12 were surrounded by one fence. The wire was provided partly by U. Wannihamy (A2:6) with wire taken from the fence to plot 1, and partly by K. Dingiri Banda (A2:B2) from the end section of plot 15.

It was at first intended that one fence should surround *kamata* nos. 1, 2, 3, 4, but that another separate fence should be put around *kamata* nos. 5, 6, 7, 8, 9, 13, and post-holes were actually dug with this in view. In the case of *kamata* no. 1, the owners of each stack agreed to produce 18 fathoms of fencing material. However, in order to provide his section of the fence to *kamata* no. 1, S. Subasinghe (A1:5) proposed to dismantle the portion of the *elapata* fence which contained his wire (by virtue of his ownership of plot 6). This section of fence happened to be adjacent to *kamata* no. 13 where it was serving a useful purpose. After a lot of argument Subasinghe agreed to leave his fence standing, on the understanding that U. Kuda Pinhamy (B2:E3), owner of *kamata* no. 13, would provide substitute wire to fence *kamata* no. 1.

Such careful particularity of the precise obligation falling on each individual plot-holder and tenant is just what we should expect in view of the extreme elaboration of the 'fair shares' principle in other parts of the system. But what was interesting was that, despite all the careful calculation, Kuda Pinhamy did *not* produce the wire. The final arrangement was that one fence encircled all the ten *kamata*.

Now, to myself, as an outsider, it was obvious from the first that this was the most economic arrangement, and my notes record my astonishment that the owners of *kamata* nos. 1–4 should have been ready to go to the trouble to separate themselves from the others. The separating fence, had they erected it, would have served no functional purpose; it would merely have expressed the feeling of structural opposition which distinguished compounds A1 and B1 on the one hand from their 'enemies' in compounds C and D on the other. Yet the fact that, at the end of the argument, the two sets of *kamata* were separated not by a fence, but only by a row of posts, is also significant and part of a recurring pattern. It is an index of how ephemeral such oppositions are.

For it must always be understood that, in this society, the social solidarity between members of a single *pavula* or between members of a single *gedara* (compound group) is never clear cut. The local community is so small in scale that, for most practical day-to-day purposes, the boundaries between the different social groupings must, almost of necessity, be blurred at the edges.

I originally defined a compound as an area within the *gamgoda* area fenced off by itself (p. 97). And certainly the fences existed and the villagers were highly conscious of their existence. They repeatedly complained to me of how the fences stood for lack of sociability and of how, 'in the good old days', there were no fences and everyone lived together in brotherhood and amity. Yet the separation provided by the fences was an idea rather than a fact. In 1954 nearly all the fences had gaps in them and there was hardly anywhere a gate which could be closed.

The ambiguity of social commitment which is associated with the absence of unilineal descent makes it understandable that fences assume a symbolic importance. An individual feels that it is important to know for certain who is on 'our side of the fence' and who is on the other. But when it really comes to the point everyone knows very well that life would become impossibly complicated if people could not go through the fences whenever they liked.

Or to put it another way, the fences, both real and ideological, only apply to the narrow and special context of inherited property. When we are dealing with economic situations in which inheritance rights do not critically discriminate one individual from another we find that the various kinship principles summarised at the beginning of this section (p. 243) become irrelevant.

The remainder of this chapter is, therefore, taken up with two pieces of ethnography which provide the negative evidence. Tank fishing and chena cultivation are *not* organised according to kinship principles.

SECTION B: TANK FISHING

The fact that a *panguva* is primarily a share to tank water rather than a share to land has the logical consequence that the *pangu* system extends to the fishing rights in the tank. Some of the smaller tanks dry up completely during long spells of dry weather. These contain only mudfish and the fishing rights here are of negligible value. But the larger tanks very seldom dry up completely and many of them contain large numbers of very delectable fish. The annual fish harvest represents an important item in the economy of the average village.

It is, at all times of the year, possible to catch fish in the shallow waters at the back of the tank. Individual shareholders go after such fish using plunge baskets and other devices. Fishing by torchlight is often quite successful. Individual fishing of this kind is, however, a sport rather than a serious business.

But twice a year towards the end of the irrigation season when the waters in the tank reach their lowest point, there is a much more serious type of fishing. The level of the water even at its deepest is then reduced to only two or three feet, while the water area has been reduced to a narrow zone immediately behind the bund (see Plate 1). This narrow shallow band of water contains the whole fish population of the tank, and the fish can be caught very easily by the plunge-basket technique.

The custom is that, as the water falls, the Vel Vidāne, observing the state of affairs, erects a leaf-decorated pole (*bol pola*) in the bed of the tank. This is a sign to declare that all individual fishing must cease. The restriction has the sanction of a magical taboo. I was told that anyone breaking the taboo might expect shortly afterwards to be attacked by a crocodile. It was said that formerly this duty and right of erecting a *bol pola* was one of the perquisites of the Gamarāla. Whether all three Gamarāla held this right or only one particular Gamarāla at a time was not clear. Today the duty falls on the Vel Vidāne by virtue of a government instruction.

As the water falls further, so that an individual can wade right through the tank at all levels, the Vel Vidāne begins to seek agreement among the *pangu* holders on the holding of a collective fishing. As soon as 50 per cent of the *pangu* holders can agree among themselves, the Vel Vidāne announces, some days in advance, the date of the fishing party. This fishing is reserved primarily for actual *pangu* holders, but such *pangu* holders may introduce their friends and relatives as assistants. A successful fishing party is likely to consist of thirty or more individuals. Some of these form a close line across the tank and drive the fish into one corner; the remainder of the party, armed with plunge baskets,[1] set about actually catching the fish. Astonishingly large numbers of fish are caught in a very short time. The division of the spoils then follows.

I was told that in the old days, in the Pul Eliya tank, the Gamarāla took a first cut of sixty large fish. It may be remembered that in the Old Field each *bāga* consists of 60 fathoms. My own inference is that the sixty fish correspond to the 60 fathoms and that this was a perquisite for each Gamarāla and not just for one particular Gamarāla. Unfortunately I did not check this point in the field.

In the modern system the Vel Vidāne is not entitled to any equivalent perquisite. As the plunge-basket fishermen catch their fish each man strings his fish individually on to a sharp-ended loop of bamboo hooked to his waist. At the end of the fishing the fishermen all wade to the shore and count out the catch. Of every three fish one goes to the fisherman and two into the *pangu* pool. the fish belonging to the *pangu* pool are then put into one large heap and counted out 'according to the *pangu*'. If there are twenty *pangu* then there will be twenty equal heaps. The various shareholders then take out fish according to their *pangu* holding. Thus the owner of two *pangu* will take two whole *pangu* heaps, the owner of half a *panguva* will take half a *pangu* heap, and so on. Odd fish are cut up into sections to equalise the share.

The period of collective fishing lasts for three days and during

---

[1] The technique is accurately illustrated by Knox (1681/1911), p. 48.

this period all fish caught must be divided out among the *pangu* holders in the manner just described. At the end of the three-day period the tank becomes open and anyone from any village can come and fish, either as an individual or along with a party of friends. One would have imagined that by this procedure some tanks would soon be completely emptied of all fish, but apparently this does not happen. I learnt of no procedure for systematic restocking of tanks, though there may be some such arrangement. There does not seem to be any special sociological principle on which fishing teams are organised. Only men partake of this activity. While I was in Pul Eliya there was no fishing party in the Pul Eliya tank itself, for the tank never became shallow enough, but parties of Pul Eliya men visited the Diwulwewa (56) and Bellankadawala (55) tanks for fishing drives. The participants were mostly men in the 20–35 age-group, with a large number of younger boys helping in the drive. An interesting point is that the party that went to the Bellankadawala tank went on the invitation of S. Subasinghe (A 1 : 5), who happens to be a shareholder in that tank. S. Subasinghe himself, however, did not bother to join the party. In the Diwulwewa case, on the other hand, two Diwulwewa tank *pangu* holders were members of the party.

The absence of any obvious kinship patterning of the work teams needs to be considered in relation to the fact that:

(*a*) Fishing is an optional activity and there is no competition for labour. Hence the rights of a man over his *massinā* do not have to be invoked.

(*b*) The team work is *ad hoc* for one day only and, though it is work in relation to the use of tank water, the situation is not one where neighbours may be led to quarrel over water supplies. Consequently the normal restraint against co-operation with near kin (father-son, brother-brother) disappears.

SECTION C: SHIFTING CULTIVATION

INTRODUCTION

I have already pointed out in chapter II that shifting cultivation (*hēna*, or 'chena') is a matter on which villagers and the administration hold diametrically contrasted points of view.

Government regulations are framed on the theory that, in general, shifting cultivation is unnecessary and should be prohibited. Nevertheless, the government admits that a small minority of villagers have so little paddy land that they cannot support themselves and their families by the use of this land alone. For these few special concessions are allowed. The *tulāna* Headman is supposed to certify who these individuals are and then, on the basis of this certification, each man will be allowed to clear a separate one-acre plot for one season only for the specific purpose of growing dry-land food crops such as *kurakkan*. The *tulāna* Headman is supposed to be personally responsible for seeing that the one-acre allotment is not exceeded.

There are a great variety of reasons why these regulations seem unworkable and ridiculous from the villagers' point of view. First, it is obvious to the villager that it is absurd to clear chena land in small plots. Two of the major parts of the labour of chena cultivation are (*a*) the work of erecting fences, and (*b*) the work of crop watching at night. If we compare a single 9-acre chena area with one in which there are nine separate one-acre plots we find that, by separating out the total into individual holdings, the work of fencing is increased threefold and the work of night watching ninefold. Furthermore, in a small one-acre plot the loss of crops due to raids by monkeys and other pests is proportionately very much greater than in a larger field.

Moreover, whereas the government looks upon chena cultivation as an emergency method of raising additional foodstuffs, the villagers see it as primarily a means of raising cash crops. The better-off villagers who are forbidden to cultivate chena regard the privileged position of the so-called 'landless peasant' as a ridiculous injustice. Finally, since the *tulāna* Headman is not provided with an aeroplane, it is obviously impossible for him to keep a close watch on the shape and size of every small jungle clearing. The smaller the plots are required to be the more difficult it is for the Headman to keep a check. The Headman doubtless knows where all the clearings are, but he can easily profess ignorance.

The aerial photograph, Plate 1, was taken in 1956. It shows a large number of chena clearings in actual use and others which have fairly recently been abandoned. Judging by my experience of 1954 I should guess that not more than half the chenas in actual use had received any sort of licence from the government. It is also very obvious that only a very small number of these clearings are of the regulation one-acre size; most of them appear to be between four and fifteen acres in area. The photograph includes land belonging to Wiralmurippu (57), Tulawelliya (59), Kalawel Potana (61), Diwulwewa (56) and Bellankadawala (55), as well as Pul Eliya (58).

In 1954 the villagers and the administration had reached deadlock; as a result, in that particular year, no new chena licences were given out. Many villagers recultivated a number of old chenas which they had first cultivated the previous year. Some new chenas were also cultivated but these were entirely illicit. The recultivated second-year chenas fell into several distinct types. There were a few regulation, square, one-acre plots fully licensed by the government; a cluster of these (*A*) may be seen just left of the road on the bottom edge of the plate. Secondly, there was land which the user had cleared on a permanent basis with the alleged intention of asweddumising and irrigating the land. Thus the chena marked *B* had been cleared by the ever-industrious U. Sirala (A2:5) as a *vi hēna*, that is as a chena used for growing rice. This land abuts on to the same owner's encroached plot no. 150 (Map *B*, cf. p. 44), and it was his obvious intention to extend the area of his encroachment further and further into the Crown jungle.

Thirdly, there were one or two chenas of the ancient traditional type in which a number of individuals combined to share a single field. The most notable of these was the field marked *C*, lying to the south-east of the Pul Eliya main tank. I shall refer to this field as the Pul Eliya Wheel Chena.

THE PUL ELIYA WHEEL CHENA[1]

In constructing a field of this type the procedure is first to choose a convenient position as centre of the field. A small area around this focus point is then fully cleared of trees and scrub; on this is erected a tall straight post called a *mul katti*. A circle about 12 ft. in diameter is then drawn on the ground around this post. The shareholders to the chena then agree among themselves on the proportion of the total circle that each will take. The proportions are marked out by pegs on the circumference of the circle. Lines are then drawn from the *mul katti* to the pegs and these lines are then extended outwards into the jungle by means of markers. Each shareholder is responsible for clearing the segments of the circle thus allocated. He is also responsible for building that portion of the fence which is opposite the end of his particular segment. He cultivates the land in his particular segment only and in any way he chooses.

There is no obligatory co-operation between the owners of different segments except of course that the different sectors of fence must be made to meet one another. A night-watching obligation is worked out by roster as in the case of the *pangu* holders in a *bāga* system. Diagram 6 shows the condition of this Wheel Chena in October 1954. It should be remembered that conditions were slightly abnormal because this was the second year that this particular chena was being cultivated.

Some of the original shareholders had withdrawn. In particular Ukku Banda (H:3), a former son-in-law of U.V. Pinhamy (C1:W), had abandoned his wife and left the village. His sector had been taken over by B. Ausadahamy (A2:Y), his sister's

[1] The material in this section may usefully be compared with Ryan and others (1955) who describe chena cultivation in another part of the Ceylon Dry Zone.

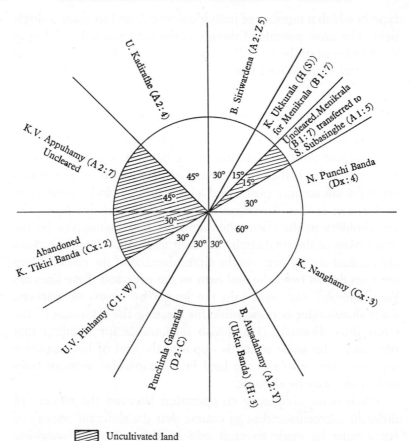

Diagram 6. Layout of Pul Eliya 'Wheel Chena', October 1954.

husband. K. Tikiri Banda (Cx:2) had abandoned his sector altogether. V. Menikrala (B1:7) had leased part of his holding to K. Ukkurala (H(S)) and presented the other half to S. Subasinghe (A1:5). The *tulāna* Headman, K.V. Appuhamy (A2:7), was trying hard to give his section away. The point of this manœuvre was that the original owner is responsible for doing his share of night-watching, whether he clears his land or not.

In this particular case it will be seen that all the segments have been obtained by dividing a particular angle of arc into either halves or thirds, so that all resulting angles are either 15°, 30°, 45° or 60°. The information I obtained suggests that this simple kind of geometry is the rule.

In discussing the membership of this Wheel Chena group no one suggested that any principle of equal representation between the different *bāga* groups was involved. It will be noticed, however, that nearly all the compound groups are in fact represented. The group includes representatives from:

Compound A2: K.V. Appuhamy (A2:7), U. Kadirathe (A2:4), B. Siriwardena (A2:Z5).
Compound A1: S. Subasinghe (A1:5).
Compound D2: Punchirala Gamarāla (D2:C).
Compound D1: N. Punchi Banda (Dx:4).
Compound H: B. Ausadahamy (A2:Y), Ukku Banda (H:3).
Compound B1: V. Menikrala (B1:7).
Compound C1: U.V. Pinhamy (C1:W), K. Tikiri Banda (Cx:2), K. Nanghamy (Cx:3).

It was obvious that the villagers were rather proud of the fact that they still preserved this ancient traditional way of doing things, and it seems to me likely that the traditional principle of 'fair shares for all compounds' tended to be given a special prominence whenever they resorted to this traditional procedure. But I must stress also the negative side of the case; this co-operative team is in no sense a group of close kin; it is certainly not a single *pavula* group. V. Menikrala (B1:7) and U.V. Pinhamy (C1:W) in particular have long been bitter enemies. U. Kadirathe (A2:4) and Punchirala Gamarāla (D2:C) likewise are the very antithesis of close friends. But then the group is not really a *co-operative* labour team at all—there is no sharing of economic rewards and responsibilities. Principal shares of land having been allocated, each individual then works his own piece to the neglect of everyone else in the field; the whole thing is simply an adaptation of the principles of the *pangu* system to the conditions of chena cultivation.

Indeed the villagers themselves recognised this; for they described to me another 'traditional' (*purāna*) layout for a chena field which they described as a *pangu hēna*. The description is illustrated in Diagram 7, which shows the layout in the case of a field with six equal *pangu*. The field as a whole is laid out in a rectangle, and divided into eight parallel strips of equal width. The six central strips are allocated one to each *pangu*; the two end strips are treated as *elapata* and subdivided into six equal sections— one for each *panguva*. The idea is to equalise the amount of fencing liability for each *panguva*—though this equalisation is not perfect. In the diagram case, *pangu* 2 and 5 have slightly less fencing than the other 4 *pangu*. The villagers said that this layout for a chena is today seldom used, and the aerial photograph seems to confirm this.

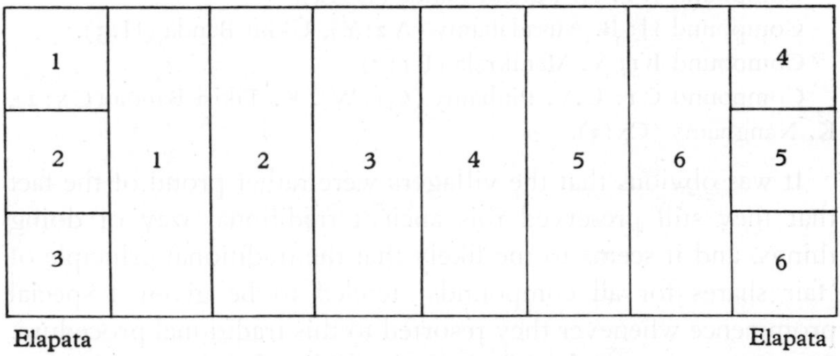

1							4
2	1	2	3	4	5	6	5
3							6

Elapata   Elapata

Diagram 7. *Pangu* chena: ideal schema.

To return to the Wheel Chena, the more obvious kinship connections between the participants are shown on Chart *g*. The conclusions which can be drawn from this are largely negative. I think it is probable that in the first instance, when the field was first cleared in 1953, U. Kadirathe (A2:4) and his friends took one half of the field and Punchirala Gamarāla (D2:C) and his friends the other half, but I cannot state for certain that this is what happened.

Some of the kinship links were certainly relevant; thus B. Siri-wardena (A2:Z5) himself said that he got his share by the favour of his 'grandfather', U. Kadirathe (A2:4), and Ukku Banda (H:3), K. Tikiri Banda (Cx:2) and K. Nanghamy (Cx:3) all got their shares from their *māmā*, U.V. Pinhamy (C1:W); but N. Punchi Banda's (Dx:4) participation cannot be explained simply in terms of kinship. It probably stems from the very close economic links existing between V. Menikrala (B1:7) and Punchi Banda's father, M. Naidurala (Dx:Y).

There is no overall systematic pattern such as can be observed in the distribution of *paravēni* holdings in the Old Field or in the

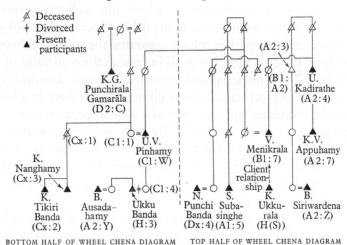

Chart *g*. Kinship connections between participants in Pul Eliya 'Wheel Chena' 1953–4. Closest known links.

organisation of *kayiya* teams at threshing time. In the chena situation the territorial context, though nicely patterned, is quite impermanent and *ad hoc*.

In the irrigated fields the scarcity of labour and the scarcity of water together force the individual to exploit to the utmost those rights over neighbours and kinsmen which are latent in the total structure; and in this situation the kinship system is seen to operate in a definite and consistent way in accordance with a set of rules. But in chena cultivation, as practised here, there are no economic scarcities which force men to co-operate so that the manifestations of kinship association are random and without significance.

CHAPTER VIII

CONCLUSION

What then has been demonstrated by this meticulous examination of a very limited range of facts? In this final chapter I shall attempt my own assessment of where this volume stands in relation to other current work in the field of social anthropology.

The crucial distinction which separates the social anthropologist from the ethnographer is his interest in the constraint of the individual. The ethnographer is content to record 'custom', that is to say the facts which are generally true of a society in a broad sense; the individual appears only as a stereotype, a creature who conforms to custom unthinkingly and without motive. In contrast, the social anthropologist stresses that custom is synthetic and quite distinct from the behaviour of individuals; a large part of modern anthropological 'theory' is concerned with the implications of this dichotomy.

There have been several distinct approaches to this issue which differ according to the empiricist and idealist bias of the writer's underlying philosophy. Is the 'social thing' which constrains the individual a tissue of ideas or of objective facts? The several arguments can all be traced to Durkheim.

In the immediate post-war period the strongest influence in British social anthropology emanated from Oxford, where the views of Radcliffe-Brown and Evans-Pritchard were dominant, with Durkheim's *Division of Labour* and Maine's *Ancient Law* as primary sources. Individuals were presumed to be born free into a society composed of corporate institutions, the relations within which and between which provide a paradigm of social existence. The structural shape of such a corporation is intrinsically self-perpetuating and is independent of the individual life-span of its particular members. Social structure is thought of as a network of relationships between 'persons', or 'roles'. The stability of the system requires that the content of such relationships shall be permanent. In such a society every individual who fills a role finds himself under jural constraint to fulfil the obligations inherent in that role. More crudely, the customs of a society are seen as providing a body of moral norms worked out in behaviouristic form; the discrepancies between individual behaviour and customary behaviour are due simply to the inability of the average man to live up to the moral demands of his society. He is represented as knowing very well what ought to be the case, but as devising immensely complicated fictions which will absolve him from the inconveniences of virtue.

Evans-Pritchard's accounts of Nuer practices with regard to descent, residence and sacrifice provide numerous examples of what I have in mind. It may be remarked that this whole analysis rests on the premiss that behaviour, as observed by the anthropologist, must of necessity make sense in terms of an equilibrium system. The reader should remember that both the sense and the equilibrium are purely pragmatic assumptions—they are convenient for certain practical purposes. There may well be situations in which these functionalist premisses are best abandoned.

There is another line of thought, which also comes from Durkheim, which stems from the thesis that the social is that which is *quantitatively* normal. In the *Division of Labour* norms are jural norms, rules of behaviour supported by sanctions; in *Suicide* the norm is a statistical average. Throughout the later writings both of Durkheim himself and of his followers this same ambiguity between normative and normal constantly recurs. In British anthropology it corresponds in some ways to the opposition between the Radcliffe-Brown and the Malinowski versions of functionalist doctrine.

In Radcliffe-Brown's schema Society is something other than a sum of individuals, for Society has the power to impose its will upon the individual through the operation of the sanctioned rules which constitute the structure of enduring corporate groups. The social anthropologist is expected to concentrate his attention upon the nature of these rules and the manner by which they are enforced.

In contrast, in Malinowski's system, despite the underlying assumption that every custom serves a utilitarian purpose and the emphatic assertion that the individual is not a 'slave to custom', no clear distinction ever emerges between customary behaviour on the one hand and individual behaviour on the other. Custom is what men do, normal men, average men.

It follows that custom, in Malinowski's conception, is like Durkheim's 'suicide rate', a symptom; it is not something imposed by rule, nor is it itself coercive, it simply corresponds to the state of affairs. Custom 'makes sense' not in terms of some external, logically ordered, moral system, but in terms of the private self-interest of the average man in that particular cultural situation.

Malinowski here evaded many issues, and the crucial one of just *how* the social fact of normal behaviour can emerge from a sum of seemingly arbitrary individual choices is one which the social anthropologist cannot legitimately avoid; but at least he did not invoke a mysticism to explain away what we do not understand.

The currently fashionable structuralist concept of 'social solidarity' seems to me to be precisely such a mysticism, for it has lately begun to be treated as an ultimate explanatory device, an absolute virtue towards which all social activity is of necessity directed. The magical potency of this concept has now been expanded to the point at which Gluckman finds it sensible to explain warlike deviation from customary behaviour as itself a form of custom which has the purposive function of enhancing social cohesion (Gluckman, 1955, especially chap. 11). This kind of double-talk can be made very persuasive, but it is a purely scholastic argument; it has no more scientific value than the comparable double-headed dogmas of the psycho-analysts.

A third way of thinking about the distinction between custom and individual behaviour derives from the difficult Durkheimian notion of 'collective representations'. Here the thesis is that 'the sacred' and the 'profane' are distinct categories of verbal and non-verbal behaviour and that the former is, as it were, a 'model' for the latter. In some developments of this argument, ritual is looked upon as providing an 'outline plan' in terms of which individuals orientate their day-to-day behaviour. The divergencies of individual behaviour from any standard norm are not then the result of moral error or of unenlightened self-interest, but arise simply because different individuals, quite legitimately, fill in the details of the ideal schema in different ways.

As I made clear in an earlier volume (Leach, 1954), this last type of approach, despite its manifest idealist pitfalls, offers a number of attractions. It disposes of the twin functionalist fictions that social systems are intrinsically in stable equilibrium and that all parts of such a system are mutually consistent. Furthermore, it allows the anthropologist to take cognisance of social adaptation to changing circumstances.

But, in my view, the strict Durkheimian proposition that 'things sacred' and 'things profane' are quite separate categories, applicable to sets of events which are distinct both in time and place, is not tenable. The category distinction, to be useful, must apply to aspects of all behaviour rather than to separate items of total behaviour. 'Rituals', through which the members of a society manifest to themselves the model schema of the social structure within which they live, occur all the time, in ordinary everyday affairs just as much as in situations which are explicitly ceremonial.

No doubt it is true that, on the occasion of a wedding or a funeral or a coronation or a degree-taking ceremony or of any similar formal function, the structural relationships between the participants are quite explicitly and consciously dramatised, and therefore easy to observe, but, unless such representations are to be regarded as mere play-acting and pretence, the same kind of structural patterning should be observable in ordinary everyday affairs.

In this book I have attempted to demonstrate this principle. The facts which have been discussed cover only a part of a single institutional aspect of the life of Pul Eliya villagers. The subject-matter of the book is the relation between land use and kinship within that very narrow territorial framework. But my objectives are those of a social anthropologist, not of a geographer; I have sought to demonstrate that the notion of 'structural relationship' is not merely an abstraction which the anthropologist uses as a paradigm to simplify his problems of description. The social structure which I talk about in this book is, in principle, a statistical notion; it is a social fact in the same sense as a suicide rate is a social fact. It is a by-product of the sum of many individual human actions, of which the participants are neither wholly conscious nor wholly unaware. It is normal rather than normative; yet, since it clearly possesses some degree of stability, we are still faced with Durkheim's problem—what relates a suicide rate with the motivations of an individual suicide? What is it about the Pul Eliya social system which persists?

When I started writing this book, this seemed to me to be my principal problem—I wanted to understand the principles of structural continuity in this small-scale community which lacked any obvious type of exclusive on-going corporation. There were no unilineal descent groups, no secret societies, no sects; what then were the continuing sets of relations which kept the society in being? It was only gradually that I came to realise that this whole formulation was altogether too much in the tradition of Radcliffe-Brown and the Oxford structuralists. Why should I be looking for some social entity other than the individuals of the community itself?

Because the structuralists assume that the individual is constrained by *moral* forces, it necessarily follows that the constraint is social, and we are led directly into the Durkheimian mystique which attributes the characteristics of deity to Society regarded as a corporation. But if we repudiate the emphasis on moral rules and jural obligation then the problem becomes much simpler. The constraint imposed on the individual is merely one of patterning and limitation; the individual can do what he likes as long as he stays inside the group. The group itself need have no rules; it may be simply a collection of individuals who derive their livelihood from a piece of territory laid out in a particular way. The continuing entity is *not* Pul Eliya *society* but Pul Eliya itself—the village tank, the *gamgoda* area, the Old Field with its complex arrangement of *bāga* and *pangu* and *elapata*. For purely technical reasons, connected with the procedures and efficiency of irrigated rice agriculture, the arrangements of the Pul Eliya ground are difficult to alter. They are not immutable, but it is much simpler for the human beings to adapt themselves to the layout of the territory than to adapt the territory to the private whims of individual human beings.

Thus, as I stated at the beginning, Pul Eliya is a society in which locality and not descent forms the basis of corporate grouping; it is a very simple and perhaps almost obvious finding, yet it seems to me to have very important implications for anthropological theory and method.

My denigration of 'kinship structure' in favour of 'locality structure' does not rest simply on an assertion. I claim that, by the detailed presentation of the facts, I have demonstrated, for the careful reader, that what I assert to be the case is so. But having made the demonstration, at least to my own satisfaction, I am filled with scepticism. How many of the elegant structural analyses, which British social anthropologists have presented over the past twenty years, would really stand up to such microscopic treatment?

Let me be clear in my insinuations. Contemporary British social anthropologists very rightly pride themselves on the meticulous detail of their field researches, and, as functionalists, all of them operate with contextualist premisses; but for the structuralist follower of Radcliffe-Brown the context is transcendental. Behaviour takes place within a social structure which, it is maintained, is no less real because it cannot be objectively perceived. Durkheim understood, as some of his successors have not, that such a 'social structure' must necessarily be credited with the attributes of Deity. The anthropologist with his wealth of detailed knowledge of the behavioural facts claims an intuitive understanding of the jural system which holds these behaviours in control. When he writes his structural analysis, it is this private intuition which he describes rather than the empirical facts of the case. The logical procedures involved are precisely those of a theologian who purports to be able to delineate the attributes of God by resorting to the argument from design.

Of course it is all very elegant, but it is not a demonstration; the structuralist anthropologist, like the theologian, will only persuade those who already wish to believe.

I am not wishing to suggest that the notion of *social*, as distinct from *material*, context is wholly without value, but it is a concept which must be used with great discretion. It is essentially a metaphysical idea, and like other such ideas it can very easily be stretched to explain, or explain away, anything you choose.

Primarily this book is offered as an example of the analysis of a particular peasant society which lacks a unilineal descent system. As such, I think it has some merits whatever may be the theoretical prejudices of the anthropological reader. But as regards theory, my purpose is to introduce a wider scepticism. It is not merely that, in societies lacking unilineal descent, some such analytical process as this becomes appropriate, but that potentially this same method, applied to societies *with* unilineal descent, might produce disconcerting results. It might even be the case that 'the structure of unilineal descent groups' is a *total* fiction; illuminating no doubt, like other theological ideas, but still a fiction.

Whether this be so or not, it is high time that social anthropologists considered the possibility; they need to take another look at the basic assumptions of the structuralist thesis. Is it, for example, due to empirical fact or to theoretical bias that, in the spate of Africanist writing on systems of kinship and marriage, the emphasis has been all on kinship to the neglect of marriage? Common descent results in social solidarity, marriage differentiates and is the ultimate source of all social fission; the argument in its various manifestations is now well known (Fortes, 1953).

'Social solidarity', as Radcliffe-Brown and most of his followers have used it, is a deceptive, unanalysed concept. It does not follow that those who have common interests are the most likely persons to act in co-operation; nor does the fact that two individuals are placed in the same category by third parties necessarily impose upon them any solidarity of interest or of action. In Pul Eliya, full siblings belong by birth to the same household, and hence to the same compound group, and they necessarily have closely similar territorial rights of all kinds. This means that full siblings must learn to 'fit themselves to the ground' in much the same way, yet, from the start, full siblings are rivals for the same material assets; every man will be the gainer by the death of his brother. In contrast, relations to affinity, which lack common territorial interest, are likely to maximise economic and social co-operation. There is a *kind* of social solidarity both between siblings and between affines, but we need to make a distinction.

Local group endogamy is not the survival of archaic caste prejudice, it is the necessary corollary of the fixed layout of the cultivated fields and the equal property rights accorded to both men and women. In chapter IV we saw how the people of Pul Eliya, the Pul Eliya *minissu*, stressed their membership of a common *variga*—a group of endogamous kin; but we also saw that membership of this common *variga* did not really depend upon common descent. Anyone who was acceptable as a Pul Eliya landowner and was also acceptable in the capacity of brother-in-law to an existing Pul Eliya landowner would, in practice, be treated as of 'our *variga*'. The test of *variga* membership never turns upon an issue of descent; it is always a question of whether or not a particular sexual relationship between a man and a woman is to be accepted as establishing affinal links between the man and the woman's kinsmen. And the critical factor here is whether or not the man can assert a claim to any kind of property right, either in the Pul Eliya *gamgoda* area or in the Pul Eliya Old Field.

The Old Field in particular, because of the way in which it is laid out and the impossibility of any accidental alteration to this layout, provides for the villagers a visual model of their community. The repeated assertion that the community consisted of three families (*pavula*) and that, in the old days, there had been three Gamarāla, was simply a projection of the *bāga* arrangements

303

of the Old Field. It did not correspond to the actual facts as any living inhabitant of Pul Eliya had ever known them.

On the other hand, the recent and quite sudden development of large areas of *sinakkara* and *badu* land had radically altered the territorial nature of the place. In 1954 it was no longer logical that the Pul Eliya villagers should think of themselves as organised around the Old Field and the *gamgoda* area exclusively. They were fully conscious of this; when they spoke of the Old Field as *purāna*, they did not merely mean 'traditional', they also meant 'old fashioned'. Yet, without the Old Field, the Pul Eliya community itself would be without a *raison d'être*; kinship alone could not hold the community together. I noted in chapter III that, under official stimulus, the villagers had all enthusiastically applied for *badu* land house-sites in scattered parts of the village territory far away from the present *gamgoda* area. Although I do not believe that, when it came to the point, any villager would actually make the move which such applications imply, the applications are themselves significant. The villagers understood that, with the recent changes in land tenure, co-residence in the *gamgoda* area is no longer a socio-economic essential. That they should contemplate scattering confirms my assertion that 'kinship solidarity' is here an image of the pattern of landholding and not vice versa.

There is nothing in the least novel about this point of view; I am simply asking my anthropological colleagues to get back to first principles. Structuralist anthropologists are far too much inclined to dichotomise their material. Just as Durkheim tried to distribute actual behaviours between his polar categories 'sacred' and 'profane', so too the structuralists try to polarise 'things social' and 'things material'. Running right through the literature of structuralist anthropology there is an underlying assumption that the social structure of a society and the material environment are two 'things' of comparable kind. Although intrinsically interconnected, the two 'things' have independent existence and are both 'real' in a comparable sense.

But this antithesis is false. Society is not a 'thing'; it is a way of ordering experience (Beattie, 1959, p. 55). My criticism is directed against such points as these:

(a) Evans-Pritchard in writing *The Nuer* (1940) clearly tried to integrate the analysis of 'ecology' (chs. 1–3) with the analysis of 'social structure' (chs. 4–6). In practice each half of the book is autonomous and makes sense without reference to the rest.

(b) Fortes (1945), p. 143, remarks: 'lineage and locality are interwoven and interdependent factors of Tale social structure. But they are functionally discrete factors' and, again (p. 171), 'every defined social group' has 'an intrinsic connection' with 'a specific locality'. Yet Fortes finds it useful to define the groups without reference to locality.

(c) Mitchell (1956) in a chapter entitled 'The Lineage Framework of Villages' manages to polarise 'social groups' (based in matrilineal descent) and 'villages' (based in locality). Evidently, lineages are thought of as 'existing' independently of villages, and considered to be a 'social' phenomenon in a sense that villages are not.

(d) The whole body of assumptions implicit in the design and construction of *African Systems of Kinship and Marriage* (1950) which are summed up in Radcliffe-Brown's assertion that 'The reality of a kinship system as a part of a social structure consists of the actual social relations of person to person as exhibited in their interactions and their behaviour in respect of one another' (p. 10).

In contrast, I want to insist that kinship systems have no 'reality' at all except in relation to land and property. What the social anthropologist calls kinship structure is just a way of talking about property relations which can also be talked about in other ways.

I doubt whether any of my colleagues would deny this, but somehow they have worked themselves into a position in which kinship structure is treated as 'a thing in itself'; indeed a very superior sort of thing which provides a self-sufficient and self-maintaining framework for all that we observe.

My protest is not directed against the study of kinship, for this is by far the most sophisticated tool of analysis which the social anthropologist possesses, but against attempts to isolate kinship behaviours as a distinct category explainable by jural rules without reference to context or economic self-interest.

Of course every social anthropologist recognises that societies exist within a material context which is partly natural—terrain, climate, natural resources—and partly man-made—houses, roads, fields, water supply, capital assets—but too many authors treat such things as nothing more than context, useful only for an introductory chapter before getting down to the main job of analysing the social structure. But such context is not simply a passive backcloth to social life; the context itself is a social product and is itself 'structured'; the people who live in it must conform to a wide range of rules and limitations simply to live there at all.

Every anthropologist needs to start out by considering just how much of the culture with which he is faced can most readily be understood as a direct adaptation to the environmental context, including that part of the context which is man-made. Only when he has exhausted the possibility of explanation by way of normality should it be necessary to resort to metaphysical solutions whereby the peculiarities of custom are explained in terms of normative morality.

APPENDIX 1

DESCRIPTION OF A 'VARIGA-SABHA'

The following account is based in part upon a description given to me in person by the accused, Arlis, in advance of the actual event, and in part upon an eye-witness description by my interpreter who was sent to observe the proceedings.

The court met at Kalawel Potana (61), a mile and a half from Pul Eliya, and it was concerned with the Vanni-Väddā *variga*. The interpreter told me about the circumstances:

'Vannakulasuriya Arlis Fernando is a carpenter practising at Minhettigama. He comes originally from Colombo and about eighteen months ago set up house with a Vanni-Väddā woman from Kalawel Potana. They have a child about five months old. Arlis is doing a good business and is well satisfied with his condition; he wishes now to make his marriage regular so that his own children can marry his wife's relatives when they grow up. Since he is a stranger in these parts he has to claim entry into his wife's *variga*. He has arranged that a relative of his wife, one Kirihamy Lēkama of Tulawelliya, has protested to the President of the *variga* court complaining that he, Arlis, has transgressed the rules of *variga* endogamy. All villages in the Vanni-Vaddā *variga* have been notified and all titled members of that *variga* have been invited to attend as members of the court.'

The court which actually assembled numbered six; two of these were from Tulawelliya, two from Medagama, one from Palugollewa and one from Hunpolayagama. The court members bore the titles Lēkama and Undiyarāla. Only five members of the court were actually titled *variga* officers, the sixth was a co-opted member and was a member of the Village Committee. The following was the sequence predicted to me by Arlis in advance of the proceedings:

'The fine will be 550 *ridi* (that is Rs. 137.50). Of this sum one quarter will go to the Bulankulame Disava. The cost of the feasting and of gifts to members of the court will also be borne by Arlis. The court will draw up a warrant certifying that Arlis has been duly fined and thereafter admitted to the *variga*. This warrant will be signed by all members of the court and afterwards the head of the court will take it with a gift of betel leaves and money to Bulankulame Disava, who will also sign it. The warrant duly signed will finally be returned to Arlis as a certificate of status. In former days Arlis himself would have been taken to Bulankulame Disava by the court president and presented to him.'

The following refers to the actual, as opposed to the expected, sequence:

'The court assembled at Kalawel Potana on Friday evening and debated all night. A feast was provided in the morning at Arlis's expense. Of the court, consisting of six persons, three took the side of the accused and three took the side of the opposition. The opposition argued that while it would be perfectly respectable for one of their girls to marry with a local Goyigama, they could not allow such a girl to marry with someone who was quite unknown. After hot argument on this point the court called for evidence. Two *massinā* of the girl were then produced who both swore that they had visited the home of Arlis in the Colombo district and there discovered that his family were a most respectable Goyigama family. As is obvious from Arlis's full name this was a pure fiction; everybody knew perfectly well that Arlis was of the Karava caste; everybody also knew that the *massinā* had never been anywhere near Colombo. The court, however, now declared, and the Lēkama duly recorded, that since Arlis was of Goyigama origin the breach of *variga* rules could be excused on payment of a fine. Arlis's hospitality had been so lavish that they reduced the fine to a mere 150 *ridi*, that is Rs. 37.50. The members of the court signed the certificate and the president of the court was instructed to proceed to Bulankulame Disava's house in Anurādhapura and obtain his signature to the certificate; from there it will be forwarded to Tulawelliya and Arlis will have to collect the certificate from Tulawelliya. A portion of the fine money will go to Bulankulame Disava, another portion to the Washerman who has played a part in the ritual proceedings. Each of the court members also obtains a share of the fine, but these shares are not personal perquisites. The share that a court member takes back home with him must be minutely divided up so that every house-holder in each respective village gets a portion, even if it is nothing more than one betel leaf. In this way every villager in the whole *variga* is committed to acceptance of the verdict. The house in which the court met was ceremonially decorated by the Washerman, also when the members sat down to eat the Washerman spread ritual cloths across their knees; it is for such ritual services as these that he obtains his reward. The uniform of the court officers was presented to them individually by Bulankulame Disava at the time of their appointment. In this *variga* it consists of (1) a cane, (2) a peaked cap, (3) a silk cloth worn over the shoulder, (4) a white waist cloth. No shirt or vest is worn. This particular combination of ritual clothing indicates the relatively low caste status of the Vanni-Väddä group. In addition to the six court members there were, in all, forty members of the *variga* attending the court session: all of them of course were acting as witnesses of the admission of Arlis to the *variga*.'

The proceedings of the court as a judicial institution were immediately followed by the formal wedding of Arlis and his bride. All those who had attended the judicial proceedings were present as guests at the wedding.

The record brings out very clearly three important principles:

(1) The *variga* court proceedings, though having the appearance of an accusation against Arlis, are in fact designed from the start simply to admit him to the *variga*.

(2) The head of the whole proceeding is quite explicitly the Bulankulame Disava as hereditary lord of the whole area. Up to 1938 Bulankulame Disava was the local Ratēmahatmayā.

(3) What matters in the whole proceedings is that appearances shall be right rather than facts. Everybody knew that the *massinā* in the case were bearing false witness.

For analogous material see Pieris (1956), pp. 254–7.

APPENDIX 2

THE TROUBLES OF
RANHAMY GE PUNCHIRALA (X:4)

When I first arrived in Pul Eliya the villagers had no precedent for coping with an Englishman who planned a prolonged stay. The problem of where I should live evoked agitated discussion. Clearly no one wanted me to live inside the main village area. A sly suggestion from Naidurala (Dx:Y) that perhaps the Village Headman (A2:7) would let me live in his garden was quickly voted down on the grounds that the site was too damp. But the opposite extreme, that I had best be kept right outside in the jungle, was too inhospitable; the site was dry and private, but I might be attacked by elephants! The compromise which put me in the derelict village dispensary (see p. 45) suited everyone.

I soon discovered that my immediate neighbours were the only other complete outsiders resident in the community. On the one side there was the schoolmaster, on the other R. Punchirala (X:4). Inevitably I saw a great deal of Punchirala, and his troubles fill many pages of my note-books. His 'case' illustrates so many of the themes which have been running through this book that it seems worth while to give the story at length.

On the face of it the root of the trouble is an issue of caste, and the conventional anthropological approach would be to argue that Punchirala was in difficulty over land and water *because* of his questionable caste and kinship status. And this is precisely how the villagers themselves tried to explain the matter. But caste and kinship are phenomena in the field of ideas compared with which such matters as digging irrigation ditches and going to law are objective items of behaviour. In the end it seemed to me that all the complicated arguments about Punchirala's kinship status amounted simply to a way of talking about a quarrel over land and water. Had Punchirala himself been of a less litigious nature, or had his wife been slightly less inclined to insult her neighbours, there would have been no problem. We cannot understand a trouble case of this sort without going into the intricacies of the kinship pattern; but the kinship pattern is not the

310

cause of what happens, it merely provides a framework of ideas in terms of which actual behaviour may be justified. The model of correct behaviour which is provided by the kinship ideology sets limits to what may be considered reasonable behaviour; but it does not finally determine what men do.

I shall recount the story in two halves, first as an issue of caste, secondly as an issue of land and water, and I shall present both in chronological sequence. In my note-books the material is recorded in quite a different way; the latest events appear first while the caste issues and the land issues are inextricably mixed up. The reader needs to remember not only that it is the end rather than the beginning of the story which is currently important, but also that the caste–land dichotomy of my story roughly corresponds to an administrative change.

From one point of view the whole tale is a long story of litigation, but whereas the first part of the case consisted of litigation in the *variga* court (and was therefore couched in the language of caste and kinship), the later phases of the same case have been brought before the civil administration in the persons of the Government Agent, the D.R.O. and the V.C.O. and have, therefore, been couched in the language of agricultural economics and title to land. Punchirala (X:4), the central figure of the story, was well known to the Anurādhapura District Office (Kachcheri) as one of the most persistent litigants in the whole area; the Pul Eliya villagers' description of him as a man of wrong *variga* was another way of saying the same thing. From both points of view he was a man who did not fit, and an infernal nuisance!

THE CASTE ISSUE

Early in this century Pul Eliya had a village priest who came from Nawana in Kurunegala District. He resided in the *Vihāra* compound. In the same compound there lived one Ranhamy (X:1), who worked as a gardener and general servant for the priest and who also came from the Nawana area, as did his wife (X:2). The precise caste status of this man is not clear; the personal names of his kinsmen indicate that he was a Goyigama. He certainly had no connection with the Pul Eliya *variga* and may have belonged to a Goyigama sub-caste which owed traditional service duties to the priesthood (see Ryan, 1953*a*, pp. 100–1 on Nilamak-karaya).

The priest was a relative of the present Kadawatgama High Priest but was, at that time, unrelated to the people of Pul Eliya. Later a lay cousin of the priest (also called Ranhamy (C:N)) came to live in Pul Eliya and married Walli Etani (C:7), daughter of Kadirathe Gamarāla (D2:C). No one made any fuss. They seem to have gone through the formality of a *variga* court case and a formal marriage ceremony; in the outcome the present Pul Eliya villagers now say that the Kadawatgama High Priest is of their *variga*.

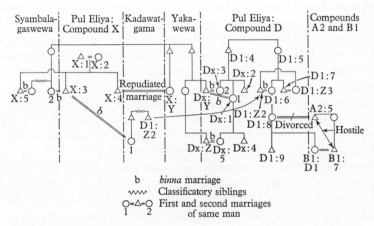

b   *binna* marriage
ᘯᘯ   Classificatory siblings
○=△=○ First and second marriages
1   2   of same man

Chart *h*. Genealogy illustrating case history material in Appendix 2.

Ranhamy (X:1), the gardener, was a popular character. When the Pul Eliya priest died and the *Vihāra* compound was left empty the Vel Vidāne of the day (Appurala Vidāne (A1:W)) helped him to purchase a *sinakkara* house-site on Crown land (house-site 1: compound X); this was in 1921. He was not provided with any agricultural land.

When his eldest son R. Mudalihamy (X:3) grew up, the Temple connection proved useful and the Kadawatgama priest arranged for a *binna* marriage in Kadawatgama (47). This was around 1935. This marriage failed, though only after some years, by which time the issue of Ranhamy's (X:1) *variga* had become so contentious that it seemed politic to go further away. Mudalihamy (X:3), around 1937/8, married *binna* into a well-to-do family in Syambalagaswewa (85); this marriage was successful and later his youngest brother (X:5) married Mudalihamy's wife's 'sister' (also in *binna*).

R. Mudalihamy's second wife's mother had come from Yakawewa (43) and, through this connection, his younger brother Punchirala (X:4) arranged a *binna* marriage with S. Ran Manika (X:Y) of Yakawewa. She was mother's brother's daughter to Mudalihamy's wife. This was around 1938/9.

Punchirala's wife's father's brother's son, M. Naidurala (Dx:Y), then living in Yakawewa, was already working land in Pul Eliya which belonged to his wife (Dx:1). Punchirala's marriage was thus of a different kind from those of his brothers. Neither the Syambalagaswewa nor the Kadawatgama marriages were likely to affect Pul Eliya land rights, but if Punchirala's children were to marry Naidurala's children, as they would be expected to do, since they were affines, *their* children would have the status of Pul Eliya *minissu*.

The Yakawewa people seem to have had similar objections. However, the marriage had the approval of Punchirala Gamarāla (D 2:C), the senior living member of Pul Eliya compound D, and also of the Pul Eliya Vel Vidāne, Mudalihamy Baddarāla (B 1:3), who was an officer of the *variga* court. The *variga* court duly met and fined R. Punchirala (X:4); Punchirala paid the fine and became thereby, in his own estimation, a fully qualified member of the Pul Eliya *variga*.

But evidently the court's decision was not generally acceptable for, on the death of Mudalihamy Badderāla (B 1:3) which occurred around 1940, the case was somehow or other reopened. This time the *variga* court disintegrated without being able to produce any agreed ruling and a major row ensued. Naidurala (Dx:Y) and his 'brother-in-law', R. Punchirala (X:4), fled from Yakawewa and in 1941 set up house in Pul Eliya compound Dx. This land, which Naidurala now holds on *badu* lease, had previously been held by Punchirala Gamarāla (D 2:C) on similar terms. At the same time J. Punchirala (Dx:2), Naidurala's wife's brother, who had until this time been living in Pul Eliya compound D 1, found it politic to leave home and go to live with his wife's people in Watarekkewa (21).

At this time Ranhamy (X:1), the gardener, was still alive and still living in compound X, but he evidently kept out of the dispute. At his death his son, R. Punchirala (X:4), moved from compound Dx to compound X.

In 1954 R. Punchirala still laid great stress on the fact that he was Naidurala's *massinā*, and Naidurala did not deny the relationship. But R. Punchirala was never invited to any family or village gathering (other than a house-building *kayiya* in Naidurala's compound). In contrast Naidurala had become so wealthy and influential that, in the Vel Vidāne's estimation, he was the fourth senior individual in the village—the official 'Pangu List' (see p. 184) placed Naidurala immediately after the Vel Vidāne (B1:7), the Village Headman (A2:7) and the ex-Vel Vidāne (A2:4).

Meanwhile J. Punchirala (Dx:2) had returned from Watarekkewa and was living in compound Dx with Naidurala; Naidurala's son, N. Punchi Banda (Dx:4), had built himself a house in compound D1.

In 1954 R. Punchirala (X:4) held land totalling 2 acres (plot 118) and his Syambalagaswewa brother R. Mudalihamy (X:3) owned ¾ acre (plot 111), leased *andē* to R. Punchirala. Neither brother owned any land in the Old Field. In the 'old days', before the days of *sinakkara* and *badu* plots, the kind of ostracism which the Pul Eliya villagers applied would have forced R. Punchirala to leave the village.

Since he had not done so, but had instead fought back with every legal means he could lay hands on, a kind of guerrilla warfare had developed, with the unanimous villagers on one side and the embattled R. Punchirala, relying on government protection, on the other. But the issues involved were not simply those of caste purity. Nor was the Kadawatgama marriage of R. Punchirala's brother quite so irrelevant as I have here implied.

THE LAND AND WATER ISSUE

To understand the territorial context of R. Punchirala's troubles we need to start elsewhere and to remember that the long-term factionalism of the community as analysed in chapter v has ranged compound D with compound C in opposition to the alliance between compounds A and B. In 1920 luck was running strongly in favour of the A+B group as represented by the Vel Vidāne, Appurala Vidāne (A1:W) and his son-in-law, W. Mudalihamy (B1:3).

This was a period when the possibility of purchasing *sinakkara* fields gave an outstanding advantage to the Vel Vidāne and his close friends. The government authorities were eager to award *sinakkara* grants, so the main problem from the villagers' point of view was that of irrigation. It was no good applying for land until you could be certain of a water supply. Around 1919 Punchirala Gamarāla (D2:C), who had his eye on the land now represented by plots 138–47, had tried his hand at constructing an irrigation channel which would feed this land, but he got his levels wrong, and the water flowed the other way. Next year, when U. Kadirathe (A2:4) tried his hand at the same task, the new trace proved entirely satisfactory and it became plainer than ever that compound A was being favoured by the planetary deities. Observing this, A. Mudalihamy (D1:Z2) took the unprecedented step of marrying off his daughter Ukkuhamy (D1:8) to U. Sirala (A2:5), Kadirathe's younger brother, instead of reserving her for someone in compound C as precedent might have suggested.

In 1921 Kadirathe and his three brothers (U. Sirala (A2:5), U.G. Pinhamy (H:A2), U. Wannihamy (A2:6)) and their new *māmā*, A. Mudalihamy (D1:Z2), formed a partnership and obtained a *sinak-kara* grant to the 9-acre block represented by plots 141–7, and the following year they applied in the same way for the $4\frac{3}{4}$-acre block represented by plots 138–40a. Of the total $13\frac{3}{4}$ acres, the allocations were: Kadirathe 5, Sirala $1\frac{1}{2}$, U.G. Pinhamy 4, Mudalihamy 2, Wannihamy $1\frac{1}{4}$. Kadirathe's extra share was because of his skill as irrigation engineer; U.G. Pinhamy got extra because his father-in-law Appurala Vidāne (A2:W) put up part of the capital; Wannihamy got least because he was only a boy of 10. A. Mudalihamy (D1:Z2) provided the capital for Sirala's share and K. Murugathe (A2:3) found the money for Wannihamy.

Meanwhile similar developments were taking place on the other side of the Old Field. In 1922/3 Appurala Vidāne (A2:W) in partnership with K. Velathe (B1:6) and P. Jangurala (D1:4) acquired the *sinak-kara* land represented by plots 120–3, 125–7. Here again compound D1, in the person of P. Jangurala, was allied with compounds A and B instead of with compound C.

But Punchirala Gamarāla (D2:C) was still influential. He made life so unpleasant for his D1 group neighbours that when P. Jangurala died in 1924 his 'son', A. Mudalihamy (D1:Z2), purchased a house-site right outside the village and went to live there.

As time went on A. Mudalihamy's relations with his son-in-law Sirala (A2:5) deteriorated but even so, around 1938/9, he married one of his granddaughters to Sirala's sister's son, V. Menikrala (B1:7), thus further consolidating his alliance with the dominant faction in the community.

Now A. Mudalihamy (D1:Z2) had come from Kadawatgama and, in an exchange marriage, his brother-in-law, K. Pinhamy (D1:7) had married Mudalihamy's sister, A. Sitti Etani (D1:Z3). This latter couple, who had originally lived *binna* in Kadawatgama, joined up with A. Mudalihamy (D1:Z2) in Pul Eliya around 1936.

It was about this time that R. Punchirala's eldest brother (X:3) had married *binna* in Kadawatgama. The girl in question was a distant niece ('brother's daughter') to Mudalihamy. This placed him under a potential caste taint in much the same way as M. Naidurala (Dx:Y) later became tainted by his 'sister's' marriage to R. Punchirala (X:4). Moreover, since Naidurala's wife and Mudalihamy's wife were cross-cousins, the whole of Pul Eliya compound D1 had become indirectly tainted by these two wrong *variga* marriages.

At this point, that is around 1938/40, a series of disasters made it evident that compound D1 was altogether out of favour with the planetary deities.

The usual Pul Eliya version was that K. Pinhamy (D1:7) unearthed some temple treasure while assisting his cross-cousin J. Punchirala (Dx:2) to cultivate (illicitly) part of plot 124. He had been chased home by the spirit guardian of the treasure and that night he and his daughter died in agony. A Mudalihamy (D1:Z2) died a few days later. At this time Mudalihamy's *sinakkara* land was all on *andē* to his son-in-law U. Sirala (A2:5), who chose this moment to divorce his wife Ukkuhamy (D1:8) and misappropriate the land. A violent quarrel ensued between Sirala and the members of compound B1, particularly V. Menikrala (B1:7), who had been expecting his wife to inherit a part of Mudalihamy's land. (For other aspects of Sirala's quarrel with Menikrala, see p. 116.) What followed is obscure.

Ukkuhamy's relatives sued Sirala in the government court, but meanwhile Sirala had adroitly managed to transfer the title of the land to his elder brother U.G. Pinhamy (H:A2), a circumstance which was aided by the fact that the Vel Vidāne Mudalihamy (B1:3) had just died and been succeeded by Sirala's brother, Kadirathe (A2:4). Sirala spent a period in gaol, but afterwards got the land back (or at any rate most of it). The bitter enmity between Sirala and his son-in-law Menikrala (B1:7) dates from this point in the story.

The sudden collapse of the fortunes of compound D1 through death and litigation provided the spark to generate caste and witchcraft animosities. A. Mudalihamy's widow, K. Punchi Etani (D1:6). drove her sister-in-law A. Sitti Etani (D1:Z3) out of the house, saying that she must have been responsible for the deaths of Mudalihamy

(D 1:Z 2) and Pinhamy (D 1:7). At the same time the Yakawewa people expelled M. Naidurala (Dx:Y) and R. Punchirala (X:4). The real connection between the two cases is remote, but the common element of caste taint was present in both of them and this served to canalise the animosities of Pul Eliya public opinion.

By a complex process of reasoning the deaths of Mudalihamy Badderāla (B 1:3), A. Mudalihamy (D 1:Z 2), K. Pinhamy (D 1:7) and Pinhamy's daughter were all held to have been 'caused by' the wrong *variga* marriages of Ranhamy's sons (X:3 and X:4).

But the caste scandal would soon have been forgiven had not R. Punchirala (X:4) got himself entangled in a major economic feud with the members of compounds B 1 and A 2.

Here we must go back again. The development of Plot 3 D (plots 108–17) under the leadership of Appurala Vidāne (A 1:W) has been outlined at the beginning of chapter VI. Plot 111 and the uncleared strip 'b' (see Map *F*) were there allocated to Appurala Vidāne's half-brother Kirihamy (W:5). Appurala Vidāne also had a foster-daughter Kiri Etani, who married one P.V. Bandathe (Z(A 1)) in Walpola. Kirihamy mortgaged his land to a trader Antoni in Wiralmurippu and then married *binna* in Kadawatgama where he struck up a friendship with R. Mudalihamy (X:3), who was then married there. On his deathbed Kirihamy gave the mortgage deed to Kiri Etani, but at the same time suggested to R. Mudalihamy that, since P.V. Bandathe was blind, he might be able to buy out the rights. R. Mudalihamy in fact purchased the mortgage deed and later redeemed the land, thus becoming a Pul Eliya landowner. This was land which, in the ordinary way of things, should have passed to the direct heirs of Appurala Vidāne, that is to members of Pul Eliya compounds A 1 and B 1.

By 1954 R. Mudalihamy (X:3) was safely out of the way in Syambalagaswewa, but he still owned the land in plot 3 D which was regularly leased *andē* to his brother R. Punchirala (X:4). Thus the quarrel with the heirs of Appurala Vidāne continued unabated.

To make matters worse R. Punchirala (X:4) had become the owner, on *badu* title, of plot 118. Many years ago K. Velathe (B 1:6) had sought to purchase this land on *sinakkara* grant and had actually 'asweddum-ised' it and cultivated it 'illicitly' for several years. Then the Land Office had ruled that this land lay outside the boundaries of Pul Eliya village and title had reverted to the Crown. But around 1946 the Land Office had changed their policy about village boundaries and had allocated the plot *badu* to R. Punchirala (X:4). Velathe's son V. Menikrala (B1:7) had appealed but lost his case. So R. Punchirala had added to his troubles by earning the enmity of the Pul Eliya Vel Vidāne.

Although by 1952 R. Punchirala had personal title to plot 118, and *andē* title to plot 111, his enemies could still make things very difficult for him by cutting off his water supply.

The obvious way to irrigate plot 118 would be to draw off water from the bottom corner of plots 116–17 (see Map *F*), but these belonged to Punchirala's enemies, V. Menikrala (B1:7) and A.V. Punchi Etani (B1:A1).

After a series of lawsuits on the subject, R. Punchirala constructed an irrigation ditch δ–γ through the uncleared strip 'b' (Map *F*) which belongs to his brother R. Mudalihamy (X:3). He then tried to tap this into the main channel α–β which feeds the strips of plot 3D. Again he ran into the difficulty that in order to reach the main channel his feed channel must at some point cross land which was owned or claimed either by Menikrala (B1:7) or by the descendants of Appurala Vidāne (A1:W). Punchirala constructed his channel but his opponents blocked it up again. They were always careful to stick to their strict legal rights. The block was always made on private land, never on Crown territory.

In 1953 R. Punchirala had got to the point of threatening murder, but he had somehow or other made his peace with V. Menikrala (B1:7). His enmity with A.V. Punchi Etani (B1:A1) continued. He had arranged to extend his channel through to plot 124 (Map *B*).

The point of this is that Punchirala's 'brother-in-law' Naidurala had lately been redeveloping plot 124. This is, strictly speaking, 'encroached Crown land'. It is also, by reputation, haunted land, and it was through digging here that K. Pinhamy (D1:7) had met his death (see p. 316). M. Naidurala (Dx:Y) had ingeniously restored a small tank known as Kana-hiti-yawa (K.H.Y. on Map *B*) which he claimed would supply his encroached field. In actual fact by a private arrangement with the Vel Vidāne he also drew water from the main tank.

In 1954, Punchirala's channel δ–γ had been extended north and tapped into Naidurala's channel from Kana-hiti-yawa. It was quite obvious that Naidurala found this extremely inconvenient from every point of view, but R. Punchirala was his *massinā*. Naidurala did not assist Punchirala to dig the ditch, but he did not block it up when it had been dug. Whether this really marked R. Punchirala's final victory

I do not know. If he goes on residing in Pul Eliya he will permanently remain an outsider until he can behave in a sufficiently politic manner to marry off one or more of his children to a Pul Eliya resident.

So long as there is no such marriage alliance everyone will continue to point out that he is not of 'our *variga*'; he is not a recognised relative. But a switch of attitude could easily take place. In 1954 his eldest son was already 14 years old. If it should suit everyone's convenience, the caste issue would vanish overnight. I should not be surprised to learn that by this time R. Punchirala's son has married the daughter of his 'enemy' V. Menikrala.

If we look at the whole story in its historical perspective as I have presented it here we see that the initial crisis was really the divorce of S. Jaymanhamy's parents, U. Sirala (A2:5) and Ukkuhamy (D1:8) and the total disintegration of compound D1 which followed. Yet despite lawsuits, witchcraft accusations and all the rest, S. Jaymanhamy (D1:9) remained Sirala's heir, and in 1954 there was something of a *rapprochement* between father and son. In that year Sirala and Jaymanhamy worked a *vi hena* together, an unprecedented event which evoked much favourable comment in the village.

To the reader it may seem that Sirala's divorce and R. Punchirala's troubles are independent events, but from the village point of view they were, in some rather undefined way, aspects of the same thing. It was not accidental that in the year that U. Sirala began to make peace with Jaymanhamy, M. Naidurala's family should start moving back into compound D1 and R. Punchirala's water problems should at last find a partial solution.

It was on the same day that I had been discussing with B. Ausadahamy (A2:7) this favourable turn of events that Ausadahamy remarked for the first time that S. Jaymanhamy's father-in-law (a resident of Kadawatgama) was after all a distant '*ayiya*' ('elder brother') of R. Punchirala; however, he did not take the further step of admitting his own quite close relationship with R. Punchirala's wife.

The point I want to make is that R. Punchirala's caste troubles were quite 'real' in that they affected the behaviour of his neighbours, but since they corresponded to nothing substantial, they might disappear at any time.

The *variga* ostracism which kept R. Punchirala in the status of outsider was not simply a private game played by the Pul Eliya villagers for their own amusement, but part of an agreed pattern of behaviours.

One day there came to visit me from Yakawewa a certain Appuhamy. I asked him specifically whether he had any close relatives in Pul Eliya, to which he replied that there was only Naidurala (Dx:Y) who was his 'brother' (father's brother's son). When he said this, R. Punchirala's wife Ran Manika was actually in sight, working in her garden 20 yards away. Later I verified that this Appuhamy and Ran Manika were half-siblings with a common father, but that Appuhamy regularly declined to recognise the relationship. Yet here again the exclusion was only of a provisional kind; Ran Manika's banishment had not prevented her from inheriting Yakawewa land.

If R. Punchirala were to be recognised as a fully qualified Pul Eliya resident it is quite certain that Ran Manika's Yakawewa relatives would accept the position and adjust their behaviour accordingly.

INDEX TO PERSONAL NAMES

(See Genealogical Charts *h* and *i*)

Code no.	Name and description	Place of birth
	Compound A	
A:1	Naidurala Gamarāla I (died *c.* 1875)	Unknown
Z:A	Kiri Naidurala. Supposedly *massinā* to A:1	Unknown

Sub-compound A 1

Residents

A1:1	Kadirathe. Former Vel Vidāne, son of A:1. Gamarāla; Vel Vidāne 1887–8	Pul Eliya
A1:2	Kadirathe ge Kirihamy. Son of A1:1	Pul Eliya
A1:3	Tikiri Etani II. Daughter of A1:1	Pul Eliya
A1:4	A.V. Sirala. Son of A1:3; Gamarāla. Vel Vidāne of Wiralmurippu *c.* 1930–40	Pul Eliya
A1:5	S. Subasinghe. Son of A1:4	Pul Eliya
A1:6	P. Ran Banda. Daughter's son of A1:3	Pul Eliya
A1:W	Appurala Vidāne. Husband of A1:3. Gamarāla; Vel Vidāne 1908–26	Wiralmurippu (57)

Non-residents

B1:A1	A.V. Punchi Etani. Daughter of A1:3	Pul Eliya
B1:8	M. Ran Manika. Daughter of B1:A1	Pul Eliya
W:5	Kirihamy (W). Half-brother of A1:W. Not on Chart *i*; perhaps same as W:3	Wiralmurippu (57)
Z(A1)	P.V. Bandathe. Resident of Walpola; husband of Kiri Etani a foster-daughter to A1:W. (Not on Chart *i*)	Walpola

Sub-compound A:2

Residents

A2:1	N. Ranhamy. Daughter of A:1	Pul Eliya
A2:2	Tikiri Etani I. Daughter of A2:2	Pul Eliya
A2:3	K. Murugathe. Son of A2:Z3 and A2:Z4	Pul Eliya
A2:4	U. Kadirathe. Second son of A2:2. Vel Vidāne 1940–51	Pul Eliya
A2:5	U. Sirala. Third son of A2:2	Pul Eliya
A2:6	U. Wannihamy. Fourth son of A2:2, adopted son of A2:3	Pul Eliya
A2:7	K.V. Appuhamy. Son of A2:4. *Tulāna* Headman since 1952	Pul Eliya

Code no.	Name and description	Place of birth
A2:8	M. Tikiri Etani. Daughter of A2:3	Pul Eliya
A2:9	Rathanawathy. Daughter of A2:B2, daughter's daughter of A2:3	Pul Eliya
A2:10	S. Punchi Manika. Daughter of A2:5 by his second wife	Pul Eliya
A2:B2	K. Dingiri Banda. Father of A2:9; son of B2:5	Pul Eliya
A2:C1	P. Herathamy. Husband of A2:10; son of C1:W	Pul Eliya
A2:H	P. Sumanawathy. Daughter of H:A2, daughter's daughter of A2:2; wife of A2:Y	Pul Eliya
A2:P	Kumari Etani. Wife of A2:3	Periyakkulam (33)
A2:Y	B. Ausadahamy. Husband of A2:H; 'step-brother' of Y:1	Yakawewa (43)
A2:Z1	Kirihamy I. Husband of A2:1	Punewa (25)
A2:Z2	Kapurala ge Ukkurala. Husband of A2:2	Ambagahawewa (86)
A2:Z3	Kapurala ge Kandathe. Younger brother of A2:Z2; husband of A2:Z4	Ambagahawewa (86)
A2:Z4	Tutti Etani. Wife of A2:Z3; daughter of Z:Z1; half-sister of B2:E2	Unknown
A2:Z5	B. Siriwardena. Husband of A2:9	Watarakkewa (21)

Non-residents

B1:A2	U. Walli Etani. Daughter of A2:2	Pul Eliya
B1:7	V. Menikrala. Son of B1:A2; Vel Vidāne since 1951	Pul Eliya
D1:9	S. Jaymanhamy. Son of A2:5 by his divorced first wife D1:8	Pul Eliya
Bel:A2	Name not recorded by me; daughter of A2:B2; full sister of A2:9; wife of Bel:3; resident in Bellankadawala (55)	Pul Eliya
Y:A2	K. Ran Manika. Daughter of A2:4; wife of Y:1; resident in Yakawewa (43)	Pul Eliya
Z:A2	Dingiri Etani I. Daughter of A2:1	Pul Eliya

Compound B

B	Name unknown (Gamarāla of Meda bāga around 1850)	Unknown
C:B	Name not recorded by me; daughter of B; second wife of Naidurala Gamarāla II	Unknown

Sub-compound B1

Residents

B1:1	Punchirala Badderāla. Son of B; Gamarāla; probably died before 1860	Unknown

Code no.	Name and description	Place of birth
B1:2	Punchirala Badderāla ge Wannihamy. Son of B1:1	Pul Eliya
B1:3	W. Mudalihamy. Badderāla; son of B1:2; Vel Vidāne 1927–40	Pul Eliya
B1:4	Name not recorded. Sister to B1:2; married to B1:Z2, see p. 205	Pul Eliya
B1:6	K. Velathe. Son of Z:B1; husband of B1:A2; resided in Pul Eliya, compound B1	Kumbukgollewa (34)
B1:7	V. Menikrala. Son of B1:6 and B1:A2; Vel Vidāne since 1951	Pul Eliya
B1:8	M. Ran Manika. Daughter of B1:3 and B1:A1	Pul Eliya
B1:A1	A.V. Punchi Etani. Wife of B1:3; daughter of A1:W	Pul Eliya
B1:A2	U. Walli Etani. First wife of B1:6; daughter of A2:4	Pul Eliya
B1:B2	Maniki Etani. Cross-cousin and wife of B1:2	Pul Eliya
B1:D1	S. Ran Manika. Full sister to D1:9 and Cx:D1; wife of B1:7	Pul Eliya
B1:Dw	M. Herathamy. Husband of B1:8; brother's son of F:Dw	Diwulwewa (56)
B1:Z1	Name not recorded. Wife of B1:1	Unknown
B1:Z2	Badderāla ge Kirihamy. Also known as Vilava-Kirihamy and Vilo-Kirihamy; husband of B1:4	Vilava

Non-residents

Bel:B1	Name not recorded. Sister (?half-sister) of B1:3; wife of Bel:1	Not recorded
Cx:B1	V. Punchi Etani. Elder sister to B1:7; first wife of Cx:1	Pul Eliya
J:B1	W. Sithi Etani. Daughter of B1:2; first married to J:2, later married to B1:6	Pul Eliya
P:B1	M. Dingiri Banda. Son of B1:3, married *binna* at Periyakkulam (33) to wife of same compound as P:B2	Pul Eliya
Z:B1	Name not recorded. Sister of B1:2; married *dīga* in Kuda Kumbukgollewa	Pul Eliya
W:J	P. Ran Etani. Daughter of J:B1; step-sister of B1:7; married *dīga* in Wiralmurippu	Pul Eliya?

Sub-compound B2

Residents

B2:1	Name not recorded. Wife of B2:Z1, full sister of B1:1 and C:B	Pul Eliya

323

Code no.	Name and description	Place of birth
B2:2	A. Menikrala. Son of B2:1	Pul Eliya
B2:3	A. Pul Etani. Daughter of B2:1	Pul Eliya
B2:4	K. Ukkurala II. Son of B2:1; half-brother of B2:2 and B2:3	Pul Eliya
B2:5	U. Kapuruhamy. Son of B2:3	Pul Eliya
B2:6	K. Menikrala. Second son of B2:5	Pul Eliya
B2:7	K. Wannihamy. Youngest son of B2:5	Pul Eliya
B2:A2	K. Punchi Etani II. Wife of B2:5, full sister of A2:3	Pul Eliya
B2:Cx	K. Pemawathy. Wife of B2:7, full sister of Cx:2	Pul Eliya
B2:D1	Dingiri Etani. 'Sister' to D1:2; wife of Z:Z1 and B2:E1	?Pul Eliya
B2:E1	Kirihamy (E). Heir to compound E; second husband of B2:D1	Pul Eliya
B2:E2	K. Walli Etani. Daughter of B2:E1; wife of B2:4; heir to compound E	Pul Eliya
B2:E3	U. Kuda Pinhamy. Son of B2:E2; heir to compound E	Pul Eliya
B2:Z1	Appurala I. First husband of B2:1	Unknown
B2:Z2	Kawrala. Second husband of B2:1	Unknown
B2:Z3	M. Ukkurala. Husband of B2:3	Unknown, probably 'wrong *variga*'

Non-residents

A2:B2	K. Dingiri Banda. Eldest son of B2:5	Pul Eliya
P:B2	Name not recorded. Daughter of B2:1 and mother of A2:P; married *dīga* in Periyakkulam (33)	Pul Eliya
W:B2	K. Appuhamy. Third son of B2:5. Married *binna* in Wiralmurippu (57)	Pul Eliya

Compound C

Residents

C:1	Name unknown. Gamarāla of the Pahala bāga around 1850	Unknown
C:2	Naidurala Gamarāla II. Gamarāla; son of C:1	Unknown
C:3	Kadirathe Gamarāla. Gamarāla; son of C:2	Pul Eliya
C:4	Velathe Vel Vidāne. Gamarāla; Vel Vidāne 1889–95; son of C:2; half-brother of C:3	Pul Eliya
C:5	V. Kirihamy. Gamarāla; mentally deficient; son of C:4	Pul Eliya
C:6	Appurala Vedarāla. Son of C:3; full brother of D2:C	Pul Eliya

Code no.	Name and description	Place of birth
C:7	K.G. Walli Etani. Full sister of C:6 and D2:C; wife of C:N	Pul Eliya
C:B	Name unknown. Second wife of C:2; mother of C:4 and H:1	Pul Eliya
C:D	Name unknown. First wife of C:2; mother of C:3	Unknown
C:N	Ranhamy (N). *Massinā* of former village priest; husband of C:7	Nawana
C:Z1	'Kirihamy'. Second wife of C:3; 'wrong *variga*'; mother of C:Z2	Wewelketiya (11 miles east of Medawach-chiya)
C:Z2	Mudalihamy. Son of C:Z1 and Z(C); brought up in house of C:3	Wewelketiya
C:Z3	Name not recorded. First wife of C:3; said to be a 'sister' of D1:2	Not recorded

Non-residents

C:Z1	Name not recorded. Second wife of C:3	Wewelketiya
C:Z2	Mudalihamy (W). Child of C:Z1 by an early liaison with Z(C); reared by C:3	Wewelketiya
C:Z3	Name not recorded. First wife of C:3; said to be a 'sister' of D1:2	Not recorded
F:C	Name unknown. Wife of F:1; full sister of D1:C; half-sister of C:2	Pul Eliya
W:C	Name unknown. Wife of W:1 (Wiralmu-rippu); mother of W:4; full sister of C:2	Unknown
D1:C	M. Kirihamy I. Half-brother of C:2; brother-in-law of F:1	Unknown
Z(C)	Name not recorded. First husband of C:Z1; father of C:Z2; 'wrong *variga*'	Wewelketiya
Z:C	A.V. Bandathe. Son of C:6; married *binna* outside Pul Eliya	Pul Eliya
H:1	Naidurala Gamarāla ge Ukkurala (Ukku-rala Vidāne). Vel Vidāne 1896–1907; half-brother of C:3; full brother of C:4	Pul Eliya

Sub-compound C1

Residents

C1:1	M. Sinni Etani. Daughter of C:Z2; wife of C1:W	Pul Eliya
C1:2	M. Kirala. Son of C:Z2	Pul Eliya
C1:3	M. Herathamy. Son of C:Z2, mentally defective	Pul Eliya
C1:4	P. Ran Menika. Daughter of C1:1; wife of H:3	Pul Eliya
C1:W	U.V. Pinhamy. Son of H:1	Wiralmurippu (57)

APPENDIX 3

Code no.	Name and description	Place of birth

Non-residents

A2:C1 — P. Herathamy. Son of C1:W — Pul Eliya

Sub-compound C2

C2:D2 — P. Kapuruhamy. Son of D2:C by his first wife; adopted son of C:7 — Pul Eliya

Sub-compound Cx

Residents

Cx:1 — M. Kirihamy II. Son of C:Z2; full brother of C1:1 and C1:2 — Pul Eliya

Cx:2 — K. Tikiri Banda. Elder son of Cx:1 — Pul Eliya

Cx:3 — K. Nanghamy. Younger son of Cx:1 — Pul Eliya

Cx:B1 — Name not recorded. First wife of Cx:1; sister of B1:7 — Pul Eliya

Cx:D1 — S. Podi Menika. Daughter of A2:5; full sister of D:9; wife of Cx:2 — Pul Eliya

Cx:Y — A. Ranhamy. Second wife of Cx:1; mother of Cx:2, Cx:3 — Yakawewa (43)

D1:Z3 — A. Sitti Etani. Widow of D1:7; resides as client of Cx:3 (see pp. 57, 316) — Kadawatgama (47)

Non-residents

B2:Cx — K. Pemawathy. Wife of B2:7; sister of Cx:2 and Cx:3 — Pul Eliya

Z:Cx — K. Ran Manika. Sister of Cx:2 and Cx:3; married *dīga* in Karapikkada — Pul Eliya

Compound D

D — Name unknown. Supposed Gamarāla of the Meda bāga around 1850 — Unknown

C:D — Name unknown. Daughter of D; wife of C:2 — Unknown

Sub-compound D1

Residents

D1:1 — Name unknown. 'Brother' of C:D — Unknown

D1:2 — Kadira Velathe Mohottāla. Son of D1:1 — Unknown

D1:3 — K.V.M. Kiri Etani. Daughter of D1:2 — Pul Eliya

D1:4 — P. Jangurala. Son of D1:3 — Not recorded

D1:5 — Name not recorded. Daughter of D1:3; wife of D1:C — Not recorded

D1:6 — K. Punchi Etani. Daughter of D1:5 — Pul Eliya

D1:7 — K. Pinhamy. Son of D1:5 — Pul Eliya

D1:8 — M. Ukkuhamy. Daughter of D1:6; first wife of A2:5 — Pul Eliya

Code no.	Name and description	Place of birth
D1:9	S. Jaymanhamy. Son of D1:8 and A2:5	Pul Eliya
D1:C	M. Kirihamy. Half-brother of C:2, husband of D1:5	Pul Eliya
D1:Z1	Pinhamy (Z). Husband of D1:3	Not recorded
D1:Z2	A. Mudalihamy. Husband of D1:6; full brother of D1:Z3	Kadawatgama (47)
D1:Z3	A. Sitti Etani. Wife of D1:7; full sister of D1:Z2 (now resides as widow in compound Cx) (see pp. 57, 316)	Kadawatgama (47)

Non-residents

All members of compound Dx other than Dx:Y and Dx:Z

B1:D1	S. Ran Manika. Full sister to D1:9; wife of B1:7	Pul Eliya
Cx:D1	S. Podi Menika. Full sister to D1:9; wife of Cx:2	Pul Eliya
J:1	Kirihamy ge Punchirala. Son of D1:C	Pul Eliya

Sub-compound D2

Residents

D2:C	K.G. Punchirala Gamarāla. Gamarāla; son of C:3; full brother of C:6 and C:7	Pul Eliya
D2:1	P. Kirala. Son of D2:C by his second wife	Pul Eliya
D2:Bel	M.V. Ranhamy. Wife of D2:1; daughter of Bel:1	Bellankadawala (55)
D2:Z	R. Kiri Etani. First wife of D2:C; 'wrong *variga*'	Tammane Elawaka (54)

Sub-compound Dx

Residents

Dx:1	J. Guni Etani. Elder daughter of D1:4; first wife of D1:Y	Pul Eliya
Dx:2	J. Punchirala. Son of D1:4	Pul Eliya
Dx:3	J. Kiri Etani. Younger daughter of D1:4; second wife of D1:Y	Pul Eliya
Dx:4	N. Punchi Banda. Son of Dx:1 and Dx:Y	Pul Eliya
Dx:5	N. Ran Manika. Daughter of Dx:1 and Dx:Y	Pul Eliya
Dx:Y	M. Naidurala. Husband of Dx:1 and Dx:3	Pul Eliya
Dx:Z	P. Kalu Banda. Husband of Dx:5; sister's son of Dx:Y	Ralapanawa

Compound E

This compound has been left uninhabited for several generations owing to alleged haunting, the owners residing in sub-compound B2 (see entries B2:E1, B2:E2, B2:E3 under sub-compound B2). The last actual resident of compound E was E:1 Appurala (?). Father of B2:E1.

Code no.	Name and description	Place of birth

Compound F

Residents

F:1	Kapurala Vedarāla. Brother-in-law of D1:C	Unknown
F:C	Name not recorded. Wife of F:1; half-sister of C:2; full sister of D1:C	Unknown
F:2	Ukki Etani. Daughter of F:1	Pul Eliya
F:Dw	K.V. Kapuruhamy. Shopkeeper; son of Dw:F	Diwulwewa (56)
F:D2	P.G. Ukkuhamy. Daughter of D2:C; full sister of C2:D2; wife of F:Dw	Pul Eliya

Non-residents

All members of Diwulwewa group (compound Dw)

Compound G

Residents

G:1	B. Appuhamy. Son of G:Z1 and G:Z2	Pul Eliya
G:Z1	Dingiri Etani II. Adopted daughter of A1:W	Yakawewa (43)
G:Z2	A. Bandathe. Husband of G:Z1; not otherwise closely related to Pul Eliya group. Has relatives in Walpola (63)	Not recorded

Compound H

Residents

H:1	Naidurala Gamarāla ge Ukkurala. Ukkurala Vidāne; son of C:2; full brother of C:4; Vel Vidāne 1896–1907; originally resident in compound C	Pul Eliya
H:2	Bandi Etani. Adopted daughter of H:1	Periyakkulam (33)
H:3	P. Ukku Banda. Son of H:A2 and H:2	Pul Eliya
H:A2	U.G. Pinhamy. Eldest son of A2:2	Pul Eliya
H(S)	K. Ukkurala. A man of 'wrong *variga*' related by indirect affinal ties with Bel:1. Now resides in compound H as client to H:A2	Doubtful

Non-resident

A2:H	P. Sumanawathie. Daughter of H:A2; wife of A2:Y	Pul Eliya

Compound J

Residents

J:1	Kirihamy ge Pulingurala. Son of C:D1	Pul Eliya
J:2	Punchirala Animuttirāla. Son of J:1 and F:2; later resided in Bellankadawala (55)	Pul Eliya

Code no.	Name and description	Place of birth
J:B1	W. Sithi Etani. Full sister to B1:3, step-mother to B1:7, mother of W:J; first married to J:2 then to B1:6	Pul Eliya

Non-resident

W:J	P. Ran Etani. Daughter of J:2; step-sister of B1:7; married *dīga* in Wiralmurippu	Pul Eliya

Bellankadawala group (compound Bel)

Residents

Bel:1	U.V. Menikrala. Son of F:2 and H:1; half-brother of J:2	?Pul Eliya
Bel:2	Name not recorded. 'Sister' of Bel:1	Not recorded
Bel:3	M.V. Tikiri Appu. Son of Bel:1; husband of Bel:A2	Bellankadawala (55)
Bel:4	M.V. Ran Manika. Daughter of Bel:1	Bellankadawala (55)
Bel:5	W. Nanghamy. Son of Bel:2	Bellankadawala (55)
Bel:Cx	K. Pinhamy. Son of Cx:1 by Cx:B1; first husband of Bel:4	Pul Eliya
Bel:Z	P. Kapurala. Second husband of Bel:4	Pahala Gama

Non-residents

D2:Bel	M.V. Ranhamy. Daughter of Bel:1; wife of D2:1	Bellankadawala (55)
Y:Bel	Not recorded. Daughter of Bel:2; married *dīga* in Yakawewa to Y:2, an 'elder brother' of Dx:Y	Bellankadawala (55)

Diwulwewa group (compound Dw)

Residents

Dw:F	Kadirathe Vedarāla. Son of F:1	Pul Eliya
Dw:1	K.V. Punchi Etani. Daughter of Dw:F	Diwulwewa (56)
Dw:2	K.V. Mudalihamy. Son of Dw:F	Diwulwewa (56)
Dw:D2	P.G. Menikrala. Son of D2:C; full brother of C2:D2; husband of Dw:1	Pul Eliya
Dw:W	W. Punchi Etani. Wife of Dw:2 and mother of B1:Dw; daughter's daughter of W:3	Wiralmurippu (57)

Non-residents

B1:Dw	M. Herathamy. Son of Dw:2; husband of B1:8	Diwulwewa (56)
F:Dw	K.V. Kapuruhamy. Shopkeeper; son of Dw:F	Diwulwewa (56)
Z:Dw	K.V. Sirala. Son of Dw:F; now resident in Syambalagaswewa (not shown on genealogy)	Diwulwewa (56)

Code no.	Name and description	Place of birth

Wiralmurippu group

Relationships between Pul Eliya and Wiralmurippu (57) residents are very close and complex. Only a few Wiralmurippu residents have been given code numbers.

Residents

W:1	Vela Vidāne. Vel Vidāne of Wiralmurippu around 1885–90; brother-in-law of C:2	? Pul Eliya
W:2	Kandathe Vedarāla. Father of A1:W; 'came from same compound as W:1, believed to have been his *massinā*'	Wiralmurippu (57)
W:3	Kirihamy. A 'father's brother' of B1:6; mother's mother's father of B1:Dw	Wiralmurippu (57)
W:4	V. Punchi Etani. Daughter of W:1 and mother of C1:W	Wiralmurippu (57)
W:5	Kirihamy. 'Half-brother' of A1:W; probably identical to W:3	Wiralmurippu (57)

See also compounds *A1, B1, B2, C, C1, J, Dw* and Chart *d* (p. 140).

The Pul Eliya 'wrong variga' group (compound X)

(Shown on genealogy in Appendix 2, but not on main genealogy)

X:1	'Ranhamy the Gardener'. Came from Nawana area as a servant to the village priest	Randänigama
X:2	Wife to X:1	Randänigama
X:3	R. Mudalihamy. Eldest son of X:1 and X:2; in 1954 married *binna* in Syambalagaswewa	Pul Eliya
X:4	R. Punchirala. Second son of X:1 and X:2; in 1954 resident in Pul Eliya	Pul Eliya
X:5	Youngest son of X:1 and X:2; in 1954 married *binna* in Syambalagaswewa	Pul Eliya
X:Y	S. Ran Manika. Member of Pul Eliya *variga* by birth; father's brother's daughter of M. Naidurala (Dx:Y); mother's brother's daughter of first wife of X:3	Yakawewa

Individuals not directly affiliated to any of the compound groups

Y:1	B. Hetuhamy. Vel Vidāne of Yakawewa; son-in-law of U. Kadirathe (A2:4); 'brother' of B. Ausadahamy (A2:Y)	Yakawewa
Y:2	Name not recorded. A 'classificatory brother' of M. Naidurala (Dx:Y); son-in-law of the sister of U.V. Menikrala (Bel:1)	Yakawewa

22-2

APPENDIX 4

DEMOGRAPHIC INFORMATION

Table 13. *Population statistics (official census figures)*

Year	'Families'*	Males	Females	Total individuals
1871	14	27	23	50
1881	13	22	18	40
1891	21	37	32	69
1901	19	36	33	69
1911	25	46	45	91
1921	24	66	49	115
1931	27	—	—	87
1941	20	—	—	82
1954†	32	78	68	146

* The figures listed under 'families' are recorded variously as 'families' and 'houses'.

† The figures for 1954 are based on a head-count, but the figure 32 for 'families' is somewhat arbitrary. Elsewhere in this book I have listed 39 'family heads' (see pp. 55–8).

The drop in the total population between 1921 and 1931 seems to have been partly due to the colonisation of the Bellankadawala *olagama* during this period and also to the results of an epidemic. The Pul Eliya tank was breached at one time during the 1920's and this may have had an effect on the population.

Table 14. *Demographic composition of Pul Eliya population in 1954. Approximate distribution by age*

Ages	Male	Female	Total
0–5	28	20	48
6–10	9	8	17
11–15	5	9	14
16–20	2	5	7
21–25	9	6	15
26–30	4	8	12
31–35	8	2	10
36–40	3	2	5
41–45	1	2	3
46–50	2	2	4
51–55	3	2	5
56–60	0	1	1
61–65	1	1	2
66–70	0	0	0
71–75	3*	0	3
	78	68	146

* These three old gentlemen claimed to be 71, 73, and 74 years old respectively. Ages between 66 and 70 seem more likely.

REFERENCES

Abbreviations:

A.A.—*American Anthropologist.*
A.R.—*Administration Reports*, Ceylon Government (annual).
Colombo, G.P.—Government Printer, Colombo.
J.C.B.R.A.S.—*Journal of the Ceylon Branch, Royal Asiatic Society* (Colombo).
J.R.A.I.—*Journal of the Royal Anthropological Institute* (London).
S.P.—*Sessional Papers* (Ceylon Government).

Ariyapala, M. B. (1956). *Society in Mediaeval Ceylon* (Colombo).
Beattie, J. H. M. (1959). 'Understanding and Explanation in Social Anthropology', *British Journal of Sociology*, vol. x, pp. 45–60.
Bibliography (1951). *Bibliography on Land Tenure and Related Problems in Ceylon* (Colombo, G.P.).
Brohier, R. L. (1934–5). *Ancient Irrigation Works in Ceylon* (3 vols., Colombo, G.P.).
Carter, Charles (1924). *A Sinhalese–English Dictionary* (Colombo).
Cartman, James (1957). *Hinduism in Ceylon* (Colombo).
Codrington, H. W. (1938). *Ancient Land Tenure and Revenue in Ceylon* (Colombo, G.P.).
Coomaraswamy, A. K. (1905). 'Notes on some Paddy Cultivation Ceremonies in the Ratnapura District', *J.C.B.R.A.S.*, vol. xviii, pp. 413–28.
—— (1956). *Mediaeval Sinhalese Art* (New York; original edn. 1909, Broad Campden, Gloucestershire).
Dickson, Sir J. F. (1870–2). 'Reports of the Service Tenures Commission', *A.R.*
—— (1873). 'Report on the Nuvarakalāviya District', *A.R.*
Dumont, L. (1957). 'Hierarchy and Marriage Alliance in South Indian Kinship', *Occasional Papers of the Royal Anthropological Institute*, no. 12.
Durkheim, E. (1947). *The Division of Labour in Society*, trans. George Simpson (Glencoe).

334

Durkheim, E. (1951). *Suicide: A Study in Sociology*, trans. J. A. Spaulding and George Simpson (Glencoe).

Evans-Pritchard, E. E. (1940). *The Nuer* (Oxford).

—— (1951). *Kinship and Marriage among the Nuer* (Oxford).

Farmer, B. H. (1957). *Pioneer Peasant Colonization in Ceylon* (London).

Firth, Raymond (1929). *Primitive Economics of the New Zealand Maori* (London).

Fortes, M. (1945). *The Dynamics of Clanship among the Tallensi* (London).

—— (1949a). *The Web of Kinship among the Tallensi* (London).

—— (1949b). 'Time and Social Structure: An Ashanti Case Study' in M. Fortes (ed.), *Social Structure: Studies Presented to A. R. Radcliffe-Brown*, pp. 54–84 (Oxford).

—— (1953). 'The Structure of Unilineal Descent Groups', *A.A.* vol. LV, pp. 17–41.

Freeman, J. D. (1958). 'The Family System among the Iban of Borneo' in Jack Goody (ed.), *The Developmental Cycle of Domestic Groups* (Cambridge Papers in Social Anthropology, no. 1), pp. 15–52 (Cambridge).

Furnivall, J. S. (1939). *Netherlands India: A Study of Plural Economy* (Cambridge).

Geiger, W. (1950). *The Mahāvamsa*, trans. W. Geiger (Colombo, G.P.).

Goonesekere, R. V. W. (1958). 'The Eclipse of the Village Court', *The Ceylon Journal of Historical and Social Studies*, vol. I, pp. 138–54.

Gluckman, Max (1955). *Custom and Conflict in Africa* (Oxford).

Hayley, F. A. (1923). *A Treatise on the Laws and Customs of the Sinhalese* (Colombo).

Hocart, A. M. (1924–8). 'The Indo-European Kinship System. Part I: The Sinhalese System', *Ceylon Journal of Science*, section G, vol. I, pp. 179–204.

Ievers, R. W. (1880). 'Customs and Ceremonies Connected with Paddy Cultivation', *J.C.B.R.A.S.*, vol. VI, pp. 46–52.

—— (1899). *Manual of the North-Central Province, Ceylon* (Colombo, G.P.).

Kapuruhamy, K. A. (1948). 'Rata Sabhāva', trans. P. E. Pieris, *J.C.B.R.A.S.*, vol. XXXVIII, pp. 42–68.

Knox, Robert (1911). *An Historical Relation of Ceylon* (Glasgow; original edn. 1681, London).

Leach, E. R. (1954). *Political Systems of Highland Burma* (London).

—— (1955). 'Polyandry, Inheritance and the Definition of Marriage', *Man* (London), Art. 199.

—— (1959). 'Hydraulic Society in Ceylon', *Past and Present* (London), no. 15, pp. 2–25.

Lewis, J. P. (1884). 'The Language of the Threshing Floor', *J.C.B.- R.A.S.*, vol. VIII, pp. 331–64.

—— (1884–6). 'On the Terms of Relationship in Sinhalese and Tamil', *Orientalist*, vol. I, pp. 217–23; vol. II, pp. 64–9.

Maine, Sir H. S. (1883). *Ancient Law* (9th edn., London).

Malinowski, B. (1927). *The Father in Primitive Psychology*, Psyche Miniatures, no. 8 (London).

Mendis-Gunasekera, A. (1914). 'Sinhalese Terms of Relationship', *J.C.B.R.A.S.* vol. XXIII, pp. xix–xxii.

Mitchell, J. C. (1956). *The Yao Village* (Manchester).

Murdock, G. P. (1949). *Social Structure* (New York).

Nevill, Hugh (1887). 'The Wanniyars', *The Taprobanian* (Colombo), vol. II, pp. 15–21.

'Papers' (1869). 'Papers on Service Tenures', *S.P.* vol. XVIII.

Park, J. H. W. (1908). 'The Irrigating Capacity of Tanks', *Transactions of the Engineering Association of Ceylon*.

Parker, H. (1909). *Ancient Ceylon* (London).

Phear, Sir John B. (1880). *The Aryan Village in India and Ceylon* (London).

Pieris, Ralph (1956). *Sinhalese Social Organisation: The Kandyan Period* (Colombo).

Radcliffe-Brown, A. R. (1935). 'Patrilineal and Matrilineal Succession' *The Iowa Law Review*, vol. XX, no. 2.

—— (1950). Introduction to *African Systems of Kinship and Marriage*, A. R. Radcliffe-Brown and Daryll Forde, eds. (London).

—— (1952). *Structure and Function in Primitive Society* (London).

'Report' (1869–76). 'Report of the Service Tenures Commission', *S.P.* 1869–70; 1874–6.

—— (1935). 'Report of the Kandyan Law Commission', *S.P.* vol. XXIV.

Rhys-Davids, T. W. (1871). 'Report on Nuvarakalāviya', *A.R.*

Ryan, Bryce (1953a). *Caste in Modern Ceylon* (New Brunswick).

Ryan, Bryce (1953*b*). 'The Sinhalese Family System', *Eastern Anthropologist*, vol. VI, pp. 143–63.

—— (1958). *Sinhalese Village* (Coral Gables, Florida).

Ryan, Bryce with Chandra Arulpragasam and Cuda Bibile (1955). 'The Agricultural System of a Ceylon Jungle Village', *Eastern Anthropologist*, vol. VIII, pp. 151–60.

Sarkar, N. K. and Tambiah, S. J. (1957). *The Disintegrating Village: Report of a Socio-Economic Survey conducted by the University of Ceylon*: Part I (Colombo).

Seligman, C. G. and B. Z. (1911). *The Veddas* (Cambridge).

Stevenson, H. N. C. (1954). 'Status Evaluation in the Hindu Caste System', *J.R.A.I.*, vol. LXXXIV.

Tambiah, H. W. (n.d. [1956]). *The Laws and Customs of the Tamils of Jaffna* (Colombo).

Tambiah, S. J. (1958). 'The structure of Kinship and its Relationship to Land Possession and Residence in Pata Dumbara, Central Ceylon', *J.R.A.I.*, vol. LXXXVIII, part I.

Tennent, Sir J. E. (1859). *Ceylon* (2 vols., London).

Weber, Max (1947). *The Theory of Social and Economic Organization*, trans. A. R. Henderson and Talcott Parsons (London).

Wickremasinghe, A. A. (1924). *Land Tenure in the Kandyan Provinces* (Colombo).

Wittfogel, K. A. (1957). *Oriental Despotism* (New Haven, Yale University Press).

Yalman, N. O. (1960). 'The Flexibility of Caste Principles in a Kandyan Community' in E. R. Leach (ed.), *Aspects of Caste in South India, Ceylon and North West Pakistan*. Cambridge Papers in Social Anthropology, no. 2 (Cambridge).

GENERAL INDEX

338

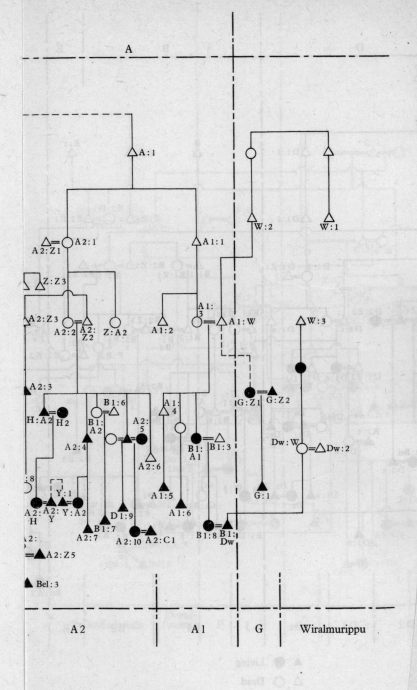

apitals A–F in
line indicates